PATH THROUGH
CHRISTIAN LIVING

BY JOHN POWELL, S.J.

WITH

MICHAEL H. CHENEY, M.A.
LOYOLA HIGH SCHOOL
LOS ANGELES, CALIFORNIA

TABOR®
PUBLISHING
Allen, Texas

NIHIL OBSTAT
Rev. Glenn D. Gardner, J.C.D.
Censor Librorum

IMPRIMATUR
Most Rev. Charles V. Grahmann
Bishop of Dallas

October 2, 1994

The nihil obstat and imprimatur are official declarations that a book or pamphlet is free of doctrinal or moral error. No implication is contained therein that those have granted the nihil obstat and the imprimatur agree with the content, opinion, or statements expressed.

Send all inquiries to:
Tabor Publishing
200 East Bethany Drive
Allen, Texas 75002–3804

Printed in the United States of America

ISBN 0–7829–0451–3 (Student Text)
ISBN 0–7829–0452–1 (Manual)

1 2 3 4 5   98 97 96 95 94

Contents

PATH THROUGH CHRISTIAN LIVING

LIVING THE CHRISTIAN LIFE FULLY

The most persistent and restless desire of my life is to be fully human and fully alive. On the other side of the coin, my deepest and most haunting fear is the possibility of wasting the glorious opportunity of life. My personal prayers vary according to the experience and needs of each day, but one prayer is never omitted: "O God, my Father, don't let me die without having really lived and loved!" This is my hope and prayer for you too. My desire to see you live fully is the reason for this book. I have found something good, energizing, and life-giving, and I want to share it with you.

What I want to talk to you about is life and the freedom to be ourselves. Saint Irenaeus, one of the great saints of the second century, said, "The glory of God is a human being who is fully alive!" Yet psychologists and students of human nature tell us that the average person achieves only ten percent of his or her potential to live, to learn, to love, to enjoy, and so on.

Where does the other ninety percent go? Cardinal Newman once said, "Fear not that your life shall come to an end; rather fear that it will never have a beginning."

What happens to our human potential? Why don't we live more fully? Why don't we savor every moment of this great opportunity called life? According to many psychologists, the reason we do not live up to our potential and enjoy our human life to the fullest is because of our attitudes, or vision of reality.

Each of us has a vision of reality that controls everything else about our life. That vision is the way we look at reality. It is the way we look at ourselves, at other people, at life, at the world around us, and at God. Such a vision is inside you and there is likewise one inside me— but there is a different vision in each of us.

It is that vision of reality that controls and regulates our ability to live and to enjoy. The ability of every human being to participate in life, to join the dance of life, to sing the songs of life is controlled by this vision—by the way each of us looks at reality.

I would like to suggest that ninety-five percent of our suffering grows out of a wrong or distorted way of looking at reality—a wrong way of looking at myself, a wrong way of looking at you and other people, a wrong way of looking at life, a wrong way of looking at the world, and a wrong way of looking at God. These distortions cause most of our suffering.

fully alive people get out of themselves.

> *Jesus reveals to us what it means to be truly human and, at the same time, he reveals to us the kind of God we have.*

I think that this is what John the Baptist had in mind when he roared out of the desert to announce the coming of his cousin, Jesus. He said, "You've got to have a change in your way of thinking!" John said, "You have to reform, re-form the way you look at reality. You've got to have a change in your vision! It's the only way you can really grow. When you are willing to change your way of thinking, when you are willing to open your mind to a new view, a new vision, then come on down and let me pour water over your head. The water will symbolize the washing away of your old ways of looking at things and the growth of a new vision."

Now, when Jesus finally arrived on the scene, he was saying the same thing as John the Baptist. Jesus said, "What makes you happy is your basic attitude. All happiness and health begin with the way you look at things. Happiness isn't guaranteed by circumstances or possessions. Happiness is guaranteed only by your possession of the truth, by seeing things as they really are."

John the Baptist and Jesus are offering us the truth: Our participation in the happiness of a full and human life is determined by our personal perception of reality. In other words, if our attitudes are healthy and realistic, then our lives will be that much more full, happy, and alive. On the other hand, if our attitudes, our vision of reality, are crippling, distorted, and unhealthy, then these attitudes will have a negative effect on our lives. Jesus claimed himself to be "the Way, the

Truth, and the Life." He offers us the Master Vision of Reality. We believe that his vision, his unique way of looking at reality, is the truth that sets us free. Consequently, if we are to change—to grow—we must first change our basic vision, or perception of reality.

In *Path Through Christian Living* we will discuss and develop in greater detail ways in which we can grow into the fullness of Christian living. Precisely we will look at (1) what precisely this vision of reality is, (2) how this vision controls everything about our lives, (3) where we get our vision of reality, (4) what specific ways we can use to get in touch with and to revise our vision, and (5) what the Christian vision of SELF, OTHERS, LIFE, the WORLD, and GOD is. We begin first by taking a look at a portrait of what it means to be fully human and fully alive.

A Portrait of the Fully Alive Human Being

Some time ago a friend told me of an occasion when, vacationing in the Bahamas, he saw a large and restless crowd gathered on a pier. Upon investigation he discovered that the object of all the attention was a young sailor making the last-minute preparations for a solo journey around the world in a homemade boat. Without exception everyone on the pier was vocally pessimistic. All were actively volunteering to tell the ambitious sailor all the things that could possibly go wrong. "The sun will broil you! . . .

You won't have enough food! . . . That boat of yours won't withstand the waves in a storm! . . . You'll never make it!"

When my friend heard all these discouraging warnings to the adventurous young sailor, he felt an irresistible desire to offer some optimism and encouragement.

As the little craft began drifting away from the pier toward the horizon, my friend went to the end of the pier, waving both arms wildly like semaphores spelling confidence. He kept shouting: "**Bon voyage!** You're really something! We're with you! We're proud of you! Good luck!"

Sometimes it seems to me that there are two kinds of people. There are those who feel obligated to tell us all the things that can go wrong as we set out over the uncharted waters of our unique lives. "Wait till you get out into the cold, cruel world, my friend. Take it

from me." Then there are those who stand at the end of the pier, cheering us on, exuding a contagious confidence: "***Bon Voyage!***"

The history of psychology has been very heavily populated by learned people who have worked mainly with the sick, trying to discover what made them sick and warning the rest of us about the things that can go wrong. They have been well intentioned, and their good efforts have no doubt benefited all of us. However, an honored place in this history of psychology must certainly be awarded to the "father of humanistic psychology," the late Abraham Maslow. He did not concern himself primarily with the sick and the causes of sickness. He devoted most of his life and energies to a study of the healthy ("self-actualizing" people) and asked about the causes of health.

Abe Maslow was definitely a **Bon Voyage type**. He was more concerned with what can go right than with what can go wrong, more anxious to lead us to the wellsprings of a full human life than to warn us about crippling injuries which we might sustain while trying to move along.

In the tradition of Maslow's humanistic psychology, I would like to begin now with a verbal portrait of people who are fully alive and offer some observations about what makes them healthy.

By way of a general description, fully alive people are those who are using all of their human faculties, powers, and talents. They are using them to the full. These individuals are fully functioning in their external and internal senses. They are comfortable with and open to the full experience and expression of all human emotions. Such people are vibrantly alive in mind, heart, and will. There is an instinctive fear in most of us, I think, to travel with our engines at full throttle. We prefer, for the sake of safety, to take life in small and dainty doses. The fully alive person travels with the confidence that if one is alive and fully functioning in all parts and powers, the result will be harmony, not chaos.

Fully alive human beings are alive in their external and internal **senses**. They see a beautiful world. They hear its music and poetry. They smell the fragrance of each new day and taste the deliciousness of every moment. Of course their senses are also insulted by ugliness and offended by odors. To be fully

alive means to be open to the whole human experience. It is a struggle to climb a mountain, but the view from the top is magnificent. Fully alive individuals have activated imaginations and cultivated senses of humor. They are alive, too, in their **emotions**. They are able to experience the full gamut and galaxy of human feelings—wonder, awe, tenderness, compassion, both agony and ecstasy.

Fully alive people are also alive in their **minds**. They are very much aware of the wisdom in the statement of Socrates that "the unreflected life isn't worth living." Fully alive people are always thoughtful and reflective. They are capable of asking the right questions of life and flexible enough to let life question them. They will not live an unreflected life in an unexamined world. Most of all, perhaps, these people are alive in **will** and **heart**. They love much. They truly love and sincerely respect themselves. All love begins here and builds on this. Fully alive people are glad to be alive and to be who they are. In a delicate and sensitive way they also love others. Their general disposition toward all is one of concern and love. And there are individuals in their lives who are so dear to them that the happiness, success, and security of these loved ones are as real to them as their own. They are committed and faithful to those they love in this special way.

For such people life has the color of joy and the sound of celebration. Their lives are not a

Fully alive people see a beautiful world. They hear its music and poetry.

perennial funeral procession. Each tomorrow is a new opportunity which is eagerly anticipated. There is a reason to live and a reason to die. And when such people come to die, their hearts will be filled with gratitude for all that has been, for "the way we were," for a beautiful and full experience. A smile will spread throughout their whole being as their lives pass in review. And the world will always be a better place, a happier place, and a more human place because they lived and laughed and loved here.

The fullness of life must not be misrepresented as the proverbial "bowl of cherries." Fully alive people, precisely because they are fully alive, obviously experience failure as well as success. They are open to both pain and pleasure. They have many questions and some answers. They cry and they laugh. They dream and they hope. The only things that remain alien to their experience of life are passivity and apathy. They say a strong "yes" to life and a resounding "amen" to love. They feel the strong stings of growing— of going from the old into the new—but their sleeves are always rolled up, their minds are whirring, and their hearts are ablaze. They are always moving, growing, beings-in-process, creatures of continual evolution.

Five Essential Steps to Fuller Living

How does one get this way? How do we learn to join the dance and sing the songs of life in all of its fullness? It seems to me that the contemporary wisdom on this subject can be distilled and formulated into five essential steps to fuller living. These are normally taken in the order suggested, and each one builds upon previous accomplishments. As will be obvious from a description of the steps, while each one builds on and grows out of the previous steps, none is ever fully and finally completed.

To be fully alive means to be open to the whole human experience.

Each will always remain an ideal to keep us reaching. In terms of a vision, or basic frame of reference, each of the five steps is essentially a new awareness or perception. The more deeply these perceptions are realized, the more one is enabled to find the fullness of life.

Briefly, and before discussing each, the five essential steps into the fullness of life are these: (1) to *accept* oneself, (2) to *be* oneself, (3) to *forget* oneself in loving, (4) to *believe*, (5) to *belong*. Obviously all growth begins with a joyful self-acceptance. Otherwise one is perpetually locked into an interior, painful, and endless civil war. However, the more we approve and accept ourselves, the more we are liberated from doubt about whether others will approve of and accept us. We are freed to be ourselves with confidence. But whether we are authentic or not, loving and living for oneself alone becomes a small and imprisoning world.

We must learn to go out of ourselves into genuine love relationships. Of course the genuineness of these relationships will be directly dependent on one's ability to be authentic, to be himself or herself. Having been led out of self by love, one must then find a faith. Everyone must learn to believe in someone or something so deeply that life is charged with meaning and a sense of mission. And the more one dedicates oneself to this meaning and mission, the more such a person will develop a sense of profound and personal belonging and discover the reality of community. Let us now look at each of these steps more closely.

"Be gentle with yourself."

Desiderata

1. To Accept Oneself. Fully alive people accept and love themselves as they are. They do not live for the promise of some tomorrow or the potential that may someday be revealed in them. They usually feel about themselves as they are the same warm and glad emotions that you and I feel when we meet someone whom we really like and admire. Fully alive people are sensitively aware of all that is good in themselves, from the little things, like the way they smile or walk, through the natural talents they have been given, to the virtues they have worked to cultivate.

When these people find imperfections and limitations in themselves, they are compassionate. They try to understand, not to condemn themselves. "Beyond a wholesome discipline," Desiderata says, "be gentle with yourself." The wellsprings for the fullness of life rise from within a person. And, psychologically speaking, a joyful self-acceptance, a good self-image, and a sense of self-celebration are the bedrock beginning of the fountain that rises up into the fullness of life.

2. To Be Oneself. Fully alive people are liberated by their self-acceptance to be authentic and real. Only people who have joyfully accepted themselves can take all the risks and responsibilities of being themselves. "I gotta be me!" the song lyrics insist, but most of us get seduced into wearing masks and playing games. The old ego defense mechanisms are built up to protect us from further vulnerability. But they buffer us from reality and reduce our visibility. They diminish our capacity for living. Being ourselves has many implications. It means that we are free to have and to report our emotions, ideas, and preferences. Authentic individuals can think their own thoughts, make their own choices. They have risen above the nagging need for the approval of others. They do not sell out to anyone. Their feelings, thoughts, and choices are simply not for hire. "To thine own self be true . . ." is their life principle and life-style.

3. To Forget Oneself in Loving.
Having learned to accept and to be themselves, fully alive people proceed to master the art of forgetting themselves—the art of loving. They learn to go out of themselves in genuine caring and concern for others. The size of a person's world is the size of his or her heart. We can be at home in the world of reality only to the extent that we have learned to love it.

Fully alive men and women escape from the dark and diminished world of egocentricity, which always has a population of one. They are filled with an empathy that enables them to feel deeply and spontaneously with others. Because they can enter into the feeling world of others—almost as if they were inside others or others were inside them—their world is greatly enlarged and their potential for human experience greatly enhanced. There are others so dear to them that they have personally experienced the "greater love than

this" sense of commitment. They would protect their loved ones with their own lives.

Being a loving person is far different from being a so-called "do-gooder." Do-gooders merely use other people as opportunities for practicing their acts of virtue, of which they keep careful count. People who love learn to move the focus of their attention and concern from themselves out to others. They care deeply about others. The difference between do-gooders and people who love is the difference between a life that is an on-stage performance and a life that is an act of love. Real love cannot be successfully imitated. Our care and concern for others must be genuine, or our love means nothing. This much is certain: There is no learning to live without learning to love.

4. To Believe.
Having learned to transcend purely self-directed concern, fully alive people discover "meaning" in their lives. This meaning is found in what Viktor Frankl calls "a specific vocation or mission in life." It is a matter of commitment to a person or a cause in which one can believe and to which one can be dedicated. This faith commitment shapes the lives of fully alive individuals, making all of their efforts seem significant and worthwhile. Devotion to this life task raises them above the pettiness and paltriness that necessarily devour meaningless lives.

When there is no such meaning in a human life, one is left almost entirely to the pursuit of sensations.

fully alive people learn to go out of themselves in genuine caring and concern for others.

Everybody needs
a place called home.

One can only experiment, looking for new "kicks," new ways to break the monotony of a stagnant life. A person without meaning usually gets lost in the forest of chemically induced delusions, the prolonged orgy, the restless eagerness to scratch without even having an itch. Human nature abhors a vacuum. We must find a cause to believe in or spend the rest of our lives compensating ourselves for failure.

5. To Belong.   The fifth and final component of the full life would no doubt be a "place called home," a sense of community. A community is a union of persons who "have in common," who share in mutuality their most precious possessions—themselves. They

know and are open to one another. They are "for" one another. They share in love their persons and their lives.

Fully alive people have such a sense of belonging—to their families, to their church, to the human family. There are others with whom such people feel completely comfortable and at home, with whom they experience a sense of mutual belonging. There is a place where their absence would be felt and their deaths mourned. When they are with these others, fully alive people find equal satisfaction in giving and receiving. A contrary sense of isolation is always diminishing and destructive. It drives us into the pits of loneliness and alienation, where we can only perish.

Our care and concern for others must be genuine, or our love means nothing.

The inescapable law built into human nature is this: We are never less than individuals but we are never merely individuals. No person is an island. Butterflies are free, but we need the heart of another as a home for our hearts. Fully alive people have the deep peace and contentment that can be experienced only in such a home.

So this is the profile, the portrait of fully alive men and women. Having succeeded in taking the five steps just discussed, their basic question as they address themselves to life is: How can I most fully experience, enjoy, and profit from this day, this person, this challenge? People like this stand eagerly on the growing edge of life. In general they will be constructive rather than destructive in their words and actions. They will be flexible rather than rigid in their attitudes. They will be capable of constant and satisfying relationships. They will be relatively free from the physical and psychological symptoms produced by stress. They will perform well, in reasonable proportion to their talents. They will prove adaptable and confident when change is thrust upon them or when they have to make a decision that will change the course of their lives.

We would all want to be like these people, and all of us can be more like them. In the last analysis, it is a question of vision. It is our perceptions that make us fragmented or whole. Health is basically an inner attitude, a life-giving vision.

Bon Voyage!

Part One

Our Vision of Reality—

Assumptions and Theses

Who Am I?
Who Are They?
What Is Life For?

1 *The Vision: What You See Is What You Get*

The assumption and thesis of vision therapy is that each of us has a unique and highly personalized perception of reality, a way of looking at things, a vision. Accordingly, we are each as happy, healthy, and alive as this vision of reality allows us to be.

May I ask you to run a short homemade movie on the screen of your imagination? Imagine that you come home some dark night and, to your horror, you see a thirty-five foot snake on your front lawn. Your heart begins to pound wildly and adrenaline starts pumping into your bloodstream. You quickly grab a garden hoe and in your frenzy you hack the writhing snake into small pieces. Satisfied that it is dead, you go inside and try to settle your nerves with a warm drink. Later, lying in bed, even with your eyes closed, you can still see the wriggling form on the front lawn.

The next morning you return to the scene of the snake slaying and find, again to your horror, that there had never been a snake on your front lawn. That which lies in pieces before your eyes was simply the garden hose which had been left out on the lawn. It was always a hose, of course; but last night for you it was a snake. What you saw last night was a snake, and all your actions and reactions followed from what you saw. The fear, the hoe, the struggle, the effort to calm down—all followed from the vision of a thirty-five foot snake. (The end of our homemade movie. Please turn on the house lights.)

What this exercise of imagination was meant to illustrate is that all our emotional and behavioral actions and reactions follow from our perceptions. In the snake drama, we were talking about a vision seen with the eyes of the body. But we also have an inner vision of reality, a highly personal and unique way that each one of us perceives reality—a vision seen with the eyes of the mind. We look at the various parts of reality through the eyes of our minds, and no two people ever see those parts of reality in exactly the same way. You have your vision. I have mine.

The important fact is this: We always act and react according to what we see. If I see a thirty-five foot snake—even though it is really a garden hose—my glands and my emotions, my hands and feet and palpitating heart all react to the "snake" I see.

And so, the way we see things shapes the kinds of experiences we have. For example, if I see you coming toward me and I perceive you in my mind's eye as a dear friend, a warm feeling will come over me, a smile will light up my face.

Our attitudes are capable of making the same given experience either pleasant or painful.

I will reach out to shake your hand or to embrace you. However, if I see you approaching me and I perceive you as hostile, intent on hurting or robbing me, my physical, emotional, and behavioral reactions will be just the opposite. It all depends on how I perceive or see you.

There was an old Roman philosopher, Epictetus, who lived shortly after our Lord. I don't suppose the man or his message was too popular, but he kept saying to the people, "It isn't your problems that are bothering you. It is the way you are looking at them. It's all in the way you look at things!" Epictetus may not have been revered for repeating this refrain, but, you know, I think he was right. It is all in the way we see or look at things. One thirsty person can look at a half-filled glass of water and gleefully observe, "Oh, good! It's half full." Another thirsty person might well look at the same glass and dejectedly moan, "Oh, nuts! It's half empty." We all remember the rhyming couplet: "Two men looked out from prison bars. One saw mud, the other stars." It's all in the way we look at it.

Perceptions and Attitudes

There are many things that we perceive again and again in very much the same way. Pretty soon such repeated perceptions get to be a habit. For example, it may be that a certain man has always perceived money as very important. He can

never forget the day he lost a dime in first grade or the day he collected his first paycheck. Whenever this man made money, won money, found money, he was greatly elated and congratulated himself. But whenever he spent money or lost money, he felt very dejected. This way of looking at money, after it has been repeated many times, becomes a habit. The man in question has an habitual way of perceiving the reality of money: It is very important and looms very large in his vision. And this is what I call an attitude. Our lives are shaped and governed by our attitudes.

Up in your head and mine are thousands of these attitudes. Sometimes I think of them as the lenses of the mind through which each of us sees reality in his or her own way. These lenses can shrink or magnify, color, clarify or obscure the reality seen through them. And there is a different lens for every different part of reality. Some of us magnify certain things and diminish others, but no two of us ever see anything in exactly the same way. What is most important, I think, is that our actions and reactions are determined by something inside us, by the way we see reality, by our attitudes.

Our attitudes are truly the lenses of the mind through which we perceive reality. However, there is another comparison that helps me more fully understand the force of attitudes. I imagine our attitudes as jurors sitting in the jury box of the mind, poised, and ready to interpret all the evidence that is brought before them. These juror-attitudes

"It isn't your problems that are bothering you. It is the way you are looking at them."

Epictetus

are ready to pronounce verdicts and to suggest appropriate actions and reactions.

For example, I look into the mirror and I see new wrinkles or gray hairs: unmistakable evidence that I am growing old. This evidence, coming through my senses, reaches my mind. There the proper and duly appointed juror—my attitude toward aging—rises, evaluates the evidence, makes a pronouncement, and suggests an appropriate reaction.

Perhaps the juror-attitude quotes Robert Browning:

"Grow old along with me!
The best is yet to be,
The last of life for which
the first was made.
Our times are in his hand."
Rabbi Ben Ezra

Browning's own attitude suggests that the most appropriate reaction would be a sense of satisfaction, and would perhaps result in a serene smile that results from the reflection that "these are the best of times . . ."

Or the juror-attitude could be very different. It could quote Dylan Thomas:

"Do not go gentle into that
good night,
Old age should burn and rave
at close of day;
Rage, rage against the dying of
the light."
*Do Not Go Gentle
into That Good Night*

Such an attitude seems to interpret the evidence harshly and angrily, even to the point of suggesting that the appropriate response would be a disappointed frustration and rebellion. "Just when

I get over the hump, I'm also over the hill! And it had to happen during the Pepsi generation when you're supposed to 'think young!' " If this is my attitude, I might as well walk away from the mirror, dejectedly thinking about a facelift or a hair rinse.

It all depends on the way I look at the process of aging. It all depends on the lens through which I look at aging. It all depends on the juror-attitude toward aging in my mind. The important thing that we must observe and absorb until it really sinks in is that our attitudes shape our reactions, emotional as well as behavioral.

Sometimes in my university classroom, I try this experiment to illustrate the same point. I ask my students, "If one of you suddenly stood up and stamped angrily out of this classroom, reading me out and writing me off, how would I react? How would I feel? What would I say or do?"

My classes have always been eager to respond. Usually, one student says, "You would be very *angry*. You would say, 'Get that person's name and number. He's not going to get away with this!' " Another student suggests, "No, you would probably feel *hurt*. You'd wonder, 'How could you do this to me? I was doing the best I could.' " Still another member of the class usually proposes, "You would probably feel *guilty*, and would accuse yourself of failing. You would want to apologize, and would wonder what you had done wrong. 'What did I do? I must have said something that infuriated that person.

Hey, come back; I'm really sorry!' " I usually find one of my students who suggests, "You'd feel *compassionate*, sorry for the angry, departing person. You'd say something like 'Poor fella! He just isn't ready for this yet.' "

I am always pleased to have these various and different reactions. Actually, I think that each suggestion is a projection of the attitude (and consequent reactions) of the suggester. We tend to think that everybody would react to given situations just as we do, but this just isn't true. Our attitudes are always unique. By the way, if you are wondering, I'm not sure how I would react. Whenever someone walks out on me, I always presume that he or she is going to use the washroom. The fact is that I might well react in any of the suggested ways. However, this I know: My reactions would reflect my attitudes—my attitude toward myself and my presentation, my attitude toward rejection by others, and perhaps my attitude about the necessity of pleasing others.

The central and critical realization is that my reaction, whatever it might be, is not determined by the person walking out on me, but by something inside me. My reaction is determined by my own inner attitudes. A reaction can be *stimulated* by thousands of things, but *my specific* reaction is *determined* by the way I perceive the person or thing or situation which is stimulating a reaction in me.

So when I wonder about my emotional and behavioral reactions to life and its events, I have to investigate my own inner attitudes. It is completely counter-productive to take inventory of someone else's attitudes rather than my own. If I resort to blaming others, I will never learn much about myself. It is futile to ask, What got into him? Instead, if I wish to grow, I have to confront the question, How am I looking at this? I have to realize that something in me passes judgment, dictates my reactions, and makes the experience growthful or embittering.

From where I now stand I would say that this is the essential difference between a growing and a nongrowing person. If I am willing to see my reactions as a reflection of my own inner attitudes, I am definitely moving toward self-knowledge and human maturity. Of course, I would rather blame my negative reactions on someone else or on something else. I might even resort to blaming the position of the stars: "My moon just wasn't in the right house!" However, if I give in to this temptation, I will be stunting my own growth as a person. "The fault, dear Brutus, is not with our stars, but with ourselves . . ." (Shakespeare, *Julius Caesar*) The initial and essential step toward full human maturity is the honest and gutsy admission that I am acting and reacting because of something in myself: my own habitual way of perceiving persons, things, situations. All my reactions are the result of my inner attitudes.

"The fault, dear Brutus, is not with our stars, but with ourselves . . ."

Shakespeare, *Julius Caesar*

Attitudes in Action

In my book *Fully Human, Fully Alive,* I told the story of the sudden death of a car which I was driving on a busy Chicago expressway. Standing on the shoulder of the expressway, alongside the unresponsive automobile, I glanced down into the ravine on one side of the expressway, noting the high fence and dense foliage at the bottom. Looking out across the expressway, I was faced in that direction with six lanes of whizzing traffic. The result in me was instant panic. I did not know what to do. What I did not reveal about this episode in that other book was that several months later a woman who works with me (Loretta Brady) came late for a meeting. "Sorry," she said, "my car broke down." I made sympathetic enquiries only to find out that her car broke down at the very same place where my own tragedy occurred. (Shades of the "Bermuda Triangle!") I know it sounds a bit contrived, but it is actually true.

"What did you do?"

"I climbed down the hill on the west side of the expressway!" she chirped with a slightly triumphal smile.

"Isn't there a big fence at the bottom of that hill?"

"Yes, I climbed over it!" (The triumphal smile widening)

"You did! Then what?"

"I went under the overpass, found a phone, and called for help."

(Long painful pause)

"Could I ask you a personal question: How did you feel when you were doing all this?"

(So help me God) "Exhilarated!"

(So help me God) "Oh, I hate you!"

As you can tell, I like to repeat this story, mostly for my own benefit. What the incident drives home for me is that my inner attitudes—the lenses, the jurors—determine the nature of my experiences and ultimately make my life happy or unhappy, pleasurable or painful, exhilarating or panic-filled. I really need to absorb and remember this. In order to remind myself of this crucial realization, I have a sign in my mirror (the first thing I see every morning) which reads: "You are looking at the face of the person who is responsible for your happiness today!" It's all in the way we look at it, Epictetus! I presume that this truth is what Abraham Lincoln had in mind when he said in one of his most quoted statements: "People are about as happy as they decide they are going to be." It also seems to be what William Cowper, the poet, had in mind when he wrote:

"Happiness depends, as Nature
    shows,
Less on exterior things than
    most suppose."
"Table Talk"

You must have heard the story—and it is just a story— of the identical twin boys. One was a hopeless optimist: "Everything is coming up roses!" The other boy was a sad and hopeless pessimist. He was sure that Murphy, as in "Murphy's Law," was an optimist. The worried parents of the boys brought them to the local psychologist.

He suggested to the parents of the boys a plan to level the boys off. "On their next birthday, put them in separate rooms to open their birthday gifts. Give the pessimist the best toys you can afford, and give the optimist a box of manure." The parents followed these instructions (remember, this is only a fable) and carefully observed the results. When they peeked in on the pessimist, they heard him audibly complaining:

"I don't like the color of this computer . . . I'll bet this calculator will break . . . I don't like this game . . . I know someone who's got a bigger toy car than this . . ."

Tiptoeing across the corridor, the parents peeked in and saw their little optimist gleefully throwing the manure up in the air. He was giggling:

"You can't fool me! Where there's this much manure, there's gotta be a pony!"

The story is meant to illustrate that it's all in the way we look at things. And it all depends on what we are looking for, because we inevitably find that which we are looking for.

The Good News: We Can Change Attitudes

The good news is, of course, that we are free to change our attitudes and consequently our lives. Attitudes are no more than practiced or habitual ways of perceiving some part of reality. We can break old habits and make new ones. We can drop in, over the eyes of our minds, a different set of lenses. We can retrain our mental jurors. We can look for and find a new and brighter outlook, and consequently enjoy a fuller and happier life.

The great William James was a Harvard-trained physician and professor. He soon discovered in his medical investigations that a person's outlook or way of seeing things has a profound influence on physical health. He realized that most of the patients who consulted him with a physical complaint really needed a revision of outlook. So James took up the study of psychology and eventually wrote a *minor masterpiece* called *The Principles of Psychology*. In this book Dr. James wrote: "The greatest discovery in our generation is that human beings, by changing the inner attitudes of their minds, can change all the outer aspects of their lives."

As you know, this same William James has written books on religion and the advancement of human spiritual frontiers. In these books James repeatedly insists that our happiness depends not so much on what happens *to* us as what happens *in* us. When we meet life and its circumstances positively and triumphantly, then no matter what comes we will have learned the master secret of living. The way we see, interpret, and react to whatever happens to us is the important thing. Sometimes the very worst thing that may happen *to* us can bring about the best thing that could ever happen *in* us. And we must assume this responsibility for what happens in us. We must assume responsibility for our attitudes. Only if we accept this responsibility can we grow through the various circumstances of life. This was the message of William James.

More recently a psychiatrist at the University of Pennsylvania, Dr. David D. Burns, has written a testimony to the same truth. In his excellent book *Feeling Good: The New Mood Therapy*, psychiatrist Burns reminds us that everything depends on our perceptions, the way we see things. He insists that we always feel and act the way we think; our attitudes shape all that follows from them. If our attitudes are distorted and crippling, our thinking is illogical and dysfunctional. In this condition we soon begin to experience a whole range of burdensome, oppressive emotions, and these are reflected in our behavior. The monkeys on our back are really born in our minds. Our distorted perceptions become our merciless tyrants. We become the tortured prisoners of these crippling attitudes, which will torment us as long as we tolerate them.

Another psychiatrist, the well-known Viktor Frankl, is basically teaching the same thing in his system of "Logotherapy." A former student of Frankl's, Dr. Robert C. Leslie, author of *Jesus and Logotherapy*, recalls these words from a conversation with Dr. Frankl: "Everybody can be helped, if not directly by psychoanalytic approaches, then indirectly by helping the patient to change his attitude."

Changing our attitudes can change our lives.

> *The good news is, of course, that we are free to change our attitudes and consequently our lives.*

Leslie then adds by way of explanation:

> The tendency in medical circles is so to focus attention on the symptom that the underlying attitude is lost sight of. It is the assumption of Logotherapy, however, that many symptoms (although, obviously not all) are the direct result of unhealthy attitudes, and that often relief can be accomplished by changing the attitude rather than by treating the symptom. . . .
>
> It is to be noted that in so focusing the attention on the attitude and away from the symptom, attention is directed to the future rather than to the past. The implication is that whatever the conditions have been in the past that caused the symptoms, the important factor is not so much the uncovering of an underlying conflict responsible for the symptom as it is the adoption of an attitude which makes possible a handling of the symptom.[1]

In his own, best-known book, *Man's Search for Meaning,* Dr. Frankl writes:

> Logotherapy is neither teaching nor preaching. It is as far removed from logical reasoning as it is from moral exhortation. To put it figuratively, the role played by the Logotherapist is rather that of an eye-specialist than that of a painter. A painter tries to convey to us a picture of the world as he sees it; an ophthalmologist tries to enable us to see the world as it really is. The Logotherapist's role consists in widening and broadening the visual fields of the patient so that the whole spectrum of meaning and values becomes conscious and visible to him.[2]

Still another of the great psychiatrists, Dr. Carl G. Jung, writes in his book *The Practice of Psychotherapy*, "The task of psychotherapy is to correct the conscious attitudes and not to chase after infantile memories."

What Drs. Burns, Frankl, Leslie, and Jung are saying is that we are fully free only when the lenses of our attitudes allow us to see reality clearly, only when we can find meaning and value in ourselves, in our fellow human beings, in life and in death. Very often we encounter people who sound as though they have swallowed a *mechanistic* view of humans. We hear people say resignedly, "This is the way I am. It was this way in the beginning, is now and ever shall be." They seem to be saying that when human beings are stimulated in a given way, the response is automatic and mechanical, and in no way free. Such people do not seem to be aware of the possibility of seeing things differently, of cultivating new attitudes. They do not seem to acknowledge the hope-filled truth that we can break old and crippling habits of perception and cultivate new, life-giving habits.

A (Saintly) Example

When I am thinking about the force and effects of our attitudes, I often think of the life and especially of the death of one of my favorite role models, Sir Thomas More, lawyer and saint. For me, this man is a living refutation of the mechanistic, the-way-it-is thesis. His living and especially his dying are a testimony to the effect of our attitudes on our reactions.

Coming face to face with death usually strips us of our pretenses. Death is the ultimate test of attitudes, I would think. The humor of Thomas More going to his death by decapitation has always impressed me very deeply. It is reported that his last words to his doleful executioner were a request for a little help up the stairs of the execution platform.

Sir Thomas More assured the poor man that he could take care of himself coming down. "See me safe up. For my coming down I can shift for myself." And he is said to have added, "And let us pray for each other so that we will all meet merrily in heaven."

To me this man's dying is more than a triumph of virtue, which it certainly was. It is also a marvelous illustration of a Christian attitude toward death and honor. As you remember, More was dying as a matter of principle and conscience. He once compared personal honor to water cupped in one's hands. "Once your spread your fingers even slightly, it is difficult to recap-

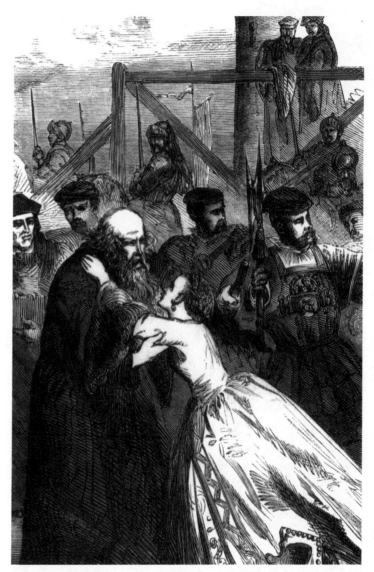

Margaret Roper taking leave of Sir Thomas More.

ture your honor." When I grow up (attitudinally), I want to turn out like Thomas More.

All that we have been saying about the radical role of attitudes in shaping our lives is generally known and accepted by psychology. The way we perceive reality through the lenses of our attitudes has a profound influence on our emotional, physical, and relational health.

[1] Robert C. Leslie, *Jesus and Logotherapy* (Nashville: Abingdon Press, 1965), p. 94.
[2] Viktor Frankl, *Man's Search for Meaning* (New York: Washington Square Press, 1969), p. 174.

Jesus, the Word of God, offers us a master vision.

Great minds from Epictetus to Viktor Frankl seem to insist on this. However, what our philosophers, psychologists, and psychiatrists do not have within their scientific resources is a master vision, a vision to which we can compare our own in an effort to locate our distortions and to acquire the healthy attitudes that will help us to live and to die as fully alive people like Thomas More. This is the precise significance of the Word of God, as it comes to us in the person and vision of Jesus. Jesus offers us just such a master vision.

However, before we consider this master vision of Jesus, we must first consider how our attitudes, our perception, or vision of reality controls all aspects of our lives.

The fully human person preserves a balance between "interiority" and "exteriority." Both the extreme introvert and the extreme extrovert are off balance. Such introverts are almost exclusively concerned with themselves. They become the center of gravity in their own private universes. Because of their preoccupation with themselves, they are distracted from the vast world outside themselves. The extreme extroverts, on the other hand, pour themselves out, move from one external distraction to another. Their lives are not at all reflective, and consequently there is little interior deepening. As Socrates once said, "The unreflected life isn't worth living." The first condition of human growth is balance.

Balanced "interiority" and "exteriority" is what is meant by integration of personality. We are all of us capable of exaggeration; we can turn too much inward or outward. We can become slaves to our sense pleasures without reflection on our peace of soul or upon our social need to love and give love to others. Or we can exaggerate by becoming prisoners of "intellect," alive only from the neck up.

When we live fully in all our faculties, and harmonize all our powers, human nature will prove constructive and trustworthy.

From *Why Am I Afraid To Tell You Who I Am?*

FOR FURTHER REFLECTION
Chapter 1: The Vision: What You See Is What You Get

Review

1. What does Epictetus, the Roman philosopher, mean when he says "It isn't your problems that are bothering you. It is the way you are looking at them. It's all the way you look at things!"?

2. All attitudes are thoughts, but not all thoughts are attitudes. Explain the difference between attitudes and thoughts.

3. Explain: "A reaction can be stimulated by thousands of things, but my specific reaction is determined by the way I perceive that person or thing or situation which is stimulating a reaction in me."

4. Explain William James's excerpt from *The Principles of Psychology:* "The greatest discovery in our generation is that human beings, by changing the inner attitudes of their minds, can change all outer aspects of their lives." *

5. How does the phrase "This is the way I am. It was this way in the beginning, is now and ever shall be" contradict the assumption and thesis that our attitudes determine our happiness or unhappiness?

Discuss

To what extent does your outlook on life affect your emotional reactions, your physical health, and your social adaptive behavior?

Scripture Activity

"No one lights a lamp and then hides it or puts it under a bowl; instead, it is put on the lampstand, so that people may see the light as they come in. Your eyes are like a lamp for the body. When your eyes are sound, your whole body is full of light; but when your eyes are no good, your whole body will be in darkness. Make certain, then, that the light in you is not darkness. If your whole body is full of light, with no part of it in darkness, it will be bright all over, as when a lamp shines on you with its brightness." (Luke 11:33–36, GNB)

Read the passage and summarize its main point. Tell how the passage relates to the chapter, and share one or two thoughts that entered your mind when you read it.

Processing These Ideas about the Importance of One's Vision

1. *Reflect upon and write about* an experience of yours that illustrates that "a change in attitude determines a different reaction." (Examples: seeing a group of people approaching you only to discover they are your friends; a person asking to see and speak with you after school; a stranger approaching with a question, and so on.)

2. *Interview an adult* (parent, teacher, coach, and so on.) and ask that person to give examples from his or her own life of how a different perception or attitude about a certain person, place, or thing changed his or her original reaction. Record your findings.

2 *The Vision That Shapes Our Lives*

How does it happen that a vision, a way of perceiving reality, can control everything about our lives? One way to answer this question is to think about the layers of your life and person as the layers of a cake. At the very bottom is this **vision**, the way you perceive reality. It is active in you all the time. It is like a cassette, and it is always playing. It is always saying: This is who I am. This is who other people are. This is what life is for. This is what the world means. This is who God is. The CD player of your vision is always playing silently inside you.

From this vision, the intellectual perception of yourself, others, life, the world, and God, grow all of your emotions, the whole emotional pattern of your life. This is your second layer—your **emotions**.

If you are an emotionally stable and happy person, it is an indication that your vision is good. If you are habitually sad, if your life feels consistently dreary, then I would suggest that your vision needs some refocusing; your vision needs examination and reevaluation.

I knew a teacher of little children, who one day got an anonymous note from one of her fifth graders. She was very upset and angry because the note read, "If you feel all right, would you please notify your face?"

When you think about it, emotions are not like coughs or sneezes. They do not just happen. You do not just happen to feel good or feel blah. There is always a perception under your feelings. There is always the vision of yourself, other people, life, the world, and God that is producing these emotions.

For example, if I think of you as a friendly audience, not in any way hostile or eager to judge me, and if I think of myself as having something worthwhile to say to you, then my emotions naturally will be very peaceful. I will feel very good and secure at this moment. On the other hand, if I think of myself as not having much to say since I am really a phony; and if I think that I have no substantial content to offer; and if I think of you sitting there, eager to judge how incompetent and inadequate I am, then naturally I am going to feel threatened and very insecure.

Do you see that it is the perception under the emotion that causes the emotion? We do not just have emotions. When we feel wrongly, it is because of our vision, the way we see ourselves, and so forth.

The next layer to be considered is the **body**. The emotions send out signals into the body. Negative emotions make us tense. Positive emotions make us relaxed and peaceful.

A way of perceiving reality can control everything about our lives.

According to the Academy of Psychosomatic Medicine, ninety percent of all our physical illnesses have psychological roots. Rooted in what? Rooted in our vision, in the way we perceive reality.

The next layer to be considered in this chain of effects beginning with our vision is our **behavior**. We all build up a way of acting, an adaptive behavior. Have you ever asked yourself, "What is my way of acting, of adapting to reality?" Do people tell you that you are shy? Are you aggressive? What are you? What am I? Whatever we are, in our conduct and communication, it no doubt represents a reaction to the way we perceive reality. Our social adjustments or behaviors are based on our visions of reality. If you are shy, it probably means that you perceive yourself as not having much to offer. So you build a wall called shyness. You chose it because you did not want to expose yourself.

Or if you find other people as being hostile, you probably find yourself backing away from life. You are afraid of interaction with others because of the way you perceive them. Whatever way you act, whatever your adaptive behavior is, is determined by your vision.

What is your adaptive behavior? Perhaps you are humorous, always telling jokes. Keep them laughing. It could be a protective device. That way you never have to reveal yourself, do you? Or perhaps you are a gossiper. "Did you hear about . . . ?" This is another device that saves

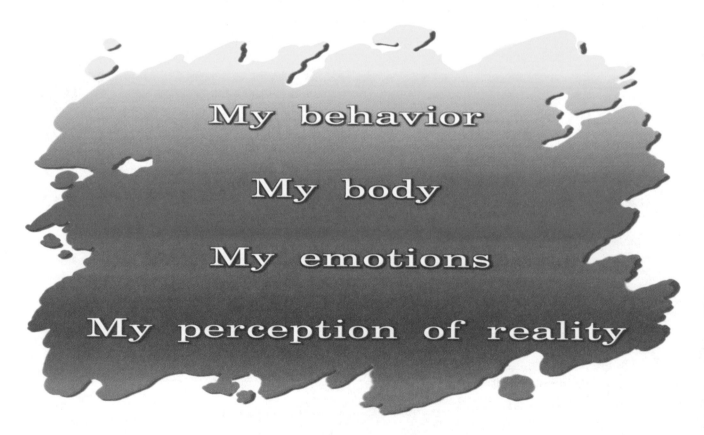

My behavior

My body

My emotions

My perception of reality

you from revealing your true self. All this goes back to the vision, to the way you look at reality. The vision translates itself into appropriate emotions, and the emotions flow into bodily tension and relaxation, and the ultimate result is an adaptive behavior designed to cope with the reality perceived in the vision. Lastly, depending on your ability to relate to others, you are free or not free to make use of your talents. For most of us, ninety percent of that talent goes down the drain because of the way we think about reality. We have never really learned to see in ourselves the glory of God, a person fully alive, a person who is really good, a person who has much to offer. We find other people threatening, and we refuse to trust them. The golden rule becomes: "Do it unto others before they do it unto you." We buy this distorted vision, and it cripples us. It paints us into a narrow little corner of life, and we become shriveled.

Our Basic Mind-set

There is one other result of this vision, which has great and pervasive influence on the quality of a human life. I would like to call this result a "basic question," or "mind-set." It consists of a disposition in advance, or anticipation. Some people are sure of eventual failure whenever they attempt anything. "Old arsenic lips! Everything I kiss falls over dead." Each of us eventually develops a habitual, individual attitude as we approach life: persons, events, specific situations, work, study,

and play. The question each of us habitually asks is always an outgrowth of his or her vision, or frame of reference. Sample basic questions: (Is yours listed in the margin?)

Of course, the basic question with which each of us approaches the various persons and situations of life is not applied in all situations with absolute universality. Most of us are capable of some variation. But the vision that shapes our personalities is a habitual outlook, and we are creatures of habit. Habit makes us repetitive. The natural, human tendency to unity and a unified approach leads us into habitual rhythms, cycles, and reactions. At any rate, the point is that the basic question, or mind-set, is a consequence of one's fundamental vision of reality.

The basic question of the fully alive person, I would suggest, is this: ***How can I enjoy this person, place, situation, or challenge?*** No suggestion of hedonism or self-centeredness is intended. Nor is there any intention of limiting the joy in enjoying sensual pleasure or emotional satisfaction, though these would be included. The essential condition for true satisfaction requires that we remain fully active in all of our parts and powers—senses, emotions, mind, will, and heart. I cannot indulge my senses or emotions at the expense of shutting down my mind or turning off my heart.

In the question, "How can I enjoy this?" there is implied a strong positive mental attitude, a spirit of creativity. This basic question is also multidimensional:

What do I have to fear?

How could I get hurt?

What do I have to do to meet the expectations of others?

How could things go wrong?

Will I have to make any decisions, meet any deadlines, or take any responsibility?

Will I look good or bad in the eyes of others?

How can this bring me attention?

What "strokes" (rewards) are in it for me?

Will I have to reveal myself?

There won't be any trouble, will there?

"How can I get and give the most? How can I grow through this and help someone else to grow? How can I most deeply "live" this experience? What are the opportunities for loving and being loved this day, this encounter, this situation?"

We Can Change Our Vision

The glory of God is the person who is fully alive, and only ten percent of our potential ever comes to life. The obvious question is, "What do you do about this?" If it really is a vision, if it is really the way we think that either shackles or liberates us, what can we do about it?

What we have to do is work with our vision. We must become more and more aware of its contents, discover its distortions, and replace faulty perceptions with those that are true. The truth alone can make us free. But before discussing how we can identify and revise our vision of reality, let us first look at how we got our vision. Afterwards, we will look at what we can do about crippling or distorted attitudes within our visions of reality. There is something you can do about it. You can become the glory of God, a person fully alive.

FOR FURTHER REFLECTION
Chapter 2: The Vision That Shapes Our Lives

Review

1. What are the five categories that make up one's vision of reality?

2. Powell analogously compares our lives with four layers. Explain the interconnectedness of these four layers beginning with the first layer: one's vision of reality.

3. How does a person's vision of reality affect his or her emotional health? Give an example to illustrate your answer.

4. How does one's vision affect his or her physical health? Give an example.

5. How does one's behavior reflect one's vision?

Discuss

1. How would you describe your vision of yourself?

2. How does your vision of reality affect your vitality for living?

3. In what situation is it easiest for you to be yourself? Why?

4. In what situations is it most difficult for you to be yourself? Why?

5. Are there times when you prefer not to be yourself? Explain what your attitude is during these times.

Scripture Activity

"As Jesus and his disciples went on their way, he came to a village where a woman named Martha welcomed him in her home. She had a sister named Mary, who sat down at the feet of the Lord and listened to his teaching. Martha was upset over all the work she had to do, so she came and said, 'Lord, don't you care that my sister has left me to do all the work by myself? Tell her to come and help me!'

"The Lord answered her, 'Martha, Martha! You are worried and troubled over so many things, but just one is needed. Mary has chosen the right thing, and it will not be taken away from her.'" (Luke 10:38–42, GNB)

Our Scripture passage above shows two women behaving quite differently in the presence of Jesus. Given what you have learned in this chapter, formulate (it's alright to guess) what the underlying attitudes of Martha and Mary might have been. Conclude by explicitly stating how this passage relates to the chapter.

Processing These Ideas about the Vision that Shapes Our Lives

A personal experience of emotional or behavioral discomfort. Recall an experience of yours when a person, situation, or a thing stimulated an emotional or behavioral reaction of discomfort in you. Try to put into words what you believe your underlying attitude was that caused the discomfort. Afterwards, analyze whether or not this underlying attitude was healthy or unhealthy.

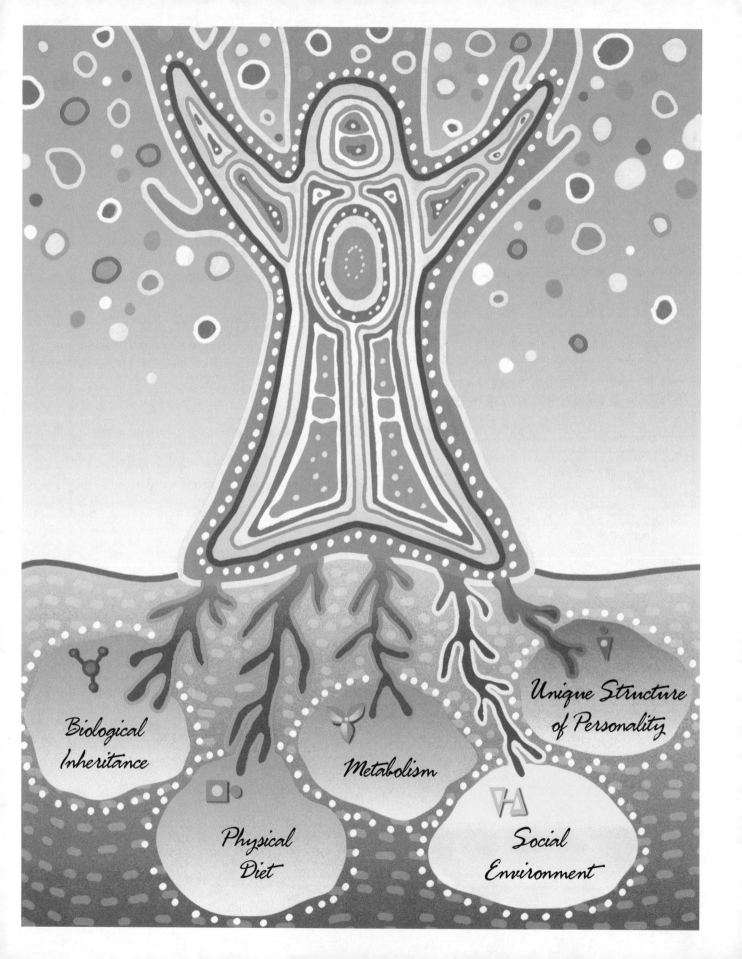

3 *The Sources of Our Vision*

We have a vision of reality that determines whether we will be fully alive or not. This vision determines the emotional pattern of my life, the tension or relaxation and health of my body. It determines my adaptive behavior, the quality of my inner personal relationships, and the use of my talents. Everything grows out of this vision. Where does each one of us get our vision? Why are some people more fully alive than others? Why do some people have a healthy vision, an expanding vision, a releasing vision while other people live as shriveled persons in a small and dismal world? Why are some people like that? The question before us, then, is, **What are the sources of one's vision of reality**.

If we could compare a human being to a tree, we would find under ground level at least five major roots. These roots nourish and tend to shape the total development of the person. They include a person's biological inheritance (brain, nervous system, and so forth), physical diet, metabolism, social environment, and a unique structure of personality. All of these affect to a great extent the way people will perceive themselves and the world around them.

There is an undeniable, even if somewhat mysterious, interaction of body and mind. It is undeniable that mental and emotional states affect the health of the body. Anxiety can precipitate an attack of asthma. I am personally convinced that health is basically an inner attitude. However, there is no doubt that bodily conditions, conversely, can affect psychological states. Anemia or an imbalance in the chemistry of the brain can bring on depression. This depression of physical origin can consequently distort the way one perceives reality. In other words, our vision of ourselves and the world around us can be profoundly influenced by physical factors.

After making this acknowledgment, I limit this present discussion of human visions and their origins to the psychological, environmental influences.

Family Messages

As infants—and later children— begin to discover and interpret reality, they are acquiring a vision that is largely shaped by parents and other family members. Children may distort some family messages, and their most impressionable stages may unfortunately coincide with darker days in the life of their families. They may not hear what others intended to say, or they may be most open to parents and others during periods when they are least apt to transmit a healthy outlook.

What are the roots of one's vision of reality?

Many people have differing thoughts about God.

However, for better or for worse, a child's first tentative vision will by and large be that of his or her parents and family.

Children will see themselves very much as their parents and other relatives have seen them. They will learn to fear the things that their parents fear, to love that which they love, to value whatever they value. This process of osmosis by which children absorb into themselves the parental vision of reality actually begins with intrauterine or prenatal experiences. The peace or turbulence of a mother while she is carrying her child is transmitted to the child through blood-chemistry changes and muscular contractions. The child records these messages in his or her developing brain cells and nervous system. The mother's tranquillity and her traumas become the child's. The mother is saying to her child through these bodily messages that the world is safe and peaceful or that it is dangerous and insecure. To some extent, at least, these messages will affect the child's evaluation of reality and the basic vision with which he or she will begin life.

The newborn are living question marks. From the very moment children receive the gift of life, they also begin to receive answers and evaluations. Along with these answers and evaluations an emotional coloration is supplied: "Living in this world is difficult; the appropriate response to life is depression." Or, "Life is an exciting adventure; the appropriate response is a sense of eagerness and exhilaration." Children are generally docile and ready to accept the evaluations and suggested emotional responses that their parents communicate to them.

Of course these perceptions, interpretations, and suggested emotional responses are not swallowed whole or all at once. Repetition is the mother of learning. The dynamics in the development of a vision are these: A child, in a definite human situation and in response to definite stimuli, thinks a certain thought, for example: "I have no worth of myself. My only worth is to please others." In successive, repeated situations of a similar nature, the child thinks this same thought, repeatedly perceiving the supposed fact of personal worthlessness and the need to please. The original perception is reinforced by each incident. After sufficient repetition, what was at first a thought and only a questionable fact becomes an attitude and a conviction.

When this happens, the original perception has become a part of the child's vision. His or her emotional responses and behavior will correspond to this habitual perception. The child will be sad and constantly seeking the approval of others. It is another example of the fact that we humans are creatures of habit. Our habits define us. Our thoughts crystallize into attitudes, and our attitudes coalesce into a habitual frame of reference, a way of looking at things, a vision.

Both in the transmission of messages and in the ways they are received, the combinations and variables are infinite. Consequently, people develop unique visions and act very differently. For example: Through coded or explicit parental messages children, rightly or wrongly, may perceive their worth to reside in causing no trouble, or in getting good grades, or in being quiet, or in looking nice, or in being brave, and so forth, ad infinitum. Whether children have heard the messages correctly or not, whatever they have heard will have a profound effect on their lives.

In terms of the fullness of life, these early perceptions are extremely important. If children perceive themselves to be affirmed by their parents for what they look like, succeed at, or avoid doing, they will be trapped into frustrating visions and lives. To the extent that they are loved unconditionally they will perceive in themselves real worth identified with their persons and not with appearances or accomplishments. If they perceive only conditional love, which will be withdrawn as soon as they stop fulfilling the imposed conditions, they will perceive themselves as worthless. They will feel "used." The emotional response to this conditional love will probably be a blend of anger, insecurity, and a strong need for approval.

Inherited Visions

A baby's first question concerns self: **Who am I?** The perceived answers to this question, and consequent perception of self, will be the most important of all the parts of the vision that is being formulated. If children are loved or perceive themselves to be loved for themselves, they will develop a good self-image and be on their way to fulfilling lives. If they are loved for what they look like or can do for others, they are on their way to diminished lives.

The second question of children is about others: **Who are they?** Parents will answer this question more by example than precept. Children watch and listen for answers. They watch the expressions on the faces of their parents and listen to the inflections of their voices as they talk to and about other people. Parental reactions are repeated; messages are reinforced; child thoughts become adult attitudes. Eventually they know: Other people are essentially good or bad, friendly or angry, trustworthy or suspicious, safe or dangerous. They feel secure in this knowledge. If you can't believe your parents, whom can you trust?

Again it should be noted that the combinations and variables are infinite. For example:

All people are basically good if they are treated well.

Being loved leads to a good self-image. A good self-image leads to a fulfilling life.

Or
Some people are all right, but test thoroughly before trusting.
Or
People will be good to you if you are good to them.
Or
Carefully measure what you are giving and what you are getting. You won't be a sucker.

The third category in the total vision that opens or closes a person to the fullness of life is life itself. The child asks: **What is life for?** Who is a success and who is a failure at life? What is the most important thing to do in and with life? What is a full and satisfying life? The answers received will become an integral part of the child's first vision and evaluation of reality. The child's first goals and ambitions will be drawn from this frame of reference.

The general attitudes and value systems of one's parents are deciphered from their actions as well as their lecturing, from their reactions of satisfaction and disappointment as well as their stated principles. Their example more than their words will carry an indelible message to the growing child about the nature and purposes of life. The life situation of the parents during these early formative years of a child is very important. It may be that the parents are generally well adjusted and possessed of reasonable goals and value systems. But it may also happen that financial reverses, health problems, or one of many possible traumas can tip them off balance for prolonged periods. The life messages transmitted to their children during these periods will probably be filled with distortions.

Eventually the child will be graduated from the home and family situation, but the old parental messages will continue to play softly on the CD player of the brain: "Life is . . ." "Success is . . ." "The most important thing is . . ."

There will also be transmitted an ***attitude toward the physical world*** in which we live. Blessed are the children who receive a life-giving, energizing vision of the universe. They will be taught to wonder, to be filled with curiosity, to admire. Their leisure will be filled with nature walks, stargazing, planting gardens, bird-watching, and collecting rocks or seashells. They will learn to care for their own pets, to distinguish species of flowers and trees as well as cloud formations.

Sad are the children of parents who have no time for such "nonsense." (Unfortunately, many parents know that summer has arrived only because someone has turned on an air conditioner.) Such people are preoccupied with grubbing out a living, with making ends meet, and with watching sports spectaculars on television. "Mabel, did you hear what the kid said? He wants a new pair of binoculars for bird-watching! That's really a good one! No kid of mine will ever be a bird-watcher." Children of such parents will begin life with a "deprived" outlook. They will be able to see only a dingy little world. They will hear only the sound of the air conditioner and the voice of the announcer, endlessly describing a game that some athletes are playing on a field somewhere . . . somewhere they aren't.

Who am I?
Who are they?
What is life for?

Inherited Vision of God

Finally, in the last category of reality, the child will receive an **inherited vision of God**. Many people have differing thoughts about God, who God is, what God does, and so forth. I do not have any last or even late work on the subject. I would deal here only with one truth about God, which is an unquestionable part of all Jewish and Christian teaching:

the love of
God for us.

There are two ways that God can be presented. One is very healthy; it will affirm a child and invite him or her to live more fully. The other is unhealthy; it can only threaten a child and diminish his or her prospects for life. In this second, distorted (as it appears to me) version, God loves us only conditionally. God loves us if, and only if, we make ourselves pleasing by obeying all God's laws. However, if we fail—in thought, word, or deed—God will immediately withdraw love. We will feel at once the shadows of divine displeasure falling across our lives. If we fulfill the condition of perfect faithfulness, God will then love us. If not, God will certainly vomit us out. It is a pretty heavy load to lay on a young mind and heart. If children later reject belief in this God, they are certainly one step closer to the truth.

The truth of God, as I find it in Jewish-Christian teaching and personally believe it, is that God loves us *unconditionally*. God says through his prophet Isaiah, "I have loved you with an everlasting love! . . . If a mother should forget the child of her womb, I would never forget you. . . . I have carved your name on the palms of my hands so I would never forget you." Of course we can refuse God and reject that love. If you ever offered your love to someone who did not want it, you will know what this means. Such a rejection of God's love constitutes the reality of sin. However, God changelessly continues to offer us his changeless love. God is not diminished in any way by our rejection. God's arms are always open to receive us.

The ideal of unconditional love was dramatized for me in a story recently related by a well-known psychologist. It seems that a troubled married couple consulted a counselor. The wife complained that her husband was loving only when she kept their house in perfect order. The man agreed that this was true, but maintained that he had the right to expect a house in perfect order when he returned from a hard day's work. The wife countered: "But I need to know that he loves me whether the house is clean or not, just to have the strength to clean the house." The counselor agreed with her.

Children should not be taught that they have to win, earn, or be worthy of love—either the love of God or the love of parents.

Real love is a gift.
Real love is unconditional.

What is a full and satisfying life?

Many people have differing thoughts about God.

There is no fine print in the contract. There is no price of admission. Simply: "I love you!" (I have described this ideal of love at greater length in my book *The Secret of Staying in Love*.) The God I know would say to the person striving to earn or be worthy of God's love: "You have it backwards. You are trying to change so that you can win my love. It just doesn't and cannot work that way. I have given you my love so that you can change. If you accept my love as a gift, it will enable you to grow. You need to know I love you whether you do your best or not so that you will have the strength to do your best."

Revising Our Inherited Vision

At any rate, Margaret Mead is right: The child has to learn from early teachers "degrees of approach and withdrawal . . . whom that child can touch, in whose arms comfort and warmth can be sought, and where distance is the safer course." Children learn who they are and what they are worth, who other people are and what they are worth. Children learn to cherish life as a beautiful opportunity or to despise it as a drudgery. They discover that the world is wide and warm and beautiful, or they walk along with eyes cast down through an unexamined world. It is all a matter of the vision they inherit. This vision is certainly the most important legacy of a child's parents and first teachers.

Inevitably children will revise this inherited vision. Their own observations and experiences will to some extent contradict, enlarge, and modify the pictures that were drawn for them. We have said earlier that the key to revising and modifying one's first vision—the key to growth as a person—is openness and flexibility. We called rigidity the trap to be avoided. Obviously, the more open and flexible a person is or becomes, the more he or she will be able to change the inherited vision and eliminate the distortions that diminish capacity for the fullness of life.

The rub is that some message of flexibility or rigidity is also a part of one's inherited vision. Parents transmit a disposition to rigidity or flexibility depending on their own willingness to risk and revise. If they are open to the new evidence that daily living constantly presents to us, their children will perceive this as an appropriate response. However, if parents are unwilling to live with doubt and are consequently rigid, their children will probably see this as the safer course. They will, in the beginning at least, imitate their parents in these inflexible postures.

For example: If a little girl comes home in tears after a disagreement with a playmate, her father may bellow some rigid, categorical sentiment such as: "I told you that kid's no good! Her whole family is no good!" Or, "You can't get along with anyone. From now on just stay home!" Or, "Stay away from those Catholics (or Protestants or Jews or blacks or whites)!"

For the kind of person who says these things, "all the evidence is in" on all questions. He is the personification of rigidity, and rigidity is the formula for nongrowth. It is also contagious. Rigid parents tend to beget rigid children.

Fortunately, as we grow up, new influences and other messages come to us from significant other persons. There is a constant turnover of new evidence in our lives. Through these sources we can modify inherited tendencies to rigidity and inflexibility as well as the other distortions in our inherited visions. But it isn't easy. Just to be aware of one's vision is very difficult.

The most profound problem of change probably lies at an even deeper level. The vision I work with gives me certainty. It makes sense of life. It gives life predictability and gives me a basis for adjustment to reality. With my vision, for better or for worse, I can cope. Without it, where would I be? What would happen to me if I gave it up in search of a new vision? It is now time to discuss these important questions.

We have a vision of reality which determines the emotional patterns of our lives, our physical responses, and our behavioral reactions and actions.

God loves us unconditionally.

In short, something inside of us, namely, our attitudes about self, other people, life, the world, and God determine all my actions and reactions.

We began by asking why some people seem to have healthy, life-enriching visions while others have visions that shackle and stifle their lives. From what we have seen the answer to this question has much to do with the original attitudes we inherited from our parents and/or significant others around us. It is this vision of reality that we inherited early on in our lives, that we took to school with us and tested out. Based on new evidence or experiences we either reinforced or modified our original attitudes. But, now we are faced with additional questions: How do we know whether or not the attitudes we have now are distorted or unhealthy? Are there responses, indicators, or symptoms that help us to determine whether or not our attitudes are healthy or unhealthy? These questions lead us to the systematic approach to personal growth and spiritual development which we call "vision therapy." In the next chapter, we will consider one specific method of vision therapy. We begin by asking, "What's in me?"

Parents transmit a disposition to rigidity or flexibility, depending on their own willingness to risk and revise.

FOR FURTHER REFLECTION
Chapter 3: The Sources of Our Vision

Review

1. Who are the primary sources of a person's vision of reality?

2. How do we initially acquire attitudes about ourselves, others, the meaning of life, the world, and God?

3. How do the attitudes that we receive early in life become modified by attending school and associating with others? Explain and give examples to illustrate your point.

4. Explain: "It's not so much what people say, it's what one hears that counts." Or "Children are excellent observers but poor interpreters."

5. Why is it that some people do not modify their original unhealthy attitudes even though they have evidence on the contrary?

Discuss

1. Give examples from your own experience that might support the statement: "Children are excellent observers but poor interpreters."

2. How did you develop your vision? What did you receive from your parents? What did you develop on your own?

3. In what ways do parents and teachers communicate that everyone is in charge of his/her life?

4. If you really believed that "the present moment is the most important moment in life," how would you approach life?

5. "What determines the way I am at any moment in my life is my vision. If I change my vision— I change." How does this statement apply to your life?

6. Is change in personal behavior possible at any age? Explain.

7. What are some conditions that make behavioral change possible?

Scripture Activity

"At once Jesus made his disciples get into the boat and go ahead of him to Bethsaida, on the other side of the lake, while he sent the crowd away. After saying good-bye to the people, he went away to the hill to pray." (Mark 6:45-46, GNB)

Spend some quiet time today in prayer. Reflect on the different sources of your vision of reality and thank God for all the healthy attitudes you have acquired. Ask God to fill you with openness and insight so that you may begin to get in touch with any attitudes that need to be revised according to his vision of reality.

Processing These Ideas about the Importance of One's Vision

1. *My vision of others.* In acknowledging that our attitude of other people is originally inherited or influenced by our parents or the significant adults in our life, describe what your attitude of others was. Afterwards, explain how you might have modified this attitude based on your personal experiences or associations. For example: racism toward, stereotypes or generalizations about other people.

2. *My vision of life.* Look over the list of possible attitudes about "What life is for." Indicate which most closely resembles your present attitude. Explain how this attitude about life determines to a large extent how you react emotionally or behaviorally to circumstances or people.

Part Two

GETTING IN TOUCH WITH AND REVISING ONE'S VISION

4 *What's in Me?*

The crucial insight and realization, which opens up a whole new dimension of personal growth, is this: Something in me—my attitudes, my vision of reality—determines all my actions and reactions, both emotional and behavioral. Something in me is writing the story of my life, making it sad and sorrowful or glad and peaceful. Something in me will ultimately make the venture of my life a success or failure. The sooner I acknowledge this, taking responsibility for my actions and reactions, the faster I will move toward my destiny: the fullness of life and peace. This fullness of life and peace is our legacy from the Lord.

I must not let this remain a matter of words, a lip-service admission. I must ask myself if in fact I really believe this. Am I really convinced that my inner attitudes evaluate the persons, events, and situations of my life and regulate all my reactions? If so, I must press on and ask, "Do I truly believe that it is within my power to change these attitudes, wherever necessary, in order to have a full and meaningful life?" If I am convinced on both scores, then I must close all the escape-from-reality doors and walk bravely down the corridor of personal responsibility. I must resist the ever-present temptation to blame other people, to complain about the past and present circumstances of my life. In a true sense, I must become "the master of my fate," and under God take responsibility for my own happiness.

The key and profitable question is not: Will this day bring me my desires? It is not: Will I get the breaks? Nor is it: How can I change all these people who surround me and shackle me and carry me along in their stream? The only key and profitable question is this: What is in me? It is not, as we have heard William James insist, what happens *to* me but rather what happens *in* me that will shape, color, and write the story of my life.

Now I don't think that you and I should think that we have to begin tearing down all the bricks of our existing mental structures. I rather suppose, in fact, that most of our attitudes are reasonable and healthy. We probably suffer from only several distorted attitudes. Also, we should recognize that the few which do pinch and prove painful have somewhere along the course of our lives been learned from others. Even though we were not always correctly understanding what they were saying, we did learn our first, inherited attitudes from our parents. Of course, there is no question of blame here, only of understanding.

> *Something in me is writing the story of my life, making it sad and sorrowful or glad and peaceful.*

45

Discomfort and the Need for Change

When these supposedly few neurotic attitudes actively distort our vision and cripple our responses, the result is always some form of DISCOMFORT! This discomfort can be (1) *physical:* We get tense and develop a headache or a skin rash, or we experience a knot or nausea in the stomach. We might come down with frequent head colds and find ourselves susceptible to various viruses. The discomfort can also be (2) *emotional:* We might frequently feel ill at ease, intimidated, anxious, inferior, guilty, depressed, angry and upset, afraid, frustrated, and so forth. Finally, the discomfort can be (3) *behavioral:* In this case we feel uncomfortable in the recognition of our own undesirable behavior. Examples: For a long time I have refused to talk to someone, or I don't tell others how I really feel. I pout and punish others by my silence. I pretend to be happy, but inside I know that it is just an act; actually I am hurting badly. I am immobilized; I haven't been able to do anything for several days now. Or I can't seem to make and keep friends. I am not able to tell others that I love them, even when I really do care very much for them. All of these, I would think, are behavioral symptoms of crippling and distorted attitudes.

The symptomatic discomfort, then, is reflected either physically, emotionally, or behaviorally, or perhaps in all three ways at the same time. Most of the time the discomfort is in fact experienced in all three ways. However, some of us are more aware of what our bodies are telling us. Others among us are better at listening to feelings. And finally, there are many of us who are not very good at physical or emotional awareness, but we do know that things are just not right with the way we are acting, reacting, and relating to others.

It is extremely important that we do not run away from our discomfort, but rather enter into and examine it. The discomfort is a signal, a teacher offering us a valuable lesson. The way to enter into our discomfort profitably and find the source of our difficulty is usually by asking, What is in me? I must ask myself, How am I looking at myself, at this other person, at this situation? My physical, emotional, and behavioral reactions are ultimately a result of my outlook. They are an outgrowth of my attitudes. In most moments of discomfort, I am feeling the effect of my attitudes in my body, in my feelings, in my actions and reactions. It is very important that I trace this discomfort to its cause: What is in me? How am I perceiving myself, another, this circumstance? The honest answering of these questions will explain my bodily, emotional, and behavioral reactions.

After I have located the attitude in question, then I must ask another question: Is there a different way to see myself, to see this other person or this situation? Can I think of a way that would be more realistic, healthier, more Christian? I must reflect that there are other people who would somehow remain peaceful, optimistic, gentle, and unruffled if they were in my shoes at this time. How would they perceive this moment and circumstance in my life if they were me? How would Jesus suggest that I look at myself, at this other person, at this situation?

The Process of Change: Case Examples

Examples of this process, like life situations, are innumerable. But let's examine a few cases here, and then perhaps we can outline others from our own life situations.

Case #1 (awareness of a distorted attitude through physical discomfort): I am tense and nervous. The back of my head and neck ache. I know that these physical reactions almost always occur when I am in a classroom. Sometimes I react this way just before an examination, or when I am in some other way being tested and evaluated. I don't test very well because I always "choke" during examinations. Basically, I suppose that the emotion which stimulates these physical reactions is fear. I am really afraid that I will be called on or tested and I will reveal my ignorance in some stupid statement. I dread the very thought of such failure and embarrassment. Failing at anything is always very torturous for me. It is like being hit again in a place that is already bruised. I am always tense and nervous at the thought that I will be found wanting and inadequate.

Diagnosis of distortion:
In the last analysis, each of us must become aware of his or her own individual discomfort and come to his or her own conclusions. Only Cinderella can tell if the shoe really fits or where it hurts. However, we can speculate that the attitude underlying the physical discomfort described here has to do with the way this person sees himself or herself. This person seems to perceive his or her personal worth as measured by ready knowledge and intelligence and by the judgment of public opinion. People who measure themselves in this way see themselves as slaves standing on the auction block, hearing their worth estimated by the public bidders. They are indeed slaves, enslaved by the fear that others will test and reject them. They are slaves of the attitude that a person's intrinsic worth is measured by achievement and by the recognition of others.

In search of an alternative attitude: Having located the source of the physical tension in this attitude, the uncomfortable person should reflect that there are others who do not seem to be affected in this way.

The reflection might sound something like this: "There are others who aren't even as smart as I am who actually seem to enjoy class and who seem to be able to take examinations in stride. There are those who don't go into a tailspin, as I do, when they make a public mistake. There are even some who can laugh at their own blunders. I wonder what these people are thinking.

Do not run from your discomfort.

Apparently they look at these situations in which I experience so much physical discomfort very differently than I do."

Healthy attitude: It is always crippling to play the comparison game, comparing my looks, my brains, or my accomplishments with those of others. The comparison game is the sure way to a poor self-image. The truth is that I am the one and only me! Furthermore, all people are mistake-makers. We humans learn by trial and error. We learn by making mistakes and learning from them. Besides, the only real mistake is the one from which we learn nothing. Thomas Edison tried two thousand different materials in search of a filament for the light bulb. When none worked satisfactorily, his assistant complained, "All our work is in vain. We have learned nothing." Edison replied very confidently,

"Oh, we have come a long way and we have learned a lot. We now know that there are two thousand elements which we cannot use to make a good light bulb."

Comment: I know that I have correctly uncovered my sick and crippling attitude and that I have replaced it with a healthy vision if and when the physical discomfort of tension greatly subsides or disappears. The same thing is true with emotional or behavioral discomfort.

CASE #2 (awareness of a distorted attitude through emotional discomfort): I feel alone and lonely most of the time. It is like the whole human race is holding a picnic and I wasn't invited. It seems that the only way I can get any attention is by being needy, by bleeding all over the place. It is really very depressing. I guess I just haven't got it.

Diagnosis of distortion: A person who feels this way probably perceives himself or herself as unattractive and unlovable. Imprisoned by this perception of ugliness, such a person can pine away a lifetime, wishing to be better looking, more intelligent, wittier, and so forth. Many people see lovability in these terms. Actually, what makes a person attractive and lovable is being loving, truly caring about other people, going out to read and respond to the needs of others. The perpetually lonely person usually does not realize this.

In search of an alternative attitude: There are other people who don't feel as isolated and lonely as I do. Many of them do not seem to have a better natural endowment of gifts than I do. So what do they have that I don't? What do they do that I don't? How do they think of and approach social relationships? I really should ask them.

Healthy attitude: It is truly caring for others that makes a person lovable. And I have at least some capacity for this: to get out of myself, to go out in personal caring to try to meet the needs of others. A loving person is a lovable person. What I am is really what I do with what I've got. My isolation and estrangement are really self-imposed. I have been sitting in this dark room, waiting for someone to come in and light up my life. I have to get out, to read and respond to the needs of others around me. Only then will I present to others the lovable person that I truly am. If I go out to others in a sincere and consistent way, I will certainly be loved and appreciated.

CASE #3 (awareness of a distorted attitude through behavioral discomfort): It really bothers me that you can't trust anyone anymore, not even your own family. Sooner or later people let you down. They'll do it every time. I have given up on having heroes or models. Everybody I've ever looked up to turns out to have clay feet. Even the religious people who go to church all the time are in fact hypocrites. They don't practice what they preach. I'm so disgusted with people. I just try to avoid them as far as possible. I say as little as I can to other people. There is no one I trust. I feel safer this way.

Diagnosis of distortion: It would seem that this person gives strong indications that he or she is a demanding perfectionist, at least with regard to others but most probably also with regard to self. In the thinking of such a person, the norm by which all people must be judged is absolute perfection. However, as has been noted, people are mistake-makers. That is why we put erasers on pencils. Even Saint Paul complained, "I see the right thing, I approve it, and then I do just the opposite. There is another law warring in my members." (See Romans 7:14–25.) It is also true that we become angry at and disgusted with others only when our expectations have somehow been disappointed. If we entertain the expectation that everyone should be perfect, our lives will probably be very painful. The fact is that no one is perfect. So rather than try to pull the whole world up to our unrealistic expectations, it would be a much wiser course of action to lower our expectations and to realize that the human condition is one of weakness. And, with Saint Paul, all of us can truly say, "This is my condition, too."

Finally, the process of human maturity is a gradual process. None of us is ever really and fully "grown up." It would be an unrealistic expectation to demand this in ourselves or in others. We are pilgrims, always on the way, but never really there. "So please be patient," the sign reads, "God is not finished with me yet."

A healthy attitude leads to less discomfort.

In search of an alternative attitude: There are others who live in the same world as I do. They cannot be blind to all the human frailties and imperfections that surround us and are a part of life on planet Earth. I wonder what they think when people disappoint them. They somehow seem to accept it and go on. Their expectation of others is apparently not the same as mine. I will have to ask some of these people what they are thinking, how they cope, and how they manage to keep up real relationships of love. Above all, I want to know how they manage to forgive and to go right on, almost as though nothing had ever happened.

Healthy attitude: It is true that the human condition is one of weakness. Every human being experiences weakness, fragility, and brokenness. Every one of us has to live with personal regrets. The only pertinent and real questions are these: Can I accept myself and others in this human condition of weakness? Can I ever learn to take myself and other people where we are? If I lower my unrealistic expectations to meet the reality of the human condition, I will consequently be more pleased by the goodness that I find in people and less disappointed with the weakness that is in all of us.

Also, each of us finds what he or she is looking for. The person who looks for weakness will certainly find it, in the self and in others. However, there is a lot more to each of us than our weakness. Deep down, most of us are basically well-intentioned. But this isn't always obvious. Our intentions don't always come through in our actions. Still we usually mean well even if we can't always do well. In order to love, one need not be blind but rather supersighted. The loving person must look past the surface weaknesses and find the essential goodness in self and in others. However, this finding can come only to those who are looking, looking more for goodness than for weakness.

* * *

As mentioned, examples could go on endlessly. But it might be more helpful at this point for you to put the book down and work through some personal discomfort (physical, emotional, or behavioral) and see if you can uncover its attitudinal roots. Then see if you can articulate a healthy attitude to replace the unhealthy one.

The main points to be realized are these: Discomfort may often be a sign of a crippling or distorted attitude. Our way of looking at something shapes our reactions to that reality. If the reaction results in discomfort, this may be an indication that the reality is not being seen in its proper, Christian perspective. The discomfort may be physical, emotional or behavioral; but whatever it is, the discomfort could be saying something to us that we really need to hear if we are to grow and to be happy, if we are to live the full and peaceful life for which we have been created.

I think it is important to realize that sometimes the experience of discomfort is *not* the result of a distorted attitude. There are very real human aches and pains that are a part of living and loving which do not imply or result from distorted attitudes. Allowing for this, I still think that ninety percent of our human discomfort is neurotic, that is, it results from a distorted and unrealistic way of seeing things. I think that ninety percent of our suffering is done on the way to the dentist and not in the chair. At any rate, when we are uncomfortable, we should always try to trace that discomfort to its attitudinal roots, to the way we are seeing things. After the attitude has been clearly recognized, we can then ask ourselves if this is a healthy and Christian way to see the reality in question. Is the discovered attitude one that I would want to recommend to another? Do I want to keep it for myself?

Among My Own Attitudes of Affliction

It has been said, and I truly believe it, that each of us harbors a core of several disjointed and crippling attitudes that tend to make us uncomfortable and to make our lives a struggle rather than a celebration. Of course, each person has to confront his or her own tyrants, but I would like to share with you now several distorted attitudes which I have found at the center of my own discomfort. I am sure that I have not yet made the new, corrective Christian attitudes completely habitual as yet, but I'm working on it. Also, I hope that my

sharing will prime the pump of your own attitudinal inspection and revision. Remember: Only after we have discovered and revised our distorted attitudes will we be free to live the full and peaceful life to which our Lord calls us.

DISTORTED ATTITUDE #1: Being overresponsible.

For a long time I saw myself as responsible for helping everyone who came to me in need. After I recognized this attitude and tendency, I slowly learned to laugh a bit at my delusion. I playfully called it my "Messianic Complex." While suffering from this attitude, I could not say "no" without a guilty feeling that I had turned away from someone in his or her hour of need. This overresponsible attitude also led me to believe that I had to have an answer for everyone who had a question. I had to provide a solution for everyone who had a problem. As you might well imagine, and as I know from experience, the overresponsible person becomes a tense and driven person. He frequently experiences emotional frustration and weariness. More and more he tends to relate to others only as a "helper." He allows others to lean on his strength while remaining weak in themselves. He cultivates a clientele of people who need him. His nerves are a bit frayed at times, but he feels good about all the people who could not possibly survive without him.

The new attitude I am cultivating: I am only one very limited person who has just two hands and twenty-four hours a day.

Human maturity is a gradual process.

If I am to stay sane and healthy, I need time to relax and enjoy, to think and to pray. It is better to refer people in need to others rather than to play at being a savior of all humankind and do a poor job. Also, problem-solvers almost always fall into the trap of becoming "enablers." They enable others to remain weak and immature. Enablers do for others what others could do for themselves. Enablers do not challenge others to grow stronger by working out their own problems. It is, of course, more loving to challenge others to grow by finding their own answers than to provide those answers ready-made. The truth is: "Give people a fish and they can eat for a day. Teach them to fish and they can eat for a lifetime."

It has been said that it is often easier to act yourself into a new way of thinking than to think yourself into a new way of acting. When we begin to act on a new insight, the hardest steps are the first ones. As I began acting on this insight into my own overresponsibility, I found the tendency gradually leaving me, as though the monkey was slowly being lifted off my back. I began to act more like a fellow pilgrim than a mini-messiah. Admittedly, it was very difficult at first because changing a habit is always hardest in the beginning. However, I soon noticed that the world didn't stop, and no one died because I resigned my messiahship. The best part: I found out that I was more peaceful and that I was helping others to realize their own strengths and to use their own resources more effectively.

We suffer more on the way to the dentist than in the chair.

DISTORTED ATTITUDE #2: *Being intolerant of conflicting positions and opinions.*

For a long time I harbored and practiced the attitude that it was essential that everyone agree with me, at least on issues which I regarded as important. The truths that I held as fundamental to belief in God and to human decency were, as I saw things, never to be challenged. Being outspoken, I often entered into conflict and heated arguments. The results were almost always unfortunate. Others remained unconvinced and I always felt drained by the conflict and emotionally upset in the wake of arguments.

The new attitude I am cultivating: Formerly I saw myself as the bold defender of absolute truth. I am now trying to accustom myself to a new set of lenses through which to see such matters. I am trying to recognize and to realize the relativity of truth: There are different ways of looking at the same truth, just as there are different sides from which to view a statue. Formerly I thought it was a part of my loyalty to my own convictions to speak up always, without compromise and without exception. I was not so determined to listen. I felt obliged to set the matter straight. Now at last I am learning that a win-lose debate almost always alienates others. Such debates seem to lock both parties deeper into their fixed and rigid positions. I also discovered that others will listen to me only to the extent that I am willing to listen to them. Again, by putting this new insight into practice, I am learning a new way of thinking. I am learning that empathic listening leads to a deep and rewarding sharing. And sharing is the essence of true human communication, which in turn is the heart of all human relationships. Finally, if I really do have a part of the truth that is worth sharing, the chances of success at communicating it are greatly increased by such an empathic sharing. A win-lose debate rarely has this happy outcome.

DISTORTED ATTITUDE #3: Taking myself too seriously. I just can't think of any other way to say it: I simply and for a long time took myself too seriously. Someone once said, and I can identify with the one who first said it: "I know of no man who has given me more trouble than myself." I also heartily endorse the new beatitude: Blessed are they who can laugh at themselves; they shall never cease to be entertained.

Looking through the lenses of my former attitude, I thought that everything I attempted, every speech I delivered, every class I taught, and all the words I spoke were vitally important because they would be carved in stone and remembered forever. I had to be good, stimulating, insightful, intelligent, and convincing because there was so much at stake. The very course

and flow of human history would forever be affected by the pebbles I threw into its stream. Consequently, I felt dejected by failure, saddened by the apparent or real rejection of my person and/or my ideas. I was frustrated even by partial success because partial success always seemed to imply partial failure. The very Kingdom of God seemed to hang in the balance, to depend on me and my efforts.

Listening leads to an appreciation of situations with many shades.

The new attitude I am cultivating: As a Christian I must try to realize that God's strength comes through my human weakness. Saint Paul himself writes:

> But to keep me from being puffed up with pride because of the many wonderful things I saw [his mystical visions], I was given a painful physical ailment, which acts as Satan's messenger to beat me and keep me from being proud. Three times I prayed to the Lord about this and asked him to take it away. But his answer was: "My grace is all you need, for my power is greatest when you are weak." I am most happy, then, to be proud of my weaknesses, in order to feel the protection of Christ's power over me. . . . For when I am weak, then I am strong.
>
> *2 Corinthians 12:7–10 (GNB)*

God's Kingdom has historically been built on failures as well as successes. I remember some years ago studying Jeremiah, who never really succeeded at anything. The poignancy of his repeated failures is deepened by the fact that he didn't want to be a prophet in the first place. At one point, Jeremiah buries his face in his hands and moans: (see margin).

Somehow I think that Jeremiah, good and holy though he was, might have missed an important point. God can call us to what seems to be failure. God can build successes out of our failures. Certainly Jeremiah and his prophecy have helped millions of people about whom Jeremiah could never have dreamed. And God can purify us and our motivation by allowing us the frustration of failure, at least as we humans judge success and failure. I would think that Christians are called to do their reasonable best in any attempt and then leave the results to God.

I see myself as needing an attitude that has a wide-angle lens. I need to take the "longer and larger view." I have taken myself too seriously because I have held the picture up too close to my face. I have lost perspective. I have to back away, in moments of prayer and reflection, to realize that God's strength operates through my weakness, that God writes straight with my crooked lines.

Mother Teresa of Calcutta, who has given her life to the destitute and derelict of India, was once asked, "How do you measure the success of your work?" The saintly, aged woman looked puzzled for a while, and then responded, "I don't remember that the Lord ever spoke of success. He spoke only of faithfulness in loving. The Lord has called me to faithfulness in love. This is the only success that really counts." We are worth only what we are worth in God's eyes, no more, no less.

> *"Why is my suffering continual, my wound incurable, refusing to be healed? Do you mean to be for me a deceptive stream with inconstant waters?"*
>
> *Jeremiah 15:18 (Jerusalem Bible)*

Summary

God calls us to the fullness of life. A deep, personal peace is the promise and legacy of Jesus to his followers. When the fullness of life and personal peace are interrupted by discomfort, whether it be physical or emotional or behavioral, the experience of discomfort is an invitation to personal introspection and reflection. What is in me? is the necessary and sometimes painful question that must be asked. I cannot change others, the world about me, the weather, or the position of the stars. I can change myself. In reflection and prayer, I can trace my discomfort to its attitudinal roots. I can look clearly at what is in me. And this is the area of my attitudes which I can control and change. There may be times when my attitude is found to be in full harmony with my Christian faith. But most of the time, if you are like me, you will find a neurotic and un-Christian attitude at the source of your discomfort.

And so I have to ask myself about alternative attitudes. I have to go out to others in my need, to explore the mind and attitudes of another who does not seem to be afflicted with my discomfort. It may also help to record in a journal a written description both of the old attitude to be unlearned and the new attitude to be acquired.

Have you ever felt that you were standing with another at an important fork in the road of that other person's life? If so, you probably sensed that if the person chose the less traveled road, it would make all the difference. I have that same feeling about this question we have been discussing. Each of us stands, I think, at the fork of a road in life. I can take the road of blaming: the other people in my life, the "way I am," the situation in which I find myself, the weather, the stars, and so forth.

In order to eliminate a distorted pattern of thinking, a crippling attitude, we have to work out a simple and direct statement of the truth which will replace the error in our crippling attitude. This statement is called a "counterlogic" or a "counterchallenge." The use or process is called "countering." Recent research calls this method "Voluntary Cortical Inhibition," or "VCI." We voluntarily inhibit old thought or brain (cortical) patterns. When an effective counterlogic is found, it is used as a weapon of attack, to attack the falsehood in our habitual thinking.

For example, if I am tempted to think and feel like a nonperson, a nobody, every time this thought or feeling rises in me, I stop or inhibit it with my counterlogic: "I am somebody. I'm the one and only Me!"

Thought and expression are so closely bound together in us that they are like hand in glove. Whenever we are thinking something, we are unconsciously verbalizing our thought. If we change the verbalization, we will change the thought too. Like hand in glove, if I change the position of my hand inside my glove, the position of the glove will change with it. Likewise, if I verbalize my new attitude, my thinking will move with it. The more I say, "I am somebody," the more I will think it. And the more I think it, the deeper-rooted the new habit will become. Eventually, it will become a part of me. The old, crippling, life-restricting thought patterns are by a conscious decision inhibited and replaced by new, life-giving attitudes.

From the audio program, *The Fully Alive Experience*

God calls us
to the fullness
of life.

This road of assigning responsibility for my reactions to others is a dead-end road. At its end there is only death: the death of my growth and development as a Christian, the death of peace, the death of what might have been.

I have a sense that we can also choose the road marked, "What's in me?" Of course, there are some zigs and zags, some bumps and sharp turns in that road. There will be mountains to be climbed, waters to be crossed. Along that road we may feel very burdened at times with the tasks that honesty imposes upon us. But if we choose that road, we will eventually become whole by becoming profoundly Christian. We will be brand-new beings, new creations. We will become more like the Christ of our faith. And we will experience his peace, and possess the fullness of life that Jesus has promised as his gift and legacy to believers.

*We will be
brand-new beings,
new creations.
We will become more like
the Christ of our faith.*

FOR FURTHER REFLECTION
Chapter 4: What's in Me?

Review

1. According to the chapter, why is the question "What's in me?" such an important one?

2. When we have unhealthy attitudes, there are clues, reactions, or symptoms that take place. What are these clues that indicate that we might have unhealthy attitudes?

3. Describe the process and steps of vision therapy that are proposed in this chapter.

4. In your own words, analyze the distortions in attitude of the three **Case Examples** of (a) failure, (b) being left out, and (c) isolation from others. Describe a **healthy attitude** toward these three cases.

Discuss

1. Our vision of reality consists of both positive and negative attitudes. What are the clues or symptoms that might indicate that we have negative and crippling attitudes?

2. Who are the models in your life who have the attitudes that you most want to acquire? Give concrete examples of their attitudes.

3. Is all discomfort a sign of unhealthy, negative attitudes? In other words, can discomfort also acquire healthy attitudes?

Scripture Activity

"They came to Bethsaida, where some people brought a blind man to Jesus and begged him to touch him. Jesus took the blind man by the hand and led him out of the village. After spitting on the man's eyes, Jesus placed his hands on him and asked him, 'Can you see anything?'

The man looked up and said, 'Yes, I can see people, but they look like trees walking around.'
Jesus again placed his hands on the man's eyes. This time the man looked intently, his eyesight returned, and he saw everything clearly." (Mark 8:22-25, GNB)

How does this miracle connect with what you are learning in this chapter? How might you be similar to the blind man in the story in light of your perception of reality?

Processing These Ideas about "What's in Me?"

1. *My own attitudes of affliction.* In this section of the textbook subtitled **Among My Own Attitudes of Affliction,** John Powell describes three of his distortions and the new attitudes he is cultivating. Using the same pattern, state and describe one of your distorted attitudes and then describe the new attitude that you are cultivating. It will be helpful to organize your paper under two headings: (a) **Distorted Attitude:** Describe the attitude as clearly as you can. (b) **The new attitude I am cultivating:** Describe your new attitude as clearly as you can.

2. *Vision therapy: "Process Sheet."* (Your teacher will be distributing this exercise sheet to you.) Using the same distorted attitude you identified above, do the following. First, state the **activating agent.** Second, record your **emotional reaction** and **resultant behavior.** Third, complete the **verbalization** and **visualization** sections. Then, state the same vision distortion that you worked on in Exercise 1 in the Vision section of the process sheet. Now you are ready to revise that vision. In the section **If the distortion in my vision is**: state your vision distortion again. Afterwards, revise your vision by **Countering, Modeling, Stretching,** and **Praying.**

5 We Must Learn to Be Goodfinders

In the last chapter we asked "What's in me?" The question led us to the realization that there is something inside of us that causes all our emotional, physical, and behavioral actions and reactions. The cause of our reactions are our attitudes, our vision of reality. Accordingly, whenever we become aware of emotional, physical, and/or behavioral discomfort in any situation of our life, then we must ask ourselves, "What's in me?", that is, "What underlying attitude is at the root of my reaction or response?" Once we have identified the attitude in question, we then make a diagnosis of the distortion and determine what is unhealthy and crippling about our attitude. When we have clearly identified our distorted attitude, we must then search for an alternative attitude. We do this by asking whether or not there is another way of looking at myself, at this person, or at this situation? We might ask questions such as, "Can I think of a way that would be more realistic, healthier, more Christian?" "How might Jesus suggest that I look at myself, at this other person, at this situation?" In our search for this alternative attitude, it is also helpful to reframe the experience and attempt to find the good in it. In short, if vision therapy is to be effective in our lives, we must become "goodfinders." As goodfinders we will then more easily discover the healthy attitude that needs to become part of our vision of reality in order to continue on the road to becoming fully human and fully alive.

The Common Denominator of Happiness

A few years ago some researchers decided to study the success of happiness in a purely scientific way. So they sought out the 100 most successful and contented people they could find. Then they went to work interviewing these 100 blessed souls. All information gleaned from these interviews was dutifully and carefully fed into a giant computer. The hope was to discover what all these people might have in common. The scientific interviewers were seeking to find the common denominator of human happiness.

At first the scientific search for this common denominator proved to be quite discouraging. These most successful and contented people did not seem to have anything in common—certainly not education or background. Some were grade school dropouts, while others had received doctorate degrees.

Goodfinders are those who look for and find what is good in themselves, in others, and in all situations of life.

59

Some had come from wealth, while others had to rise above the poverty into which they were born. Of all the categories, the nearest thing to a common denominator was that 70 of the 100 persons interviewed had come from small towns, population under 15,000. However, in the final tally of all the information in the computer, the search was rewarded with success. In fact, it ended in a blaze of satisfied discovery. The scientists found that each and every one of the 100 subjects was a . . . well, was a "goodfinder." However, the word *goodfinder* had to be invented to describe this common trait.

Definition of a Goodfinder

By definition, a goodfinder is one who *looks for* and *finds* what is good in him or herself, in others, and in all the situations of life. It is probably true that we usually do find whatever we are looking for. If we set ourselves to find evil, there is plenty of it to be discovered. On the other hand, if we seek to find goodness, there is also much goodness waiting for our discovery. If we look for imperfections in ourselves and in others, the search will no doubt be successful. However, if we look beyond the weak and the foolish things and seek to find the good and beautiful things that no one else had ever looked quite far enough to find, our search will be rewarded with success. It all depends upon what we are looking for. "Two men

Many of life's greatest opportunities come into our lives disguised as problems.

looked out from prison bars. / One saw mud and one saw stars."

An old country preacher once exclaimed, "People are always trying to explain the problem of evil. Well, there certainly is a lot of evil to be explained. But there is another problem. How can we explain all the goodness in this world?" The preacher was right, I think. How can we explain the people who are faithful in keeping their promises? How do we explain human devotion and a caring life spent in the service of others? How do we explain heroism? There is a lot of goodness, and often it is found in unlikely persons and places.

I have tried to imagine what would happen if a priest, a poet, and a politician were to walk down the same street together. They would each look for and find something different. The priest might think about all the souls in the high rises, and wonder about their lives and what God is doing in those lives. He might ask difficult questions about the providence of God. The poet has meanwhile been absorbed with the beauty of the overhanging branches, a veritable tunnel of trees. He sees the nuances of shades, exults in the riot of colors. He walks down the street in rapture. The politician's eyes scan the same high rises, and he mentally calculates, "There are a lot of votes up there." He wonders about who the ward leader is, and whether or not someone is trying to register all these voters. The priest, the poet, and the politician all look for and find something different in the very same experience.

Looking for the Good in Myself and Others

To be a true goodfinder, I must set my own sights on the many gifts of God to me. I should slowly make a "lover's count" of my blessings. I should look for and find all the goodness and the giftedness with which the Lord has blessed me. I must face the obvious fact that whatever I have is God's gift to me. I should be happily grateful for these gifts that are a part of me.

People are something like wildflowers. Their goodness and beauty can be so easily missed or taken for granted. Sometime everyone should pick a wildflower and study it carefully. There are delicate veins in its leaves. The petals are so fragile, the blossom so beautiful. It has a beauty all its own.

In the words of Roy Croft, "I love you . . . for passing over all the foolish, weak things that you can't help dimly seeing in me, and for drawing out into the light all the beautiful belongings that no one else had looked quite far enough to find."

People, too, need a closer look. But we do have to look beyond the weak and foolish things that cover the goodness in most of us. We must go in search of the beauty that no one else has ever looked long enough or far enough to discover. However, let all goodfinders be forewarned: Others will think of you as naive or Pollyannaish. The world at large cannot easily believe in the optimism of goodfinders.

It has often occurred to me that the function of a crisis in a human relationship is really a challenge. Most people in such a relationship seem to go along for a while on a plateau of peace. Then there is the storm or the silence of a crisis. Maybe it all starts with the fear of intimacy or with simple boredom. Or it could be that there is a win-lose rhythm, a struggle for dominance. As the Chinese say, a crisis is both a danger and an opportunity.

Most crises are a warning signal, I think. The crisis is signaling the partners to find each other at a deeper level of discovery. You may well have experienced this at some time in your life. Do you remember a time when you felt estranged from someone close to you? You wondered if love was over. There were angry words, wounded feelings, and a long, smoldering resentment. Then you got sudden word that the other person was seriously sick or badly hurt. All the surface conflict and consequent estrangement seemed to vanish. You rushed to the side of the other person. You poured out parts of your own depths that you didn't know existed. A new and deeper bond was forged in that moment. The tinsel of shallow love mellowed into gold. You had found each other at a deeper level. It was a new beginning in the relationship.

Finding Good in All Situations of Life

It has been said that our biggest opportunities will probably come into our lives disguised as problems. Problems have a way of challenging us, of calling out of us coping capacities of which we were unaware. Problems can jolt us out of our predictable routines but only to introduce us to a life of new possibilities. In the end, we probably profit more from suffering than we do from success. But I feel sure that the extent of benefits derived is determined by our habitual mindset. We must be ready to look for and find good in all the situations of life.

Recently I heard that a friend of mine was arrested for a minor traffic violation. This woman is the mother of five children, and a very dear and gentle person. At any rate, she was driving to a department store in a suburb of Chicago. A large and overserious policeman stalked into the store after her and demanded to see her driver's license. He said that she had made an improper turn before arriving at the store. When she asked him to tell her that he was only joking, he (honestly) arrested her. While he was handcuffing her, he swung her arm around behind her. It struck him, and so he added the charge: "Striking an officer." Then, believe it or not, he called for backup help. My friend was taken to the police station, strip-searched, fingerprinted, and put into a cell.

finding the goods.

I had heard all these details before I actually saw my friend. When I told the story to a lawyer friend, he gasped, "This is a lawyer's dream. It has a 'quick million' written all over it." He wanted to know if the woman in question had a lawyer.

Then I had a chance to hear the whole story again, firsthand. My friend assured me that "it was one of the most meaningful experiences of my whole life. I told the officers that I finally understood how Jesus must have felt. I assured them that during the week before Easter when we recall his suffering, I would be much more understanding than ever before. They kept insisting, 'We're only doing our duty, Ma'am.' And I kept reassuring and thanking them."

By the way, I did ask her if she intended to file a lawsuit against the suburb or maybe against the arresting officer. She replied, "Oh, no. The arresting officer was just a poor boy who overreacted. Do you know, he kept calling me 'Ma'am,' but once he slipped and said 'Mom.' Somehow I'm sure he was just looking for a mother."

We speak of having to "reframe" our difficult experiences in order to find the good in them. I suppose that the term comes from the reframing of a painting. The frame brings out certain details that might otherwise have been missed. When we reframe an experience, we go back over it to look for the silver lining in the dark cloud, to focus on the lessons learned, the advantages derived. Many psychotherapists ask their clients

Problems may jolt us into
new possibilities.

to repeat a story of misfortune. Only in the repetition, the client is asked to tell the same story as one of opportunity and profit. For example, James Whistler, the painter, wanted to be a career soldier until he flunked out of West Point. He was so depressed by his failure that he took up painting as therapy. The singer Julio Iglesias wanted only to be a soccer player until he was hurt and temporarily paralyzed. A nurse brought him a guitar to help him pass the time. It almost seems that when one door is closed, another is opened. The important thing is to be a goodfinder.

God, the Ultimate Goodfinder

At the time of Jesus, the world was a cold and cruel world. The rich spent their idle time in endless orgies, the poor lived in a grinding poverty. Two-thirds of all the people in that world were living in a subhuman form of slavery. The favorite sport of that world was watching two gladiators fight until one of them was fallen with wounds or exhaustion. At this point the victorious gladiator would look to the spectators for further instructions. The spectators would then hold money or jewels in one hand, and with the thumb of the other point upward or down. The upthrusted thumb meant, "This money or these jewels are yours if you spare him. He was a vicious competitor and will come back to entertain us again." The down-pointing thumb was a signal that urged the victor, "Kill him. He was uninteresting. Put your sword through his throat."

Historians of the time tell us that when the victorious gladiator would transfix his fallen victim, there would arise a shout of celebration that would rock the whole city. It was as though a home run had been hit in a major-league baseball park during a World Series.

This was the world of which the Scriptures say: "God so loved the world that he sent his only begotten Son into the world, so that anyone who would believe in him would not die but would have eternal life. God sent his Son into the world not to judge or condemn it, but to love it into life" (John 3:16-17). The coming of Jesus into this world was the supreme act of goodfinding. The world that God found "very good" at creation was, for all its misery, still very good. Deep down inside every human heart, God resides and recognizes the goodness and giftedness that lies buried there.

We who are made in the image and likeness of God will share in God's happiness to the extent that we become goodfinders. There is even scientific, computerized proof for this.

There is a problem. Although we must learn to reframe our experiences, to become "goodfinders," yet there remains a problem. How do we know if our vision is correct? How do we know that people who think well of themselves are on the right track? How do we know that people who think well of others are not just naive? In other words, how do we know when our vision of reality is the right one?

I would like to suggest that the questions we are now asking lead us to the feet of God. These questions will help us to understand the importance of the Word of God, that is, the Scriptures, and the great Word that God uttered into the world, God's Son Jesus. He alone can offer assurance of a correct vision.

Belief in Jesus offers what psychologists can never provide: a master vision. Jesus himself said that if we would accept and live his message, if we would make his vision our own, we would become the fully alive people he calls us to be. The person and vision of Jesus are the truth that sets us free from the inner distorted attitudes that keep us from being fully human and fully alive.

God always finds good.

FOR FURTHER REFLECTION
Chapter 5: We Must Learn to Be Goodfinders

Review

1. Define a "goodfinder."

2. Explain: "Many of life's greatest opportunities come into our lives disguised as problems."

3. What is the technique of "reframing"? How does this technique support the assumption and thesis of vision therapy?

4. How did Julio Iglesias and John Whistler reframe their experiences?

5. How is God the Ultimate Goodfinder?

Discuss

1. In terms of your own self-attitude, are you a goodfinder? Do you tend to look for what is good or what is bad in you?

2. In your general approach to others, do you notice other people's good qualities or are you more aware of their faults, weaknesses, and limitations?

3. Describe a personal experience of "crisis." Explain how the experience posed itself as either an "opportunity" or a "danger."

4. Describe how you or a person you know quite well "reframed" an experience and found the good in it.

Scripture Activity

"Love is patient and kind; it is not jealous or conceited or proud; love is not ill-mannered or selfish or irritable; love does not keep a record of wrongs; love is not happy with evil, but is happy with the truth. Love never gives up; and its faith, hope, and patience never fail." (1 Corinthians 13:4–7, GNB)

A goodfinder is one who looks for good in oneself, in others, and in all situations of life. Think about a difficult person in your life. Look beyond the difficulties you have with that person and attempt to look for his or her goodness. Construct a prayer asking God to help you to love and understand this person more effectively and to acquire the attitude of "goodfinding."

Processing These Ideas about Being a "Goodfinder"

The Meaning of Quixote's code.[1]

1. ***How is Don Quixote a model of a "goodfinder"?*** Share whether or not you could personally live by this code Why or why not?

CODE OF HONOR
> Call nothing thine except thy soul.
> Love not what thou art, but only what
> thou may become.
> Do not pursue pleasure, for thou may
> have the misfortune to overtake it.
> Look always forward; in last year's nest
> there are no birds this year.
> Be just to all men, courteous to all women.
> Live in the vision of the one for whom all
> great deeds are done . . .

2. ***Journalize about self.*** Write several paragraphs describing your own three best qualities. Let it be the beginning of a lover's count of personal blessings.

3. ***Journalize about another.*** Write a second set of paragraphs describing the three best qualities of someone you don't like.

4. ***Reframe a recent experience of crisis in your life.*** Tell a friend or confidant the story of a recent trauma or disappointment, but in the context of opportunity and advantage. Recall the things you learned from experience. Go over it and describe the good results, the profit derived from this experience.

---

[1] This should be assigned only if the class has seen *Man of La Mancha.*

6 Vision Therapy and Religious Faith

If you were to take the sum total of all the authoritative articles ever written by the most quali- fied of psychologists and psychiatrists on the subject of mental hygiene—if you were to combine them and refine them and cleave out the excess verbiage—if you were to . . . have these unadulterated bits of pure scientific knowledge concisely expressed by the most capable of living poets, you would have an awkward and incomplete summation of the Sermon on the Mount.

Psychiatrist James T. Fisher,
*A Few Buttons Missing:
The Case Book of a Psychiatrist*

One of the main assumptions of vision therapy is that there is a knowable "reality." We need some version of reality by which we can judge the rationality of our thoughts and to which we can conform our vision or belief system. But who is to say what reality is? Cynics are sure that they are in touch with reality in suspecting everything, trusting no one. Naive persons are convinced that everybody is really a true-blue Boy or Girl Scout at heart. Poets swoon at the beauty of a lake or forest. Others see only a lot of water or lumber. What is reality? Who has conceived it correctly?

Psychologists are reasonable and honest in facing this problem. There are many slightly different solutions. Some suggest that we use a "universal consensus": Reality is that which most people think it is. There are others who offer the pragmatic solution of "what works" as a criterion of reality. There are still others who speak only of an "individual and personal" reality, suggesting that each person has his or her own reality. It is true, of course, that all of us perceive reality, whatever it is, in our own uniquely rational and uniquely irrational ways.

But the practical question persists. How am I to see other human beings? Are we really brothers and sisters in a human family, or are we enemies on a common battlefield? Is there such a thing as a free commitment of love, or are we really determined and predestined to become whatever it is that we will become? Is life governed by the pleasure principle, the power principle, or the programming principle? Is this life all that there is, or is there really a glorious hereafter? Perhaps the answers to these questions would not make a radical difference in my life-style, but they would definitely have some influence on my thoughts, choices, and perspectives. But in these matters, who is to say?

What is reality?

Jesus Christ Is the Answer

Those who believe in revealed religions have a very definite criterion of reality. They are convinced that God has directly told us through revelations some very important things about who God is, who we are, about our relationship to one another, about the purpose of life and the significance of this world. There is no logic, of course, either to prove or disprove the authenticity of this revelation of God. Ultimately, the test of faith is always religious experience, which is highly personal and individual. Most believers have at some time felt the touch of God, a conversion-to-faith experience in which they have found a new and distinct peace, power, and presence. The intuition of faith, in this moment, surpasses the reach of all natural logic and scientific knowledge.

This has certainly been my experience, as I have related it in my book *He Touched Me*. Because of my own religious background and personal experience I have accepted the message of Jesus Christ as the master vision of reality. For me the message and person of Jesus are the source of objectification for my own vision of reality. They are the basic norm for my judgments and choices. I have chosen to live my life in the light of this revelation. I want to be God's man and to do God's work: I want to help build a world of love and a human family of mutual understanding.

An evangelist friend of mine told me that when Jesus became real to him as a teenager, he sneaked into his high-school classroom before the start of the school day and printed on the chalkboard in huge letters: JESUS CHRIST IS THE ANSWER! When he returned later with the other students for the beginning of class, he discovered that someone else had printed under his statement: YEAH, BUT WHAT IS THE QUESTION? "Yeah," he thought, "what is the question?"

As his life progressed, my friend found that there isn't only one question. As psychiatrist Viktor Frankl says it should, life asks many different questions of us. Life asks how much we can love, how much we can enjoy and endure. Life asks us if we love ourselves and if we love our fellow human beings. Daily living asks us to distinguish between what is really important and what is unimportant in life: to choose priorities. Life demands that we exercise the judgment of conscience: to choose whatever seems right and to avoid whatever seems wrong. Perhaps the most profound question asked by life is the question of significance and meaning. All of us have to find some purpose or mission in life which will confer upon us a sense of personal distinction and worth. We need to believe that our lives will make a difference for someone or for something.

Of course, there are no patented, simple answers that flow out of automated machines. The German poet Rainer Maria Rilke counsels us to be patient toward all

> *Most believers have at some time felt the touch of God, a conversion-to-faith experience in which they have found a new and distinct peace, power, and presence.*

that is unsolved in our hearts. He suggests that we must learn to love the questions themselves while waiting for and working out the answers. Growth is always a gradual process even if there are glittering moments of insight and a divine revelation.

Alexander Solzhenitsyn ended his Nobel lecture on literature with the Russian proverb: "One word of truth outweighs the whole world." Saint John, in the prologue of his Gospel, says that the one Word of truth has been spoken by God:

> In the beginning the Word already existed; the Word was with God, and the Word was God . . .
>
> The Word was the source of life, and this life brought light to people. The light shines in the darkness, and the darkness has never put it out . . .
>
> The Word became a human being and, full of grace and truth, lived among us. We saw his glory, the glory which he received as the Father's only Son.
>
> *John 1:1, 4–5, 14, GNB*

My evangelist friend, now an old man, tells me that he now knows much more about the many questions which life asks. Life has questioned him about his values and priorities, about his visions and dreams, about his courage and capacity to love. "But," he said to me, looking over his glasses, "to all the questions life asks: Jesus Christ is the answer!"

I am sure that he is right. Of course, this does not imply that the answers which Jesus applied to the problems of his life and times can be imported and applied without any change to the problems of our very different lives and times. Jesus asks us to be as concerned and loving to our world and times as he was to his. However, because all conduct ultimately is the result of a vision, the important thing is to grasp the basic vision of reality that Jesus had, his inner attitudes and belief system. This is the ultimate source of human health and happiness. These Jesus has communicated to us through his message and in his person:

> "I am the light of the world. Whoever follows me will have the light of life and will never walk in darkness."
>
> *John 8:12, GNB*

There is an interesting dialogue between Jesus and his contemporaries recorded in the eighth chapter of John's Gospel. Jesus makes the point that only the truth, the full acceptance of reality, can make a person free.

> "If you obey my teaching, you are really my disciples; you will know the truth, and the truth will set you free."
>
> *John 8:31–32, GNB*

When his hearers profess puzzlement at this idea of liberation by truth, pointing out that they have "never been anybody's slaves," Jesus repeats that he is himself the source of true freedom:

One word of truth outweighs the whole world.

"If the Son sets you free, then you will be really free."

John 8:36, GNB

True health resides principally in one's vision, in one's deepest attitudes; it is not merely the absence of symptoms. Likewise, true freedom has its roots in one's basic vision of reality; it is not merely the absence of coercion from external forces. I see the person of Jesus liberated by a vision that results in a startling freedom: He is free enough to love and to associate with prodigals and prostitutes, and at the end to express a quaking fear and still die freely as an act of love.

What is the vision of Jesus which lies under his message and manner of life? Whatever else it is, it is certainly a call to the fullness of life.

"I am come in order that you might have life—life in all its fullness." *John 10:10, GNB*

The Master Vision of Jesus

At the risk of seeming presumptuous, I would like now to describe some of the central features of the vision of Jesus, as I see them. I think that the message, the life, and the person of Jesus are saying to us:

1. God is love. This means that all God does is love. As the sun only shines, conferring its light and warmth on those who stand ready to receive them, so God only loves, conferring light and warmth on those who would receive them. This means that God does not have anger. God does not punish. When we separate ourselves from God by our sin, all the change takes place in us, never in God. God is unchangeably loving. Love is sharing, the sharing of one's self and one's life. God's intention in creating us in this world was to share life with us. In nurturing this life in us, God calls us to be a human family, to become a community of love, each wanting and working for the true happiness of all.

2. You are loved by God, unconditionally and as you are. God has assured you through the prophets and through the Son that even if a mother were to forget the child of her womb, God would never forget you. Your name is carved in God's palms, inscribed indelibly in God's heart. You do not have to win or earn or be worthy of God's love. It is a "given." Of course, you can refuse to accept it. You can separate yourself from God's love for a while or even for an eternity. Whatever your response, all during your life and at every moment of your life God will be there offering love to you, even at those times when you are distracted or refusing it.

Wherever you are in your development, whatever you are doing, with a strong affirmation of all your goodness and good deeds, with a gentle understanding of your weakness, God is forever loving you. You do not have to change, grow, or be good in order to be loved. Rather, you are loved so that you can change, grow, and be good. Your realization of this unconditional love is extremely important. You must remember people like:

Peter the Rock, who was often a sandpile, a loudmouth, a man who had denied even knowing the one who had loved him most.

Zacchaeus, who was a runt, who offered to collect taxes for Rome from his own people for a "kickback" from the take.

Mary Magdalene, who was a "hooker."

James and John, who were mama's boys and pretty ridiculous at times, such as the time when they wanted to destroy a whole town which had given them a poor reception. The "Sons of Thunder," they were laughingly called.

Andrew, who was pretty naive. He thought five loaves and two fish were enough for five thousand people.

Thomas, who was an all-star bullhead.

Martha, who was a twitch, worrier, and complainer.

The woman taken in adultery, who was pretty frightened until Jesus saved her life and forgave her sin.

The thief on the cross, who said what might have been his first prayer and was promised immediate paradise.

The blind man, who didn't know who Jesus was but only that he himself was blind and now he could see!

The paralyzed boy, whose body needed healing but who first needed to have his sins forgiven.

The prodigal son, who was pretty heartless but who came home when he was hungry into his father's open arms and open heart.

Saul of Tarsus, who was hell-bent on destroying Christianity until he took that road to Damascus and found a loving Lord.

God was in Jesus, loving them, affirming them, forgiving them, encouraging them, challenging them all the way into greatness, peace, and the fullness of life: and millions more like them, and like us.

3. The providence of God rules the world. Jesus is the Lord of human history. At times you may experience the feeling that everything is falling apart. You wonder: What is the world coming to? What am I coming to? How will I make ends meet? Who is going to push my wheelchair? You do not consciously define or defend the thought, but sometimes you may be tempted to imagine God's back to the wall, furious and frustrated at the fact that everything has gotten out of hand.

> God, who is love, has made you in God's image and likeness. Love is your calling and destiny.

"King Christ, this world is a leak; and lifepreservers there are none" (e. e. cummings). In the words of Saint Paul: "Jesus is the Lord!" You must remember that this world, the course of human history and human destiny are in his hands. He is in charge of this world. He alone has the game plan, total knowledge of the human situation and the power to turn things around completely. Do not try to make yourself the Messiah to all people or caretaker to the world. You are not equipped to cover so much territory or bear such a burden. Reflect upon these words until they have formed a new insight in you and have become deeply embedded in your vision: Then Jesus said to his disciples:

> "And so I tell you not to worry about the food you need to stay alive or about the clothes you need for your body. Life is much more important than food, and the body much more important than clothes. Look at the crows: they don't plant seeds or gather a harvest; they don't have storage rooms or barns; God feeds them! You are worth so much more than birds! Can any of you live a bit longer by worrying about it? If you can't manage even such a small thing, why worry about the other things? Look how the wild flowers grow: they don't work or make clothes for themselves. But I tell you that not even King Solomon with all his wealth had clothes as beautiful as one of these flowers. It is God who clothes the wild grass—grass that is here today and gone tomorrow, burned up in the oven. Won't he be all the more sure to clothe you? What little faith you have!
>
> "So don't be all upset, always concerned about what you will eat and drink. (For the pagans of this world are always concerned about all these things.) Your Father knows that you need these things. Instead, be concerned with his Kingdom, and he will provide you with these things."
>
> *Luke 12:22–31, GNB*

4. You are called to love: your God, your self, and your neighbor. God, who is love, has made you in God's image and likeness. Love is your calling and destiny. It is the perfection of your human nature. Love is also a gift of God, the highest gift of God's Spirit. It is necessary that you realize the importance of loving yourself. There has to be some kind of logical, if not chronological, priority to loving yourself. If you do not love yourself, you will be filled with pain, and this pain will keep all your attention riveted on yourself. Agony constricts our consciousness. If you do not love yourself, you cannot truly love either God or your neighbor. So you must learn to do the same things for yourself that you would do in loving others: You must acknowledge and affirm all that is good in you. You must gently try to understand all that is weak and limited. You must be aware of and

try to fulfill your needs: physical, psychological, and spiritual. As you learn to love yourself, you must also learn to balance concern for yourself with concern for others. "Whatever you do for the least of my brothers and sisters you do for me." But remember that your success in loving will be proportionate to your openness in accepting the love and affirmation of God. It will likewise be proportionate to the love that you have for yourself. In the end, the success of your life will be judged by how sensitively and delicately you have loved.

5. I will be with you. God says: I am covenanted, committed forever to love you, to do whatever is best for you. I will be kind,

encouraging and enabling, but I will also be challenging. At times I will come to comfort you in your affliction. At other times I will come to afflict you in your comfort. Whatever I do, it will always be an act of love and an invitation to growth. I will be with you to illuminate your darkness, to strengthen your weakness, to fill your emptiness, to heal your brokenness, to cure your sickness, to straighten what may be bent in you, and to revive whatever good things may have died in you. Remain united to me, accept my love, enjoy the warmth of my friendship, avail yourself of my power, and you will bear much fruit. You will have life in all its fullness.

6. Your destiny is eternal life. God says: By all means join the

Look how the wild flowers grow: they don't work or make clothes for themselves. But I tell you that not even King Solomon with all his wealth had clothes as beautiful as one of these flowers.
Luke 12:27, GNB

6. Your destiny is eternal life.
God says: By all means join the dance and sing the songs of a full life. At the same time, remember that you are a pilgrim. You are on your way to an eternal home which I have prepared for you. Eternal life has already begun in you but it is not perfectly completed. There are still inevitable sufferings. But remember that the sufferings of this present stage of your life are nothing compared to the glory that you will see revealed in you someday. Eye has not ever seen, nor ear ever heard, nor has the mind ever imagined the joy prepared for you because you have

and to love at all times. Someday you will come up into my mountain, and then for you all the clocks and calendars will have finished their counting. Together with all my children, you will be mine and I will be yours forever.

This is, as I see it, the basic vision proposed in the Gospels (the good news) of Christians. It offers a perspective of life and death—a vision of reality—that is reassuring and at the same time challenging. It provides a needed sense of security, but also meaning and purpose in life. It gives us a basic frame of reference to understand ourselves, our brothers and sisters in the human family, the meaning of life and the world, and God as our loving Father. For the believer it offers a vision of reality or belief system through which all the activating events of our human lives can be interpreted and evaluated. It is a reassurance of what reality is by the Maker of all that is.

This vision of religious faith remains for some people a sweet but mere construct, only a pair of lovely rose-colored glasses to tint and tone down the harsh

opened yourself to the gift of my love. On your way to our eternal home, enjoy the journey. Let your happiness be double, in the joyful possession of what you have and in the eager anticipation of what will be. Say a resounding "Yes!" to life

demands of reality. Again, the decisive factor is personal religious experience, the touch of God. One must be actively engaged with and educated by the Holy Spirit, who alone can make a person a believer. Faith is not a matter of logical reasoning or a natural acquisition. It is a matter of experience. Only God's Spirit can provide the needed religious experience. Only the touch of grace can make the Christian message more than a code of conduct and comfort for pious and plastic people.

It cannot be repeated too often that a living faith is not a human skill or acquisition. We do not pick up "believing" as we would learn, for example, to play the piano. We must be touched by the Spirit of God. The difference in one who has been touched in this way is so profound that Saint Paul calls this person a "new creation." Such a one is, as we say, a new person. Paul calls a life which has not been touched and transformed by the Spirit "life according to the flesh." The life of a person who has been renewed by the Spirit lives a "life according to the Spirit."

Jesus says that it is the Spirit who gives us a certain instinct or intuition that we are affirmed by God. It is through the Spirit that we know we are beloved children. It is the Spirit who calls out of our hearts the tender and loving words: "Father!"

Even if we did once know Christ in the flesh, that is not how we know him now. And for everyone who is in Christ, there is a new creation; the old creation has gone, and now the new one is here. It is all God's work. It was God who reconciled us through Christ and gave us the work of handing on this reconciliation. In other words, God in Christ was reconciling the world to God.

Paul himself is so deeply moved by the reality of this complete transformation that he expresses his personal experience in the line: "so that it is no longer I who live, but it is Christ who lives in me." (Galatians 2:20, GNB)

We have said that we need a vision when we look out at reality through the eyes of our mind. When we perceive ourselves, other people, life, the world, and God, we have to make some kind of an interpretation or evaluation. We need some kind of order and predictability because we cannot abide chaos. It is the touch of the Spirit that provides the kind of focus and clarity that we need in order to see clearly and to live fully.

In the first words of the first book of the Bible, Genesis, the Spirit of God is depicted as bringing the order of creation out of the primordial chaos.

"In the beginning, when God created the universe, the earth was formless and desolate. The raging ocean that covered everything was engulfed in total darkness, and the Spirit of God was moving over the water." (Genesis 1:1–2, GNB)

It is by this Spirit that confusion and chaos are transformed into the loveliness of creation. Eight chapters later, in the narration of the Flood, it is the same Spirit of God that causes the waters of the flood to subside. Again God restores the order of creation out of the watery confusion and chaos. Through the prophet Joel, God promises that "I will pour out my Spirit on everyone" (Joel 3:1; quoted in Acts 2:17, GNB).

> We do not pick up "believing" as we would learn, for example, to play the piano. We must be touched by the Spirit of God. The difference in one who has been touched in this way is so profound that Saint Paul calls this person a "new creation."

It is this same Spirit of God who comes on the day of Pentecost to transform the disciples of Jesus from cowardly and confused men into clear-headed and convinced apostles. The chaos of their confusion is replaced by great clarity of purpose. It is the Spirit of God who directs the Christians of the early Church. The Spirit's action appoints leaders, heals the sick, melts hearts, and enables people to love one another in an overwhelming release of power that will renew the face of the earth.

This touch of the Spirit transforms everything in a person and in his or her world. The person is indeed a new creation. The revelation of God, which might otherwise seem to be a fiction, is clearly a fact: a vision of reality. The touch of the Spirit results in a deep harmony, peace and order, replacing a kind of primordial chaos in a human being's inner vision of reality. Consequently, all the emotional and behavioral patterns of the person touched by the Spirit are deeply affected. There is a new sense of integration and wholeness. The person experiences that "unity which the Spirit gives by means of the peace that binds" (Ephesians 4:3, GNB). As a new creation, this man or woman is enabled by the Spirit to walk into the beautiful world of God and into the fullness of the life to which God has called God's children.

> *The Spirit's touch gives harmony and peace.*

What Is to Come?

In the following pages I would like to describe this joy-filled and liberating master vision of Jesus, as I understand it. I know very well that our Christian understanding of Jesus, his message and vision, is progressive. Each generation stands on the shoulder of the previous generation. Like pygmies standing on the shoulders of giants, we of this generation should understand the person and vision of Jesus better than previous generations. And those Christians who will come after us should see more clearly than we do the meaning of his person and message. I can only share with you, my sisters and brothers in Christ, the Jesus whom I know and his vision as best I can understand it at this time in my life and at this point of human history. I trust that there will be others who have more profound insights than I do. I trust that there will be others who will take up where I must leave off, who will see and understand the person and vision of Jesus more clearly than I do. However, I do want to share with you the insights that are helping me to become a more peaceful and a more fully alive believer. Of this one thing I am certain: To the extent that you and I truly understand and live the vision of Jesus, we will be that much more free to live, to love, to grow, and to experience the fullness of life that Jesus holds out to us.

FOR FURTHER REFLECTION
Chapter 6: Vision Therapy and Religious Faith

Review

1. There is a dilemma because psychologists cannot decide on which attitude should be considered "healthy." Some suggest that we arrive at a "universal consensus." Others suggest that "what works" is sufficient as the criterion of reality. While others speak of "a personal" reality, suggesting that each person has his or her reality. Given this dilemma, how does religious faith and Jesus' vision of reality help decide what attitude is healthy?

2. Explain Victor Frankl's statement "Life asks us questions."

3. What does Powell's evangelist friend mean when he states, "To all the questions life asks: Jesus Christ is the answer!"?

4. Briefly explain the following:
   a. God is love.
   b. You are loved by God, unconditionally and as you are.
   c. The providence of God rules the world. Jesus is the Lord of human history.
   d. You are called to love: your God, your self, and your neighbor.
   e. I will be with you.
   f. Your destiny will be eternal life.

5. What is religious faith?

Discuss

1. Give examples of how life questions you.
2. Describe what you believe is the most common attitude the media has of other people. How does it differ from Jesus' vision of others?
3. How is Jesus' attitude of the meaning of life different from the attitude of consumerism?
4. How is your faith related to your vision of reality?
5. What would life be without faith?
6. How can you make Jesus' vision yours?
7. How do you check the accuracy of your vision of reality? What is an inaccurate vision?

Scripture Activity

"Jesus spoke to the Pharisees again. 'I am the light of the world,' he said. 'Whoever follows me will have the light of life and will never walk in darkness . . . If you obey my teaching, you are really my disciples; you will know the truth, and the truth will set you free . . . If the Son sets you free, then you will be really free.'" (John 8:12, 31–32, 36, GNB)

Processing These Ideas about Vision Therapy and Religious Faith

1. **The be-attitudes and my life.** Take each of the Beatitudes from Matthew 5:3–12 and show how by making them an integral part of your life, you can shape a larger and truer vision of life. Write out your ideas.[1]

   Example: I want to work for peace because . . .
   I want to be merciful to others because . . .

2. **The master vision of Jesus.** What is Jesus' vision of reality? Try to describe in writing Jesus' vision of how you should see: (a) yourself, (b) other people, (c) the meaning of life, (d) the world, and (e) God.

3. **Letting life question you.** Review your day and share in writing how life has questioned you today. In other words, how has life (activating agents) exposed your attitudes? Conclude by stating what attitude you became aware of when life questioned you. For example: A man comes up to me and asks for money. If I react nervously, life is asking me "Who are other people?" My reaction suggests that my attitude toward strangers is that they are threatening or untrustworthy. Now it's your turn to share how life has asked you questions.

---

[1] This exercise was taken from *Free to Be Me.*

THE CHRISTIAN VISION

OF ONESELF

7 *The Christian Vision of Self*

An Experiment: The Empty Chair

Before we explore the question about how we Christians are to think of ourselves, I would like to ask you to do another experiment. (By the way, thanks for your patience with me and my experiments.) I would like you to close your eyes after you have finished reading the instructions. Imagine a chair at a distance of about ten feet from yourself. Please notice the appearance of the chair: its height, width, color. Notice, too, the type of chair: straight back or rocker, upholstered or wood, and so forth. After the chair becomes very vivid to you in your imagination, let someone you know very well come out of the wings of the stage of your imagination and sit in the chair. Please look carefully at this person, and notice the way this person looks at you. You will then register a "felt sense" of the person. Become aware of your total, unified reaction to this person: physical (bodily), emotional, perceptual. All of your previous experiences with this person will feed into this "felt sense." All the things you have ever thought or judged about this person—your previous emotional reactions, your stored memories of past experiences with this person—will all shape and color and contribute to your reaction.

After you record this reaction, see the first person getting up and leaving. Then a second person whom you know very well comes and sits in the same chair. Again, you consciously record your "felt sense" of this second person. You can compare it with your previous reaction, the "felt sense" of the first person. After you have finished with the two persons, let a third person come from the wings of the stage and sit in the chair, face to face with you. This third person is yourself. Notice and become more and more aware of your "felt sense" of yourself. Notice and remember the immediate reaction you have to yourself: warm or cold, heavy or light, enjoyable or painful, a sense of attraction or revulsion, and so forth. The main thing is to record your "felt sense" reaction to all three persons, the last of whom is yourself. Please review these instructions and then put the book down for now. When you get back, I would like to make a few suggestions about the significance of the results of your experiment.

* * *

The exercise you just conducted was an effort to get at your "self-image." Imagining the other two people was just a warm-up, getting you used to the awareness of a "felt sense."

We cannot love others unless we love ourselves.

The real test was the reaction to yourself that you experienced. Your thoughts and judgments, your feelings and memories of yourself all fed into and determined that reaction. Recall now: Did you like or dislike yourself? Did you feel warm and friendly, turned on or off by the image of yourself? What would you like to have said to yourself? What did the face and the body language of "the other you" seem to be saying to you?

I recall that the first time I did this experiment, the "me" that I saw looked tentative and uneasy, as though he was bracing himself for impending criticism. I instinctively felt very sorry for him. Suddenly it dawned on me that I have always been my own severest and constant critic. I have never been able to review my own personal performances. I can't watch myself on video or listen to myself on a recording. It has even been painful for me to read the words that I have written. The critic in me has always been commenting: "Why did you say that? Why didn't you use a different illustration? Your voice is high pitched and nasal! That idea does not come through clearly!" When I realized this, during the chair fantasy, I remember apologizing to myself: "Hey, I'm sorry. I have never really been an affirming friend to you. I have been only a negative critic. From now on, I am going to try to be a friend, to notice and to tell you about your strengths as well as your weaknesses, about your gifts and your goodness as well as about your limitations and failures."

Each of us acts out his or her self-image.

The Most Important Attitude and Its Effects

There is no doubt that the attitude each of us has toward himself or herself is the most important of all our attitudes. We have earlier compared an attitude to a lens of the mind. To continue with this comparison, the lens or the attitude one has toward self is *always* over the eyes of the mind. Other lenses or attitudes may be superimposed when we are reacting to something else, but this lens-vision of self will affect favorably or unfavorably the way we see everything else. Depending on what we are dealing with, our various attitudes are always ready to interpret, evaluate, dictate an appropriate response. However, it is important to realize that the attitude toward self is *always* in play, always affecting our other attitudes, always coloring the way we see every part of reality. It is, without a doubt, the basic or fundamental attitude in each and every one of us.

Perhaps the most critical function and result of this attitude toward self is this: Each of us acts out his or her self-image. For example, if I perceive myself as a loser, I act like a loser. I approach each new person or situation with a loser mentality. All my expectations are colored by this "loser" perception of myself. And, as we all know, the expectation is often the mother of the result. Our expectations of failure give birth to our actual failures. And when in fact we do lose or fail, we are then confirmed in our original self-defeating attitude.

"You see, I told you I was no good! I failed again." It is indeed a vicious circle.

There is a story in Native American folklore that illustrates this truth very clearly. According to the legend, a brave came upon an eagle's egg that had somehow fallen unbroken from an eagle's nest. Unable to find the nest, the brave put the egg in the nest of a prairie chicken, where it was hatched by the brooding mother hen. The fledgling eagle, with its proverbial strong eyes, saw the world for the first time. Looking at the other prairie chickens, he did what they did. He cawed and scratched at the earth, pecked here and there for stray grains and husks, now and then rising in a flutter a few feet above the earth and then descending again. The eagle accepted and imitated the daily routine of the earthbound prairie chickens. And he spent most of his life this way.

Then, as the story continues, one day an eagle flew over the brood of prairie chickens. The now aging eagle, who still thought he was a prairie chicken, looked up in awed admiration as the great bird soared through the skies. "What is that?" he gasped in astonishment. One of the old prairie chickens replied, "I have seen one before. That is the eagle, the proudest, the strongest, and the most magnificent of all the birds. But don't you ever dream that you could be like that. You're like the rest of us and we are prairie chickens." And so, shackled by this belief, the eagle lived and died thinking he was a prairie chicken.

So, too, does each of us live and die. Our lives are shaped by the way we perceive ourselves. The all-important attitudes by which we perceive and evaluate ourselves tell us who we are and describe the appropriate behavior for such a person. We live and we die according to our self-perception.

There is still another very important effect of the attitude toward self. This attitude determines not only how we act but also how others will treat us. No doubt you remember the nasty kid in grammar school, who pinned a sign on your back that read: "Kick me!" (And other nasty kids obliged.) Well, it seems to be true that our attitudes toward ourselves, the way we perceive ourselves, compose a message or sign also. Only this sign that you and I hold out in front of ourselves is something like an announcement of who we are. It tells other people who we are and invites a definite reaction. Like the children at school, most people treat us accordingly. If my sign says that I'm not much, that's about how much attention, respect, and affirmation I will get: not much! On the other hand, if the sign composed by my attitude toward self says that I am a person who deserves respect, I will be treated with respect by others.

A postscript has to be added to what has just been said about this "sign" that is composed and held out in front of us, reflecting our attitudes toward ourselves. We may consciously try to pretend, to develop a public personality that belies what we truly think and feel about ourselves.

We may try to camouflage our anxiety by an outward show of arrogance. We may pretend confidence when we are trembling inside. However, most people see through our transparent masks. We have a sense, don't we, that tells us when another is being "real" and when that person is striking a public pose. We want to ask the braggart, "Are you trying to convince us or yourself?"

Subconsciously, in a thousand ways that we might try to hide, we publicly reveal our self-image. We tell people, as clearly as if there were a visible sign held out for all to see, what we truly think about ourselves. And most people, reading our giveaway signs with instincts that are partly conscious and partly subconscious, treat us accordingly. Human intuition can be frighteningly accurate. People are much more perceptive than perhaps we realize. And so, when troubled people come to a counselor to ask how they can change the other people with whom they are dealing, the counselor almost always gives the same advice: "Change yourself. Change your own attitude toward yourself, and other people will automatically change their treatment of you."

Love of Self and Love of Others

Finally, it is a fact that we cannot love others if we do not love ourselves. The commandment of the Lord is to love our neighbor as we love ourself. A psychological version of this commandment might well read: "Love yourself and you will love your neighbor. Refuse to love yourself and you won't be able to love your neighbor." The Jesus I know insistently tells us to put away our pan scales, to stop measuring output versus input, to make love the rule and motive of our lives. "Love one another as I have loved you." Further, Jesus assures us, "If you do this, you will be very happy." (See John 13:17.) However, it is crucial to realize that our attitude toward self regulates

---

The importance of one's self-image is aptly illustrated in the fairy tale Rapunzel. It is the story of a young girl, imprisoned in a tower with an old witch. The young girl is in fact very beautiful, but the old witch insistently tells her that she is ugly. It is, of course, a stratagem of the witch to keep the girl in the tower. The moment of Rapunzel's liberation occurs one day when she is gazing from the window of the tower. At the base of the tower stands her Prince Charming. She throws her hair, long and beautiful tresses, out of the window (the root-ends, of course, remain attached to her scalp), and he braids the hair into a ladder and climbs up to rescue her. Rapunzel's imprisonment is really not that of the tower. She is imprisoned by the fear of her own ugliness that the witch has described so often and so effectively. However, when Rapunzel sees in the mirroring eyes of her lover that she is beautiful, she is freed from the real tyranny of her own imagined ugliness.

This is true not only in the case of Rapunzel but with all of us. We desperately need to see in the mirror of another's eyes our own goodness and beauty, if we are to be truly free. Until this moment, we, too, will remain locked inside the prison towers of ourselves. And if the thrust of love requires us to be outside ourselves and to be preoccupied with the happiness and fulfillment of others, we will not love very much until we have had this vision.

From *Why Am I Afraid To Love?*

---

our active capacity for loving others. The hard fact is that only to the extent that we love ourselves can we truly love others, God included.

If our attitude toward self is crippling, our capacity to love is proportionately diminished. The pain of a poor self-image is like the noisy strife of a civil war inside us. It magnetizes all our attention to ourselves and leaves us little freedom to go out to others. When we are hurting, even from a simple thing like a toothache, we have only a diminished availability for others. If our attitude toward self leaves us with an ache of emptiness, we have no strength or desire to go out to others. However, as our attitude toward self grows more positive and supportive, our pain is proportionately reduced and we are to that extent more free to read and respond to the needs of others around us. In short, the better the self-image, the larger the capacity for loving. On the contrary, the greater the distraction of pain, the smaller will be our capacity to love and care about others.

A memory from my own past convinces me of this truth. My career as a teacher was launched on a bright September morning in a boys' high school. We novice-teachers were instructed to be very businesslike, efficient, masterful, clear, inspiring, and spellbinding. We were warned that we should not smile until Christmas. Otherwise, those adolescent rascals would run away with us. On that bright September morning, I remember the butterflies in my stomach and the trembling hope that I would be able to remember my own name. During that whole first year of teaching, a real baptism by fire, the only question that preoccupied me was, How am I doing? My main interest in teaching well and in preserving an atmosphere of discipline was centered mainly on my own desire to succeed as a teacher. I was so busy reading and responding to the needs of my own insecurity that I had only a small capacity left over to read and respond to the needs of the young men whom I was teaching.

Gradually I realized that I was in fact a good and competent teacher. (Permit me a moment of immodesty, okay?) As I came more and more into the possession of self-confidence, my inner anxieties about personal success and my fear of failure abated. Proportionately, my capacity to care about the needs and concerns of my students started growing. I felt myself moving slowly but certainly from the self-centered question, How am I doing? to the more loving question, How are you doing?

It is very much this same way with our attitude toward self. If we focus mainly on our limitations, if we remember vividly our failures and see in ourselves only doubtful value, we will be preoccupied with ourselves. We will always be asking the nervous question, How am I doing? The inner anxiety, the sense of inferiority, the fear of failure will leave very little freedom and availability to read and respond to the needs of others.

Stop measuring, stop judging.

However, as we slowly and certainly come to a healthier attitude toward self, we will find an increased capacity to care about those others whom Jesus has asked us to love.

My List of Likable Qualities

I am personally convinced that only by truly loving myself will I be able to love my neighbor and my God; and this love is my life ambition and my life wager. And so, in balance with my efforts to fulfill the needs of others and contribute to the kingdom of God, I consciously work at improving my self-image. My own deepest desire is, with grace of God, to make my life an act of love. And I know that this is the first and indispensable step: I must love myself. I must try to recognize and appreciate the unique gifts that God has given me. And so, I have made out an alphabetized list of everything I like about myself. (I alphabetized the list so I wouldn't repeat too often.) My list includes everything from the color of my eyes and my love of music to the deep, instinctual compassion that I feel for those who are suffering.

I keep this list in the center drawer of my desk for two reasons. The first is that it is close at hand for reading when I tend to get down on myself. It is also easily available when I discover a new likable quality in myself. The second reason is a bit more facetious. I tell others that I keep this list in the center drawer of my desk in the event of my own sudden death. It will furnish some ideas for the person who is assigned to write my obituary. The presence of this list in my desk also provides for another contingency. When others come to see me and seem to be suffering from problems that arise because of a crippling attitude toward self, I suggest that they write out such a list. When they express astonishment or disbelief, exclaiming that I cannot be serious about this, I show and let them read my list. (P.S. There are currently about three hundred entries on my list!)

Also, when people offer me a compliment, my own tendency is semihumorously to ask them "to expand on that," because it will help me increase my self-appreciation and my gratitude to God, who has been so good to me. The bottom line is this: My only chance to love you and God is based on my ability to appreciate and love myself. And so I work at it. Loving ourselves is our only chance for a happy life. If a person truly loves himself or herself, not much can make that person seriously unhappy.

Such a person will have a built-in insulation against harsh and unkind criticism. Such a person can truly accept and enjoy being loved by others.

In addition to all this, if I truly love myself, I am with someone I like twenty-four hours a day. On the other hand, if I do not love myself, not much can or will make me happy. I will feel crushed by criticism because I will secretly believe that I deserve it. I will not be able to take in compliments or truly accept the offer of love from others because I will reason, "If you really knew me, you would not love me." If people insist on loving me, I will question their motives and wonder about their angles. The dark shadows and distortions of a crippling attitude toward self, the way I perceive myself, discolors and distorts everything else I see. To me it is obvious that a healthy attitude of self-appreciation is essential for a peaceful soul and a happy life.

The Danger of Conceit or Pride

At this point we might ask, Can a person love himself or herself too much? I would like to suggest that the answer, with one important qualification, is most probably "No!" Self-centeredness is not the result of self-love, but the product of pain, the result of a poor self-image.

A self-centered person has a toothache—an ache of emptiness inside. This person attempts to fill the aching emptiness with bragging, name dropping, posing as an authority on all questions great and small. What may look like an excess of self-love in fact represents an absence of self-love. Erich Fromm rightly maintains that self-ishness and true love of self are at opposite ends of the spectrum. One does not suddenly slip over from true self-appreciation into the trap of selfishness. In fact, the greater the self-appreciation, the less danger there is of selfishness.

There is one important qualification to which I have already alluded. What I am about to say represents a relatively recent insight for me. For a long time, it seemed to me that there was some opposition between love of self and the Christian virtue of humility. My former understanding of humility required a person to deny resolutely anything good about self, and to focus all one's conscious attention on personal faults and failings. I sensed, even while doing this, that it was a course of psychological self-destruction.

So I was delighted to find that one of the Fathers of the Church, Saint Ambrose, bishop of Milan in the late fourth century, had a very different idea of humility. He proposed that the "perfect expression of humility" is found in the Magnificat of Mary, the mother of Jesus.

According to the gospels, the setting was this: Mary's cousin, Elizabeth, was about to give birth (to John the Baptist). It was a Jewish custom that all women relatives should come to such an expectant mother, at the time of her delivery, to offer their help. I suspect that besides wanting to help, Mary was also anxious to share the secret of her womb with her cousin. At any rate, shortly after the announcement of the angel to her, Mary sets off on the seventy-five-mile journey from Nazareth to Ain Karim, a southwestern suburb of Jerusalem. When Mary arrives, Elizabeth is surprised: "Why should such an honor come to me, that the mother of my Lord should come to visit me?" Mary, we might well imagine, falls into the warm embrace of her cousin and explains:

> "My soul magnifies the Lord, and my spirit rejoices in God, my Savior. For he has smiled upon me, his little servant girl, and now all generations will call me 'blessed' because he, the mighty and holy one, has done such great things in me. Holy is his name." *Luke 1:46–49*

Saint Ambrose found in these words the perfect expression of humility. The virtue of humility first of all implies a grateful appreciation of all God's gifts. Second, it involves an acknowledgment that all these gifts of God are pure gifts. None of us has any claim on God. All of God's gifts to us are totally the result of God's goodness and not in any way the result of our worthiness. God has smiled down upon and has endowed each of us with such unique gifts that anyone who truly knows us will know that we are indeed "blessed" by our Father. If we did not appreciate our unique gifts, we would certainly be failing in gratitude to our good and generous God.

Once a wise old teacher was speaking to a group of young and eager students. The teacher gave them the assignment to go out and find by the side of some lonely road a small, unnoticed flower. The teacher asked them to study the flower for a long time. "Get a magnifying glass and study the delicate veins in the leaves, and notice the nuances and shades of color. Turn the leaf slowly and observe its symmetry. And remember: this flower might have gone unnoticed and unappreciated if you had not found and admired it." When the class returned, after carrying out the assignment, the wise old teacher observed: "People are like that. Each one is different, carefully crafted, uniquely endowed. But . . . you have to spend time with them to know this. So many people go unnoticed and unappreciated because no one has ever taken time with them and admired their uniqueness." In a true sense, each one of us is a unique masterpiece of God.

The One and Only You

Obviously—and I hope this suggestion is not misconstrued as an exercise in narcissism—the place and the person with whom to begin is oneself. Carl Jung says that we all know what Jesus said about the way we treat the least of God's children. But then Jung asks, "What if you were to discover that the least of the children of God is . . . *you?*" If you were judged only on how well you have appreciated and loved yourself, the least of God's children, would you get a glowing and affirmative judgment?

Most of us have a constant struggle with a sense of inferiority. We tend to play a painful comparison game. "So and so is smarter than I . . . This other person is stronger, more beautiful, or more athletic than I . . . That other person over there is more musical, although I am richer and have more clothes . . . ," and so forth. It goes on endlessly, and each new person we meet offers a new contest of comparison.

True appreciation of our personal uniqueness offers each of us the truth that sets us free from these endless and painful contests. God says to each of us: "You are unique, the one and only you. From all eternity and into all eternity, there will be only one you. I have loved you with an eternal love. I do not get new ideas nor do I lose old ones; so the thought of you has always been in my mind. And the image of you has always had a special, warm place in my heart. You have been given an important role to play in my world. You have a unique message to deliver, a unique song to sing, a unique act of love to bestow. This message, this song, and this act of love have been entrusted exclusively to the one and only you."

The Word of God assures us: *There were many other possible worlds I could have created. Yes, I could have made a world without you. But, don't you realize this, that I didn't want a world without you? A world without you would have been incomplete for me. You are the child of my heart, the delight of my thoughts, the apple of my eye. Of course, I could have made you different—taller, shorter, born of different parents, born in a different place and into a different culture, endowed with a different set of gifts. But I didn't want a* different *you. It is this* you *that I love. Just as every grain of sand on the seashore and every snowflake that falls in wintertime has its own unique composition and structure, so are you composed and structured as no other human being has ever been. It is* this *you that I love, that I have always loved and will always love. If you should ever get down on yourself and feel that you are the type that only a mother could love, please remember this: "Even if a mother should forget the child of her womb, I will never forget you!"*

> *You are unique, the one and only you.*

Seeing Oneself through the Eyes of a Critic

One final thought about the attitude toward self. Though most of us are publicly defensive when criticized by another, privately we are usually our own worst critic.

To illustrate how we are our own worst critic, I want to share a letter I received from one of the participants who attended *The Fully Alive Experience* seminar given by Loretta Brady and myself.

Your seminar advertised for "emotionally stable people in search of further growth." Well, I sneaked in. I have always been a psychological basket-case, complete with frequent hospitalizations, suicide attempts, and the continuous care of a psychiatrist. I knew, however, as I left the *Fully Alive Experience,* that I was cured, that my troubles were at last ended. A month later, by mutual agreement, I terminated with my psychiatrist. I have not needed his help for a full year now.

The transforming, healing insight was this: I had always viewed myself through the eyes of a critic. I was constantly reproaching myself, scolding myself for failing, being disappointed in the way I looked, regretful about the things that I did. I kept a careful log of all my mistakes both by commission and omission. I always saw myself through the lenses of a relentless and heartless critic. The juror in the court of my mind was forever finding me "guilty on all counts."

I saw clearly that my attitude toward myself was utterly destructive. In the wake of this insight, for the first time I felt truly sorry for myself. The compassion I had extended only to others I finally extended to myself. Of course I don't want to wallow in the swamps of self-pity. But I did promise myself that in the future I would try to be a true friend, that I would look for the gifts more than for the limitations, for the beauty more than for the ugliness, for the goodness in me more than for my regrets.

I didn't write to you immediately to tell you about this for fear that it was an emotional high that would quickly vanish like a cruel mirage. Since a year has elapsed now I feel safe in sharing this with you. I have indeed been healed. I am not only functional but alive. I am happy and free at last. Thank God!

At a subsequent Fully Alive weekend, one of the participants admitted to me: "I have to tell you that I did not come to this weekend primarily for myself. I just wanted to find out what happened to my friend [the author of the letter just quoted]. Believe me, my friend is now a changed person: optimistic, full of energy, in love with life."

You and I can profitably ask ourselves: What do I see when I look through the lens of my attitude toward myself? Am I more a critic or a friend? Do I look beyond the surface blemishes to find the truly beautiful and unique person that I am? Or do I play the destructive "comparison game"? What verdict does the juror of my mind pass on me: "good at heart" or "guilty on all counts"?

The Intolerable Burden of Perfectionism: "Be Perfect . . ."

I remember what a great and endless consolation it was for me to find out that the often used quotation, "Be perfect as your heavenly Father is perfect" (Matthew 5:48), is really a mistranslation. The context of this quotation is the challenge of Jesus to love our enemies. The Lord points out that we must try to be worthy children of a heavenly Father, who "causes his sun to rise on the bad as well as the good, and his rain to fall on the honest and the dishonest alike." The challenge God extends is not to be perfect, which is impossible for us mistake-makers, but to be as tolerant and loving and forgiving as our heavenly Father is!

I remember sitting with this scriptural passage and with this insight for a long time, breathing great sighs of relief that God was not really asking the impossible (perfection). It was as though a very heavy burden had been lifted from my shoulders. I suddenly realized that God was not challenging me to be perfect but to be patient, to be tolerant and understanding of weakness, in others and especially in myself.

You are unique.

I felt sure that Jesus was asking me not for perfection but for presence, to share my life with him, much as married couples promise each other in their wedding vows. Jesus was not insisting on instant or even ultimate perfection. He was inviting me into a covenant much like marriage. Married couples equivalently say to each other, "We have and will experience the human condition of weakness. We will inevitably fail each other at times. But we are going to make it *together*." It is something very much like this that the Lord asks of all of us and that we Christians promise to him in our faith commitment: "We are going to make it . . . *together!*"

A healthy Christian attitude toward self acknowledges and accepts the human condition of fragility. But we always see ourselves walking through life hand in hand with the Lord, feeling glad to be who we are, knowing that he accepts and loves us as we are.

Our Father who is mighty has indeed done great and beautiful things in us and for us, and holy is God's name. Only through the lenses of this vision can we find the peace and joy that are the legacy of Jesus. Only if we see ourselves in this way can we experience the fullness of life that he came to bring us.

"My soul magnifies the Lord, and my spirit rejoices in God, my Savior. For he has smiled upon me, his little servant girl, and now all generations will call me 'blessed' because he, the mighty and holy one, has done such great things in me. Holy is his name."

Luke 1:46-49

FOR FURTHER REFLECTION

Chapter 7: The Christian Vision of Self

Review

1. Explain: "The attitude each of us has toward ourself is the most important of all our attitudes."

2. How does our self-image determine how others will treat us?

3. Comment on the statement: "It is a fact that we cannot love others if we do not love ourselves."

4. Is it possible to love yourself too much? Why or why not?

5. How are self-love and self-centeredness at opposite ends of the spectrum? Explain the difference between the two.

6. How does comparing yourself to others depreciate and demean the "One and Only You"?

7. According to the chapter, Jesus' command to "be perfect as your heavenly Father is perfect" (Matthew 5:48) is a mistranslation. How should this command be interpreted?

Discuss

1. What are some techniques you can use to know yourself better?

2. How do you express your self-image?

3. Why is it sometimes difficult for you to communicate to others who you are?

4. Why do people sometimes fake it? Cover the truth? Play a role?

5. Give some examples that show how you sometimes make it difficult for others to be who they are.

6. What happens when your vision of self differs from someone else's vision of you?

Scripture Activity

"And Mary said, 'My soul magnifies the Lord, and my spirit rejoices in God my Savior, for he has looked with favor on the lowliness of his servant. Surely, from now on all generations will call me blessed; for the Mighty One has done great things for me, and holy is his name." (Luke 1:46–49, NRSV)

Reflect on the above passage. In writing, comment on how this is a statement of a good self-image of Mary. Conclude by formulating a short prayer asking Mary to help you learn to appreciate the "One and Only You."

Processing These Ideas about the Christian Vision of Self

Feelings about self. On a rating scale of 1 (lowest) to 10 (highest) how would you rate yourself? To call up your truest and most habitual feelings about yourself, it may help to close your eyes for minute, and to see yourself coming out of a door, meeting there with a group of others and relating to them. Watch and listen to yourself. Watch your typical reaction when a favor is asked of you, when a compliment is paid to you, when you are criticized, when the group laughs at you. Did you like or dislike yourself as you watched and listened? How did you seem to compare with the others? Did you feel sorry for yourself in some ways? Are there any questions you would like to ask yourself? Would you like yourself as a friend? Did you seem to be understood or misunderstood by others, liked or disliked by them? After you have isolated your feelings about yourself, record your emotional reaction to the feelings you experienced. For example: "I liked myself but feel embarrassed to acknowledge this." Or, "I disliked myself, and it makes me feel very discouraged."

8 We Must Accept Ourselves As We Are

We tend to hold on to things, including ideas. We are reluctant to give up ideas like who I am. Yet giving up some old ideas is essential to growing. I must learn how to let go of the static image of who I think I am. If I am to grow, I must get unhooked from my past. I must come to realize that I am the one and only me, a person in process—always and forever learning, changing, growing. The only important reality is who I am right now. I am not who I used to be. I am not yet who I will be. And above all I must know this: I am who I am supposed to be, and I am fully equipped to do whatever it is I am supposed to be doing with my life.

The Signs of Self-acceptance

First and foremost, self-acceptance implies a *joyful* satisfaction in being who I am. Simply being resigned to being who I am is only a "for better or for worse" kind of acceptance. It can be discouraging. If I am to be a happy person, I must learn to be happy about who I am. But this is not a simple matter. You see, all of us have an "unconscious" level of the mind. It is a hiding place or a mental burial ground for those things we don't like to face or can't

live with. The unfortunate truth is that we do not bury these "eyesores" dead but alive. They continue to influence us. But we are not aware of them or their continuing influence on all our thoughts, words, and actions.

And so it is not a simple matter to confront myself with the questions: "Do I really accept myself? Do I enjoy being who I am? Do I find meaning and satisfaction in being who I am?" The answers that come forth easily and quickly are not fully trustworthy. However, there are reliable signs, or symptoms, of the truth. These signs of self-acceptance will be apparent in my daily living. I would like to list here ten signs that I think are apparent in those who truly and joyfully accept themselves as they are.

1. Self-accepting people are happy people. Strangely, the first sign of true self-acceptance is happiness itself. It sounds like a vicious circle, doesn't it? Yet people who truly enjoy being who they are always have good company. They are with someone they like twenty-four hours a day. On good days and bad, that familiar, delightful person is always there. Not much can make them unhappy. If others are critical or unloving, those who truly love themselves will really believe that there has been a communication problem.

> *I must come to realize that I am a person in process—always and forever learning, changing, growing.*

Or failing this, they will be led to assume that the critical or unloving person has a personal problem. They will feel sorry for, not angry at, that person.

2. Self-accepting people go out to others easily. The more we accept ourselves as we are, the more we presume that others will like us too. So anticipating their acceptance, we will like to be with others. We will walk into a room full of strangers confidently, and introduce ourselves around. We will think of ourselves as gifts to be given through self-disclosure, and of others as gifts to be received, gently and gratefully. However, if we truly love ourselves, we will also enjoy and savor the moments of solitude. It has been truly said that for those who joyfully accept themselves, being alone is a peaceful solitude. For those who do not accept themselves, being alone can mean a painful loneliness. The lonely experience a vacuum and can only look for distractions—a newspaper, a cup of coffee, a blaring radio.

3. Self-accepting people are always open to being loved and complimented. If I truly accept and enjoy being myself, I will understand it when others also love me. I will be able to accept love from others graciously and gratefully. I won't have to wrestle with the unspoken regret: "If you really knew me, you wouldn't love me." I will also be able to take in, to interiorize, favorable comments and compliments. I will be

comfortable with such compliments. I won't have to be constantly suspicious of the motives of the giver of compliments: "Okay, what's your angle?" "What do you want?" I won't have to moan sadly to myself, "Oh, you can't be serious."

4. Self-accepting people are empowered to be their "real" selves. To the extent that I truly and joyfully accept myself as I am, I will have about me an authenticity that can follow only from genuine self-acceptance. In other words, I have to accept myself before I can be myself. I will be real. When my feelings are hurt, I will be able to say an audible "Ouch!" When I love and admire another, I will be honest and open about sharing my love and admiration with that person. I won't be tortured by the possibility of misunderstanding or misinterpretation. I won't be worried about whether my feelings are mutual or not. In a word, I will be free to be me. This authenticity means that I won't have to carry around with me, as a kind of bag and baggage of life, a set of masks. I will face the honest fact: I don't have to please you, but I do have to be me. What you see is what you get. This is me, the one and only me, an original by God. There are no carbon copies anywhere. Most of us have been putting on a mask or playing a role so long that we don't know where the mask-role ends and the real me begins. But we do have a gut instinct about genuineness. We have a relieving sense of honesty when we have been our true selves.

Your story and mine did not begin with our entrance into this world. From all eternity God has thought about and loved you and me.

5. Self-accepting people accept themselves as they are right now. Yesterday's me is history. Tomorrow's me is unknown. Getting unhooked from my past and not living in anticipation of the future is far from simple or easy. But the only real self-acceptance must focus on who I am at this moment. An old humorous verse puts it this way: "Your *wasness* doesn't matter if your *isness* really am." What I have been, including all the mistakes I have made, doesn't really matter. What does matter is who I am right now. Self-acceptance of the right-now me is likewise not filled with anticipation of the me I will become. If I love or allow another to love only the potential me, this love is useless, if not destructive. It is not *unconditional,* which is an essential quality of all real love. It says only, "I will love you if you will become . . ." As good old Charlie Brown once put it, "The greatest suffering in life is to have a great potential."

6. Self-accepting people are able to laugh at themselves, often and easily. Taking oneself too seriously is an almost certain sign of insecurity. An old Chinese beatitude has it: "Blessed are they who can laugh at themselves. They shall never cease to be entertained." Being able to admit and laugh at one's own fragility and folly requires an inner security that is born only of self-acceptance. Only when I know that I am essentially good can I admit that I am also limited. I can even laugh when these limitations rise to the surface

of life and get recognized by others. "I never promised you a rose garden, did I?"

7. Self-accepting people have the ability to recognize and attend to their own needs. First of all, self-accepting people are in touch with their own needs—physical, emotional, intellectual, social, and spiritual. And second, it is true that charity in this context begins at home. If I do not love myself, I certainly cannot love anyone else. Trying to ignore one's own needs is a suicide course. I must love my neighbor as myself. However, it is almost a truism that if I truly and genuinely love myself, I will be empowered to love my neighbor, spontaneously and naturally.

Self-accepting people seek to live the kind of balanced life in which their needs are met. They generally get enough rest, relaxation, exercise, and nourishment. They refrain from all excesses and self-destructive habits like overeating, smoking, drunkenness, and the use of drugs. Also, they are able to weigh their own needs in balance with the needs, requests, and demands of others. They are attentive to the needs of others, whom they often help with compassion. However, they can also say no to others without a lingering feeling of regret or guilt. They know their own limitations and needs.

8. Self-accepting people are self-determining people. They take their cues from inside themselves, not from other people.

If I truly and joyfully accept myself, I will do what I think is right and appropriate, not what other people may think or say. Self-acceptance is relatively immune to mob psychology or the crowd spirit. It is not afraid to swim upstream when necessary. As Fritz Perls would say, "I did not come into this world to live up to your expectations. And you did not come into the world to live up to mine."

9. Self-accepting people are in good contact with reality. This kind of contact with reality is sometimes more easily explained by describing its opposite. It precludes daydreaming or imagining myself in another life as another person. I deal with myself as I really am, with others as they really are. I do not waste useless energy regretting that we are not otherwise. I enjoy and engage myself with life as it really is. I don't wander off mentally into what "might" have been.

10. Self-accepting people are assertive. The final sign of self-acceptance is what is called assertiveness. As a self-accepting person, I assert my right to be taken seriously, the right to think my own thoughts and to make my own choices. I enter all relationships only as an equal. I will not be the compulsive underdog or the compulsive helper of the helpless. I will also assert my right to be wrong. Many of us retreat from true assertiveness on the grounds that we might be wrong. We bury our opinions, refuse to make known our preferences. Joyful self-

acceptance challenges us to be assertive—to respect ourselves, to express ourselves openly and honestly. Is self-acceptance only disguised self-centeredness? There is an instinct that causes most of us to blush whenever we are told that we must love ourselves. We experience a very real fear of self-centeredness. I don't know if we still speak of "capital sins," but right at the head of the old list was *pride*. The surprising fact of the matter is that self-centeredness, or narcissism, has been shown to result from self-loathing, not self-liking. The self-centered person feels empty and tries to fill this painful void with bragging, competing, triumphing over others, and so forth. In the self-liking person, the civil war of self-acceptance is over. The guns are quiet. The darkness is gone. The pain that magnetized all attention to self has subsided. There is peace at last. There is a new freedom to go out of self to others. Only those who truly and joyfully accept themselves can achieve the self-forgetfulness of loving and caring for others.

It is in this context that Carl Jung, the great psychiatrist, said, "We all know what Jesus said about the way we treat the least of our brothers and sisters. But what if we were to discover that the least, the most needy of these brothers and sisters is *me?*" Very often, good and decent people think that being disappointed with themselves is healthy. What they see as an "angel of light" is really a temptation. "I expected to be better than I am" is a discouraging thought. It is devastating to our realization of the love God has for each of us. While self-disappointment may seem very humble and objective, it in fact undermines the experience of being loved, and it discredits any affirming comments made of me or of my achievements. Self-disappointment will silently rob me of the happiness for which I was created.

As I see it, pride and true humility begin the same way: by realizing and savoring one's own goodness and giftedness. Then virtue and vice part company. Pride claims this goodness and giftedness as personal accomplishment. Pride listens for applause, sniffs for incense. Pride is lonely without recognition and reward. Humility quietly knows that "I have nothing which I was not given." Humility is grateful, not grasping.

The Obstacles to Self-acceptance

Someone has wisely said that before we can seek an adequate solution, we have to define the problem clearly. So we ask, "Why do so many of us have such a hard time with self-acceptance?" I think the answer is that all of us have inferiority complexes. Those who seem not to have such a complex are only pretending.

We came into this world asking questions for which we had no answers. The most obvious question we asked was, "Who am I?" From birth to age five we supposedly got an average of 431 negative messages every day. "Get down from there." "No, you're too

Some years ago, a psychologist named Carl Rogers offered a revolutionizing thought to counselors. He said that everybody really has the same problem. We do, however, have different symptoms. Whatever the symptoms are, the real problem is always the same, according to Rogers. We do not understand, accept, and love others. This problem may squirt out in one symptom or another, but the problem remains radically the same. We do not offer ourselves understanding, acceptance, and love. And so Rogers suggests that instead of focusing on the symptom, we must simply accept people wherever they are. What we have to be saying to others in our lives is this: "I accept you. I understand you. I care about you." If we can extend acceptance like this to one another, we will all individually grow in self-understanding and self-acceptance.

Think about your husband and wife, your children, your parents, your friends. In a sense, we hold the destiny of those we love in our hands. If we accept and love them, they will be empowered to accept and love themselves. We are like a mirror standing in front of them, saying: "Look! You're beautiful. You're really okay. Of course, you have problems, and I'm not denying that. What I'm trying to say is that you are okay. I accept you whoever you are. I care about you." According to the Rogerian concept, when people are empowered by others to understand, accept, and love themselves, the symptomatic problems (whatever they are) will miraculously disappear! This is not something to be debated. It has to be put to work in our lives.

From the audio program, *My Vision and My Values*

small." "Give me that! You'll hurt yourself." "Oh, you've made another mess." "Be quiet, please. I've had a hard day." A friend of mine swears that until he was eight, he thought his name was "Freddy No-No." No doubt this first impression of our inadequacy has stayed with us.

It is also true that the obstacles to self-acceptance are as unique in each of us as our personal histories.

The causes and reasons I can't fully enjoy being me are somewhat different from the causes and reasons you can't enjoy being you. And so, in order to define the problem more clearly, let's start with five general categories. Which of the following is most difficult for you to accept about yourself? Which is easiest? As you continue reading, make some mental notes about the way you would rank the following in the order of your personal difficulty. Rank them from the most serious obstacle to self-acceptance to the least serious.

 my body
 my mind
 my mistakes
 my feelings or emotions
 my personality

Do I accept my feelings or emotions?

Do I Accept My Body?

Physical appearance is probably the first and most frequent point of comment and comparison. Consequently, for many of us, it has become a serious obstacle to self-acceptance. Many clinical psychologists believe that physical appearance is the most important factor in most people's self-esteem. Almost all of us would like to change at least one physical feature. We would like to be taller or shorter, have thicker hair or a smaller nose. A test of self-esteem that I once read asked me to stand in front of a full-length mirror. The instructions continued: "Then turn around and around, examining your physical

appearance with a critical eye. Then look at yourself in the mirror and ask, 'Do I like being who I am, physically?' " Sometimes, beautiful people are not packaged very beautifully. And so I must ask myself honestly, "How does my packaging affect my self-acceptance?" Anything but an honest answer is a poor place to start.

Most plastic surgeons maintain that when a physical abnormality is corrected in a patient, there is an almost immediate psychological change. The person who looks better becomes more socially outgoing, more pleasant and confident. An orthopedic physician once told me that he asks his older female patients to wear makeup and have their hair done. He makes similar, appropriate suggestions to his male patients. He smiled and added, "It's amazing how an improved appearance raises the self-image and morale of my patients."

Another part of physical self-acceptance concerns our health. Often, strong people do not come equipped with strong bodies. For genetic or other reasons, many of us have to live with some bodily affliction—weak lungs or weak eyes, spastic colons or nervous stomachs, skin problems, epilepsy or diabetes. We have to be fearless in asking ourselves how these physical disabilities affect our self-acceptance. Again, the only constructive starting point is utter honesty. Only the truth can set us free.

Do I Accept My Mind?

In almost any school or job situation, some emphasis is placed on intelligence. In our personal relationships, there is often an intellectual competition between the partners. Many of us carry inside us painful memories of being embarrassed or laughed at in a classroom or a social situation. Others looked at us almost pityingly or ridiculed our comment, question, or behavior.

So we must ask ourselves if we feel comfortable with the amount and quality of the intelligence we have been given. Am I tempted to compare myself with others on this basis? Am I intimidated by others who seem mentally quicker or more informed than I? My self-esteem and consequently my happiness may be seriously involved with these questions and my answers to them.

Do I Accept My Mistakes?

The human condition is one of weakness. This is why there are erasers on pencils. We are all mistake makers. God has equipped his animals and birds with infallible instincts. We human beings have to learn most things by trial and error. An old sage once said, "Try to learn from the mistakes of others. You won't live long enough to make them all yourself." Most of us take it for granted that if you haven't made a mistake, you have probably never made a discovery. Obviously, the only real mistake is the one from which you have learned nothing. Mistakes are learning experiences. So welcome to the club!

As with most virtues, the spirit of understanding and tolerance begins at home. Somehow most of us have to come to a point of ego-desperation before we can offer ourselves a gentle understanding. We have to hit the proverbial bottom before we can begin to rise again.

So I must ask myself: Where am I? Have I let go of rehashing my "mistake-riddled" past? Have I let go of the feelings of embarrassment about my failures and regrets? Can I honestly and with peace say, "This is the person I used to be, the old me. It is not the person I am now, the new and present me"? Most of us do not realize that we have learned from our past mistakes and that we have outgrown some of our immaturities. Do I realize that the *old me* has taught the *new me* many things?

The trap here is to identify with the dark side of my person and the mistakes of my past. It is to think of myself as I once was. It's something like the person who was fat as a child, but who has become slender as an adult. The important question is, Do I think of myself as fat or thin? Clearly, growth requires change, and change means "letting go." How difficult or easy is this for you? Remember, we have to start with a ruthless honesty or we may never come to the truth. And without the truth there is no growth, no joy.

Do I Accept My Feelings or Emotions?

Mood swings are common to most of us. One moment we may feel "up," the next "down." But some feelings are quarantined out of existence by our early programming. For example, I always found it hard to admit fear because my father insisted that "a man is not afraid of anything or anyone." Some of us feel obliged to repress the emotion of jealousy or feelings of self-satisfaction. Someone has somehow taught us that these emotions are simply not allowed. One valid emotion that is almost universally condemned is self-pity. We have all either heard or made the accusation, "Oh, you're only feeling sorry for yourself."

It seems to be true that we handle emotions according to what we think about them. And so we must ask: Are there emotions active in me that I allow to become an obstacle to joyful self-acceptance? Can I feel fear, hurt, anger, jealousy, resentment, self-satisfaction, or self-pity without getting involved in self-condemnation and self-criticism? Are there feelings I would like to conceal in the hope that they will just go away?

Do I Accept My Personality?

Without going into detail, I think it is safe to assume that there are personality types. These types seem to be partly genetic and partly the result of early programming. Of course, within each personality type, there are healthy and unhealthy individuals. And there is always room for growth. However, the basic type is usually pretty well set in us. Some of us are extroverts, others introverts. Some are born leaders, others are loyal followers.

Some are quiet, others talkative. Some of us are funny, others can't even read a joke well. Some are thick-skinned, others very sensitive. But each of us is unique, different from all others. Our very gifts distinguish us. Our limitations define us. From what I know of my basic personality type, am I happy to be me? Does my basic personality seem attractive or regrettable to me?

To better understand my personality, it might help to make a list of the five qualities that describe me best: quiet, plain, diplomatic, funny, verbal, emotional, involved, lonely, joyful, troubled, and so forth. Then I should ask a close but very honest friend to make a similar list of qualities that best describe me, capture my personality. Putting the two lists together should give me a starting point. My personality is me-in-action. Do I like what I see, or am I a disappointment to myself? Would I want to change my personality radically, or am I satisfied with who I am? Would I choose someone like myself for a close friend?

Ways to a Healthy Self-esteem

Self-esteem is a choice. In the same way that we can decide to esteem (hold in high regard) a friend despite his or her faults, limitations, and weaknesses, we can also choose to accept and esteem ourselves. We can choose to accept our total self: our bodies, minds, mistakes, feelings or emotions, and personalities. True self-acceptance necessarily means that we must choose to accept all

that we are. According to what we have learned so far, one way we can improve our self-images and increase our self-esteem is to use vision therapy, i.e., to replace any negative messages or attitudes about ourselves with healthier and more life-giving attitudes.

Another way to help bring about and enjoy higher self-esteem is to practice the **Ten Requisites for Affirmation**.

These ten requisites are based on the assumption that we need to see reflected back to us from the eyes of another person: "You're beautiful!" Like the young Rapunzel in Grimm's fairy tale, we too need Prince/Princess Charmings who will reflect back to us our own individual worth, beauty, and goodness. Now it is important to point out that people do not give us worth, beauty, and goodness; they only affirm and reflect back to us that we have them. Consequently, in order to receive this feedback, this affirmation from others, there are ten guaranteed requisites for affirmation. And I guarantee you. If you challenge yourself to actually put them into practice, not only will you be affirmable, but you will be affirmed. Like magic, this affirmation from others will help you get in touch with your beauty, worth, and goodness, and in turn increase your own self-appreciation and self-esteem.

Requisites for Affirmation

1. Have fully and express freely all your emotions, positive and negative. Only then will you have a sense that others really know you.
2. Be yourself. Let your criteria of conduct and communication be who you really are, what you really think and feel and want.
3. Be assertive. Practice self-esteem. Insist on your right to be taken seriously and respected as a person. Balance your efforts to fulfill your own needs with your efforts to fulfill the needs of others. Do not be a compulsive pleaser or voluntary underdog.
4. Desist from all attempts at self-affirmation: like bragging, acquiring things to impress, competing, gamesmanship, dealing in status symbols, name-dropping, gouging and clawing for fame or power in order to prove self.
5. Think of yourself in positive terms. Be more aware of your strengths than your weaknesses, of your accomplishments than your failures.
6. Be gentle with yourself. Be more ready to understand than to judge.
7. Do not be controlled by fears and crippling inhibitions. Act against them. Stretch!
8. Do not judge others or make assumptions about their intentions.
9. Look for what is good in others and express your appreciation. Offer both evaluative ("That is a very fine poem!") and appreciative ("It really moved me very deeply.") feedback. Be a chronic affirmer.
10. Love others. Seek to find your happiness in theirs. Begin with empathy.

Many of these requisites for affirmation will be developed even more fully throughout the course. But for now, what is important is that you actually challenge yourself to put them into practice. They are some of the hardest practices of this course, but likewise they are some of the most rewarding too. Go for it! You can do it!

FOR FURTHER REFLECTION

Chapter 8: We Must Accept Ourselves As We Are

Review

1. List the ten signs of a self-accepting person. Describe each sign briefly.

2. According to the chapter, what are the causes of the inferiority complex?

3. If you were to categorize the obstacles to self-acceptance, what would these five basic categories be?

4. How does one improve his or her self-image?

Discuss

1. From the list of the five categories of obstacles to self-acceptance, which do you find troublesome or an obstacle toward your own self-acceptance?
2. Who in your life has affirmed and affirms your self-worth?
3. How do you respond to constructive criticism and/or to genuine compliments?

Scripture Activity

"One of the scribes came near and heard them disputing with one another, and seeing that he answered them well, he asked him, 'Which commandment is the first of all?' Jesus answered, 'The first is, "Hear, O Israel: the Lord your God is one; you shall love the Lord your God with all your heart, and with all your soul, and with all your mind, and with all your strength." The second is this, "You shall love your neighbor as yourself." There is no other commandment greater than these.' " (Mark 12:28–31, GNB)

Why is self-love emphasized as the standard of love of others? Discuss whether love is an obligation or a privilege.

Processing These Ideas about Self-acceptance

1. *Try to describe in writing what you find most difficult to accept about yourself—and why.* Note which category of self you find hardest to accept: (a) your body, (b) your mind, (c) your mistakes, (d) your feelings or emotions, (e) your personality. Conclude by explaining what you would say to someone else who has your "problem" with self-acceptance.

2. *Compose two lists.* (a) The first is a list of all those things you consider to be your personal assets or blessings: your special qualities, physical endowments, abilities, talents, gifts, and so forth. (b) On the second list record the personal limitations and regrets that most disturb you. This second list is a kind of housecleaning. True self-acceptance must start with an honest evaluation. We must not be discouraged by our limitations, nor should we attempt to deny them. We do not celebrate our regrets or congratulate ourselves for our neuroses. True self-acceptance means accepting some painful truths about ourselves.

We are all limited human beings. Without facing that fact, we will be living in a world of pretense and fantasy. Unless we accept and face our limitations, we will not see clearly the direction of our future development and growth.

9 We Must Accept Responsibility for Our Lives

Accepting full responsibility for all our actions, including our emotional and our behavioral responses to all life situations, is the definitive step toward human maturity. However, the tendency to blame our responses on other persons or things is as old as the human race. Many of us grew up as blamers. We defended our most unacceptable behavior: "You had it coming." "You did the same thing to me." "I'm just giving you a taste of your own medicine." We learned to explain away our failures on the grounds that we did not have the right materials to work with, or we even pleaded that "our stars were not in proper alignment; the moon was not in the right house." The essential sadness is that blamers are not in contact with reality. As a result, they do not get to know themselves. They do not mature. They do not grow. It is a fact of life: Growth begins where blaming ends. *The opposite of this blaming tendency is to accept full responsibility for our lives, to* become an owner, not a blamer. *Owners know that something in them explains their emotional and behavioral responses to life. It is clearly the definitive step toward human maturity. Responsibility ensures that we will grow up.*

What Is "Full Responsibility"?

Every one of us knows from personal experience that we are not completely free. There are times when our reactions completely escape from the reins of self-control. We cannot turn our emotions on and off as though they were controlled by faucets. There are times when we just cannot be all that we want to be, do what we want to do, or say only those things we want to say. Sometimes our habits hold us captive. They seem unbreakable. Our yesterdays lie heavily upon our todays, and our todays will lie heavily upon our tomorrows. We cry when we know we should be laughing. We overeat or overdrink even when we know that this is not good for us. We pout when we know we should be talking something out. So, what's this about accepting "full responsibility"?

Granted that we are not fully free. We have all been programmed from infancy through childhood. And this programming limits our freedom. Also, we have practiced our habits so long and faithfully. Habits, too, diminish our freedom to choose. And sometimes just plain old human inertia often controls us.

> *Sometimes our habits hold us captive. They seem unbreakable.*

With Saint Paul we must admit, "I see the right thing, I intend to do it, and then I do just the opposite. There is another law warring within me."

Clearly, full responsibility does not imply full freedom. In this context, what full responsibility means is this: There is *something in me* that determines my actions and responses to the various stimulations and situations of life. It may be the result of my genes, my programming, or the force of my own habits. But it is *something in me*. I take full responsibility for that. I do what I do, I say what I say, because of something in me. Other persons or situations may *stimulate a response,* but the *nature of that response* will be determined by something in me.

First, let's take a look at the meaning of *full responsibility for all my actions.* One of my favorite illustrations is the well-known story of the late Sydney Harris. Accompanying a friend to a newsstand, Harris noted that the man selling papers was openly sullen and cantankerous. He also noted that his friend was kind and cordial in his dealing with this man. As he walked away with his friend, Harris asked, "Is that fellow always so mean?" "Yes, unfortunately he is," the friend answered. Harris persisted, "And are you always so nice to him?" "Yes, of course," answered the friend. So Harris asked the question that was stirring in him from the beginning: "Why?"

Harris's friend had to think, as though the answer were obvious. "Because," he finally explained, "I don't want him or anyone else to

decide how I am going to act. *I decide how I am going to act.* I am an *actor,* not a *reactor.*" Sydney Harris walked away, mumbling to himself, "That's one of the most important realizations and accomplishments in life: to be an actor, not a reactor."

Full Responsibility and Transactional Analysis

Eric Berne and Thomas Harris are the two psychiatrists who have originated and popularized what is called Transactional Analysis. They say (perhaps more elaborately) the same thing as the friend of Sydney Harris. The theory of Transactional Analysis tells us that there are three components in all of us: *parent, adult,* and *child.* The *parent* in us is a collection of all the messages and programming recorded in us in the early years of life. The *adult* in us is our own mind and will, which make us capable of thinking for and choosing for ourselves. The *child* in us is the storehouse of all our emotional or feeling responses. The psychiatrists of T.A. maintain that those emotions which were experienced most strongly in the first five years of life tend to be the most strong in us for the rest of our lives.

The T.A. theory is that we can analyze our transactions with others and can tell whether the *parent, adult,* or *child* has been in control. Human maturity, the theory continues, is achieved by keeping the *adult* in charge of making all our decisions. We must hear and edit our parent tapes, and we must fully and freely have our feelings. However, we must never let them

I'm an actor, not a reactor!

make our decisions. We must never let our parent-tape programming or our feelings *decide* how we are going to act. We must think for ourselves and choose to act in a mature way.

So accepting full responsibility does not mean that I am completely free. It does not even imply full and complete control by my *adult*. It does, however, mean that I honestly acknowledge that *something in me* determines and controls all my actions and responses. This something in me may be my parental programming overpowering my mind. It may be an explosion of emotions that deprive me, at least in part, of my freedom. So even when I am a reactor as opposed to an actor, it is still something in me that determines my reaction.

Most of us can remember times when the *parent* or the *child* has prevailed in us. Afterward we knew that the *adult* in us would have acted differently. Maybe we allowed some parental message to keep us silent when we should have spoken up. Maybe we childishly refused to apologize when an apology was in order. The *adult* in us would have spoken up, would have apologized. We recognize the difference. When my *adult* is in charge, I think independently and make rational decisions. I take my cues from within my own self. I do not let others decide how I am going to act. Whatever the case may be, I still have to acknowledge and take full responsibility for the *parent, adult,* and *child* in me. Even when I let the *parent* or the *child* decide how I am going to act, I am still directed by something in me. It is my responsibility.

Full Responsibility and Our Emotions

Now we proceed to a more difficult matter: *full responsibility for our emotions or feelings.* Many of us have grown accustomed to the myth that we are not responsible for our feelings. This may have been true of us when we were infants and even children. We did not have an adult in us to sort through our messages and emotions. In a sense we were at the mercy of those older people around us. As adults it is far from the truth. Emotions may still arise quickly and spontaneously in us. However, as responsible adults we can fully and freely experience them, and then decide how we can express them constructively and maturely. Later, perhaps in a reflective moment, we can trace our spontaneous feelings to their roots. Why did I react that way?

By definition, an *emotion* is a *perception* that results in an overflow into a *physical reaction.* Because an emotion is a perception and a consequent physical reaction to that perception, we could not have emotions if we did not have minds and bodies. For example, if I perceive you as my friend, physically I will have a comfortable and peaceful reaction to you. Emotionally I am glad to see you. However, if I perceive you as an enemy, my physical reaction will be one of fight or flight. My muscles will grow tense and my heartbeat will accelerate. I will be afraid of you and what you might be planning to do or say to me.

The behavior of the fully alive human being is always unpredictable—simply because it is free.

While I might not be free to control this emotional reaction, I do know that it is caused by *something in me:* my perception of you. This perception may be right or wrong. It may be colored by other experiences, but it is clearly something in me that directs my emotional response.

This is easily illustrated in a classroom situation. I often put this case to my students: "Imagine that one of you walks out of this classroom angrily. You express disgust with me and my teaching ability. How would I feel?" Usually my students are quick to volunteer: "You would feel angry. You would remind the student that you know his name and have his social security number." Another disagrees: "No, you would feel hurt. You know you try hard to be a good teacher. You would be sad that all your efforts would get such a response." Still another offers the opinion: "No, I think you would feel guilty. You would ask the student to come back and give you another chance. You might even try to apologize." Someone almost always suggests a compassionate response: "You would feel sorry for the kid. You would reason that no doubt there are other tensions that are getting to him."

By the end of the discussion I have usually collected ten or eleven suggestions about my possible emotional response to such a situation. (I secretly suspect that most of the students are projecting how they would feel.)

Anyway, I then suggest that I might well react in any of the ways suggested. Then I add with great emphasis, "But notice this. There really are so many possible reactions, ways I might respond. I'm not sure how I would actually respond. But this much is clear: My emotional reaction would be caused by something in me and not by the student walking out. Such a person can only stimulate *a reaction.* Something in me will determine *the precise emotional reaction* I will have. What I think of myself, how I regard myself as a teacher, the importance I attach to the matter I am presenting—all these things inside me will determine my precise emotional reaction. I must accept full responsibility for this. And this is what I mean by accepting full responsibility for my emotions."

Many of my emotional responses are good. Others tend to be self-destructive. So when I reflect upon my emotional reaction in a given situation, I go back to the perception where it all began. I can question and enlarge upon or even alter that perception. Maybe I should take another look. Maybe you were just trying to be friendly, not to embarrass me. It might be that I perceived myself to be inferior, and instead of admitting that, I might have tried to cover it up with conceit. I know this: If I question and perhaps change my perception, my emotional response will also change.

Owners Versus Blamers

In trying to account for our behavioral and emotional responses, I suppose that we have only two real choices. Either we "own" them or we "blame" them on someone or something else. But this is not a simple choice without consequences. My honesty can put me on the road to maturity, or my rationalizing will remove me from reality. If I own my responses, take responsibility for my emotions and behavior, I will get to know myself. I will grow up. If I try to explain my actions and feelings by shifting responsibility to other persons or situations, I will never get to know my real self. I will stunt my personal growth as long as I persist in this unwillingness to acknowledge my responsibility. Remember: *Growth begins where blaming ends*.

Sometime notice how differently people react to the very same person or situation. Take the case of an obnoxious or offensive person. We might be feeling anger toward this person only to discover that a third party feels sorry for this obnoxious person. It all depends on one's perception. Obviously, if I have perceived that person as deliberately malicious, my emotional response might well be that of anger or resentment. My behavioral response might be sarcasm. But if I see that obnoxious person as hurting or deprived, my reaction will probably be compassionate.

Note that in revising our perceptions or attitudes (practiced or habitual perceptions), we also revise our emotional responses.

You had it coming. I'll give you a taste of your own medicine.

It is important to remember that a perception is always at the heart of every emotion. It is that perception which will determine the nature and intensity of the emotion. It is probably true that many of my emotions are healthy and happy. However, if my emotional patterns are self-destructive or socially alienating, I may want to look at the perceptions or attitudes that are writing my life script. This is certainly a part of my "full responsibility."

Does Assuming Full Responsibility Really Make Us Happy?

This is a good if not obvious question. My own answer is, "Not automatically nor immediately." I'm sure you have heard that the truth will set you free, but first it may make you a little miserable. Unfortunately, our yesterdays do lie heavily upon our todays. Our habits can be deeply ingrained. Such habits, like "flying off the handle," can temporarily and partially limit our freedom of response. Saying that "I have a short fuse," or that "I have hot blood," is only blaming. It's really not a matter of my fuse or my blood. It's a matter of habit. Our responses of the past were probably learned from others. Worriers tend to beget worriers. Short fuses tend to run in the same families. However, our own repetition of these responses may have dug deep grooves of habit in us. Eventually, they become automatic reactions. You press this button and you get this response. We become slaves to our habits. We are the "trained animals," and habits are the "hoops" we jump through. We can easily keep responding poorly to given situations, for example, by losing our tempers. But if we allow this to become an irreplaceable habit, we tend to get stuck or arrested at that point of our personal growth. When this happens, we naturally tend to blame other persons or situations for our responses. Once we get trapped in this vicious circle, we get stuck in a place of pain. And we stay there.

However, if we assume the full responsibility described above, we are then free to recognize and revise our responses. And this is certainly the pathway to peace and personal happiness. I can't change the world to suit me, but I can change my response to the world. I can change me. *Happiness is an inside job.*

Owners, Blamers, and Self-knowledge

Ancient wisdom insists that self-knowledge is the pinnacle of wisdom. Unfortunately, if I blame my actions and feelings on someone or something else, I will learn nothing about myself. The unfortunate *blamer* keeps assigning responsibility to other people, other places, or other things: "You made me mad." "This place bores me." "Your test frightened me." "He made me feel so small." The poor blamer keeps repeating supposed facts. It is a classic ego-defense mechanism called projection.

> A perception is always at the heart of every emotion.

Once stuck here, the blamer is removed from reality. There is no possibility of growing up. The magnificence of what might have been is lost until the blamer becomes an owner. Growth begins where blaming ends.

The *owner* asks the only profitable question: "What's in me? Why did I choose to do that or feel that way?" *Notice please* that an owner does not excuse or explain away obvious misconduct on the part of others. Owners may well think of the behavior of others as regrettable or even destructive. But owners know that they can only change themselves. They may be inclined to help the offending party, but they are even more interested in their own personal response. When owners are cut off in traffic, they ask something like this: "When that other driver cut in front of me, why did I honk my horn repeatedly? Why did I get so upset and decide to give him a disgusted look at the next stoplight? What perception, attitude, or habit prompted that response? Did I see that other driver as rude and dangerous? Did it ever occur to me that he might be rushing off to a sick child in the hospital? Or even if he really is just out for himself, why don't I feel sorry for him?" If we do ask such questions, we will certainly get to know much more about ourselves.

Of course, I am not always the owner I would like to be. Like many others, I also resort to blaming, to shifting the responsibility for my own responses. But let me insert here a true story about a time when I did "own" and did learn about myself.

After class one day, two of my students almost playfully remarked to me, "Do you know that you come across to some people as a phony?" I felt anger arising in me, but I know better than to "blow my cool." I'm too controlled for that. So with the precision of a surgeon probing with a scalpel, I asked, "Oh, really, and what does *phony* mean?" They protested that *they* did not think this. They tried to apologize, but I was relentless. "Oh, I heard what you said, but I was just wondering about the meaning of the word *phony."* Eventually I coaxed out of them the response I was waiting for: "I guess it means that you do not practice what you preach."

Affecting a humble posture, I immediately pleaded guilty. "Oh, in that case, I am a phony. My ideals are just too high for me." I even quoted Saint Paul about "another law warring in my members." (I laugh when I think of myself doing all this.) Then I had to put the final bruise on them. Shylock was looking for his pound of flesh. "There is another meaning of *phony,* my friends. It is that I don't mean what I preach. To this I plead innocent. I do believe what I preach. I just can't practice it as well as I would like." After everybody was quite uncomfortable, we left one another.

The blamer that I too often am would have recalled how he gives his very life to his students. He would have wondered how anyone could be so ungrateful for his gift. He would probably have raved to others about his experience with those two "hopeless adolescents."

Happiness is an inside job!

He would have generated a lot of gastric juice, and held a grudge of resentment that would keep his blood pressure elevated. He would have dug a deeper and deeper rut for himself. I think I was tempted to do this.

Fortunately for me, on this occasion I did not for long remain a blamer. I soon became an owner. I went to my room and sat there alone with my thoughts. "Why did I get angry?" I peeled back the cover of my anger to look inside at the perception under it. After twenty minutes of self-examination, it all became clear. I got angry because I am a phony in the second sense. I recalled many times when I said things and later wondered if I really meant them. I recalled giving a great sermon about death on one occasion. "What do we have to fear? O death, where is your victory? O death, where is your sting?" In the middle of my Oscar-winning performance, I got a sudden stab of pain in the center of my chest. My stomach started tightening. Fear ran up and down my spinal cord. My panic was screaming from a place deep inside me: "This could be a heart attack." But my mouth went right on with the serene sermon.

Of course, the pain quickly passed. But later, when no one could see me, I smiled and mused to myself: "Gee, my stomach and my mouth are only sixteen inches apart, and they are not connected." I laughed to myself: "It's really hard to live with yourself after a good sermon."

Many other such recollections tumbled out of my memory. But the lasting profit was this: I knew why I was angry. My students had stumbled across an exposed nerve. I am a fraction. Part of me believes what I say. Part of me has doubts. Later, in spite of their protestations that it wasn't necessary, I apologized and explained to the two young people. I told them why I had been angry and what I had learned about myself. They said, and I agreed, "That's good, isn't it?"

I am a fraction. Part of me believes what I say. Part of me has doubts.

Blaming Is Like Active Alcoholism

In the last ten years of my life, I think I have learned more from the Alcoholics Anonymous Fellowship than from any other human source. I am not myself an alcoholic, so I feel like a lucky kid who won a free pass to the movies. I get to see the show without having to pay the admission price. One of the things I have learned is that chemically dependent people do not mature while they are drinking or drugging. It is a fact that "being in contact with reality" is an indispensable condition for growing up. When alcohol or drugs separate people from reality, those persons can no longer "tell it like it is" or "see it like it is." They are arrested in their human development. One of my college students, who had been drinking heavily for five or six years prior to his recent sobriety, continually reminded me, "You've got to remember: I didn't have an adolescence." This young man had to pick up the pieces and start to grow again after five or six years of being in an alcoholic haze.

The same thing happens to a blamer. Refusing to take responsibility for one's life and responses is a barrier between that person and reality. It is the barrier of projection and rationalization. It is a haze of ego-defense. Self-deception becomes an escape route. The blamer, like the active alcoholic, does not grow up. Active alcoholics construct their own foggy world. They are at peace only when they are "stoned." In the case of blamers, it is a world of false explanations for true facts. They search for peace by shifting the responsibility for their life and happiness to others.

Does This Apply to Everyone?

What we have been saying about full responsibility applies to all human beings, but in graduated form. When we are infants and small children, we are like soft wax, ready to take on any imprint. Our memory tapes came blank, and in this period they are being filled in. Our perceptions and emotional reactions were for the most part learned from adult influences. At least we learned from our inter- pretations of those influences.

At the same time we know that children must gradually be given freedom to think and choose for themselves. In a similar way, we must learn in graduated steps to assume full responsibility for our lives and for our happiness. It is an important part of the human process, of our human develop- mental tasks. We know what would happen if parents insisted on making all the decisions for their children until those children were twenty-one years of age. The result would be some seriously immature twenty-one-year-olds. We also know what would happen if children were taught by example to assign the responsibility for their lives to others. They would remain children all their lives.

So, full responsibility is adult responsibility. But it has to be taught early in life and assumed more and more as we get older. The penalty for refusal is to remain imprisoned in a perpetual childhood.

I am trying to practice what I preach. Sometimes I am successful. At other times I still fail. However, I am making an effort to assume full responsibility for my life and my happiness. I referred earlier to a sign in my mirror which I see and read every morning:

YOU ARE LOOKING AT THE FACE OF THE PERSON WHO IS RESPONSIBLE FOR YOUR HAPPINESS!

All of life is a process. We are all on a journey to the fullness of life. And we are meant to enjoy the trip. I am sure that the two legs on which we need to walk through life are (1) joyful self-acceptance—an appreciation of our human uniqueness, and (2) a willingness to assume full responsibility for every step and misstep along the way.

There is a parent and a child inside each one of us.

Part Three   The Christian Vision of Oneself

FOR FURTHER REFLECTION

Chapter 9: We Must Accept Responsibility for Our Lives

Review

1. What is "full responsibility"?
2. Give an example to support the following statement: "Other persons or situations may *stimulate a response,* but the *nature of that response* will be determined by something in me."
3. Describe the transactional analysis theory of three components in every individual: child, parent, and adult "tapes."
4. What does it mean to take full responsibility for one's emotions and behavior?
5. What are the benefits of being "an owner, not a blamer"?

Discuss

1. How is the concept of "taking full responsibility for one's life" connected to the assumption and thesis of vision therapy?
2. Do you agree with the statement that "growth begins where blaming ends"? Why or why not?
3. Do you know anyone who generally accepts full responsibility for his or her reactions? Is this person respected by those around him or her? As you perceive this person, do you consider him or her to be mature and happy?
4. How in the last week have you passed blame onto a person, event, or thing for your emotions or behavior? What might you do to begin to accept responsibility for your life?

Scripture Activity

"You are the people of God; he loved you and chose you for his own. So then, you must clothe yourselves with compassion, kindness, humility, gentleness, and patience. Be tolerant with one another and forgive one another whenever any of you has a complaint against someone else. You must forgive one another just as the Lord has forgiven you. And to all these qualities add love, which binds all things together in perfect unity." (Colossians 3:12-14, GNB)

Go and "be an actor, not a reactor" today. Decide on at least one concrete way you can take responsibility for your actions or reactions toward someone you have had a difficult time with. Ask God to help you to respond to that person with compassion, kindness, humility, gentleness, and patience.

Processing These Ideas about Full Responsibility

1. *Write a letter of apology.* Write to all your favorite "blamees" (one letter to cover all). This letter would include not only other persons but also groups, situations, and even inanimate things. Tell them that you are sorry for making them your scapegoats. In your letter admit that it was a big mistake to shift onto them responsibility for your responses. Reassure them that from now on you are going to be an owner. Please remember that this does *not* mean that others were faultless or flawless. It does *not* imply that certain situations were not difficult. It means only that even in dealing with flawed persons and difficult situations, we are still responsible for our own responses. It acknowledges only that something in us determines our responses. When our responses have been undesirable, we must find that "something in us" and deal with it. Our "adult" must take charge of our lives.

2. *Recall and record.* Who are some good role models of full self-responsibility in your life? Recall some people you know who are especially good at assuming self-responsibility. How does each of these people demonstrate this acceptance of responsibility in relationships? Record in writing.

10 *We Must Try to Fulfill Our Needs for Relaxation, Exercise, and Nourishment*

We human beings are not grounded angels or pure spirits trapped in a prison of flesh. Neither are we merely material beings—$1.50 worth of highly organized chemicals. It's just not that simple. The fact is that we are a magnificent oneness that has three interconnected parts: body, mind, *and* spirit. *Now this can all get very confusing at times. We want to divide and conquer. We want to uncomplicate this oversized, human mystery. We don't like this interrelationship of parts. We are reluctant to admit that the material body could influence how we think and what we choose. We are likewise reluctant to admit that mind and spirit can work out their hidden agendas on the poor body. We want to deny this kind of oneness and interconnectedness.*

Still, it is true: The twisted mind and the deprived spirit can make us physically sick. We laugh at the thought that a simple headache might be the result of a "denied" worry or a crippling attitude of the mind. But, like it or not, it is a fact: We are a mysterious oneness with three sensitively interconnected parts. The body has an effect on mind and spirit. Mind affects body and spirit. And spirit affects body and mind. And so caring for these bodies of ours is indirectly caring for mind and spirit. Such caring will always be necessary for a full and happy life.

The History of the Separation

In this matter we come by our prejudices quite naturally. The denial of the interconnectedness of our parts goes all the way back to the ancient Greek philosophers. Plato was the first to divide human nature into separate categories. He obviously thought of the mind (the thinking self) as the superior part of the human composite. He conceived the mind as separate and distinct from the body. And he concluded that the body could not influence the mind and vice versa. Then Augustine, Western civilization, and Christian thinkers all added their contributions to this impression that mind and body are separate and distinct. Finally, it was the philosopher Rene Descartes who drew a dark black line of separation between soul and body. Descartes wanted to make human nature as clear as his beloved geometry. This "Cartesian dualism" (soul/body) has lasted right up to the present day. Body is body and soul is soul. It's not mind-body-spirit = one me.

Our past may have been misleading. In us spirit and matter are not like oil and water. Like it or not, we are a mysterious oneness. Our bodies and minds and spirits are the sensitively interconnected parts of this oneness.

Caring for these bodies of ours is indirectly caring for mind and spirit. Such caring will always be necessary for a full and happy life.

Nothing can happen in one of these parts that does not somehow affect the other two parts.

For years we have entrusted our bodies to physicians, our minds to psychiatrists, and our souls to theologians. But now we can no longer maintain this neat separation. Our physicians sometimes tell us that our aches and pains are not purely physical. They are psychosomatic. In other words, our pains are in our bodies but are psychologically induced. On the other hand, our psychiatrists sometimes have to inform us that our depression results from a purely physical condition, like a chemical imbalance or vitamin deficiency. And theologians just may report that our suffering is not really a divine trial but is probably due to a distorted idea of what it means to be human. Our spiritual directors may have to go back to deal with our early psychological programming. Our spiritual problems may have originated in this early programming.

The connection between body, mind, and spirit means that a problem that originates in one part may well show up in another part. A crippling perception may cause a headache. The physical condition of inadequate nutrition may well cause psychological depression. And the unsatisfied hungers of the human spirit may well show up in the sickness of our bodies and our minds.

Our happiness requires that all three of these interconnected parts be cared for. No one can be truly

We are as sick as we are secret.

happy unless the needs of all three are provided. In this third practice, of course, we are talking mainly about the body and its needs for *relaxation, exercise,* and *nutrition.* However, because of our inter-connectedness, in talking about the needs of the body, we are certainly implying a concern for the mind and the spirit which are also essential parts of each of us.

Stress

We have already said that a physical problem can be the cause of mental and spiritual problems. It is also true that attending to our physical needs facilitates the use of mind and the functions of spirit. One of the main problems that afflicts us today is stress. It begins with some strain, tension, or temporary loss of inner harmony. It throws off our sense of balance, or equilibrium. This stress is clearly a fact of life. No one can avoid it. The events or situations that cause stress can be positive and seemingly pleasant as well as negative. Any new challenge will require some adaptation, and this alone can produce stress. Although we humans usually thrive on growth, we also crave balance and the security of our equilibrium, the serenity of a steady and unchal-lenged state. And so a new child in a family can cause as much stress as a death in the family. "Falling in love" can be as stressful as "falling out of love." However, whether its source be pleasant or painful, stress *can* easily make us very unhappy.

The four basic sources through which stress enters our lives are—
- our environment,
- our bodies,
- our minds, and
- our spirits.

As far as *environment* is concerned, there is always some challenge of adaptation. We are called upon to endure cold and heat, noise, crowding, living with one another, time deadlines, threats to personal security and self-esteem. Our *bodies,* too, offer us many challenges that result in stress: the rapid development of adolescence, the slow toll of aging, illness, accidents, sleep or diet disturbances. The *mind* and its various perceptions also can give rise to stress. For example, we perceive ourselves as inadequate or unloved. We think of ourselves as underdogs or unworthy. We conceive our failures as cata-strophic. We interpret reality as threatening. In each case the result is stress!

And finally, a deprived *spirit* can cause us great discomfort. We think we can get along without the security and comfort of faith and its overview. But without these we soon experience a painful loneliness and anxiety. We fall into a puzzling state of depression. Something in us wants to know where we have come from, what we are doing here, and where we are going. The spirit registers stress when we can't find meaning in life. We don't want to think of ourselves as mere mortals walking through the motions of meaningless lives.

We are a mysterious oneness with three interconnected parts.

Just as the body can be sick and cause stress, so the spirit can become starved and lead us into a stress-filled vacuum.

As soon as stress occurs in us, whatever its source, there are immediate biochemical changes that take place in our bodies. We experience the "fight or flight" response. Our minds perceive some kind of distress or threat. Our regulating physical centers send immediate information throughout the body. The chemicals that carry this message tell the body to speed up its organic and glandular processes to prepare us to deal with or to escape the threat. Only in the last twenty years has medical science discovered the existence of the chemical messengers known as neurotransmitters. The effect is that the pupils of the eyes dilate so we can see better. The hearing becomes more acute. Muscles tense up in order to deal with this perceived new threat. The heart and respiratory rates increase. Blood leaves the extremities and starts pooling in the torso and head. Consequently, the hands and feet grow cold and sweaty.

If the stress is prolonged, these physical conditions become chronic. Psychologically, under stress everything looms out of proportion. Things that ordinarily don't bother us become torturous. We have a hard time concentrating. Sleeping and eating are also affected by chronic stress. We can adapt either by sleeping and eating excessively or by sleeping and eating only fitfully.

Eventually, chronic or repeated stress wears down the body. It is a proven fact that stress always tends to shut down the immune system. So we get sick and we sometimes die. For example, chronic stress can also result in elevated or high blood pressure or hypertension. About 25 million Americans are thought to have hypertension, although half of this number don't even know of the condition. Stress is frequently found as the major cause for respiratory infections, arthritis, colitis, diarrhea, asthma, uneven heart rhythms, many sexual problems, circulatory problems, and even cancer. The doctors of the American Academy of Psychosomatic Medicine, which was founded in 1953, believe that 75 to 90 percent of all reported diseases are due in part to stress. The three best-selling prescription drugs in America are Valium for relaxation, Inderal for high blood pressure, and Tagamet for ulcers. Leaders in industry estimate that 50 to 75 billion dollars are lost each year due to stress-related symptoms. It would seem that many of us are like an accident or an explosion looking for a place to happen.

"Mens Sana in Corpore Sano"

The ancient Latin adage and prescription for happiness was "a healthy mind in a healthy body." Modern science, which has explained stress so clearly to us, has also insisted that we can conquer stress. The vicious circle can be broken. However, to do this, we must learn to relax, to exercise, and to eat a properly balanced diet. The ancients were right: a healthy body contributes greatly to a happy mind and a healthy spirit. These, we remember, are our sensitively inter-connected parts.

To be convinced of the importance of the physical, try to recall how you reacted to a given stimulus when you were relaxed. Then recall how you have reacted to the same stimulus when tense, tired, or hungry. Oftentimes it isn't the big things that cause us tension and stress. It's the snapped shoelace when you don't have time to find another. When driving, it is the turn you "can't miss." Stress and the tension it produces magnify all these small irritations of life. We usually don't trip over mountains but molehills. Stress and tension lure us into the telescope trap. Everything begins to look and feel oversized.

The body reacts immediately to any stress, whatever its source. Overwork, the loss of a job, a death or a divorce can easily cause chronic stress. But small things like a time deadline, a simple quarrel, or a gadget that doesn't work can throw us off balance. The message of "Stress!" is immediately carried along neuron, or nerve, tracks and stimulates an increased production of the chemicals of tension. The effects are almost immediate. When the body becomes tense, the functions of mind and spirit are immediately diminished.

Relaxation

The first step in combating stress is to relax. And the first step in learning how to relax is to recognize our stressors. At your first opportunity make a list of the people, the activities, and the situations that tend to create stress in you. Also, most of us have what is known as a "target organ" of stress. It will help you to detect stress more easily if you can identify your target organ and attend to its signals. Some of us get headaches; others get backaches. Some are troubled by stomach upsets; others get skin rashes. With me, it is my sinuses. When I begin to feel pressure in my sinuses, I know it is time to shift into a slower gear. My very personal problem is detecting stress as it builds in me. I am such a determined and driven person. A real "Type A." Stress often gathers hurricane force in me before I am able to recognize it. (I hope you are better at this than I.)

Some stressors seem to help us; others tend to diminish us. Stress in our lives has been compared to the friction of a violin bow. If there is no friction, there is also no music. If there is too much friction, there is only a painful screeching. Helpful stress gets us going. Helpful stress situations seem to excite us and energize us. I have often thought that going into a classroom to teach is a helpful stressor for me. I almost always feel stimulated by the prospect.

Chronic stress wears down the body.

Relaxing by Converting Stressors

Some stressors that tend to be destructive can be converted into helpful stressors. For example, most of us find only a destructive stress in harboring resentment. We tend to judge harshly those whom we resent. We try to avoid them, if possible. If we have to deal with them, we try to conceal our resentment, but afterward we feel drained. It has been wisely said that if you want to be a slave to someone, resent that person. He or she will be with you in the morning, throughout the day, and into the night. The resented person will eat with you and ruin your digestion. He or she will destroy your powers of concentration, ruin your good times, and deprive you of your precious peace and joy.

How do I go about converting the stress of resentment? Can it be changed into a helpful stress? Something that helps me very much is the realization that in resenting another, I have put my happiness into the hands of that person. I have given that person a very real power over me. The change from a negative to a positive charge will take place at the moment I truly take back the responsibility for my own happiness. This usually means that I must forgive the person I resent. I have to release that person from the real or imagined debt owed me, and I have to release myself from the high price of continued resentment.

I think that true and complete forgiveness depends on this insight: "Everyone makes psychological sense." There is always so much I do not know and will never know about those I tend to resent. To understand these people, I would have to know about their genes, family, education, experiences, neighborhood, and so forth. The human brain weighs three pounds, three ounces. But it stores within itself more messages than the most sophisticated computer ever built. Whenever a human being acts, all the messages that have been stored in the brain are somehow activated. They all feed into every action and reaction. So I can never be sure how much any person really needs forgiveness. Maybe if I could know all the messages fed into and stored

Some final suggestions on relaxation:

1. Find a confidant with whom you can be totally open and feel totally safe. Please don't cop out and say that you just cannot find one. With a little coaching, almost any well-intentioned person will do. Talk out all your significant and emotion-filled experiences. But be sure you let your confidant have equal time. Nobody wants to be a human garbage dump for emotional refuse.

2. Take a walk through the world of nature. Take time to examine and smell the flowers. Watch and listen to the waves of water at the lake or ocean. Look up at and admire the stars.

3. Reread a favorite book or poem.

4. Describe in a journal the most recent storm or crisis in your life, and be sure to add what you have learned from the experience. There is always a positive side to every storm or crisis.

5. Write in a journal daily. Let the subject matter concern your thoughts, feelings, and needs.

6. Remember your favorite jokes and laugh. Humor is healing.

Part Three   The Christian Vision of Oneself

in that person's brain, I would be sympathetic rather than critical. The bottom line: I just don't know.

I must always plead ignorance. Then to the extent that the person needs my forgiveness, I give it. God knows, I am myself often in need of the same understanding forgiveness that I need to offer. In the end of the forgiveness process, I will feel sorry for, not angry at, the offending person. I will be at peace because I will have released both of us from the bondage of resentment. I will have reclaimed responsibility for my own happiness. To the extent that I am able to accomplish this, my negative stress will be converted into a positive and helpful stress.

To take another example, some teachers get bent out of shape when a student disagrees with them. I have often fallen into this trap myself. There is another insight here: "In a win-lose argument, everyone loses." However, asking the student to elaborate on his or her point of view can lead to a meaningful sharing. In sharing, everyone wins. Of course, it calls for abdication from the pretense of looking as if you know everything. That's a hard act to sustain anyway. If, in spite of all this, the student is still unpleasant or arrogant, it pays to remember that "an obnoxious person is a hurting person." Such insights can well be the "converters" we need in dealing with stress.

The same kind of conversion process can be applied to the expression of feelings. First we must come to the realization that

feelings are not morally good or bad. We must also realize that it is always good for everyone to have fully and to express freely all significant feelings. Otherwise the stomach keeps score, and a bottled-up emotion becomes destructive if not deadly. We are as sick as we are secret. Of course, feelings have to be expressed in "I" not "You" statements. For example, "I felt angry," rather than "You made me angry!" Obvious insights and simple skills can produce the miracle of conversion quite easily. Harmful stress becomes helpful stress. Tranquillity replaces tension.

In a win-lose argument, everyone loses.

So, first we must learn to identify our stressors. The transformation of a negative stressor into a positive stressor is something like the experience of a miracle. What was hurtful becomes helpful. We can often gain the enlightenment and empowerment to make this conversion by talking the matter over with another. It is especially helpful if that person has experienced the same stress and has successfully gone through the conversion process.

Relaxing by Techniques

Obviously, not all negative stressors can be converted into positive stressors. For example, the death of a dear one means that we must go through a grieving process. There is no shortcut through this sorrow. There is no way to make grief pleasant. And so it is helpful to find ways to release such tensions. Whether our tensions result from major grief or from everyday stress, we all need to practice and use some helpful form of relaxation. There are many of these, and each person has to use whatever seems to help.

One common technique is to set aside some time each day for a hobby that has a pacifying, relaxing effect. At the end of each day I usually play the piano and relax. I am a musician in the same sense that a woodpecker is a carpenter. My music would definitely not relax someone who knows and loves music, but it does relax me. Other hobbies that might appeal to you are baking, gardening, reading,

talking, listening to music, collecting, looking through photo albums, writing, and so forth.

Still another popular technique is to make a daily appointment with yourself. During this appointment time, try to learn to enjoy the peace of doing nothing. See if it helps. Sit back and close your eyes. Breathe deeply, all the way in and all the way out. Imagine yourself in a place of peace, a delightful place you have actually visited or can easily imagine. Feel all your muscles unstretching. Relax and enjoy this daily appointment with yourself. It's cheaper and better than Valium.

Physical Exercise

The traditional formula for tension is, "An overactive mind in an underactive body." Daily, vigorous (if possible) exercise restores the balance. It also releases the buildup of tension. What exercise does for us physically is clear out of the brain and bloodstream the chemicals of tension. Exercise also promotes the production and flow of the chemicals that make us feel relaxed and peaceful, like the endorphines. It is very difficult to be depressed after vigorous exercise. Joggers often experience a feeling of exhilaration, commonly called runners' high. Physically, it is a neurochemical change in the body brought about by exercise.

It is interesting to note what many authors on the midlife crisis recommend above and before all: daily, vigorous exercise. Often psychological or spiritual needs assert themselves most forcibly at midlife. The result is not only the intrusion of our old friend, stress, but a vicious circle that apparently traps many of us. We get into the circle when our needs produce stress, and then the stress magnifies the needs. The result is more stress. The quickest way out is daily, vigorous exercise. Jog, swim, walk briskly, but do something!

More than fifteen years ago, I took the heart examination called a stress test. It was a blessing in disguise. I got onto the treadmill, while my heart was being monitored by an attending physician. I was convinced that the test would be a mere routine and that everything would go well. However, after six or seven minutes, the doctor stopped the machine. He asked me to sit down with my feet up. He kept listening attentively with his stethoscope to the sounds of my heart. Finally, he said that everything was back to normal. He explained that my heart had started to "palpitate." It was working very hard without achieving very much. He suggested that it might well be due to "lack of exercise."

And that was the beginning of my career as a jogger. I started out by running very slowly for a short distance. (Old men walking their dogs often passed me.) Then I would walk until I could comfortably resume running. Eventually my capacity increased, and I now jog for three or four miles every day. (I still have to be careful of those old men and their dogs.) The day

I took up jogging was indeed "the first day of the rest of my life." The "running doctor," cardiologist Dr. George Sheehan, has said that jogging may not increase the length of your life, but it will certainly improve the quality of your life. Beyond all doubt, jogging has done this for me.

The human body is a strange machine. It wears out from *lack of use*. Strangely enough, human energy comes into existence through the use of our bodies or exercise. Consequently, physical fitness contributes greatly to the energy we have to expend. Very often the best remedy for tiredness or weariness is a half hour of aerobic exercise. Inaction tends to make us sluggish. It actually leads to low energy, depression, and despair. It's hard to believe, but we can't hoard energy; that is, we can't build up our supply of energy by not using it. Of course, adequate rest is essential, but if it is not accompanied by physical activity, rest can prove depressing for most of us. Unused energy, like untapped potential, turns into a destructive force. I think it is safe to say that everyone can profit from physical exercise. We can all increase our energy supply by exercise.

Ever since researchers began examining the effects of physical exercise, its benefits have been firmly established. The death rate from cancer and heart disease has always been highest among people whose work involves the least amount of physical exertion.

An overactive mind is an underactive body.

On the other end of the spectrum, the death rate from cancer and heart problems has been lowest among those whose work involves the greatest amount of physical exertion. (Cf. *The Healing Family* by Stephanie Matthews Simonton and Robert L. Shook [Bantam Books, 1984].)

Of course, not everyone can or wants to jog. But almost everyone can walk briskly. Brisk walking has virtually all the benefits of strenuous exercise. Like jogging or swimming, brisk walking raises the metabolism so that the body burns up calories at a faster rate. It improves muscle tone and the efficiency of the heart. Exercise has also been found to lessen the buildup of plaque in the arteries, to lower blood pressure, and to slow down the aging process. With all these obvious benefits, exercise has to be a considerable factor in human happiness.

Stress and tension are greatly reduced by regular physical exercise. Consequently, those who exercise see a peaceful and proportioned world. They tend to have a healthy perspective. They think more clearly, remember better, and are more cheerful, pleasant, and optimistic. Of course, getting started may be the most difficult part. But the eventual rewards are enormous.

> *The human body is a strange machine. It wears out from lack of use.*

Nourishment: The Engine Won't Work Unless Properly Fueled

If we are to be happy and fully alive, good nutrition is absolutely essential. Keeping fit through right eating is very important. The human engine just won't run smoothly unless it is properly fueled. I know that it sounds overdramatic to link our social ills to nutrition. However, from crime and insanity to divorce and drug addiction, there is a connection. The late Adelle Davis, one of the most respected nutritionists of our times, wrote:

> We can expect all of these social problems to increase, involving ever larger percents of our population, unless our nutrition is markedly improved. I am not saying for a minute that faulty nutrition is the *only* cause of these social ills . . . but inadequate nutrition is still a vital factor which has received, as Dr. Margaret Mead puts it, "nearly total inattention." (*Let's Eat Right to Keep Fit* [Harcourt Brace Jovanovich, 1970], p. 248)

The body is obviously the instrument through which the mind and spirit work. One dramatic instance and proof of this is brain damage. The powers to know and choose are powers of the mind and spirit. But if the brain is damaged, as in the case of accident victims or punch-drunk boxers, the powers of the mind and spirit can be very limited. Likewise, it is true that if the brain is nutritionally deprived, the same effects will follow in proportion. In the case of prolonged alcoholism, the brain eventually turns to "mush." Another example: vitamin B 6 is necessary for the normal functioning of the brain. When this vitamin is withheld from diets in an attempt to starve cancer cells, convulsions result both in children and in adults.

An Eastern Parable

There is an Eastern parable of a horse, carriage, and driver that is a good illustration of the human condition and human interconnectedness. The carriage in this parable is the human body. The horse represents the human emotions, and the driver is the mind.

If the system does not function well, the first thing to check out is the care and condition of the carriage. If it has not been oiled and exercised, it may be that parts of the carriage are rusty or rotting. Maintenance may be poor, and lack of proper care and usage may have created further deterioration.

An Eastern parable illustrates human interconnectedness. A carriage in the parable is the human body. The horse represents human emotions, and the driver is the mind.

This carriage has a built-in system of self-lubrication. The bumps of the road are supposed to help circulate these lubricants. However, if the carriage has not been cared for or exercised, it may be that many of its joints have become frozen or corroded. Its appearance may even be shabby and unattractive. Obviously, for safe and efficient travel the carriage must be well maintained.

Consequently, many psychotherapists recommend a program of relaxation, nourishment, and exercise as a starting point. If the ride through life is proving uncomfortable, the first place to check out is the maintenance of the carriage (body). It may well be that the problem is here. If problems persist, a good psychotherapist will then proceed to check out the horse (emotions) and the driver (mind). However, "seemingly deeper" problems often disappear after the body has been properly relaxed, nourished, and exercised.

There is much in our historically rooted prejudices that wants to deny the interaction of body, mind, and spirit. And yet this sensitive interconnectedness is daily dramatized in our own experience. When we are overstressed, we become irritable. When we are physically underexercised, we get "down" emotionally. We lose the capacity to think clearly. Under prolonged stress, the very spirit in us is likewise stifled. Attending to our own physical needs for relaxation, exercise, and nourishment makes great sense. Without this care, the quality of our lives is greatly reduced. The world just doesn't make sense, and life begins to feel like a painful treadmill. We begin to ask, "What's it all about, anyway?'

We are a mysterious oneness with three sensitively interconnected parts. The body has an effect on mind and spirit. Mind affects body and spirit. And spirit affects body and mind.

FOR FURTHER REFLECTION

Chapter 10: We Must Try to Fulfill Our Needs for Relaxation, Exercise, and Nourishment

Review

1. Give examples that support the concept that our minds, bodies, and spirits are interconnected to such a sensitive unity that nothing can happen in one of these parts without affecting the other two parts.

2. If an interconnectedness of the mind, body, and spirit exists, then what *needs* must be taken care of if a person is to be happy and fully alive?

3. How does the health of your body affect your mind?

4. If the needs of the "spirit" are not fulfilled, how does that affect your mind and body? Give examples to support your explanation.

5. What are the four basic sources through which stress enters our lives? Give examples from the four sources.

6. Identify and explain the three ways a person may convert stress.

7. What are the benefits of good nutrition? What happens when a person does not fulfill his or her need for adequate nourishment?

Discuss

1. How does traditional religious thought and practice come out of the "separation of body and soul" understanding?

2. The words *wholeness, holiness,* and *health* all come from the same Latin word. The implication is that a holy person is one who is whole and healthy. Does this seem to be the case when you look at past examples of holiness?

3. What changes in your life would have to take place if you were to decide to fulfill your needs for relaxation, exercise, and nourishment?

4. In light of fulfilling these needs, which area of your life do you feel needs the most attention?

5. In the past month, how have you experienced stress?

6. Do you know of other techniques or ways that one might get rid of or convert stress? Share the techniques that you know.

Scripture Activity

"Come to me, all of you who are tired from carrying heavy loads, and I will give you rest. Take my yoke and put it on you, and learn from me, because I am gentle and humble in spirit; and you will find rest. For my yoke I will give you is easy, and the load I will put on you is light." (Matthew 11:28–30, GNB)

Read and reflect on the above passage and on the times when you felt stressed or physically tired. Summarize its main message and comment on how it relates to the chapter.

Processing These Ideas about Fulfilling Our Bodily Needs

Make a list. (Are you ready for another list?) This time you are asked to list the things you have done in the last week to care for your body. Use the categories of *relaxation, exercise,* and *nutrition.* Then give yourself a mark for your body-caring efforts. **A** = awe-inspiring. **B** = beautiful. **C** = coming along. **D** = dragging along. **F** = fooling yourself.

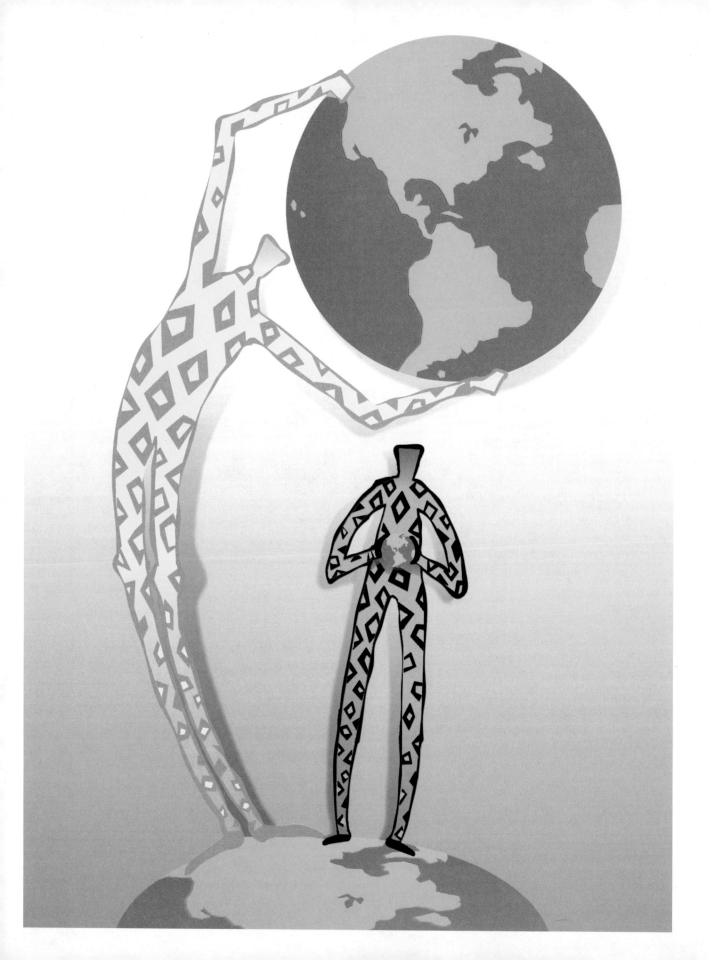

11 We Must Stretch by Stepping Out of Our Comfort Zones

We are all pilgrims, beings in process. Each one of us must march bravely to a personal drummer, climb our personal mountains, struggle for a destiny that is ours alone. I am I and you are you. Sometimes it seems much safer just to follow the good old beaten path. It feels safer to be a member of a flock. The "road less traveled" always seems so risky. But we are all pilgrims, each on the way to a personal, private destiny. There is no "one road for all." We are each gifted with an enormous but unique potential. However, in our rendezvous with destiny, we have to take chances, run risks, get rejected and be hurt, be knocked down and get back up on our feet. We must learn to survive defeats. It is all so wild, so terrifying, so adventuresome.

Pilgrims on their way to a promised land, it would seem, have to be, above all, courageous and very tough. Sometimes it will feel as though determination alone compels us to go on. It is so tempting just to find a place in the sun and stay there. The fertile imagination can and will make up a thousand rationalizations: "That's just not me." "This is just as good." "Why try something new?" We can send out a thousand small distress signals. Bleeding hearts will surely see them and rush to our rescue. Our rescuers will also make excuses for us. They will assure us that they like us just as we are, that there is no need to try for something more.

So we are doomed to stay in the same place. We do the very same things we have always done. Our actions and reactions become very predictable. Some will call us dependable. Others will be able to see that we are paralyzed by our fears. We are stagnant and stifled. Each day becomes a carbon copy of the previous. Each year begins to look very much like the last one. Our bones ache a little more. New wrinkles mark our faces. There is less energy. But otherwise we are just the same person we have always been, living in a world without challenges or change.

> *Repeated stretching will usher me into a new and larger world.*

A Definition of Terms

Each of us lives for the most part in the safe confines of a comfort zone. As long as we stay within that area, we feel secure and we know what to do. We are well practiced at the things inside the circle of this comfort zone. There are certain emotions we can easily express because we are comfortable expressing them. Others are just outside our comfort zone, and still others seem impossibly distant. Some actions come easily and comfortably.

We can do them, as it were, with one hand behind our backs. But others tend to terrify us. We can break out in a rash just thinking about them. Our comfort zones even extend to the clothes we wear. We are comfortable wearing certain fashions and certain colors, but there are others in which we would feel too conspicuous or too plain and, therefore, ill at ease.

One of our obstacles to growth is that we tend to rationalize these comfort zones. Successful rationalization always begins with a laundering of our language. We must pick just the right words. So we say, "That's just not me." "That's not my style." "I would just not be comfortable doing that." The most successful rationalization is simply to say, "I just can't." It has a certain "finality" about it. If we were to say "I won't," others might ask us why. But when we say "I can't," people tend to leave us alone. If you can't, you just can't. Ah! Alone in my sweet comfort zone.

The deliberate stepping out of our comfort zones is what we mean by "stretching." Right at the top, however, a qualification should be made. We stretch when we try something that is *right and reasonable*. We don't undress in public or hurt or embarrass someone else just to stretch. Stretching challenges us to do something that seems right and reasonable, but from which we have always been inhibited by fear. For example, I would like to give a speech in public, or I would like to express my true feelings. However, I have always felt too intimidated

to try it. This would be a good area in which to stretch.

Obviously, all growth involves some stretching. I have to attempt new things if I am to change. At first, I may feel clumsy, awkward, and more than a little self-conscious. But every time I try the same stretch, I will be a little more comfortable. Finally, what was once outside my comfort zone will now be within it. Repeated stretching will usher me into a new and larger world. I will be much more free. Eventually I will develop a "stretch mentality." I will actually enjoy trying new things. The old fears and crippling inhibitions that once painted me into a small corner of life will seem so stupid. I will even wonder why I ever let myself be terrorized by such toothless animals.

Stretching can be compared to being born. Have you ever seen a delivery? The newborn baby looks as though it would rather return to the warm womb from which it came. But the womb was in fact very confining. The baby had to be wherever its mother was. Now the baby has come into a new world, a larger world. With time and a little practice, the baby will be able to explore this bigger world. The person who is determined to stretch is by the force of that determination introduced into a larger world. Such a person can then explore that larger and more magnificent world. The cramping confines of a comfort zone gradually give way to the fullness of life and happiness.

Now we can obviously *think* our way into a new way of *acting*. For example, as I learn to think of myself as competent, I am empowered to attempt more and more difficult things. However, stretching involves a reverse process. Stretching means *acting* my way into a new way of *thinking*. For example, I don't think I can give a speech in public. My concept of myself does not include this ability. Somehow I just don't think that "I have it." Then one day I stretch. I give a speech, and everyone tells me how good it was. I gradually learn to think of myself as a speaker. I have acted my way into a new way of thinking about myself. All of us have had a similar experience, I think. Do you remember the first time you were able to swim without the support of another? "I can swim!" you shouted to the whole world. The same thing was true of the first cake you baked or the first time you hit a home run. You did something for the first time, and your concept of yourself changed. Previously, you were sure that you were a person who couldn't, and now you think of yourself as a person who can! Another victory for stretching.

Areas for Stretching

The possibilities are as large as the world a person wants to live in. But there are certain areas that for many of us seem to need special consideration. The first of these is *the expression of emotions*. It has been demonstrated again and again that the bottling up of our feelings inside us is self-destructive. We just can't get away with it. What we don't speak out we will act out.

We will act out our unexpressed feelings on our own bodies by getting headaches or ulcers. We will act out our pent-up feelings on innocent third parties. Or we will pout or harbor a grudge that will gradually poison us. But we won't get away with the suppression of our feelings. We need to tell others how we truly feel. The penalty for refusal is unhappiness. The stretching in this area calls for the mature, the right and reasonable expression of our feelings. Please see the chapter on communication (practice 8) in *Will the Real Me Please Stand Up?* (Powell and Brady, Tabor Publishing, 1985) to learn the needed techniques for doing this. Or for a fuller study of the question, look at the appropriate guidelines proposed in that book.

A profitable area for stretching could be included under the title "Things I have always wanted to do but have been afraid to try." All of us have at some time dreamed about reaching for a star. But our fears, especially the fear of failure, have always restrained us. Of course, our fears are largely subjective and personal. What some of us fear to try, others may find very natural and easy. But let me include here some typical challenges: giving a speech, telling others how grateful we are, disagreeing with a teacher or a boss, going sailing, flying through the skies, learning a musical instrument, speaking up when silence would be so much easier, taking dancing lessons, writing a letter of praise or protest to a publication. What have you always wanted to do, but were afraid to try?

Stretching means acting my way into a new way of thinking.

Certainly included in areas for stretching would be *personal authenticity,* or *realness.* Such authenticity calls for listening to what is going on inside us and in a mature way laying it on the line.

If I am uncertain inside, then what I have to do is admit my uncertainty. If I don't understand something, then I must admit that I really don't understand it. When I know that I am gifted at doing something, and my talent is needed, then I must step forth and volunteer. I will, always in a mature way, make known my needs. I will not be afraid to ask favors from others. And if something hurts, I will say an audible "Ouch!" Eventually, I will be able to retire my repertoire of masks and pretenses. I will be honest and open and real! And I am nothing if not real. This is certainly a right and reasonable goal to set for myself.

An additional area for stretching would be *relationships.* Relationships are essential for a full and happy life. However, for many of us, starting a relationship is difficult. It would be a good place to stretch. This usually involves introducing oneself to another. "You look like a person I would like to know." Oh, gulp, we think. Well, do it anyway. A relationship also and eventually involves sharing "secrets" and doing things together. The stretching to initiate relationships challenges us to open up, to admit one's secrets, to extend invitations, to risk rejections, to take one's chances.

Of course, there are numerous "little stretches" that all of us should attempt. You know, the kinds that don't cost us much inner crunch or struggle. You are no doubt familiar with the saying "No pain, no gain." So you ask, "Why bother with these almost costless stretches?" It is true that these smaller stretches might seem insignificant. Still, if undertaken regularly, they nudge us out of our old, familiar grooves. And just that small movement can cause great ripples of change and growth. Little by little, we move from being a person who is trying to stretch to a stretching-type, adventurous person. Little by little, we find ourselves living in a much larger, more exciting world. We find ourselves living every moment as new and fresh.

Among the small stretches we might try would be these: Take a rainy day nap. Make an appointment with yourself to relax and reflect. Make a list of things to be done today, and stick to it. Do a favor for someone anonymously. Write a song or a poem. Sincerely compliment someone who never compliments you. Say no to a request without giving in to guilt feelings. Spend some time talking to a child. Hold someone's hand. Try something you might fail at. Go slow when you feel rushed. Give away something that you feel attached to. C'mon. Go for it!

It has been calculated by the students of human nature that the average person uses only 10 percent of his or her potential. Ninety percent of what might have been dies quietly of frustration by fear and inhibitions. Stretching works to improve these odds. Without stretching, we will forfeit 90 percent of life's beauty, goodness, and giftedness. We will go to our graves with 90 percent of our potential goodness and giftedness unused. Sad, eh? Ninety percent of our potential sealed into our coffins with our own mortal remains.

All of us have "comfort zones," the areas in which we are comfortable. These comfort zones apply to the way we dress, the emotions we can comfortably express, the things which we will try, the depths to which we reveal ourselves, our openness to change, and so forth.

As long as we stay within these comfort zones, we just keep repeating what we have always done. We don't change. We don't grow. Every day is pretty much like the day before, and every tomorrow is pretty much like today. Our days are all "carbon copies" of one another.

We like our comfort zones, even though they definitely shrink the world in which we live. We know our way around inside our comfort zones. We know how to cope with the things we encounter in our familiar comfort zones. We feel "safe" there.

If you promise me that you are going to stay within your comfort zone, I will be able to tell you what you will be like at the end of your life. You'll be just what you are now, only more so.

If you promise me that you are going to stretch, to step outside your comfort zone, I cannot predict your future. The sky is the limit.

From the audio program, *The Fully Alive Experience*

Stretching: Reaching for the New, Leaving the Old

Something that pays off quickly and rewards us immediately usually comes easily. Unfortunately, most stretching requires time and repetition. We usually don't kill the dragons of our fears with one stroke of the sword. However, if we stay with it, we will experience a growing sense of ease and peace in doing what we could never do before.

I have clear recollections of my own early shyness. But, fortunately for me, kind and loving people challenged me.

> Ninety percent of what might have been dies quietly of frustration, by fear, and inhibitions.

So I got into debating, and I entered elocution and oratorical contests at school. I thought I might die or at least faint from embarrassment during my first appearances on the stage. But after a while and with perseverance, most of the shyness began to disappear. Now it is almost completely gone. (Every once in a while I experience a shy little kid somewhere deep down inside myself. He blinks and wants to know if all this is real.) But don't forget: Growth is always a gradual process, a bridge slowly crossed and not a corner sharply turned.

I remember reading about the liberation of the Nazi concentration camps by the Allied Forces at the end of World War II. It seems that many of the prisoners came hesitantly out of their prison barracks, blinked in the sunlight, and then slowly walked back into those barracks. It was the only life they had known for such a long time. They were accustomed to think of themselves as prisoners. They couldn't imagine themselves as free. So they weren't able to adapt immediately to acting like free human beings. I think that all of us somehow share this very human tendency. We have been imprisoned by our fears for such a long time. We go on living in a small but safe corner and, sadly, using only 10 percent of our giftedness. Then we are challenged to stretch—to take the first awkward steps out of our own personal prisons. We blink in the sunlight and want to go back silently to the things we have known, to our cramped but familiar comfort zones.

One of the relentless laws of our humanity is that when we give up one pleasure, we must be consoled by a new and, if possible, a greater pleasure. Human nature abhors a vacuum. The pleasure we give up in stretching is safety. We are stepping out over the fences and ditches of our inhibitions; we are leaving our "place in the sun." We are giving up the security of our comfort zones. Those comfort zones have always offered us an unchallenged and unchallenging existence. The substitute pleasure in stretching is freedom. We are becoming free. We are acting against our crippling fears, and this is liberating. Before stretching, we were using only 10 percent of our giftedness—the giftedness of our senses, emotions, minds, and hearts. By stretching, we are slowly coming out of our darkness into the light, out of our loneliness into love, out of our partial living into the fullness of life.

It is true, I am sure, that there is no such thing as a strong or weak will. What is strong or weak in us is *motivation*. Motivation sets our wills into action. It is the fuel of desire that moves us. Obviously, the motivation to stretch will somehow relate to our increased freedom, enjoyment, and self-actualization. All of us desire the sure and certain rewards of a fuller life and greater freedom. As we proceed to stretch, this motive becomes stronger and stronger.

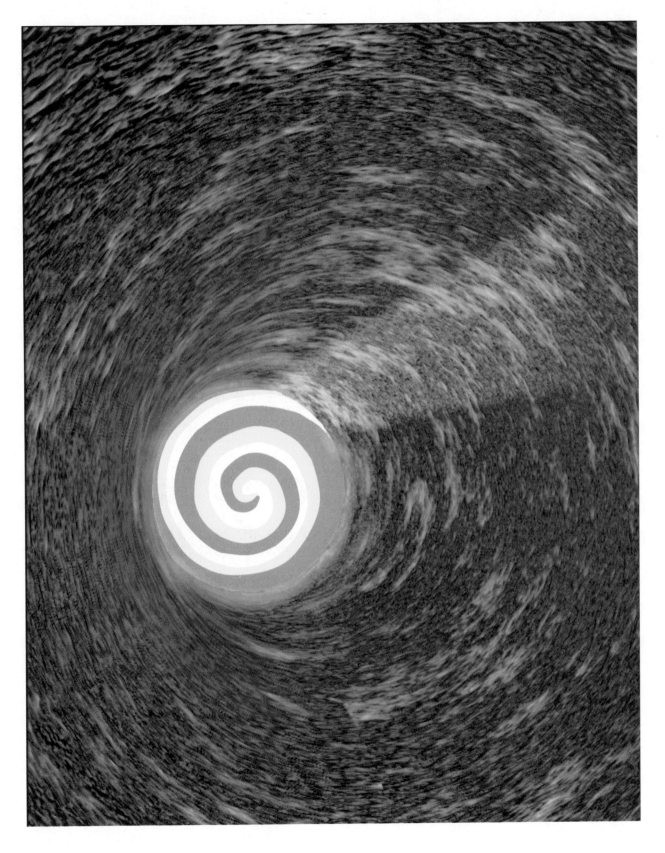

Motivating Underachievers

In every school there is a group called the underachievers. They have all that is needed except the drive or incentive to use their gifts. And in almost every school there is a class or course for these underachievers. One thing is almost always suggested in these classes: "Do something on your own. Try to stimulate your own interest. Read a book. Volunteer to do a project." Most underachievers sit on the fringe of a class, waiting for the teacher to inspire them. But three out of four teachers are simply not inspiring. It's the law of averages. The classic underachiever gets used to sitting on the curbstones of life, having one identity crisis after another. He or she keeps mumbling, "Who am I? What am I worth? Who cares anyway?" It's like sitting in a rocker. It doesn't get you anywhere, but it gives you something to do.

Until the underachiever is persuaded to stretch, this limbo of a half existence will go on. But with stretching, the underachiever will experience an enthusiasm that will build on itself. When we become involved in something, our very activity generates further enthusiasm. And enthusiasm feeds on itself. It naturally increases and multiplies. Stretching overcomes our inertia, and from there on we gradually become self-motivating.

*We are each gifted
with an enormous but unique potential.
However, in our rendezvous
with destiny, we have to take chances,
run risks, get rejected and be hurt,
be knocked down and
get back up on our feet.*

FOR FURTHER REFLECTION

Chapter 11: We Must Stretch By Stepping Out of Our Comfort Zones

Review

1. Define "comfort zone."
2. Define "stretching." What are the qualifications for constructive stretching? Why are these qualifications measurements for constructive stretching?
3. Describe the two ways of stretching: (a) thinking your way into a new way of acting, and (b) acting your way into a new way of thinking. Offer two examples that will differentiate each way of stretching.
4. How does stretching get us in touch with our potential and lead to happiness?

Discuss

1. Generally, what would work better for you: thinking your way into a new way of acting, or acting your way into a new way of thinking about yourself? Explain.
2. In what area do you feel you need to stretch the most: (a) the expression of emotions, (b) things you have always wanted to do but have been afraid to do, (c) personal authenticity (realness), or (d) starting a new relationship?
3. In terms of "little stretches" that do not cost us much inner struggle, which do you feel would be the most profitable for you at this time of your life: (a) taking a nap, (b) making a list of things to do, and sticking to it, (c) doing a favor for someone anonymously, (d) writing a poem or song, (e) offering a genuine compliment, (f) saying no to a request without giving in to guilt feelings, or (g) trying something you might fail at?

Scripture Activity

"The Spirit of the Lord is upon me, because he has anointed me to bring good news to the poor. He has sent me to proclaim release to the captives and recovery of sight to the blind, to let the oppressed go free, to proclaim the year of the Lord's favor." (Luke 4:18–19, NRSV)

Reflect on Jesus' statement and his call that we become "bearers of good news." How does this passage from Luke challenge you to concretely "stretch beyond your comfort zones" in order to become this "bearer of good news" in your day-to-day life?

Processing These Ideas about Stretching

We have already discussed and looked at profitable areas for stretching. To be more specific and actually challenge yourself to "stretch beyond your comfort zones," pick any five of the following "stretches" and challenge yourself to actually do them. See for yourself how these stretches will release you from the small and lonely world of comfort zones. Experience the liberation of acting against your fears and painful inhibitions.

1. *An emotion I have never shared.* I will share that emotion today.
2. *A risk I have never taken.* Today I will take that risk.
3. *An achievement I have never tried.* Today I will try for that achievement.
4. *A rejection I have never chanced.* Today I will take that chance.
5. *A need I have never admitted to anyone.* Today I am going to admit that need.
6. *An apology I have never been able to make.* Today I will make that apology.
7. *An affirmation I have never offered.* Today I am going to offer that affirmation.
8. *A secret I have never shared.* Today I will share it with someone.
9. *A hurt I have never revealed.* Today I will reveal that hurt.
10. *A love I have never expressed.* Today I am going to tell someone "I love you."

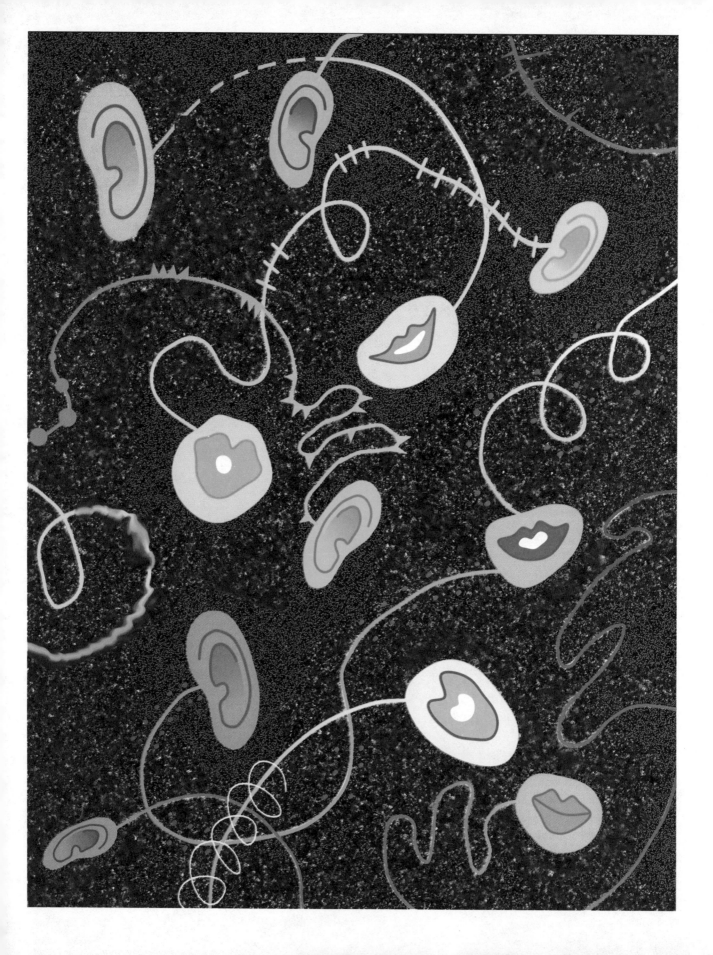

12 *We Must Seek Growth, Not Perfection*

It all seemed so noble, so generous, and if I say so myself, it even seemed so saintly: "Reach for the top. Give it your best. Don't settle for your second best."

The very rhetoric of my zeal to do my best, to be my best, sent fire surging through my veins. But the rhetoric betrayed reality. The rhetoric was unrealistic. Nothing is ever perfect. My best was always flawed.

The results of my zeal for perfection left a thick and bitter taste in my mouth. Deep inside me was a soft and long moan: "But I tried so hard. I gave it all I had. It was my best shot."

Then I pounded my fists of frustration on the earth. I waved them at the sky. But it did no good. I was left to admit that I am imperfect. I am a mistake maker. The human condition of trial and error is my condition.

I have tried all my cover-ups, my denials. I have tried to look as though I had it all together. But under all my sham and pretense, I knew all along that I could never match my dreams with my performance. I could never be perfect.

The Roots of Perfectionism

"Obsessive-compulsive" is a double-barreled diagnosis of trouble: trouble behind and trouble ahead. "Obsessive" has to do with the mind. An obsessive person thinks and rethinks almost constantly about the obsession, whatever it is. "Compulsive" refers to conduct or "doing." The compulsive person has to do, do, do. A compulsive person may wash his or her hands twenty times a day.

Now the fact is that some of us are obsessive-compulsive about perfection. And I would think that there is some of this in most of us. Even those who insist that they are not perfectionists are uncomfortable with being "mistake makers." They can recite chapter and verse of their willingness to be imperfect, but the recitation ends when they make a mistake. The extent to which we experience and act on this obsession and compulsion is the extent to which we are bound to suffer. It is not at all surprising to learn that perfectionists actually have the highest rate of depression among all human beings.

It's not what I say that matters, it's what you hear.

143

Like all of our tendencies, perfectionism has deeper, unexposed roots. Sometimes it betrays a hidden fear. For example, I may be thinking in an unconscious way, "If I am imperfect, people won't trust me" or "I won't ever be able to get ahead." Or there may be some all-or-nothing logic hiding beneath my surface thoughts: "If I am not perfect, then I am a failure." Sometimes, I secretly think (but rarely admit) that "if I am a failure, people will criticize me." Or it may be that a little voice from my past will ask in a whisper, "If I do not do a perfect job, what will Mommy or Daddy say?" It may well be that my drive for perfection is simply my way to get approval. And it may have started in early childhood, with Mommy and Daddy.

Early on in life, many of us get programmed to think this way. It may be that the message was acted out by exacting parents. They programmed us to be perfectionists by trying to be perfect themselves. Or it may be that the inclination to perfectionism was drilled into us by others who wanted to enjoy our performances vicariously. Peer pressure can be another strong factor. Many of us have had the experience of being laughed at. Afterward we secretly resolved never again to make a public mistake. The penalties are simply too painful, too embarrassing. If I am a "driven" person, someone has somehow placed expectations on me that can only become painful. Of course, it may have been a matter of my misinterpretation. But anyway, it is not what is said but rather what is heard that influences people, people like you and me.

The High Price of Perfectionism

Perfectionism always has a downward spiral. It leaves us room only for failure. Nothing ever comes off exactly as we planned it. And the end result of such failure is discouragement. Very often our frustrated hopes degenerate gradually into a disappointed anger. We act out our discouragement or anger in obnoxious ways, but they are always buried in pretense. Others would never suspect.

This self-destructive course of striving for perfection has been repeated in many lives. A young woman I met years ago admitted to me at our first meeting that she had twice tried suicide. However, she assured me that her nursing degree would definitely fill her painful sense of emptiness. Of course, she got the R.N. degree, but she was just as unhappy as before. By that time she was sure that marriage was all that she needed. A fine young man soon appeared on the scene, and they were married. But the depression that had haunted her all her life soon reappeared like a cloud over her head. At this time she was certain that children would be all that she needed. They would definitely make her happy. Soon enough she was the mother of three children. But the clear skies didn't last. It wasn't long before she was tearfully confiding in me that her children hated her. In fact, she said, her adolescent son was physically abusive to her. I urged her to seek family counseling to find out what her children were acting out. I don't think she ever accepted this suggestion.

Then a few years ago I got a long-distance phone call from her husband. "Jean is dead," he told me. "And the really sad news is that she killed herself. She drove our car into the garage and left the motor running while she waited to die. She left a suicide note on the kitchen table. In her last words to us, she said simply: 'Don't be sad. You tried.' " Jean was being waked at the time of our phone conversation. In fact, her husband was calling from the funeral home. I almost couldn't believe the objectivity in his bereavement. He knew of the occasional phone calls between Jean and me. He asked, "Did she ever mention to you that our children hated her?" "Yes," I admitted, "she did tell me that."

"Well, they did. In fact, at her wake in the next room, I can sense the relief in our children that she is gone." He continued: "She had all the goodwill in the world. She tried everything to distract herself from her pain. But she never really acknowledged the real source of that pain. She was a perfectionist. She had declared an all-out war on all forms of imperfection. She sought an unconditional surrender from the less than perfect. She hounded the children until they hated her. At least they hated the sound of her voice and the finger she pointed at them. She drove herself to physical and emotional exhaustion. It lasted for thirty-nine years. Then she died, with the simple farewell: "Don't be sad. You tried.' "

The poor man admitted that he felt very sorry for her. But he added that he also felt sorry for all those other people out there "trying to wage war with the same demon of perfectionism. They die inch by inch, day by day. And even when they never really die, as my Jeannie, they lose all zest for living. They crawl into a corner of hopelessness, and there they wait for death to say 'It's over!' " Perfectionism is indeed a suicide course.

Denial of the Demon

Most of the people I know are reluctant to admit that the demon of perfectionism has dominated them. They remember some habit of slovenliness that seems to disqualify them. Yet, these same people are uncomfortable with personal mistakes or oversights. I admit that I am myself uncomfortable, even though I am not a full-fledged perfectionist. We semiperfectionists are impatient with the mistakes and oversights of others as well as our own. We find it hard to laugh at the mistakes and weaknesses of ourselves and others. We do not comfortably accept ourselves as trial-and-error types, and we are slow to concede this privilege to others. It may not be the most virulent form of perfectionism, but it is enough to diminish the joy of living for ourselves and for those around us.

Of course, any form or degree of perfectionism is unrealistic. And somehow it seems that denial itself is a symptom of the disease.

A good way to choose growth is to set out to enjoy rather than to achieve perfection.

Once we admit that perfectionism is obsessive-compulsive behavior, we have implicitly said that perfectionism is itself a form of imperfection, the very thing we cannot live with. Obviously, a real perfectionist cannot admit that unrealistic hopes or expectations bedevil him or her. That would blow one's cover.

The Anatomy of Perfectionism

Perfectionism is humanly unhealthy. And the difference between one who is healthy and the perfectionist is that the healthy person is in control of his or her life. The perfectionist is controlled, is driven by a compulsion. The healthy person is free and chooses freely. The perfectionist is not free. He or she has to . . . must . . . should succeed, be perfect. It is a bondage, an imprisonment of the free spirit.

Perfectionism begins with a *belief*. Perfectionists believe that their worth is measured by their performance. Of course, mistakes then detract from personal worth. They also believe that the only way to impress others is by being perfect. In a sense they see themselves as solo performers. They are not part of a team but contestants on their own. The obvious *emotions* that result are fear and panic. Perfectionists fear the displeasure and the punishment of others. They know that somehow they will have to pay for possible imperfections. They will surrender the respect of others. And so the emotional groundswell results in a loneliness, sadness, and depression.

Because emotions by their nature are partly physical, there are *physical symptoms* of perfectionism. These will vary with the perfectionist and the "target organ" of the perfectionist. But there will be symptoms of stress that will probably affect sleeping and eating, and will produce tension. As a result of all these, there is a type of *behavior* by which perfectionists reinforce the original belief that started everything. Perfectionists are people pleasers, and so they work hard to meet the expectations of others. They overpromise themselves. They set unrealistic standards and have unrealistic

---

Life itself is a process and we are all "beings-in-process." None of us has yet come to full maturity; none of us has arrived at completion. We are all fractions on our way to becoming whole numbers. I remember once seeing this sign on a button a woman was wearing: "Please be patient. God is not finished with me yet." God is not finished with any of us yet. We are all en route to our full personal growth and potential. And certainly we need a lot of patience during the process—patience from ourselves and patience from others.

The process of human development and growth is much like the process of accepting death. We humans have to move at our own pace, and all during the process we need to be accepted wherever we are. We know, for example, that we cannot insist on consistently mature behavior from small children. We must let them be children and we must accept them as such. We also know that we cannot demand a rigid conformity from adolescents who are trying to learn how to think for themselves and become their own independent person. In a similar way we must learn to be patient with ourselves in the passages of the human process.

From *Will The Real Me Please Stand Up?*

expectations. They do not like to ask for help, because this would be a concession. It would be an admission of inadequacy.

Perfectionists believe that they will be accepted by others on the basis of their achievements. They think of themselves as successful if they do well, not by simply being who they are. Performance and responsibility are always more important than feelings or needs. The penalty for failure is a withdrawal of the love of others and the loss of self-esteem.

Perfectionists do not give themselves unconditional acceptance nor do they expect it from others. They do not give themselves permission to fail, so they are anxious and nervous before every performance. They do not think of others as supporting and encouraging them. They see others only as watching and ready with pen and paper to grade them.

Peaceful Acceptance of the Human Condition

Of course, there can be no reversal or healing of this obsession with perfection unless one becomes aware of the condition and the bondage that results. Perfectionism is indeed a slave master. To put one's happiness in the hands of such a master is indeed foolish. The human condition is that of weakness. We are all trial-and-error types, real mistake makers. Brute animals and fowls have been endowed with perfect instincts. They do their thing even for the first time as if guided by a built-in set of instructions. The white-tufted sparrow always builds its recognizable nest perfectly, even the first time. But we poor humans, endowed as we are with very limited instincts and the precious gift of intelligence, have to proceed by trial and error. We are prone to miscalculation. Our maturation process is a process. Our finest minds design a space capsule that explodes in space. Our best trains derail. Our airplanes crash. Our automobiles are recalled because of potentially fatal defects.

It is true that the human spirit has put a man on the moon and built high-rises that soar to dizzying heights. But for every such success there are a thousand failures. For every experiment that succeeds, a litter of failures lies on the laboratory floor. However, we continue our corporate efforts to improve. At the same time, to deny the truth of the human condition is to invite pain and frustration into our lives.

Human blessedness in this matter requires us to face and accept the truth. We are error prone. We learn by trial and error. Failure is never ultimate and absolute failure. It is only a learning experience. *The only real failure is the one from which we learn nothing.* All failure can be educational. The truth that confession is good for the soul extends to this admission of our own folly and fragility. According to the old proverb already quoted, if and when we learn to laugh at ourselves, we shall never cease to be entertained. The possibilities are infinite.

A corollary of this basic truth is that we are collaborators and not competitors. We are all in this together. Each of us should learn from the experience of others. You don't have to rerun my failed experiments. It's all part of the sage advice: "Learn from the mistakes of others. You won't have time to make them all yourself." When Henry Ford produced the first Model T, he must have known that others would improve on his design and structure. Each generation surpasses the previous, but only because it stands on the shoulders of that previous generation.

Seeking Growth

If perfection is a torturous ideal, growth is not. Growth sees life as a process during which skills are gradually developed. Learning to play the piano starts with laboriously fingering the scales over and over again. Then we proceed to melodies, and these melodies become more and more "classical" as our proficiency develops. If perfectionism seeks to arrive immediately (if not sooner), growth knows that even the journey of a thousand miles begins with a single step. Time and practice are of the essence. Actually, once we get the knack, gradual growth is much more fun than instant arrival.

What would you say if I were to propose to you this choice: You come to two doors. One is marked "instant perfection" and the other is marked "gradual growth." Which door would you prefer to go through? Surprisingly, very few, in my own experience, have chosen "instant perfection." If they go through that door, it's all over. What do you do for an encore to perfection? The journey has come to an end. If one chooses, however, to go through the door of "gradual growth," such a person will experience the joy of getting better and better, and the process will be ongoing for a lifetime. There will be the little successes of growth, without the big failure of perfectionism.

A good way to choose growth is to set out to *enjoy* rather than to achieve perfection. As I write these words for the first time, I am trying to follow my own advice. Something in me knows that there must be a better way to say all this. There may even be a perfect way. But I do not write seven or eight drafts and tear them all up in despair because they are not perfect. I rather try to enjoy this sharing with you. I read over what I have written, cross out this or that, add a word here or there. Then I think, "There. That's pretty clear. Somehow I seem to have said it better than in my previous attempts. Maybe, just maybe, what I write will help someone." That's a consoling thought.

And here is the surprise bonus. If you set out to *enjoy*, you will actually do a better job than if you are determined to make it perfect. (Maybe you don't believe that yet, but I think that someday you will.) If you are in school, set the dials of your mind to enjoy the courses you are taking as much as you can.

Perfectionism is indeed a slave master.

I'll bet the results will surprise you. If you hold a job, try to do your work with as much enjoyment as possible. You'll most likely notice an improvement in your performance. Setting out to achieve perfection, by contrast, will become stressful and demoralizing. The end result will probably be discouragement. And discouragement always wants to quit, to give it all up.

Some Antidotes for Perfectionism

1. With any obsessive-compulsive habit, it helps to distract yourself from it. So the next time you find yourself grinding your teeth trying to be perfect, direct all your thoughts to enjoying whatever it is you are doing. Be happy instead of hyper. This will create a new route for your brain waves. Such distraction from or defusing of the perfection mindset will be telling your obsessive compulsion, "You don't own me. I declare myself free from your tyranny. I am my own person, not your slave." The same declaration of personal independence can be achieved by putting a time delay on my compulsion. If I think I've got to do it right now, let it wait for an hour or even a day.

2. Desensitize yourself to the failures of imperfection. Talk over, laugh at, be open about your failures or imperfections. In this way you will eventually learn to be more comfortable with the human condition. You will also find, I am sure, that others will like you more. They will be able to identify with you. Many of us have somehow come to believe that others are impressed by our perfect performances. We think that they expect us to be perfect. So we try to look good, even when we aren't. The fact of the matter is that others, who experience the same human condition of weakness, would feel greater kinship if they knew that we are fragile and foolish, too. Admit it, and the world will applaud.

Failure is never ultimate and absolute failure. It is only a learning experience. The only real failure is the one from which we learn nothing.

FOR FURTHER REFLECTION

Chapter 12: We Must Seek Growth, Not Perfection

Review

1. What does the term *obsessive-compulsive* mean? How does the term apply to our discussion about perfectionism?
2. What attitudes are at the root of perfectionism?
3. What is the high price of perfectionism?
4. Using the four-layer "human" cake of Chapter 2, describe the anatomy of a perfectionist.
5. In your own words, describe a healthy Christian attitude toward perfectionism. Include in your description insights about (a) peacefully accepting the human condition, and (b) seeking growth, not perfection.
6. What two practical methods or antidotes are useful in dealing with perfectionism? Comment on how these antidotes deal with one's obsessive-compulsive need to be perfect.

Discuss

1. What unhealthy attitudes do you have that influence you to behave as a perfectionist?
2. Are you more aware of and impatient with your own mistakes, weaknesses, and faults, or those of other people? Why?
3. How might you be a happier person and enjoy life more if you began to become more comfortable with the human condition of weakness?
4. Which door would you prefer to go through if you had a choice: (a) one marked "Instant Perfection," or (b) one marked "Gradual Growth"? Give reasons for your preference.

Scripture Activity

"O Lord, you have searched me and known me. You know when I sit down and when I rise up; you discern my thoughts from afar. You searched out my path and my lying down, and are acquainted with all my ways. Even before a word is on my tongue, O Lord, you know it completely.

You hem me in, behind and before, and lay your hand upon me. Such knowledge is too wonderful for me; it is so high that I cannot attain it.

"For it was you who formed my inward parts; you knit me together in my mother's womb. I praise you, for I am fearfully and wonderfully made. Wonderful are your works; that I know very well. My frame was not hidden from you, when I was being made in secret, intricately woven in the depths of the earth. Your eyes beheld my unformed substance. In your book were written all the days that were formed for me, when none of them existed. How weighty to me are your thoughts, O God! How vast is the sum of them!" (Psalm 139:1–6, 13–17, NRSV)

Reflect on Psalm 139. It is a deeply moving psalm-prayer acknowledging that God knows and accepts us as we are. In the spirit of this psalm, construct your own prayer-psalm of praise and thanksgiving for the wonder of your own being. You may use any lines from Psalm 139 in constructing your own prayer-psalm, but be sure to include some statements about your desire to come to greater acceptance of your own human condition and your desire to "seek growth, not perfection."

Processing These Ideas about Perfectionism

1. *Make two lists.* On one of these lists, enumerate the advantages of perfectionism, and on the other, the disadvantages.
2. *Write in a journal.* Write about yourself as a person seeking growth rather than perfection. Whether you are seeing yourself as a student, an athlete, a member of an organization, or whatever else, describe yourself in a posture of growing rather than being perfect. Would growth be preferable and profitable for you? Write the pros and cons.

Part Four

THE CHRISTIAN VISION

OF OTHERS

13 *The Way We View Others*

People Are Basically . . . What?

Occasionally I visit a prisoner in the State Penitentiary of Illinois. I certainly don't think it would be a good idea to free all such prisoners, but I do find it emotionally difficult to see human beings locked in cages. As you may know, more than 90 percent of all the prisoners in our American prisons were abused as children. In the language of transactional analysis, they think of themselves as "not O.K.," but they also think that "you're not O.K. either." The vindictive, Papillon mentality is strong in them: "You hurt me and you're going to pay for it through your clean blue nose!" The more violent prisoners are transported wearing thick leather girdles, to which are attached strong steel handcuffs. Most of those whom I have seen were sneering, defiant, and contemptuous of the beefy trustees who were leading them around.

On the occasion of one such visit, I was being processed as a visitor (translated: questioned, searched, x-rayed, and registered on a written form). Next to me was an elderly black woman who was visiting her grandson. She was so warmly gracious and kind to everyone around her that I could not resist the comment: "I have to say this to you. You seem to live what I preach. You come across as a very loving person, and I'll bet you bring a lot of joy into this world." She smiled and thanked me. Then she added, "Father, I am a Christian. In my world there are no strangers, just brothers and sisters. Some of them I have not yet met." All of my instincts recognized the presence of this beautiful attitude in her bearing and manner. "You really believe that, don't you?" I said. She replied simply and softly, "Yes, I do." On the other hand, the prisoner whom I visit has a very different attitude toward humanity. He tells me in detail about the subhuman conduct of many of the prisoners and of his general distrust of others. His motto seems to be "Don't trust anyone, and always carry an 'equalizer.' "

If the attitude toward self is the most important one of all those that reside in your head and mine, no doubt our second most important attitude is the way we view others. Of course, whenever someone speaks of an attitude toward others, we immediately want to distinguish: "Some people like, others I don't. Some people are nice, others aren't." Still there is in us a general instinct about other people.

We must give our children roots and wings.

155

> *Our lives are shaped by those who love us and by those who refuse to love us.*

There is a general anticipation: People are basically __(what?)__ until they prove otherwise. What would your juror-attitude in charge of evaluating others fill into that blank? People are basically "good . . . bad . . . selfish . . . loving . . . kind . . . cruel . . . honest . . . deceitful . . . manipulative . . . generous . . ." and so forth. Pick one or more, but let your choices come spontaneously out of your guts and heart rather than out of the stock of memorized answers in your head. Respond out of your *real*, rather than out of your *ideal*, self.

I would like to share with you that in my own efforts at introspection and investigation of personal attitudes, this attitude toward others seems to be the one attitude in me that is most in need of work and revision. I envy people like the elderly lady at the state prison. When I grow up, I want to turn out like her. I want to think of others as my brothers and sisters, even the ones I have not yet met.

Just as you must be, I am also aware of the extremes in this matter. Some of us are rosy-cheeked, naive, and gullible. We don't seem to acknowledge the effects of original sin. Others of us tend to be sour-faced and cynical. We are sure, as we see others through our suspicious and squinting eyes, that everyone is "rotten to the core."

These are the extremes. Most of us stumble around somewhere in between them, looking for a middle ground.

The Source of Our Attitude toward Others

The first, inherited attitudes of children are usually taken in by osmosis from their parents. When we were little kids playing with our toy cars or dolls, we heard our parents talking about others. We heard them talking about the people with whom they worked and the people in the neighborhood. Their messages, expressed and implied, were recorded on our "parent tapes." These parent tapes tend to play insistently, however softly, in our heads, for the rest of our lives. If there are certain messages on these tapes which we judge to be unhealthy, we must make a conscious effort to delete them.

In addition to this parental source of our attitudes toward others, there is also the dimension of personal experience. A frightening bully in the school yard, the ridicule of our elementary school classmates, a traumatic deception by a supposed friend, an attack or abuse suffered as a child—such experiences can plant seeds of distrust and suspicion in us that do not die easily. All of us have some unpleasant experiences with others that are stored in our memory banks.

Our personal psychological development also has a profound influence on our view of others. In the normal course of human growth, the first stage of child development involves an *attachment* or *dependency*. The child becomes deeply attached to his or her mother (primarily), so that she is the indispensable source of security, comfort, and reassurance. After this period, the child usually turns to the father for *guidance*. The child at this stage needs and seeks the approval of the father, and fears his disapproval and rejection. Then comes the period of *separation*, in which the young person leaves the protection and direction of parents, and becomes his or her own mother and father. In the first stages, the parents provide roots for their children. In the last stage, the parents must assist their children by offering them wings, the wings on which they can leave the nest of security and venture forth into their own independent lives.

If a person does not successfully negotiate these broadly outlined transitions, he or she can spend the greater part of life looking for the missing pieces. Such a person can easily become overdependent on the approval and reassurance of others, or can remain indecisive, hitchhiking through life on the judgments and decisions of others. Some people remain bottomless wells in need of reassurance by others or perpetually intimidated by a supposed inferiority to others. In any case, our attitude toward others usually has deep roots in the soil of our early lives. As mentioned, the abused child comes into later life angry and filled with vendettas of vengeance. Those who come from close, affirming, and affectionate families will come into later life fully equipped with roots and wings, ready to bless and be blessed by others. "Our lives are shaped by those who love us . . . and by those who refuse to love us."

The Master Vision of Others

In the master vision, provided by the message, life, and person of Jesus, we Christians are called to be channels of love to one another. God, who is love, created us in an act of love. All goodness is somehow self-diffusive. In the act of creation God's goodness diffused itself. We all know what this diffusion of goodness means from personal experience. When we have something good—like a good joke, a good recipe, or even a bit of good news—the instinct of love is to share it. So our Father-God, experiencing in himself an ecstasy of love and happiness, wanted to share his life, his happiness, and even his home with us. From all eternity God planned this and picked out each of us to be the special recipients of God's love. We are the chosen children of God's family and of God's heart. Each of us was conceived and born into this world only because we were loved and wanted by our Father-God.

From the beginning there was a human network of veins and arteries through which this love was to be carried to all the parts of God's human family. However, somewhere, somehow, something went wrong. We call this "original sin." Sin and selfishness, hatred and homicide became a part of our human inheritance. But the call has always remained the same.

Jesus answered, "'Love the Lord your God with all your heart, with all your soul, and with all your mind.' This is the greatest and the most important commandment.

The second most important commandment is like it: 'Love your neighbor as you love yourself.' The whole Law of Moses and the teachings of the prophets depend on these two commandments."

Matthew 22:37–40 (GNB)

In the Christian vision these two commandments are really linked together. I cannot say my "yes" of love to God unless I say my "yes" of love to each and every member of God's human family. There are to be no exceptions. The French poet Charles Peguy once said that if we try to come to God alone, God will certainly ask us some embarrassing questions: "Where are your brothers and sisters? Didn't you bring them with you? You didn't come alone, did you?" These yeses of love, required by the two great commandments, are inseparable. Jesus himself made this very clear: We can refuse our love to no one.

"You have heard that it was said, 'Love your friends, hate your enemies.' But now I tell you: love your enemies and pray for those who persecute you, so that you may become the sons [and daughters] of your Father in heaven. For he makes his sun to shine on bad and good people alike, and gives rain to those who do good and to those who do evil. Why should God reward you if you love only the people who love you? Even the tax collectors do that! And if you speak only to your friends, have you done anything out of the ordinary? Even the pagans do that!"

Matthew 5:43–47 (GNB)

"Aye!" as Shakespeare once said, "there's the rub!" The two yeses of love are inseparable. In fact, Jesus never talks about loving God without adding the second part of the great commandment, namely, a love of neighbor. Also, with the exception of the great commandment itself, Jesus does not even talk explicitly about loving God. He does say that God takes as done to God's self whatever we do to the least of God's children. Jesus also instructs us that we should not offer God our gifts unless and until we have been reconciled with one another. (See Matthew 5:23–26.) Finally, Jesus insists that we cannot expect God's forgiveness for our sins unless we stand ready to forgive those who have offended us. (See Matthew 6:12.) In the message and master vision of Jesus, the principal place of encounter with God is in others: our families, friends, neighbors, acquaintances, and yes, even our enemies.

There is an old Irish ditty: "To live above with the saints we love, ah! that is the purest glory; but to live below with the saints we know, ah! that is another story." Let's face it, some people (not you or I, of course!) are hard to live with, let alone love. Those who are truly loving and caring people must see something in others that I do not.

Christians are called to be channels of love.

Two Persons in Each of Us

For myself, I think that my Christian commitment asks me to love others for themselves and not in spite of themselves. So I would suggest that there really is a vision that enables us to love people who are apparently unlovable. It seems to me that there are really two different persons in ourselves and in each of the others whom we meet. There is a wounded, hurt, and angry person: the obnoxious person. Wearing various outward appearances, it may be that this person is usually in the ascendancy in the personalities of the unlovable. This wounded, hurt, and angry person can be called out of any of us by harsh criticism, by sarcasm, by ridicule, and by put-downs. But there is also in each of us a good and decent, a caring and loving person. We are made in the image and likeness of God, and this likeness is never totally obliterated. This beautiful and loving person is called out by gentle kindness, by love and understanding.

As a newly ordained priest I volunteered to preach a week-long retreat to other priests. I felt confident at the time I accepted the invitation: "Have sermons, will travel!" But at zero hour, standing outside the chapel, watching my retreatants file past me into the chapel, I was completely intimidated. There were two bishops, and the youngest of the priest retreatants looked about fifteen years older than I. Through my saucer eyes, every single one of them looked completely confident, utterly together, and worthy of the most respectful veneration. At the time I accepted the invitation, I thought I had it all together, but when the chips were down I was wondering where I had put it.

The older priest in charge of the retreat house was standing with me at the chapel door. We were reviewing the troops together. He smiled at me as the last priest retreatant went into the chapel.

"How do you feel?" he asked.

"Terrified!" was my spontaneous and utterly honest reply.

"Why?"

"Why? You're kidding. Didn't you see them?"

"Oh, they just need what every one of us needs, a little love and a little understanding."

"Then why don't they look like it? Those fellas didn't look like they were lining up for love and understanding. Are you sure that's what they need?"

"I'm sure," he said with a knowing smile and a friendly wink.

> One of the most startling lines I have ever read in any book was in *The Diary of a Young Girl* by Anne Frank. Anne wrote the book while she was being hunted down by the Nazis. While she was literally running for her life, Anne Frank wrote in her diary, "I do believe that deep within his heart, every person is good." When I read that line and considered the circumstances under which it was written, I kept asking: "Do you really believe that, Anne Frank, do you? With all the malice that you are experiencing, in the midst of all the hatred directed towards you because you have Jewish blood in your veins, while you are in hiding and frightened by every noise, can you really believe that? Is it true that every person, deep within his heart, is good?"
>
> From the video program *Free to Be Me*

So began the retreat. During the first conference my mouth was dry and my hands were cold and clammy. Between the lines of their facial expressions I read this question: "Where did we get this kid?" I swore I could hear them thinking, "Sonny, the oils of ordination are not yet dry on your hands. When you have been over the ropes of life for a few more miles, come back and we will hear you again."

At the end of the first conference I just knew I should have volunteered for the foreign missions rather than arrogantly assume the task of preaching to my elders. However, even on that first day of the retreat, the priest retreatants began coming in to consult me. I couldn't believe it! They were so good, so humble, and some of them seemed to be hurting rather badly. One elderly, white-haired priest poured out his troubled soul to me like a small child talking confidently to his father. I remember thinking, "I hope that when I am your age I have half the humility, knowledge of self, and openness that you do." By the end of the retreat, I knew the truth beyond all doubt.

It is true and will always be true. We are all in need of a little love and a little understanding. And it is this love and this understanding that will draw out of us all the goodness and giftedness with which each of us has been blessed by God our Father. And it is probably also true that even we ourselves cannot know the depths of our own goodness and giftedness until someone else first loves us and calls these things out of us.

> Empathy asks only one question: "What is it like to be you?"

Jesus: His Understanding and Love

I am convinced that this is how Jesus loved the people of his time. I am convinced that this is how Jesus today loves you and me. It is this understanding love, which is not blind but rather supersighted because it sees beyond appearances, that the Lord commends to us when he proposes, "Love one another as I have loved you." (John 13:34)

Jesus calls the buried goodness and giftedness out of the depths of people. Just as surely as he called Lazarus, four days dead, out of his grave, so Jesus, by loving them, called the outcasts and the estranged, the lonely, and the defeated back into the fullness of life.

Little Zacchaeus was a "runt" and up a tree in more ways than one. He was a physically small man who became the chief publican at Jericho, a rich tax collector who gouged and clawed his poverty-stricken fellow Jews and sent their taxes to the pompous emperor of Rome. Nobody liked him. You and I probably wouldn't have liked him. However, one day, as Jesus was moving slowly through the crowds that always followed him, Zacchaeus climbed up into the branches of a sycamore tree just to get a look at this Jesus. He never could have dreamed what was to follow. He was astonished to see Jesus making his way toward the very sycamore in whose branches he was perched.

Then Zacchaeus heard those unbelievable words. "Zacchaeus," Jesus was calling, "I'd like to stay here in Jericho tonight.

Could I stay with you at your house?" Can you hear the thunder of excitement in the little man's heart? "He wants to stay with me!" (See Luke 19:1–10.) The crowd obviously didn't share the little publican's excited joy. The gospel says only that they "started grumbling." Zacchaeus, we are told, jumped down from the tree, and in his great, excited joy pledged half his goods to the poor. Furthermore, he promised to restore fourfold whatever he had gained dishonestly. Jesus then reassured the little man that salvation had come to his house on that day, for the Son of Man had come looking "to seek and to save" those who were lost. The buried goodness and giftedness of Zacchaeus had surfaced at the touch of Jesus and his understanding love. Somehow I feel sure that the little man and his world were never the same again.

Then there was Mary of Magdala, which was a village on the west coast of the Sea of Galilee. She is frequently identified with the prostitute who bolted into the banquet at the house of Simon the Pharisee and wept at the feet of Jesus. However, there is no scriptural basis for this identification. Nevertheless, according to Mark (16:9) and Luke (8:2), Jesus had cast seven demons out of this woman. Whatever her past, Mary Magdalene was really present and available to the needs of the Lord. Once the good and beautiful person was called forth by the understanding of Jesus, she loved boldly and recklessly. She stood bravely on Calvary as Jesus was dying (Matthew 27:56). She must have been taunted there by those

who knew of her past, and ridiculed for her new religious posture and piety. "Hey, Mary, what's all this pious stuff? We all know who you really are!" However, I feel sure that she was far too strong to be much affected by the taunting.

It was Mary Magdalene who assisted at the burial of Jesus (Matthew 27:61). Again, it was Mary who discovered the empty tomb on Easter Day (Matthew 28:1–10). The importance of Mary Magdalene in the whole resurrection story is clear in the Gospel of John (20:1–18). She seems to have been the first to see the risen Jesus. As in the case of Zacchaeus, the depths of strength and a fierce loyalty in loving had been called out of this great and strong woman by the love of Jesus. Zacchaeus and Mary of Magdala and countless others of us can truly say this to Jesus:

I love you for what you are making of me. I love you for the part of me that you bring out; I love you for passing over all the foolish, weak things that you can't help dimly seeing there, and for drawing out into the light all the beautiful belongings that no one else had looked quite far enough to find.

The Beginning of Love: Empathy

It seems to me that the key to success in so seeing and loving others is empathy. Empathy starts with an attentive listening and an intuitive reading of the uniqueness of another. Empathy asks only one question: What is it like to be you? Empathy is getting inside the skin

Empathy is walking in another's shoes.

of another, walking in his or her shoes, seeing and experiencing reality as it looks through the eyes of another. In the end, empathy offers not advice but only understanding. "Oh, yes, I hear you." If the essence of empathy is listening to and living vicariously the life experience of another, the price of empathy is this: It requires a temporary leaving of one's self, one's own thoughts and feelings, one's values and beliefs. When I empathize with you, I leave where I am and I go to be with you where you are.

The experience of most people would seem to indicate that there are not many really good listeners among us. When we try to share who we are, many others tend to leap in, reduce us and our sharing to a problem, and proceed to solve the problem. They volunteer to tell us what to do. At other times they may seem to question the sincerity of our communication: "You don't really mean that, do you?" Or they go off into a narration of their own, assuring us that they have gone through our experiences in their own lives. None of these reactions is a part of empathic listening. I know you are really hearing me only when the expression of your face registers my present feelings, only when your voice and body language say, "So that's what it's like to be you . . . I hear you."

The empathic listener does not judge, criticize, or direct, because in the act of empathy we leave our own positions, our perceptions, and most of all our prejudices. Our concentration is given totally to the

vicarious experience of another person. We break our fixation with self by getting out of ourselves and into the other's thoughts, feelings, and life situation.

When we have identified with another in this way, we are already supplying the primary need of everyone: to have someone who really understands what it's like to be me! Only after immersing ourselves in the experience of empathy can we know what we might say or do or be for another person's happiness and well-being. Loving is indeed an art. There are no automatic decisions or fixed and final formulas when we are trying to respond to the needs of another.

We might have to be tough or tender, to talk or be silent, to sit at another's side or allow that person the luxury of aloneness. Only the empathic person can master this art.

The Two Essential Gifts of Love

Whatever else love may ask of us in a given case, there are two indispensable gifts that are always a part of loving. We can always be sure that these two gifts are needed. The first is the gift of self through self-disclosure. All the other gifts of love—like flowers, jewelry, cigars, and candy—are mere tokens and symbolic expressions. The essential gift of love is always the gift of myself. If I do not give you my true and authentic self, I have given you nothing. I have given you only pretense and sham. I have let you watch my charade.

The second essential gift of love is the affirmation of the other person's worth. If I am to love you, somehow I must appreciate and reflect back to you my appreciation of your unique goodness and giftedness. I cannot interact with you without making some contribution, either positive or negative, to your all-important self-image. Nor can I so interact with you without taking away some increase or decrease in my own sense of personal worth. We are all like mirrors to one another. We perceive ourselves largely in the "feedback" of one another's reactions. We are always contributing, positively or negatively, to one another's self-image. I can know that I am

worthwhile only in the mirror of your smiling face, only in the warm sound of your voice, and in the gentle touch of your hand. And you can understand your worth only in my face, my voice, and my touch. "All they need is a little understanding and a little love!"

By way of summary, then, the eyes of love see in every other person not one but two persons: the wounded and angry, the good and gifted. It is understanding and love that call forth the good and gifted person. This is the way that Jesus loved people like Zacchaeus and Mary Magdalene and the twelve apostles into the fullness of life. The essential prelude to love is always empathy, which breaks our own self-centered fixation and provides for the other the inestimable good feeling of being understood. Having given a listening and available heart in empathy, we must go on to respond to the specific needs of those we love. The two specific needs we can be sure of are the gift of ourselves in self-disclosure and the gift of our affirmation of the other's worth.

At the beginning of this chapter, we filled in a response about people in general: People are basically __(what?)__ . One certain answer is: *needy*. No matter how much we try to conceal our need for understanding and love, we are all thirsty to be understood and hungry to be loved. Only when this thirst is quenched and this hunger filled can we be the fully alive people the Lord has called us to be. This is the way Jesus himself sees us, and this is the way his master vision invites us to see one another.

FOR FURTHER REFLECTION
Chapter 13: The Way We View Others

Review

1. What are the sources of our vision of other people?
2. How might parental sources influence our vision of other people? Give examples to support your answer.
3. How does one's personal psychological development have a profound influence on one's attitude toward others?
4. What is Jesus' vision of other people? How does his vision of others connect the two great commandments?
5. How does the concept that "there are two persons inside each of us" add a healthy insight into formulating a Christian vision of other people?
6. If there are two persons inside each of us, then how might a Christian complete the following statement: "People are basically ? until they prove otherwise"?
7. Briefly describe what it means to "understand through empathy."
8. What are the two essential gifts of love? Describe each gift of love and offer an example for each.

Discuss

1. How do you form your vision of other people? What is the most common attitude you have of other people when you encounter them? What is your basic attitude toward people who are your peers? What about strangers?
2. How does the important insight that there are two persons inside each of us challenge, change, or revise your former attitude toward other people?
3. What does the following mean to you: "When I see those people who look obnoxious or threatening to me, I say within myself, 'You are hurting . . . Deep within your heart you are good, but you are hurting'"? What kind of hurt is that statement speaking about?
4. Is it true that every person, deep down inside, is in need of love and understanding? Explain.
5. Give examples of people you know or know about who were transformed into a more loving and open person because someone offered them a little love and understanding.
6. What can you do to make sure the "good person" inside someone can be set free?

7. Who in your life has offered or is now offering love and understanding to you? What effect do these gifts have on you?

Scripture Activity

Jesus went on into Jericho and was passing through. There was a chief tax collector there named Zacchaeus, who was rich. He was trying to see who Jesus was, but he was a little man and could not see Jesus because of the crowd. So he ran ahead of the crowd and climbed a sycamore tree to see Jesus, who was going to pass that way. When Jesus came to that place, he looked up and said to Zacchaeus, "Hurry down, Zacchaeus, because I must stay in your house today."

Zacchaeus hurried down and welcomed him with great joy. All the people who saw it started grumbling, "This man has gone as a guest to the home of a sinner!"

Zacchaeus stood up and said to the Lord, "Listen, sir! I will give half my belonging to the poor, and if I have cheated anyone, I will pay back four times as much."

Jesus said to him, "Salvation has come to this house today, for this man, also, is a descendant of Abraham. The Son of Man came to seek and to save the lost." (Luke 19:1–10, GNB)

In your own words tell what Jesus is saying to Zacchaeus and what Zacchaeus is hearing. How does this free Zacchaeus?

Processing These Ideas about the Christian Vision of Others

1. **Return of the Jedi.** If you have not already done so, see the film *Return of the Jedi*. How does the film illustrate that (a) "there are two persons deep inside of us," and (b) "all we need is a little love and understanding"? Focus on the characters of Luke Skywalker and Darth Vader.

2. **Give a genuine affirmation.** Choose someone who you believe needs the gift of affirmation of his or her worth. Genuinely affirm that person and observe what his or her reaction is to your gift of affirmation.

Afterward, write what you have learned about the power of affirmation.

14 *We Must Learn to Communicate Effectively*

The human condition has been compared to a person trapped at the bottom of a deep dry well. All calls for help go unanswered. They seem to be blown away by the winds that howl at the top of the well. Hope begins to wear thin. Then, when hope seems certainly to be on its deathbed, an answering call comes from the top of the well: "We know that you are down there. We are coming with help. We will rescue you." There is an explosion of joy in the heart of the trapped person. "Thank God, someone finally knows that I am here!"

It is like this in real communication. The person who has opened up to another and has been heard no doubt feels the same sense of relief and exhilaration. "Thank God, someone finally knows what it is like to be me."

Sheltering Our Fatal Secrets

The secrets that we keep hidden inside us become the poison that makes us sick. Eventually these secrets will destroy us. Poet laureate John Berryman, who leaped to his death from a bridge, wrote the line: "We are as sick as we are secret." He alone knew what private demons drove him to his death. But the words he left behind, his life, and his death are a legacy of warning to the rest of us. By a strange kind of human internal fermentation, what we keep inside us turns to poison. Still, most of us go on sheltering our fatal secrets because we don't want to run the risk of rejection, ridicule, or condemnation.

Inside us, in the sealed vaults of our privacy, our secrets seem like smoke. Whatever I am afraid to share spreads out until I am not sure what it really is, where it begins, and where it ends. If only I could put it all out, like pieces of a jigsaw puzzle, it might make sense. It is so true that the first obstacle to communication is really inside each of us. *I cannot tell you what I am not telling even myself.* And somehow, even if I could find the courage to open up, I'm not sure what I would say.

A good place to start, of course, would be to get in touch with the fears that haunt and imprison me. What would happen if I started peeling off the layers of my pretense and exposed my hiddenness to the light of day? What if I were to tell other human beings what it is like to be me? Would they understand? A thousand questions and doubts come to haunt me. Would I lose my reputation? Would others laugh at or reject me? Would I somehow be punished for my honesty? Would they use it against me at some later time? Would they be shocked to know?

What if I were to tell other human beings what it is like to be me? Would they understand? A thousand questions and doubts come to haunt me.

Some of us fear rejection and keep a distance. If you really get to know me, you won't like me.

Would I be accused of lying? Of course I have been a phony, but would others say it bluntly? I get lost in all my questions and doubts. Somehow I recognize reality in all of them. Meanwhile, I go on with my pretense, hoping that I will get through one more day undetected. I cave in to the peer pressure. I take my cues from others. I find a mask to wear, a way to exist in this frightening world.

Communication

Communication is a nice word. Everybody seems to be for it, just as they are for love and peace. Communication has been called the lifeline of love. In its root meaning, it refers to an act of sharing. It implies that two or more persons now have something "in common" because it has been shared. In its most profound sense, communication is a sharing of the persons themselves. By our ongoing communication, you get to know me, and I get to know you. We have this in common: ourselves. Of course, it is not always a smooth and painless thing, this communication. If you are to know me, I must be willing to share with you the hidden angers that seethe somewhere in my depths. I must tell you about the humiliating fears that seem to diminish my stature. At times, too, the green head of envy will rise up between us. I will be tempted to get into a win-lose struggle for domination with you. Somehow I must be sure that you are as committed to honest and open communication as I am. I don't want you to use my openness as a pretext to scorn me or leave me. And I must be ready to guarantee that your openness will never be abused by me. And I must be ready to put aside my own agendas to listen to you, to find out what it is like to be you.

The Fears of Intimacy

If we do really commit ourselves to communication, intimacy between us is inevitable. Everyone has some fear of intimacy, and so everyone instinctively fears communication for this reason. One of the problems is that our fears are as unique as our fingerprints. Your fear of intimacy has a different shading than mine. Some of us fear *separation*. "I don't want to get too close to you because afterward you might leave me. You might die or divorce me. It is safer 'not to love than to lose.' " Others of us fear *fusion*. "If I share everything with you, what will be left for me? Will I still have my own turf, the place where I can be alone? I don't want to be like a glob of wax melted into one larger glob. I hate symbiotic relationships in which you don't know where one person ends and the other begins. That's enmeshment, not intimacy."

Still others of us fear *rejection*. "If you really get to know me, you won't like me. You will gradually lose interest once you find out all you want to know. You will find a pretext or occasion to move on to someone else." My own personal fear seems to be a fear of *responsibility*. If I get too close to another, I will feel obliged to be there for that person in his or her moments of need. But I almost always feel overextended, overinvolved. And I don't want to overpromise myself. In addition to this, I also feel a serious aversion for exposing the weak, the hurting, the wounded parts of me. My act, or role, has always been to look as if I have it all together. It is very difficult for me to reveal my total self. I don't want people to know what a fraction I am. It is the bag and baggage of my perfectionism.

Very often people, for their own reasons, head off intimacy before it can grow deep roots. An argument, sulking or pouting, carrying a grudge, or assigning someone to the "doghouse" are all excellent inhibitors of intimacy. Perhaps the main problem with this ploy is that it can convince even its perpetrators. We don't admit, even to ourselves, that intimacy is the real issue. We cover over our fear with the "sincere pretense" of anger or resentment. It does keep others at a distance. No one can really get close to a porcupine, right? What we really fear, of course, is intimacy.

Communication As an Act of Love

There are two convictions that are essential prerequisites for loving communication. The first is that we must think of ourselves as gifts to be given. The second is that we must regard others as gifts (sometimes tentatively and hesitantly) offered to us. The exchange of these gifts is *communication*. It is clearly an act of gracious hospitality to welcome another into our confidence.

To understand people, I must try to hear what they are not saying, what they perhaps will never be able to say.

Likewise, it is gracious of others to take us into the places where they live and work, and into their secret rooms. But this will happen only if communication is seen as an act of love. The only gift of any worth that I have to give you is myself. The only gift of value that you can offer me is the gift of yourself through self-disclosure. If we are not willing to run the risks involved in this exchange of gifts, we have really given each other nothing. We can have a relationship only of need, not of love. If our love for one another is to survive, communication is not really a luxury; it is a necessity.

If either of us falls into the deception of sharing self as a ploy, it will ruin everything. I must not want to communicate so that I will feel better, but only so that you may know me better. And I must not share myself with you so that you will react in the very way I had in mind. I don't share myself with you with the hope that you will feel responsible for me, or solve my problems, or feel guilty. I share myself with you only to let you know who I am and what it is really like to be me. I ask you to take my sharing in gentle and sensitive hands. But I do not have any hidden agendas. Do with it whatever you will. It is my gift to you.

We must not be deceived into thinking that communication makes one person out of two. You must always remain you, and I must always keep my own identity. You are you and I am I. We each think our own thoughts, retain our own preferences, make our own choices (and compromise only when

necessary). This is the way it was in the beginning, is now, and ever shall be. In communicating with you, I don't want to look into a mirror and find your face there. Nor do I want you to march to my drums. The beauty of our communication will be a shared celebration of our differences. We are each unique. What it is like to be me is not what it is like to be you. However, if you will take me into your unique world and share it with me, I will certainly be enriched by this sharing. And if I welcome you into my private world, you will forever be richer for having known me.

Speaking in Communication

There are so many things I have to share with you. There is my *past*. It's not a simple statement of biographical facts. I must tell you about my laughter and my tears, about my successes and my failures. I must tell you about my *memories,* the ones that have shaped and directed my life. God gave us memories so that we could have roses in December. Some of mine are suffused with sunlight. Others were recorded in darkness and play only to a sad accompaniment. I must tell you about my unique *vision of reality,* the way I see things: myself, the other people in my life, the world about me, and the God I worship and pray to. I must share, too, my *hidden secrets,* my *hopes,* and my *values.*

But somehow, more important than all of these, I must tell you about my *feelings*. Some are light,

To tell you my thoughts is to locate myself in a category. To tell you about my feelings is to tell you about me.

others are dark; some are beautiful, others seem ugly to me. But they are all mine. I can't really explain them. I can only describe them to you. I do know that my roots are many and tangled. Some of my feelings are nourished at root level. They come from places and experiences stored so deep in me that I have never really explored them. But this much I know: my feelings are mine, and when I share them with you, I have a sense of sharing my most sensitive self with you. My feelings encapsulate my whole personal history, the experiences that have shaped my vision. My feelings depend, too, on my physical condition, my food intake and sleep supply. And though we use common labels, like anger and affection, no one has ever felt as I do. Somehow I know that when I share my feelings with you, I am sharing my one and only self.

As we saw in Chapter 9, in communicating my feelings, *I assume full responsibility for these feelings.* I know that I must be, in my communication, an owner and not a blamer. Owners always make "I" statements, while blamers tend to make "You" statements. "I felt angry" is an "I" statement. It is the statement of an owner who knows that anger has arisen out of something in himself or herself. "You made me angry!" is the accusation statement of a blamer. It scapegoats the listener, shifts the responsibility for anger from the speaker onto the listener. Owners get to know themselves, and they mature. Blamers live in a make-believe but bitter world.

Some of my feelings come from experiences stored so deep in me that I have never really explored them. When I share them with you, I am sharing my most sensitive self.

Separated from reality by their blaming, they never really do get to know themselves or others. Unfortunately, they never grow up.

In trying to share myself with you, I will be tempted to cover up my vulnerable places. I will want to close off certain rooms because they contain secret weaknesses. I can so easily show you my trophy room of successes, but I don't want you to see the scars of my failures. If I do conceal my vulnerability, my weaknesses, my failures, I have not really shared my complete self with you. I have edited my sharing, shown you only the parts I wanted you to see. You will sense this, I am sure, and you will want to do the same thing. You will want to edit your sharing. But if I do put my whole self, warts and all, on the line, you will sense that I have taken a chance and have trusted you. Everything human is contagious. You will want to do the same. Like love, communication is a decision and a commitment.

Listening in Communication

True listening, empathic listening, is indeed a rarely developed talent. If you or I should encounter five good listeners in a lifetime, we would be doing very well. First of all, I should be listening because I really want to know what it is like to be you. This means I will hear much more than the words you use. I will hear the emotions that vibrate in your voice. I will see the facial expressions and notice the body language that accompany

your words. I won't be mentally preparing my own response to your sharing. At the end I will probably just nod and thank you most sincerely. I will tell you how grateful I am for your gift. I will promise to treat your confidences with a gentle respect.

Even though God gave us two ears and only one mouth, most of us are not good listeners. Most of us listen only long enough to shoot from the lip—to offer a little advice, tell an anecdote from the past, narrate a few stories of our own experiences. Sometimes we cast ourselves in the role of problem solvers. Or we take over the conversation by offering a survey of our own lives. Sometimes we expose our own inability to listen by closing off the speaker. We yawn, get visibly distracted, ask an unrelated question, or simply change the subject. Some of us find silence painful, and so we leap in to fill the gaps.

A good listener has tried in the past to be a good speaker, too. So good listeners know how hard it is to open up. If I am a good listener, I will interrupt only to ask you for a clarification of your meaning or for a detail I find missing. My interruptions will never intentionally derail you. I will try to supply the atmosphere you need to give me your gift. Obviously, it takes work and practice to become a good listener. But most of all, it requires a real capacity for empathy, a patient curiosity that wants to know what it is really like to be you.

A phrase that is familiar to most of us is "listening with the head and the heart." To be purely logical and deal only with ideas is listening

True listening is a rarely developed talent.

only with the head. It will prove very discouraging for most speakers. Someone has pleaded, "Please hear what I am not saying." Almost everyone has an instinctual understanding of this. There are times when we just can't find the right words or the courage to say those words. We have to hope that the heart of the listener will supply those meanings. It is almost a truism that the least important things in communication are the words themselves. Joy and sorrow, affection and discouragement, hope and despair are conveyed in so many ways other than words. These realities can be grasped only by the heart. And they will be grasped only by the heart that is committed to love.

Semantics and Other Problems in Communication

Words are signs. Unfortunately, the reality symbolized by the same word-sign may be different for different people. One person may be happy to be called "sweet" while another may bristle at the very thought. It is a fact: words mean different things to different people. Everyone who has ever spoken to a group knows that each person in the audience is hearing a slightly different message. For example, "I am anxious about Monday" could mean one of several things. *Anxious* could mean "fearful." It could also mean "eager" or even "excited."

Both speaker and listener must be aware of this problem. The practice called shared meaning can offer some clarification. The speaker asks the listener to relate back what he or she has heard. Then both speaker and listener can arrive at some satisfaction that the message sent is the same as the message received.

Then there is the problem of prejudice. If I am right, we are all filled with prejudices of all sorts. For example, the names we like are probably those of people we have liked in the past. The names we don't like are probably those of people we didn't like. We are prejudiced with regard to almost everything, including food, colors, styles, races, and religions. A prejudice is a premature judgment. The judgment is premature because it is made on false or incomplete evidence. In the act of prejudice, the mind exercises the closure of a judgment before it has all the facts. Usually this happens because of emotional forces, conscious or unconscious.

It is obvious that prejudice can invade and undermine communication. If I carry a little checklist with me into every conversation, I will listen to see if you agree with me, to see how you check out. Instead of listening to learn what it is like to be you, I will be running down my list to see if you are one of "the good guys." Also, prejudice may close down my mind to all that is good in you because I recall something you said years ago. I gave you a "batting average" at that time, and I refuse to reconsider. Finally, there may be something I don't like about you. It could be your appearance, your mannerisms, or your political persuasion.

Listen with the head and the heart.

If I let this one source of aversion keep me from opening to you or listening empathetically to you, I have become the victim of prejudice.

Another obstacle to communication is imagination. If something is not said explicitly, imagination tends to fill in all the missing details. For example, you may have a vision problem. So when you look at another person, you tend to squint a bit. Your eyes narrow noticeably. If you do not tell me that you like me, I will probably imagine that you don't. I can tell by the way you look at me. When imagination supplies for communication, misunderstanding is inevitable. Now this possibility imposes a burden on both speaker and listener. The speaker should try to leave as few gaps as possible for the imagination of the listener. But, the listener must also check out his or her interpretations. "I read you as being quite upset with me. Is this true, or am I just imagining it?"

The Temptation to Quit

I'm sure that everyone has seen or heard the motto "Winners never quit. Quitters never win." Apart from the "rah, rah" hype, there is a truth here that is applicable to communication. There are times when the best lines of communication fall in the midst of some storm. A misunderstanding, an argument, a rash judgment can easily interrupt the flow of good communication. I'm sure that something like this happens at intervals to everyone.

The crisis is a test of one's determination. It is also a time to claim ownership instead of making accusations and blaming others. We blamers are always tempted to think that it is a question of good or bad, right or wrong. We want to figure out who has the problem and why. Excuse me for correcting myself in public, but none of the above categories applies here. If I give up on communication, I have to take full responsibility for this. I have to say that because of something in me, I have ceased trying to understand what it is like to be you. Oh, it is possible that one of us or even both of us may have an erroneous opinion or make a false judgment. But that is no reason to go off in a sulk or demand an apology. Love is not that small, and communication is an act of love or it is nothing. Part of the decision-commitment of love, I am sure, is the decision to keep trying and the commitment to persevere in communication.

A relationship is always stronger when two people survive a crisis. It is something like a broken bone. Nature throws out additional calcium around the break, so that the bone is actually stronger after the mending process is over. Most of us are at times tempted to quit, to give up, to blame, to go off looking for consolation and understanding from someone else. I think it is highly important to reerect the lines of communication, to keep trying. The relationship will forever be stronger and more durable because of these efforts and this commitment.

Chapter 14: We Must Learn to Communicate Effectively

Review

1. Explain what the following statement says about the value of communicating effectively: "We are as sick as we are secret."
2. Define *communication*. How is it an act of love? What are the essential prerequisites for loving communication?
3. Identify and explain the four fears of intimacy. Comment on how "true loving communication" does not and should not foster these fears of intimacy.
4. There are many areas that can be shared in communication between two persons, such as one's *past, memories, vision of reality, secrets, hopes,* and *values.* But the area that will enable a person to become intimately close to another is the honest communication of his or her *feelings.* Explain why this is the case.
5. In any act of communication of one's feelings, why is it important to "accept responsibility for one's feelings" and not "be a blamer"?
6. Describe how one should listen in communication. How might semantics get in the way of true communication?
7. Explain: "Communication seeks unity, not happiness."

Discuss[1]

1. Are you comfortable or uncomfortable at the prospect of being very close to another, knowing and being known as completely as possible?
2. Intimacy has frightening aspects for everyone. What do you fear most about intimacy?
3. Can you surrender to the joy of being loved without fear of later rejection?
4. Do you find intimacy easier with people to whom you are related (family) or with friends?
5. How important to you are your friends?
6. If you had to move from your present location, how deeply would you feel the loss of the immediate presence of your friends?
7. Are you most inclined to express your love for others by deep personal sharing and confiding or by doing things for them?
8. Have you made a considerable emotional investment in your friends? Do your friends feel

---

1 Many of the **Discuss** questions in this section come from Powell's book *The Secret of Staying in Love.*

that they really know you and that you really know them on an intimate level?
9. How do you feel about your own present attitudes toward, and accomplishments of, human closeness?
10. If you had to call someone in the middle of the night in an emergency, who would you call and why?

Scripture Activity

"And whenever you pray, do not be like the hypocrites; for they love to stand and pray in the synagogues and at the street corners, so that they may be seen by others. Truly I tell you, they have received their reward. But whenever you pray, go into your room and shut the door and pray to your Father; and your Father, who sees in secret, will reward you. When you are praying, do not heap up empty phrases as the Gentiles do; for they think that they will be heard because of their many words. Do not be like them, for your Father knows what you need before you ask him. Pray, then, in this way: 'Our Father in heaven, hallowed be your name. Your kingdom come. Your will be done, on earth as it is in heaven. Give us today our daily bread. And forgive us our debts, as we also have forgiven our debtors. And do not bring us to the time of trial, but rescue us from the evil one.' For if you forgive others their trespasses, your heavenly Father will also forgive you." (Matthew 6:5–15, NRSV)

What does this passage say about communication in the love relationship between God and you?

Processing These Ideas about Communication

Locate your catastrophic fears of communication. A catastrophic fear of an object or activity usually results from the anticipation of the worst thing that could happen. Try to get in touch with your own fears of good communication. What is the worst thing that could happen if you were an open and honest person with everyone? (Obviously, this does not mean to imply that we should tell all our secrets to everyone.) What is the worst thing that could happen if you were a truly empathic listener? What is the one specific thing about "intimacy" that frightens you most?

The Christian Vision

of Life

15 *A Life Principle*

ocrates said that the unexamined life is not worth living. Sooner or later we all ask deep within ourselves: **What is life for?** It is an important and sometimes painful question. But it is a question that must be asked.

When I ask myself this question, I try to direct it to my stomach rather than to my head. My poor head has memorized so many ideal answers, and these rote responses are ready to come tumbling out as soon as someone presses the right button.

The late and great psychologist Abraham Maslow saw us in pursuit of our human goals and needs according to a definite hierarchy: a ladder with many rungs. The lower rungs of the ladder are the fundamental drives for food, shelter, safety from external threats. The middle rungs are the more precisely human set of needs and goals—the "higher order" needs of dignity, belongingness, love. At the summit of Maslow's ladder are the highest human aspirations: independence and excellence. He calls this state "self-actualization." Of course, we never reach the top, but it is precisely this that keeps us going. Maslow was convinced that we function best when we are striving for something we don't have. I think that, for the most part, this is true.

So I ask you to make with me what Dag Hammarskjold once called "the longest journey, the journey inward" to the center of your being, where answers are not memorized but are very much alive. It is a reluctant journey to which I invite you. Carl Jung, the renowned psychiatrist, once wrote:

> Wherever there is a reaching down into innermost experience, into the nucleus of personality, most people are overcome by fright, and many run away. . . . The risk of inner experience, the adventure of the spirit, is in any case, alien to most human beings.
>
> *Memories, Dreams, Reflections*

I invite you to reflect with me: What is life for?

Perhaps it would be good if each of us were to sit down and to write out a script for our lives-to-come. Try it sometime. You have a blank check. You can fill in all the amounts of success-failure, tears-laughter, long life–short life, agony-ecstasy. You have complete control over pleasure, power, money, fame, relationships. What would you consider the ideal life? What do you really want most?

Or it may help to write out a description of your "perfect day," or a list of the ten activities you enjoy most.

What is life for? It is an important and sometimes painful question. But it is a question that must be asked.

179

When you reflect on what you have written, you may find your deepest needs and longings in clearer perspective. For example, if you find that during your perfect day or in the activities you enjoy most you are alone, perhaps there is some need, buried deep inside you, for solitude or even a desire to avoid relationships.

The question is: What is life for—for you?

To Win a Place in Heaven

What you and I will become in the end will be just more and more of what we are deciding and trying to be right now.

I remember a time, many years ago, when I was in Germany trying to master the language of the "natives." I was privileged to serve for a while as a chaplain in a remote Bavarian convent. The Sister who was assigned to care for my room was eighty-four years old. Every time I left my room, even for a moment, she cleaned it. And I don't mean a superficial cleaning. She would wax the floors, polish the furniture, and so forth. On one occasion when I left my room for a short walk, I came back to find "Schwester" on her knees, putting a final sheen on her waxing job. I laughingly teased her:

"Schwester, Sie arbeiten zuviel!"
("Sister, you work too much!")

The dear and devoted little Sister straightened up (still kneeling) and looked at me with a seriousness that bordered on severity. She said:

"Der Himmel ist nicht billig!"
("Heaven isn't cheap, you know!")

God bless her. She was no doubt educated to believe, and she believed with all her heart, that life was supposed to be an ordeal, the price of eternal bliss. Heaven must be bought, and it is not cheap. I feel sure that heaven now belongs to that dear soul, who lived so faithfully according to her lights. (In fact, I think that there must be a roped-off section for special souls like "Schwester.") But I can't believe that this kind of joyless purchase of a place in heaven is really the life to which God is calling us. I do not believe that God intends that we should crawl through a dark tunnel on bleeding hands and knees to have a so-called "pie in the sky when we die." God is not a Shylock, demanding a pound of flesh for eternal life. In fact, I believe that, theologically speaking, eternal life has already begun in us because God's life is already in us. We should be celebrating this. We are the branches to Christ's vine (*see* John 15:5).

Do you remember, as I do, the famous *Salve Regina* prayer? It describes a very sad and forlorn version of human life: ". . . to thee do we cry, poor banished children of Eve, to thee do we send up our sighs, mourning and weeping in this valley of tears." I have often thought that if someone really believed this, life would be very bleak. What Jesus said was: "I have come that you might have life, life to the fullest" (John 10:10). "I have told you these things, that my joy may be in you, and your joy may be perfect" (John 15:11).

A Personal Inventory

You and I must open ourselves to the question: What is life for? We should get right down into the fabric of our daily lives. What am I doing? Is my life a series of deadlines . . . meetings . . . clearing my desk . . . answering phones . . . moving from one crisis to the next? Do I look forward to the stretch of life that is ahead of me? To next week? To the coming year? Is mine a hand-to-mouth existence? Is it a matter of "getting by"? When I wake up in the morning, is my first reaction: "Good morning, God!" or "Good God, morning!"? Am I in a survival contest? Do I feel trapped? Am I just hanging on? Am I asking: How much longer can I take this?

Some of us are afraid, as Carl Jung says, to face these questions because of what the answers might imply. We rather anticipate that someone who really doesn't understand will use our answers to tell us that we have to change our lives— to give up our present jobs, to leave our families, to move to a sunnier climate, and so forth. Of course, it may be that you or I should change something in our lives, but I think it is much more realistic and important to change something in ourselves. It may be that the parasites which are eating away inside us, depriving us of the deeper joys and satisfactions of life, should become the object of our attention.

For example, if I am a "compulsive pleaser" of others, living or dying according to the approval I get for my person or my work, then no change of life, job, family, or climate can possibly help me.

No matter where I would go or what I would do, the problem would be with me. I would still be asking those torturous questions: Did that look mean that he didn't like me? . . . She didn't smile. I guess she is unhappy with my performance . . . (A thousand etceteras.)

The same would be true of the "compulsive perfectionist," who can never experience satisfaction because nothing is ever completely perfect. Such a person is, at least internally, a ruthless critic of everything and everyone. (This person, upon entering heaven, will no doubt suggest that God spend a few bucks to fix up the place.)

We should comb through our patterns of action and reaction to locate these or similar distortions in our attitudes, and we must then work at revising those attitudes where necessary. But the more universal and more important reality to be investigated is what I would call a "life principle."

**The question is:
What is life for—for you?**

The Meaning of a Life Principle

A life principle is a generalized, accepted intention of purpose that is applied to specific choices and circumstances. For example, "Good must be done and evil avoided." If this is one of my life principles, whenever I come to a specific choice involving good and evil, my principle directs me to choose that which is good and to avoid that which is evil.

Some use pleasure as a life principle. Some use power as a life principle. Some don't feel responsibility because their fate is in the stars.

I would like to suggest that everyone has one dominant life principle. It may be difficult to lure it out of the dark, subconscious regions to face examination in the light, but it is there. There is in each of us a set of needs, goals, or values with which we are psychologically preoccupied. There is something, in all the zigs and zags of daily living, which dominates all our other desires. This life principle runs through the fabric of our choices like the dominant theme in a piece of music: it keeps recurring and it is heard in different settings. Of course, only you can answer for yourself, just as only I can answer for myself: What is my life principle?

For example, some people are above and before all else seeking *safety*. They avoid all places where danger might lurk, even if opportunity could be waiting in the same place. They will take no risks, make no gambles. They stay home at night and reveal their deepest selves to no one. It is better to be safe than sorry, they say. The same kind of thumbnail sketch could be made of a person whose primary concern and life principle is *duty, recognition, money, fame, need, success, fun, relationships, approval of others,* or *power.*

Practice Makes
a Perfect Habit

Having a life principle is a matter of psychological economy. It diminishes the wear and tear of having to make all decisions from the ground up. For example, if my life principle is *fun,* then whenever I come upon a choice or receive two invitations for the same evening, I simply have to apply my life principle: Where will I have the most fun? My fundamental option or choice is having fun. I have already, consciously or unconsciously, accepted that as a life principle. The specific options or choices are easy. I don't have to go searching through my soul to find out what it is that I am really looking for in life. I already know that. The only uncertainty with which I must deal is: Where will I have the most fun? Having such a life principle, as we said, is a matter of psychological economy.

It is very important to realize that we are creatures of habit. Every time we think a certain way, seek a certain good, use a given motive, a habit is forming and deepening in us. Like a groove that is being furrowed, each repetition adds a new depth to the habit. (Have you ever tried to break a habit? Then you know what I am trying to say.)

And so it is with a life principle, whatever it be. With each use it becomes a deeper and more permanent habit. And in the twilight of life our habits rule us. They define and dictate our actions and reactions. We will, as the old saying goes, die as we have lived.

People who in old age prove quite self-centered and demanding, as well as those who are "mellow" and tolerant, did not become so only in their last years of life. Old cranks have practiced all their lives, just as old saints have likewise practiced all their lives. They just practiced different life principles. What you and I will become in the end will be just more and more of what we are deciding and trying to be right now. There is a fundamental choice, a life principle, which will one day possess us in the marrow of our bones and the blood in our veins. It is a certainty that we will die as we have lived.

The Life Principle
of Jesus

In the so-called temptation narratives which are recorded in Luke 4:1–13, we find Jesus, at the beginning of his public life, clarifying his own life principle. More specifically, we find him rejecting three life principles suggested to him by the devil. Jesus waited until he was thirty to begin his public life, because that was the acceptable age for a man to begin his practice as a rabbi (teacher). At this time, before beginning what we call his public life, Jesus was led by the Spirit into the desert.

> Jesus returned from the Jordan River full of the Holy Spirit and was led by the Spirit into the desert, where he was tempted by the Devil for forty days. In all that time he ate nothing, so that he was hungry when it was over.

Everyone has one dominant life principle.

The Devil said to him, "If you are God's Son, order this stone to turn into bread."

But Jesus answered, "The scripture says, 'Human beings cannot live on bread alone.!' "

Then the Devil took him up and showed him in a second all the kingdoms of the world, "I will give you all this power and all this wealth," the Devil told him. "It has all been handed over to me, and I can give it to anyone I choose. All this will be yours, then, if you worship me."

Jesus answered, "The scripture says 'Worship the Lord your God and serve only him!' "

Then the Devil took him to Jerusalem and set him on the highest point of the Temple, and said to him, "If you are God's Son, throw yourself down from here. For the scripture says, 'God will order his angels to take good care of you.' It also says, 'They will hold you up with their hands so that not even your feet will be hurt on the stones."

But Jesus answered, "The scripture says, 'Do not put the Lord your God to the test.' "

Luke 4:1–12 (GNB)

The first temptation, we might say, was to accept the life principle of *pleasure*. Jesus had fasted, a total fast from all food, and was very hungry. The promise of the devil was the satisfaction of his physical hunger. The reply of Jesus was: "Other things in life are much more important than bread!"

So the devil takes Jesus up to a high place and shows him all the glittering kingdoms of the world and promises him *power* over all these places and peoples. Jesus firmly rejects this life principle: "We must worship God, and him alone." Jesus will give his heart neither to the pursuit of pleasure nor to the flattery of power.

So Satan takes Jesus up to the pinnacle of the Temple and urges him to throw himself off. "Let your Father catch you in the arms of his angels!" the devil taunts, but Jesus is resolute. He will not abdicate his personal responsibility for his life. I see this third temptation precisely in this way. It implies that we are not really free anyway. It asks us to accept a kind of determinism that rationalizes an *avoidance of respon-sibility*. Jesus is firm: "Don't experiment with God's patience."

In this clarification of his own life principle, Jesus is stating firmly: "I will not live for pleasure! I will not live for power! I will not surrender responsibility for my life and my actions!"

Life Principles: Freud, Adler, Skinner

These same three principles, rejected by Jesus, have been proposed by three of the great names in the history of psychology as *the* life principles of all human beings.

Sigmund Freud (1856–1939) has been traditionally associated with the *pleasure drive* or *pleasure principle*. In the first part of his career he thought that all neuroses were due to sexual repression. Later he realized that there are other personal factors involved, but he continued to use the word *libido* (the Latin word for "desire" or "lust") to describe the instinctual energies and desires that are derived from the so-called *id*. In the Freudian construct, the *id* represents our (animal) drives: vanity, gluttony, lust. It is the source of energy which manifests itself in emotional drives. These impulses are unrefined and primitive, bent only upon immediate gratification. Of course, Freud taught that this basic desire for pleasure had to be moderated. This moderation is done by the *superego* (censor), which means that there is a constant tension in every person between wish and morality. This tension is to be resolved by the ego (the self or the "I"). The ego is a kind of executive part of our psychological makeup, which tries to regulate our desires by adjusting them to reality. The point is that human drives are strongly animalistic—drives for pleasure, for personal gratification. Whether frustrated or moderated, the pleasure principle is the fundamental drive in all humans, according to Freud.

Alfred Adler (1870–1937) was Freud's pupil and disciple until 1911, when he left the "Master" to start his own school of "Individual Psychology," so called because he thought that every human being represented a unique psychological problem. He accused Freud of applying a general formula indiscriminately to all. More specifically, Adler believed Freud's basic error was his universal application of the assumption that frustration of *libido*

> The problem is that we are all clutching to our own life-rafts. Each of us must make a decision about how we intend to spend our lives. If we decide to spend our lives in the pursuit of our own happiness and fulfillment, we are destined to failure and desolation. If we decide to spend our lives seeking the fulfillment and happiness of others, and this is what is implied in love, we shall certainly attain our own happiness and fulfillment.
>
> People who want only their own fulfillment, or who decide to love in order that they might be fulfilled, will find that their efforts are in vain because the focus of attention remains on themselves. Persons can grow only as much as their horizon allows, and those who decide to love in order to be fulfilled and happy will be disappointed and will not grow because their horizon is still themselves. Consequently, we cannot conceive of love in any way as a means of self-fulfillment, because if we do we will still be within the treacherous vicious circle, traveling always from our own needs and through others and back into ourselves. We cannot ever use others as means. They must always be the end-object of love. We will attain maturity only in proportion to the shifting of the focus of our minds away from ourselves and our own needs and away from self-centered desire to satisfy those needs.
>
> From *Why Am I Afraid To Love?*

(the pleasure principle) was always at the heart of every human problem. However, as Adler progressed with his own thought, he fell into the same fallacy of universal application in his formula of compensation-for-inferiority. Adler saw sex and *libido* only as a setting for the *struggle to gain power.* He interpreted all relationships as struggles for power: the child trying to throw off parental authority, a husband and wife each striving for dominance, and so forth. It all begins, according to Adler, with an inferiority complex.

This complex is universal, and there is in everyone a desire to compensate for a sense of inferiority. Of course, Adler proposed that the basic desire and struggle for power, as a compensation for inferiority feelings, should be channeled into positive and useful accomplishments. But this was his assumption and interpretation: The basic drive in people is for power and accomplishment.

B. F. Skinner, a contemporary psychologist, once proposed that it is neither pleasure nor the pursuit of power that writes the script for human life. He contends that we are the irreversible result of our conditioning or programming. This logically invites us to *avoidance of responsibility* for our lives. "Operant conditioning" is based on the assumption that if we find a certain type of behavior rewarding, we tend to repeat it. If it produces negative results, we avoid it and try something else. In his book *Beyond Human Freedom and Dignity,* Skinner attempts to refute the theory that we can choose our own life principle. According to him, it is not our lot to choose anything. His is a theory of behaviorism that amounts to determinism. If one were to accept this, it would mean abdication of all personal responsibility for one's life and actions. The attitude of such a person would be to wait and see what life holds in store, to see how things turn out. One would regard his or her life story as a phonograph record, already imprinted, complete in all details, as the result of programming in infancy. During one's

lifetime the CD player is in the process of spinning out. The process is automatic. The story cannot be changed. We are predetermined. No adult really exercises either freedom or responsibility. Or so says Skinner.

Inroads into My Own Life

Of course, there is *some* truth in what each of these three men has written. (It is hard to be totally wrong.) We have only to consult our own personal experience to know that there is in us a drive toward pleasure and toward power. We are likewise aware that certain reactions, prejudices, phobias, and so forth have been programmed into us. We have to acknowledge that our freedom has been limited to some extent by the early experiences of our lives.

Still each of us has a leverage of freedom, an ability to choose, to clarify our own values, and to act on chosen motives. It is good for us to look back over the choices of the past: Which of the proposed life principles has tended to dominate my life? Has the story of my life been a pursuit of *pleasure?* Or have I been competitive, ambitious, intoxicated by the raw liquor of *power?* Perhaps neither has been the driving force in my life. It may be that there has been no driving force in my life. Perhaps I have let life roll over me. I have decided by not deciding. It may be that I have accepted the *avoidance-of-responsibility* life principle, which has led me to abdicate

I will not live for power!

Part Five   The Christian Vision of Life

responsibility for the direction and outcome of my life. (There is a consensus, by the way, that most people today have given up all serious hope that they can determine or even change their lives.)

The Christian Life Principle

In the Gospel narrative of the final Passover Feast (the Last Supper), Jesus dramatizes his own life principle and lays before the Apostles and all of us the condition of our own Christian discipleship. Almost immediately after Jesus gives his disciples the bread of his Body and the cup of his Blood, a dispute arises over "which one in their group should be considered the greatest" (Luke 22:24). After three years of tutelage under the greatest of all spiritual directors, the disciples still labor under their old delusions. They are petty, competitive, self-centered.

So in the last hours of his life, Jesus tries to remind them of his central message. He washes their feet. According to Jewish custom, if the host of a dinner was honored by the presence of his guests, he would wash their feet. If, on the contrary, the guests considered themselves honored by the invitation, the host did not wash their feet, presumably indicating his higher social status.

Christ Washing Peter's Feet
Ford Madox Brown
(1821–1893)

God's life is already within us. We should be celebrating it.

You will recall that when Jesus ate with Simon the Pharisee (Luke 7:36–50), Simon did not extend this courtesy.

So he rose from the table, took off his outer garment, and tied a towel around his waist. Then he poured some water into a washbasin and began to wash the disciples' feet and dry them with the towel around his waist. He came to Simon Peter, who said to him, "Are you going to wash my feet, Lord?"

Jesus answered him, "You do not understand now what I am doing, but you will understand later."

Peter declared, "Never at any time will you wash my feet!"

"If I do not wash your feet," Jesus answered, "you will not longer be my disciple."

Simon Peter answered, "Lord, do not wash only me feet, then! Wash my hands and head, too!"

John 13:4–9 (GNB)

During his three years with the Twelve—spending most of the time alone with them, teaching and preparing them for their mission— the central message of Jesus was the kingdom of God. Much of the Gospel narrative concerns the preaching and parables of the kingdom. If this kingdom could be briefly defined, it would certainly imply two things.

First, the kingdom is an invitation from God. It is an invitation to all humankind to come to God in an intimate relationship of love. More vividly, we might imagine God, smiling at us with a warm look of love and embrace us: "Come to me. I will be your God. You will be my People, the children of my heart!" It should be noted that this call or invitation is not extended to us merely as individuals. In the kingdom of God we are never less than individuals, but we are never merely individuals. We are the Body of Christ. We are called to come to God's embrace of love as brothers and sisters in the Lord. The invitation to the kingdom is extended to us together. I can say "yes" to God only if I say "yes" to you, my brothers and my sisters. It is one and the same "yes" which embraces my God and my human family, all in the same act of love.

Second, on our part, the kingdom of God implies a free response of love. "In the head of the book it is written of me that to do your will is all my delight. Behold I come . . . running!" When we pray in the Lord's Prayer "Thy kingdom come!" we are praying that all of us will say the big "yes" (and all the little "yeses" which will be inside it) to one another and to our Father.

It was this, I feel sure, that Jesus wanted so much to make clear to Peter and the disciples. In all his days with them, but especially at the Last Supper, in his last moments with them, he wanted to underline the truth: My kingdom is a kingdom of love! It is not a place where power rules or people compete. It is not a playground of pleasure or a haven for those who have no heart

to try. The solemn and solitary requirement for entrance into the kingdom of God is the choice of love as a life principle. There is only one badge of identification: "By this shall all men know that you are my disciples, that you love one another as I have loved you" (John 13:35).

"If you cannot accept this," Jesus was saying to Peter, "you cannot be my partner. The only power in my kingdom is the power of love!" In the wake of their silly squabbling over who was the most important, Jesus washed their feet and left them with a rather solemn reminder:

> "The kings of the pagans have power over their people, and the rulers claim the title 'Friends of the People.' But this is not the way it is with you; rather, the greatest one among you must be like the youngest, and the leader must be like the servant. Who is greater, the one who sits down to eat or the one who serves? The one who sits down, of course. But I am among you as one who serves."
>
> *Luke 22:25–27*

Jesus wants to know if the lesson has come through. He apparently found in the Apostles the same lack of understanding that I so often find in myself. In Mark's Gospel, Jesus asks the Apostles seventeen times (I once counted them!): "Are you still without understanding?" John writes:

> After Jesus had washed their feet, he put his outer garment back on and returned to his place at the table.

I will not surrender responsibility for my life and my actions!

"Do you understand what I have just done to you?" he asked. "You call me Teacher and Lord, and It is right that you do so, because that is what I am. I, your Lord and Teacher, have just washed your feet. You, then should wash one another's feet. I have set an example for you, so that you will do just what I have done for you. I am telling you the truth: no slaves are greater than their master, and no messengers are greater than the one who sent them. Now that you know this truth, how happy you will be if you put it into practice!

John 13:12–17 (GNB)

I must ask myself the same question again and again: Do I really understand? Do I really believe that Jesus calls me to accept as my own the life principle of love? Do I really understand that such a commitment is the only way to true and abiding happiness? These are the questions whose answers lie deep inside me. I must at least attempt a search of those deepest parts. My whole life is at stake.

First, the kingdom is an invitation from God. It is an invitation to all humankind to come to God in an intimate relationship of love.

FOR FURTHER REFLECTION
Chapter 15: A Life Principle

Review

1. Define a "life principle." Give examples of how a life principle provides psychological economy in making decisions and choices.

2. In the story of Jesus' temptations in the desert, Jesus rejects three life principles. Identify the three temptations he rejects, and explain how these temptations symbolically represent three distinct life principles.

3. In your own words, present the explanations of Freud, Adler, and Skinner about the life principle that is most dominant in people.

4. Briefly illustrate how each of these gospel characters approaches life based upon his life principle: (a) Herod, (b) Pontius Pilate, and (c) the man at the pool of Bethesda.

5. What is Jesus' life principle? How does Jesus illustrate this life principle during the Last Supper?

6. How is Jesus' life principle contrary to the ones proposed by Freud, Adler, and Skinner?

7. Explain: (a) "The Kingdom of God is an invitation from God," and (b) "The Kingdom of God implies a free response of love."

Discuss

1. At present, what do you believe is the ideal life? In other words, what is life for—for *you?*

2. Which of the three life principles that Jesus rejected in the desert seem to be the most dominant in our society today? Give reasons to support your opinion.

3. Which of these three life principles make the deepest inroads in your life?

4. In what situations does the attraction of *power* (in terms of recognition, praise, clout, desire for authority, influence, privileged position, success in competition, and so forth) diminish the principle of love in your life?

5. How does the attraction of *pleasure* (excessive sensual gratification) diminish the life principle of love in your life?

6. In what situations does the attraction of *avoidance of responsibility* (in terms of procrastination, reticence, indecisiveness, lack of resolution or future planning) diminish the principle of love in your life?

7. In what situations of your life has the life principle of *love* clearly predominated? Were you the happiest in those situations? Explain.

Scripture Activity

"No, the Lord has told us what is good. What he requires of us is this: To do what is just, to show constant love, and to live in humble fellowship with our God." (Micah 6:8, GNB)

How does the prophet Micah's statement relate to Jesus' life principle of unconditional love? Relate in concrete terms how you can in your everyday affairs and relationships live out Micah's message.

Processing These Ideas about the Meaning of Life

1. *Write out a script for your life-to-come.* You have a blank check. You can fill it out for whatever you want—success/failure, tears/laughter, long life/short life, agony/ecstasy, and so forth. You have complete control over pleasure, power, money, fame, relationships. What would you consider the ideal life? What do you really want most?

    After you have written out your script, determine which life principle seems to be the underlying principle of your life.

2. *Identify the life principles advertised or promoted in the media.* Look through current magazines and clip out ads and/or articles that promote the life principles of power, pleasure, and avoidance of responsibility. Comment on how each of your samples promotes one or more of these life principles.

3. *Six journal questions.* (Your teacher will be distributing the activity sheets for this exercise.) Complete the six journal entries according to the directions given. After entries one through four, you are asked to respond to the "Why?" section of each entry. You may use the vision distortions from the list of "Some Common Vision Distortions about Life" for possible responses to the "Why?" questions.

16 The Contemporary Crisis of Love

The crisis of our time
As we are beginning Slowly
and painfully to perceive
Is a crisis not of the hands
But of the hearts.
                    ARCHIBALD MACLEISH

The English author Gilbert Keith Chesterton once said that there is a double problem with proclaiming the Gospel as the "Good News." First, he suggested, it is not really "news" to many people who have heard it repeated and repeated. Second, it does not sound like "good" news to most people.

Something in me eagerly agrees. To my ears a lot of religious exhortation seems to be aimed about two or three miles above where most people really live. The level of the ideal offered is so clearly beyond reach that all we are left with is inevitable failure and the consequent guilt feelings. Of course, I am not suggesting a massive compromise of our ascetical and moral principles. Such a "cave-in" would be even worse.

The question at hand is this: Is loving really the way to human fulfillment? If I choose love as my personal life principle, will I find satisfaction and true gratification?

Are all the Gospel paradoxes about love really valid in the laboratory of life? If I seek myself and my own happiness, is it certain that I will lose both? Does the seed really have to fall into the ground and die before there can be a full and happy life? Is the Gospel beatitude of unselfish and unconditional love really the path to true human joy? These are indeed hard and practical questions—questions which are today the subject of considerable debate.

In fact, I would say that this is the major crisis facing contemporary society. Is a life of love, which involves a permanent and unconditional commitment to the happiness of another, really the way to personal satisfaction and human fulfillment? Or must one rather stay free and unencumbered from all such relationships in order to experience the pleasure, the power, and the variety of sensations which life can offer? Is personal satisfaction and gratification the most fulfilling life goal, or is the deepest meaning in life to be found only in a committed and permanent relationship of love? Should we lay our lives and our persons on the line, or is it better never to say "forever"?

"Unless you love someone nothing else makes any sense."

e. e. cummings

The Denial of Love

Love as the life principle of a meaningful existence has not been accorded the status of a beatitude by contemporary society. In fact, there is a library of recent literature challenging the life principle of love. In the life-styles chosen by many people today, and in the motives they offer for their life-styles, there is a persistent and ruthless questioning of the reality—the very *possibility*—of true, permanent human love. Books pour off the presses—many of them high on best-seller charts—proposing trendy techniques to get the most pleasure and personal satisfaction out of life. The suggested basic mind-set and only pertinent question is: *What's in it for me?*

As a result of this philosophy, many people have taken to reevaluating the investment of their lives. They have measured their life experience according to the recommended criterion: What have I gotten out of life for myself? An alarming number of these people have fallen into a regret-filled despondency as they look at their lives, their jobs, their marriages, and their families. They feel that they have been somehow defrauded, cheated of an exhilarating happiness that could have been theirs. "You only go around once. You have to grab all you can . . . for yourself." They look at what they have grabbed and it is not enough. They are haunted by the fear that they have missed all the tingling satisfactions that could have been theirs. They are sad and wonder where they went wrong. The depressing words repeat themselves slowly and sadly: Is this all there is?

Opportunistic authors have come running with reams of advice and pages of instructions on self-satisfaction and self-fulfillment. "I will turn these stones to bread. . . . I will give you these cities to rule. . . . I will free you from the struggles of personal responsibility and commitments!" These authors have given detailed instructions on taking care of Number One (me, me, me!), on getting power and keeping it, on winning by the intimidation of others. They have extolled the virtues of selfishness. They have portrayed life as a cutthroat competition and warned that "nice guys finish last!" They have deluged an already sex-drenched generation with the "how to" books, guaranteed to produce increased erotic pleasure. Sexploitation.

These authors have relegated love, marriage, and family to the oblivion of "old-fashioned" ideas. The "in thing" now is creative divorce: how to make the death of a deep relationship the birth of something bright and beautiful. One group actually wrote a ritual to "celebrate" divorce among its members. The authors have encouraged us to shift gears, to pull up old roots in order to develop exciting new selves!

They have urged us to focus all our attention on ourselves, to be our own best friends now and forever.

Underlying all these suggestions is the belief that human fulfillment is found by the direct pursuit of one's own happiness. To do this, one must be free— free from once-made promises, free from responsibilities and love commitments, free from all the claims others make upon one's life and one's love. This has led many to see their spouses and families as obstacles to their personal fulfillment.

At best these books are dehumanizing; at worst they are positively cruel. In either case they are part of a vast societal rationalization of the self-centered existence. They lie at the farthest point on the spectrum from the commitment of unconditional love. The assumption of this self-fulfillment cult seems to be that to give your word of commitment and your promise of faithfulness to another is really to surrender your own individuality and personal identity.

To me it is obvious that this is simply not true—that the very opposite is true. Unless you give your word and your promise of fidelity to another, there can be no real trust and consequently no authentic relationship or secure framework in which two people can grow.

A meaningful life can result only from the experience of love and this implies commitment and dedication to another.

The Cult of Experience Versus Unconditional Commitment

Of course, all of us should at times take inventory of our personal growth and sense of fulfillment. The question "Am I really enjoying my life?" can and very likely will reveal valuable information and put me in touch with unrealized parts of myself. If we find inside us some painful voids, we should reassess our attitudes and perhaps redirect some of our energies. But this is not the issue of contention.

The heart of the matter and the crux of the problem is this: Do we get fulfilled by trying to have all the experiences we can? Is it true that the more experiences a person has, the more developed and fulfilled he or she will be as a person? Or is the contrary true, that a person is fulfilled by making a commitment and then choosing experiences according to whether they honor, promote, and reaffirm the commitment?

Trying to choose all available experiences is like trying to mix oil and water: they just don't blend. The result is confusing, fragmenting, and disintegrating to the human person. For a fulfilling life, we must conceive reality as somehow ordered and meaningful. This implies a value structure, priorities. It is in the light of these values and priorities that we must evaluate experiences. I would like to quote from my own book on religious faith, *A Reason to Live, A Reason to Die:*

> To try to open himself to all possible experiences can only

result in an interior chaos; it would break him apart. If a man decides to be a true husband and father, to be loyal and faithful to his marriage commitment, the experience of having a mistress or visiting prostitutes will make his heart and soul a divided city. If a person is determined to grow through contact with reality, which is the only way to grow, the experience of drunkenness or hallucinogenic narcotics will be very crippling to his personal growth.

Becoming a person, therefore, involves the sacrifice of some experiences in order to experience more deeply the values which are connected with and which promote one's own destiny. Having decided what we want to be and want to do, we must exercise some selection in the experiences we seek, choosing those which are conducive to our goals and refusing those which could only detour us.

Making a commitment to permanent, unconditional love will mean for me that certain experiences, which might otherwise have been mine, are now impossible for me. The man who chooses one woman for his wife and life partner by his very choice has eliminated all other women as possible wives and life partners. It is this very elimination that frightens us on the brink of commitment. Every commitment is like every moment in life: there is a birth and a death in every moment. Something is and something else can never be again. There is a choice and a surrender, a "yes" and a "no." To love is indeed costly. To love

To love unconditionally is a life wager.

unconditionally is a life wager. In love we put ourselves on the line and there is no going back. It is at this brink that so many seem to collapse. Within arms' reach of greatness, they faint at the thought of never returning. It is the less traveled road.

The cult of experience urges us to grab all we can while passing through this world. Besides being internally confusing, such a program is a practical impossibility. It can leave us so fragmented that we might never be able to put our pieces back together again. It will certainly leave us with broken dreams and shattered hopes. If we listen to the preachers and propagandists of this cult, we will resemble the person who wants it all so badly that, in the end, everything is lost. I am reminded of the graphic description of such a person, given in *The Bell Jar* by Sylvia Plath:

> I felt like a racehorse in a world without racetracks or a champion college footballer suddenly confronted by Wall Street and a business suit, his days of glory shrunk to a little gold cup on his mantel with a date engraved on it like the date on a tombstone.
>
> I saw my life branching out before me like the green fig tree in the story.
>
> From the tip of every branch, like a fat purple fig, a wonderful future beckoned and winked. One fig was a husband and a happy home and children, and another fig was a famous poet, and another fig was a brilliant professor, and another fig was Ee Gee, the amazing editor, and another fig was Europe and Africa and South America, and another fig was Constantine and Socrates and Attila and a pack of other lovers with queer names and offbeat professions, and another fig was an Olympic lady crew champion, and beyond and above these figs were many more figs I couldn't quite make out.
>
> I saw myself sitting in the crotch of this fig tree, starving to death, just because I couldn't make up my mind which of the figs I would choose. I wanted each and every one of them, but choosing one meant losing all the rest, and, as I sat there, unable to decide, the figs began to wrinkle and go black, and, one by one, they plopped to the ground at my feet.

The ultimate delusion and cruelty of the cult of experience lie in this, that in the end we are always left with the same painful emptiness which we were led to believe we could fill. Human nature abhors a vacuum; but when empty people reach out to eat, drink, and be merry as a program of fulfillment, the hangover is worse than the hunger. The hangover is not confined to the next morning. The original emptiness becomes a deeply painful bankruptcy. Like a gull that circles over shining waters, we swoop down to be filled with the cool, refreshing waters of pleasure. But the waters of pleasure, sought for all they can give, are always bright on the surface but, sadly, only one inch deep. We always come up with sand in our mouths.

The waters of pleasure, sought for all they can give, are always bright on the surface but, sadly, only one inch deep.

Good Times Versus a Good Life

Human fulfillment and true satisfaction cannot be measured by the yardstick of "fun." This would be sadly superficial. Fulfillment and satisfaction likewise cannot be measured by counting the moments of exhilaration that can be crammed into each day. And finally, true happiness cannot be the result of a tensionless existence. Fun, exhilaration, and the absence of tension—which are all good in themselves and have a place in every life—can never add up to human fulfillment or a meaningful life.

A meaningful life can result only from the experience of love, and this implies a commitment and dedication to another. Love rejects the question "What am I getting out of this?" as the only criterion of fulfillment. Love understands by direct experience those often-quoted words of Francis of Assisi: "It is in giving that we receive." Egoistic concern and concentration on self can lead only to the loss of self. It is a strange and painful paradox that we must all learn. The most perceptive insight of contemporary personalism is that I become a person only if I receive my personhood from someone else through the gift of affirmation. If I never see myself valued by others, I will never value myself. To this the psychiatrist Viktor Frankl enjoins this absolutely necessary advice: True self-esteem and a true sense of identity can be found only in the reflected appraisal of those whom we have loved.

Giving the gift of myself in love leaves me with a deep and lasting satisfaction of having done something good with my life. I live with the sweet memory of having contributed a gift of love to the lives of others. Likewise I am left with a sense of having used well the gifts which God has invested in me. Love takes time, demands a history of giving and receiving, laughing and crying, living and dying. It never promises instant gratification, only ultimate fulfillment. Love means believing in someone, in something. It supposes a willingness to struggle, to work, to suffer, and to join in the rejoicing. I doubt that there has ever been one recorded case of deep and lasting fulfillment reported by a person whose basic mind-set and only question was: What am I getting out of this?

It is, of course, the paradox of the Gospels: satisfaction and fulfillment are the by-products of dedicated love. They belong only to those who can reach beyond themselves, to whom giving is more important than receiving.

Sometimes we are tempted to confuse "good times" with "a good life." The successful pursuit of endless "good times" is a Camelot that never existed and can never exist. It can only result in the inevitable sadness and disappointment of unfulfilled expectations. G. Marian Kinget writes:

Many a life may be regarded—and experienced by the subject—as good, yet may comprise a relatively scant measure of what is commonly called fun and enjoyment. Among those who hold an examined view of the subject, few would deny that a fair share of the goodness of life befell to such persons as Abraham Lincoln, Gandhi, Louis Pasteur, Albert Schweitzer, Dorothea Dix, Dietrich Bonhoeffer, Pope John XXIII, Martin Buber, and Martin Luther King. Hardly anyone, however, would say that these persons' lives were marked by lots of fun. Such contamination of the notion of the good life with that of a good time obscures and distorts the issue.

On Being Human

"Doing My Thing" Versus I-Thou

The tension between self-fulfillment directly sought and self-fulfillment as a by-product of loving is, in my judgment, the greatest crisis facing our society today.

There are two poetic expressions which do not precisely define these opposing positions, but seem to reflect something of their diverse spirits. The first is the familiar "Gestalt Prayer" of Fritz Perls.

I do my thing, and you do
 your thing.
I am not in this world to live
 up to your expectations,
And you are not in this world
 to live up to mine.
You are you and I am I;
If by chance we find each
 other, it's beautiful.
If not, it can't be helped.

Fritz Perls

These lines express very forcibly the human need for independence and self-expression. I must have my own thoughts and feelings and I must assert my right to express them freely. I must make my own choices and be able to live by them. No doubt these were the practical good purposes in the mind of Fritz Perls.

I feel sure that he wanted his lines to expose the clinging dependency and jealous possessiveness which are, in fact, counterfeits of true love.

At the same time his verse opens itself to serious criticism. In itself and without qualification it sounds like a creed of "subjectivism" which waves the banner-slogan: "Do your own thing!" This kind of subjectivism ignores the fact that we are interrelated and interdependent social beings. I cannot do my thing without somehow affecting you. I cannot light up my big, fat cigar if it will make you sick.

But more profoundly, this subjectivism ignores one of the deepest truths of human existence:

For a person to be is to-be-with-others. Human life and human fulfillment are essentially relational. In other words, the Perls credo reflects the human need for independence, but ignores the need for true and deep relationships. Perls prescinds from the warmth, the caring, the empathy and commitment which are so essential to loving, which is in turn so essential to the process of becoming a person.

The supplement, offered by psychologist Walter Tubbs, speaks for itself. It redresses the imbalance in the thought of Perls, giving a fuller view of the human condition. True human fulfillment is found only in relationships of love: "The truth begins with two."

Giving the gift of myself in love leaves me with a deep and lasting satisfaction of having done something good with my life.

FOR FURTHER REFLECTION
Chapter 16: The Contemporary Crisis of Love

Review

1. In what ways has contemporary society denied that a life of unselfish and unconditional love is the way toward genuine happiness and a joy-filled life?
2. How are "the cult of experience" and "good times" similar in mind-set?
3. How do the mind-sets of "the cult of experience" and "good times" ultimately lead to frustration, fragmentation, broken dreams, and disillusionment?
4. Explain the similarities of "unconditional commitment" and "a good life." In what ways do these two mind-sets form the road to true human happiness and fulfillment?
5. Compare and contrast Fritz Perls's "Gestalt Prayer" and Walter Tubbs's "Beyond Perls." How do Perls and Tubbs illustrate either (a) the belief that human fulfillment is found in the direct pursuit of one's own happiness, or (b) the belief that human fulfillment comes from making a commitment and then choosing experiences which honor, promote, and reaffirm that commitment?

Discuss

1. Is the gospel beatitude of unselfish and unconditional love really the path to true human joy?
2. Identify titles of popular books, other literary works, and films that challenge the life principle of love. If you have read or seen any of these, explain how they challenge a life of unconditional love in favor of a life of "good times."
3. When you first read Fritz Perls's "Gestalt Prayer," were you impressed with his approach to relationships and individuality? What did you like and not like about his prayer?
4. How does Tubbs's "Beyond Perls" correct the distortions in Perls's "Gestalt Prayer"? Do you agree with Tubbs's approach to life, relationships, and individuality? Why or why not?
5. All of us struggle within the spectrum of self-centeredness and self-giving. Recall situations in your life when your basic mind-set toward life was (a) "What's in it for me?" (self-centeredness), or (b) "How can I be most loving now?"

(self-giving). Analyze when you experienced yourself to be the happiest.
6. A poem by Robert Frost ends like this: "Two roads diverged in a wood, and I— / I took the one less traveled by, / And that has made all the difference." How does a life of unconditional love make a difference in a person's life?

Scripture Activity

"And one of them, a teacher of the Law, tried to trap him with a question. 'Teacher,' he asked, 'which is the greatest commandment in the Law?' Jesus answered, '"Love the Lord your God with all your heart, with all your soul, and with all your mind." This is the greatest and the most important commandment. The second most important commandment is like it: "Love your neighbor as you love yourself." The whole Law of Moses and the teachings of the prophets depend on these two commandments.'" (Matthew 22:35–40, GNB)

Compose a prayer of your own asking God to help you accept the truth that genuine human happiness is a by-product and result of a loving life. Share with God your questions, doubts, and concerns about the life principle of self-forgetfulness and unconditional love.

Processing These Ideas about the Contemporary Crisis of Love

List and compare. Write the names of the ten people you know best. Then rank these same ten people according to their active capacity for loving. Put the most loving (in your judgment) at the top of the list and the least loving (in your judgment) at the bottom. Then rank the same ten people according to their apparent happiness, peace, and contentment. Again, put the happiest (in your judgment) at the top of the list, the least happy at the bottom.

Now compare these two lists. What is your conclusion? Are the happiest people also the most loving? Does loving really make us happy? What do you think?

17 We Must Make Our Lives an Act of Love

For those who have not loved, old age is a wintertime of loneliness. The greatest human talent was buried in the ground so it would not be lost. And in the end everything was lost. No one else came or cared. There was only a loveless person and a lonely waiting for death.

For those who have loved, old age is a harvesttime. The seeds of love planted so carefully and so long ago have matured with time. The loving person is surrounded in the twilight of life with the presence and the caring of others. The bread always comes back on the waters. What was given so freely and joyfully has been returned with interest.

What Is Love?

If there is a more frequently misused word in our English language, I don't know what it is. Most young people and many of us who are old enough to know better think of love as a *feeling*. When a feeling turns us on, we speak of "falling in love." When the feeling ebbs, love is suddenly but clearly a matter of history. It's over. An infatuation, or temporary emotional attraction, can so easily be confused with love.

Another source of confusion is that almost all of us at some time misconstrue *need* for *love*. When another person comes along and fills one of our needs, we are tempted to say, "Oh, I love you." The classic expression of real love, "I need you because I love you," is very much different from "I love you because I need you." You do not earn my love by filling my emptiness, my need. My love is always my freely given gift to you.

Real love, I feel sure, is a *decision* and a *commitment*. Before I can really love someone, I must make an inner decision that commits me to whatever is best for the one I love. Love moves me to say, to do, to be whatever the one loved needs. Love may ask me to be tough or tender, to be blue velvet or blue steel. Love may ask me to confront the one I love, or it may ask me to console that person. But I must first say yes to love. I must make that decision and commitment. Whatever love asks of me, I must be ready to do. At the crossroads of every decision, I must ask only this: What is the loving thing to do?

Is this possible? Of course, it is not possible to be perfect at anything. But it is an excellent ideal. In fact, it is the only life principle that can bring us happiness.

The glory of God is a person who is fully alive.

At every moment in my life and yours, we are asking a fundamental question. This question concerns our life principle. I may be asking, "How can I make the most money?" Or it may be that I am asking, "Where will I have the most fun?" The person who has decided to make his or her life an act of love does not ask primarily about money or fun. The loving person does not ask about pleasure, does not listen for applause or sniff for incense. The basic drive of this person is simply to be a loving human being. The only question is, What is the loving thing to do? This is the decision of love. This is love's commitment.

Love at Different Levels

Of course, love can exist at many levels. Some people in my life take precedence over others. The "commitment" level is deeper in some cases, as in a marriage or family. There are strangers, acquaintances, enemies, classmates, coworkers, friends, neighbors, close friends, sisters and brothers, parents, spouses, and children. A loving person tries to read and recognize and fill the needs of all, insofar as he or she is able. However, because there are degrees of closeness, there will also be differing levels of commitment. There is an order of priority, corresponding to the level of commitment. Family before friends. Friends before strangers, and so forth.

Love of Self and Love of Others

Of course, we cannot talk of loving others without first mentioning that love begins at home. We must first love ourselves. The psychiatrist of interpersonal relationships, Harry Stack Sullivan, says that "when the happiness, security, and well-being of another person is as real or more real to you than your own, you love that person." The obvious assumption is that my own happiness, security, and well-being are real to me. In fact, to the extent that I fail to love myself, to that same extent I will be unable to love others.

If I am to be a loving person, I must weigh my own happiness, security, and well-being as well as those of another. I must balance my needs with the needs of others whom I also love. For example, I am hungry and on my way to dinner, or tired and on my way to bed. I meet you, and you express a need to talk. I have to ask you how important, how urgent it is for you to talk at this time. If it is a minor matter, I may make an appointment to see you tomorrow. My needs will take priority over yours. However, if you have just suffered a serious setback, a death in the family, or if you are suicidal, my dinner or sleep can wait. Your needs will take priority over mine. A loving person will be called on to make many difficult decisions, and this prioritizing is surely one of them.

Most of the other love decisions have to do with the "good of the one loved." What is really good for you may not be what you would prefer. You may be getting drunk, for example, and ask me to get you another drink. Or you may ask me to join you in a lie or deception. Likewise, you may be a shy person and ask me to ignore you. I must say no to all of these requests. Another example would be the case of the emotional bully. You may want to "walk all over" me or to tell me off abusively. You may try to manipulate me with your anger or your tears. Love will ask me in these cases not to give one inch. Love forbids me to be a "doormat" or a "dingbat." Love may ask me to confront you or to walk away from you. So whatever else we might say of love, it is definitely not for those who seek the course of least resistance. It is, however, for those who would be happy.

A friend of mine had been a teacher for most of his life. Once he confided to me that he had been an alcoholic for twenty years during his teaching career. During this time, he said, his family and friends made excuses for him. They were classic "enablers," enabling him to go on drinking. Others took his classes when he was too drunk or too hung over to teach. And so his self-destruction by drinking went on for all those years. "Then," he almost sighed with relief, "thank God, someone loved me with a tough love. Someone loved me enough to confront me. He stood right in front of me, and he promised that if I did not get help, he would blow the whistle on me. He said I was sick and that I

needed help. He said that he loved me too much to watch me destroy myself. That's what turned me around. So I got help."

My friend's story of being loved with a tough love reminded me of something I once heard: If a loved one comes home in a drunken stupor and falls asleep on the front lawn, the most loving and kind thing to do would be to leave the person there. It is part of his "hitting bottom." The person will change only when he or she is allowed to feel the full impact of pain, to suffer the consequences of drinking. By the way, the cruelest thing would be to turn on the sprinkler.

God's will is often mysterious.

The Third Object of Love: God

There is a third object of my love, namely, God. Besides myself and others, I must love the Lord my God with my whole mind and heart and strength. Loving God adds a new and different dimension to love. In spite of what we would like to believe, it is a fact that we cannot give God anything that God doesn't already have. God does not need us as we truly need one another. Only those who are needy experience need, and God is not needy. However, God does ask us to love one another. And Jesus promises that whatever we do for the least of God's children, Jesus will take as done to himself.

> One of the requisites that true love must fulfill is that it be unconditional.

And, of course, God does ask us to accept and to do God's will. As I see it, the bottom line in doing God's will seems to be this: Do I make my own plans and then ask God to support those plans? Or do I ask God what are God's plans, and then seek to know my place in those plans? To remind myself, I have a second sign in my mirror that thanks God for loving me, and then asks: "What have you got going today? I'd like to be part of it."

Of course, God's will is often mysterious. However, of this we can all be certain: God wants us to use fully all the gifts we have been given by God. In the second century, Saint Irenaeus wrote that "the glory of God is a person who is fully alive." Have you ever given a gift to another and then noticed that the other person never used your gift? Do you remember what you wanted to ask: "Didn't you like the gift I gave you? Why don't you ever use it?" Maybe God wants to ask us about the gifts God has given us. When we say in the Lord's Prayer, "Thy will be done!" I am certain that part of this will is that I stretch to use all my talents. I know that God wills that I should develop my senses, emotions, mind, will, and heart as fully as possible. "The glory of God is a person who is fully alive."

Something in me is sure that our love for God is measured totally by our willingness to do these two things: to love one another as we love ourselves, and to do God's will in all things.

The Three Parts of Loving One Another

It has been rightly said that there are three parts of the love we are asked to give one another. They are (1) *kindness,* (2) *encouragement,* and (3) *challenge.* Only the mind and heart of love know when each is needed by the one loved. But these three parts of love seem in general to build on one another in the order given. If I am to love you effectively, I must first of all make it clear to you that I care, that I am on your side. I am committed to be "for you." This is the message of *kindness.* Once this is established, I must go on to encourage you to believe in yourself. Letting you lean on me or hitchhike on my strength is not loving you. It is keeping you weak and dependent. I must help you to use your own strength by urging you to think and choose for yourself. This is the task of *encouragement.* And finally, after kindness and encouragement have been successfully offered, I must challenge you to put your goodness and giftedness to work. You know I care. You know I believe in you and that I am sure you can do it. Now I say, "Do it. Go ahead, do it!" It is the moment of *challenge.*

And so Erich Fromm has appropriately called *loving* an *art.* In sciences, as in recipes, there are exact measures and careful directions for procedure. Not so in love. I must artfully decide when it is time for kindness, when encouragement is needed, and when the person I love is ready for challenge.

There are no manuals of instruction, no certain answers, only my best judgment. At times I may misfire in my judgment. But I can always apologize for my failures. And others can always accept my good intentions, even when my judgment has been poor.

True Love Is Unconditional

One of the requisites that true love must fulfill is that it be *unconditional*. The opposite, conditional love, is not really love. It is a barter. "I will love you as long as . . . until . . . if you . . ." The contract is filled with fine print, and the one to whom this conditional "love" is offered is asked to conform to all the provisions. Otherwise, the contract is null and void. Conditional love is threatening. It may be taken away for one misstep. Conditional love is "panscale" love. "If you put your donation on one of the pans, I will put my contribution on the other. But I won't be cheated. I'm watching you. If you don't go 50 percent of the way, neither will I." Of course, such "love" is a counterfeit. It never survives.

I think that a lot of the anger we see in the world is the result of this conditional love. In the end, we tend to resent someone who has "loved" us in this conditional way. We feel used. We want to protest, "You never really loved me. You loved my pretty face as long as it was pretty. You loved my clean

> The commitment to love will involve me in much careful and active listening. I truly want to be whatever you need me to be, to do whatever you need done, and I want to say whatever will promote your happiness, security, and well-being. To discover your needs, I must be attentive, caring, and open both to what you say and to what you cannot say. However, the final decision about the "loving thing" must be mine.
>
> This means that my love may be "tough" love, not all sweet and coddling. You may ask me for another drink when you are already inebriated, or you may ask me to join you in some deception. Of course, if I truly love you, I must say an emphatic "No!" to these requests. If you are on a self-destructive course, like alcoholism, you will meet in me a firm and confronting love. But, when needed, my love will also be "tender." If you have tried and failed, and you just need a hand in yours in the darkness of disappointment, you can count on mine.
>
> I may read you wrongly on occasion and misjudge your needs. I have done this so often to so many in the past. But know this, that my decision is to love you and my commitment is to your true and lasting happiness. I am dedicated to your growth and fulfillment as a person. If I should fail you, for lack of wisdom or because of the abundance of weakness in me, please forgive me, try to recognize my intention, and know that I will try to do better.
>
> From *Unconditional Love*

clothes and demanded that I keep them clean. You loved my good marks and made it clear that I was not allowed to fail. You loved my abilities. But you never loved *me*. I was always walking on eggshells. I knew that if I ever failed to meet your requirements, you would treat me as a smoker treats cigarettes. You would use me up, grind me out, and throw me away."

Love and Unfaithfulness

So love is by its nature unconditional. But what if I set out to love someone and that person is repeatedly unfaithful to me? Does unconditional love just forgive again and again and continue to love? This is a good question and should be addressed, but the answer is not easy. Love certainly does not ask me to become stupid or naive. So I have to make the judgment—as best I can—about what would be the loving thing to do, to be, to say. Forgiveness is not the real issue here. Of course, I forgive you. Love sets no limits to forgiveness. The real issue is, What is best for you and for me? That is what I must do.

I must try to balance my love for myself and my love for you. I must ask, "What is the best way to preserve my own self-esteem and out of love to help you at the same time?" Love is indeed an art and not a science. There are no clear and obvious answers. Love does not promise us a rose garden.

Certainly, to write you off because you have disappointed me would be a thinly veiled form of conditional love. On the other hand, to go on trusting you after repeated unfaithfulness would not be loving you. It would only enable you to stay weak. It would also not be loving myself. It would certainly tend to undermine my own self-respect. So I have to ask myself this hard question: "Considering all the circumstances, what would be the best thing to say, to do, to be,

for you *and* for me?" At a certain point, I think, I would have to ask you to choose between faithfulness with me or unfaithfulness without me.

Love Includes . . . Love Excludes

Sometimes it is agonizing to answer the questions love asks. It may be helpful first to consider this question: What does love include and what does love exclude? Saint Paul, in his First Letter to the Corinthians, gives us a few suggestions:

> The love of which I speak is slow to lose patience.
> It always looks for a way to be constructive.
> Love is not possessive.
> Neither is it anxious to impress, nor does it cherish inflated ideas of its own importance.
> Love has good manners and does not pursue selfish advantage.
> Love is not touchy or fragile.
> It does not keep an account of evil,
> or gloat over the wickedness of other people.
> On the other hand, love is glad with all good people whenever truth prevails.
> Love does not give up on others.
> Love knows no end to its trust, no fading of its hope.
> Love outlasts everything.
> Love is in fact the one thing that will still be standing when all else has fallen.
>
> *Paraphrase of 1 Corinthians 13:4–8*

I must try to balance my love for myself and my love for you.

My own list goes something like this:

What LOVE DOES

LOVE

ACCEPTS you wherever you are

AFFIRMS your goodness and giftedness

CARES about you, wants to know that you're okay

CHALLENGES you to be all you can be

EMPATHIZES—knows what it's like to be you

ENCOURAGES you to believe in yourself

IS GENTLE in its way of dealing with you

KEEPS CONFIDENCES—your secrets are safe

IS KIND—is always for you, on your side

LAUGHS A LOT, always with, never at you

LOOKS FOR GOODNESS in you and finds it

MAKES YOU FEEL GLAD that you're you

OVERLOOKS your foolish vanities, human weakness

PRAYS for your needs and your growth

SEES good things in you that others had never noticed

SHARES itself with you, by self-disclosure

SPEAKS UP when you need someone to defend you

IS TACTFUL even when confronting you

TAKES RESPONSIBILITY for its own behavior

TELLS YOU THE TRUTH always and honestly

THINKS about you and your needs

IS TOUGH OR TENDER, depending on your needs

UNDERSTANDS your ups and downs, allows you "bad days"

What LOVE DOESN'T

LOVE DOESN'T ABUSE you or take you for granted

ASK you to march to a different drummer

BLAME you or carry angry grudges

BULLY you by anger, a loud voice, or tears

GET you into win-lose arguments

GIVE you unsolicited advice

JUDGE you or tell you "what your whole trouble is"

JUST TOLERATE you as a condescending favor

MAKE YOU PROVE yourself again and again

NEED always to be right, to have all the answers

POUT or refuse to talk to you

PUNISH you vindictively for being wrong

REMEMBER all the things you have done wrong

SEEK and call attention to itself

SHOW OFF, just to let you know where you stand

UNDERMINE your confidence in yourself

USE you for its own purposes and then discard you

VENTILATE its emotions on you as a garbage dump

WRITE YOU OFF because you didn't meet its demands

The things that are included here may help you prime your own pump. Please feel free to add, subtract, edit, and borrow. Your own list is the one that will be most meaningful to you.

Chronic Unhappiness Represents a Failure to Love

The source of most chronic unhappiness is a failure to love. All the great psychiatrists—Freud, Adler, Jung, Frankl—have said this. However, this is clearly not meant to imply that the failure is culpable or blameworthy. It may be that my early programming and experiences did not encourage me to love myself, my neighbor, or my God. I may spend much of my life paying the high price of this failure to love. However, it could be that I am only acting out my past programming and experiences. I may be failing to love because of messages that I absorbed from others and from my early life situation.

Of course, we cannot judge human responsibility. But we can say for certain that if a person does not love himself or herself, there is only misery ahead. Or it may be that, because of early programming in distrust, a person does not really love others. As long as this condition prevails, there is no real hope for happiness. Such a person lives in a sad and shrunken world that has a population of one. And I must add that the human spirit is seriously deprived without a relationship of love with a loving God. As the French author Leon Bloy once wrote, "Only the saints are truly happy."

Let us love one another, because love comes from God. Whoever loves is a child of God and knows God.

1 John 4:7

Love and the Laboratory of Life

I remember once disliking someone quite intensely. He was the proverbial drop of vinegar in my barrel of sweetness. Long after this person had gone out of my life, the upsetting memory remained. So I was delighted by the visit of a psychologist friend who maintains that if something really bothers you, you have not fully explored the cause of your unhappiness. The cause of your upset is not what you think. If it were, you wouldn't be so upset by it. So I told him about my problem, and we went through his test. First I closed my eyes and relaxed. Then I "unpacked" my brain of everything else, and went through an imaginary door. I took only the problem person and my upsetting memories with me into the room beyond the door. Soon my body was reacting, and according to directions, I dialogued with my physical reactions. What emotion did I push deep down inside myself so that it could get out only as a physical reaction? What I felt in the end was guilt, not anger. When my shoulders sagged and an audible sigh of relief passed from my lips, my psychologist friend knew that I had discovered the real cause of my upset.

What in fact I discovered was that the reason for my inner unrest was that I had never loved but only resented the person in question. I couldn't recall ever feeling sorry for him, or ever asking myself what

I could do to help him. I know somewhere deep inside myself that obnoxious people are hurting people. But I did not compassionate his hurting. I spent all my energies resenting the obnoxious symptoms. But I am learning. I know now that resentment is a form of enslavement. I know that the price of making my life an act of love means reversing a lot of my old habits and values. It is difficult, but the alternative is a life of misery—and an old age of loneliness.

Love: God's Gift to Us and Our Gift to God

There are two things I would like to say about love and God. I realize that in our pluralistic society, both of my statements will be vehemently debated. However, I believe that this discussion of a life of love would be incomplete without some inclusion of these two things. These are my beliefs: (1) Love is a gift of God, and (2) When we love, God acts.

There is much power in God if only you are connected.

Love Really Is
a Gift of God

I accept the Bible as the word of God. So I look to the Bible for answers to questions like the one we are now asking. I think that the Bible is quite clear on this point. Love is indeed a gift from God. Saint Paul talks about the three main gifts of God: faith, hope, and love. Then he proclaims that the greatest of these gifts is love. Paul says that there are many and various gifts of God, but the one we should ask for above all else is this gift of love. (See 1 Corinthians, chapters 13 and 14.)

Saint John is even more explicit. He simply says, "Let us love one another, because love comes from God. Whoever loves is a child of God and knows God" (1 John 4:7).

I think I can anticipate your next question: If love is in fact a gift of God, can those who do not believe in God really love? It would take much more time and space than we have to answer that question adequately. But let me say simply: Yes, of course, people without faith are able to love. God believes in many people who do not believe in God. In some cases God gives us gifts, such as the power to love, as a prelude to the gift of faith. At other times God simply enlightens nonbelievers in their love choices and empowers them in their love commitments. A great theologian, Karl Rahner, once referred to such people as "anonymous Christians." And the great Thomas Aquinas insisted that

"God is not limited in his gift giving to those who are sacramentally united to him."

To paraphrase Jesus, "God lets the rain fall on the crops of the believers and the nonbelievers. God lets the sun fall on the fields of the believers and also the nonbelievers." If this is true, of what value is faith? For those of us who believe, faith opens us to a loving relationship with God. It enables us to know where our gifts have come from. And, of course, faith wins us further gifts, as we learn from the story of the lady with the hemorrhages. (See Matthew 9:20–22.) To this woman and to most of the people for whom Jesus worked wonders, he said, "Your faith has made this possible." There is no point in God doing a work of power if it is not going to be recognized. And it is clear to me that it takes faith to recognize a miracle. There were many works of power Jesus could not do because there was no faith in those who surrounded him. God is something like an electrical outlet. There is much power to be had, but only if we are connected. And the connection is faith. Faith releases the power of God.

The importance of knowing that love is a gift from God is this: We will more surely receive this gift when we know that its source is God and not simply a matter of using our own powers. Most of us first have to try our own little formulas for relationships of love. Eventually we come to a moment called ego-desperation. It is a moment of admitting,

"I cannot do it by myself."
I must turn my life over to the enlightenment and empowerment of God as I understand God. I must ask God to make me a channel of God's love, to fill my wells so that I can give the thirsty a drink from my supply.

When We Love, God Acts

This is the second of my statements about God and love. I think that I did not always believe that when we love, God acts. I do now. I used to think that our actions changed things. If I defended the truth, fed the hungry, shouted from the housetops what was whispered into my ear, it would change everything. The contagion of my truth, my compassion, and my virtue would eventually envelop the whole world. These were my thoughts during my "messianic period," the time when I was playing at being God. Now I believe much more simply that when we love, God's grace flows into this world through the channel of our love: healing it, straightening its twistedness, mending its brokenness, and enlightening its darkness. We are only God's instruments.

I am convinced that when you and I accept the grace of loving and we use it, we will be fulfilling the condition for God's action. Our love is the channel through which God's healing and helping grace will flow. Most of us do not have great talent, but we can all do small things with great love. And it is this that is essential. The loving mother who has her hands full of children, the

silent monk who prays in some distant monastery, the elderly person whose vision is failing, the adolescent who worries about acne—they are all capable of accepting and putting into practice the gift of love. And when they do, God will act. Because of those who love, God will change this world.

Can We Really Love Everyone? Even Our Enemies?

I remember once arguing my case for a life of love against fifteen others. They obviously did not believe what I did. I was really trying to swim upstream that night. My friends who were arguing against me were releasing their pent-up angers. It is so easy for most of us to get into an embattled siege mentality. We get sick of people lying to us, laundering their language, twisting the truth, and falsifying the facts. We want to hate them and to fight. My friends typified these urges. They cited one case after another—all hopeless types. Their conclusion: "You just can't love some people." Secretly, I think that they were confusing *like* with *love*. And I probably wasn't clear about my meaning of love, and the many faces of love.

For all our "fight or flight" tendencies, we are called to love. Despite all our petty squabbles, the towering figure of Christ stands over our lives and over all human history. He says, "Love only your friends? Why, even the heathens do this.

God could not ask us to love people we don't even like, unless God were willing to help us and to empower us.

I am asking you to love your enemies also." It is at moments like this that we face the difficult challenges and the consequences of a life of love. We slowly come to believe that this kind of love can only be a grace or gift of God. God could not ask us to love people we don't even like, unless God were willing to help us and to empower us. So we slowly come to believe that our love is a gift of God and at the same time the condition for God's action. "This is all I command you. . . . I will do the rest."

Love Is the Truth That Sets Us Free

The happiness that can come only as a by-product to loving can be learned only by experiencing it. Such joy can only be described to the unloving, who will no doubt think of it as a fairy tale. A life that is an act of love can be presented only on a "Try it—you might like it" basis. But the alternative is clear. If a life of love is a fairy tale, the opposite is a nightmare.

Unloving people just don't care about anyone. They keep their grudges carefully labeled and stored in a memory bank. They don't trust others. And they feel safer behind an array of masks. They decide which one to wear depending on the occasion and the people present. They reason that walls are safer than bridges. Others have never passed their inspection tests. And the only people willing to enter into a relationship of sorts with them are just as cautious, just as phony, just as self-centered. It is

a prison life. There are the cages with their bars. The loneliness can get very painful at times, but there are always distractions, like kicks and sensations. But then the unloving person can only ask, "What else is there?"

I have told this story elsewhere and many times. It was one of those Copernican moments in my own life. And it has a definite point and place here. It was my personal discovery of the freeing effects of love.

I was the last speaker on a panel of three. I was very anxious to impress my audience, which was my own religious community. They had never heard me speak, and I wanted them to know what a gem was in their midst. I am rarely nervous before a speaking engagement. You see, I have a lot of mileage on my mouth. But on this night my mouth was dry and my hands were cold. I was nervous. So I prayed silently as I sat there waiting for my anticipated moment of glory. But my prayer brought no results. I was still nervous.

So I prayed again, reminding the Lord of his promise that whatever we asked in his name would be granted. But apparently not on that night. My mouth was still dry. My hands were still cold. Then I remembered the advice of an old spiritual sage who said, "If you keep asking God the same question and you do not get an answer, try another question." So I asked God, "Why am I so nervous? And why won't you do anything about it? Are you trying to tell me something?"

Now, I have no difficulty believing in a loving God who interacts and communicates with us. In fact, this is the only God I do believe in. Anyway, on that night, sitting right there in front of one hundred and twenty brother Jesuits, I know that God spoke to me. I know it was the grace of God. Somewhere, deep inside me, I heard: "You are getting ready to give another performance. And I don't need any more performances from you. Only acts of love. You want to perform for your brothers, so that they will know how good you are. They do not need that. They need you to love them, so that they will know how good they are."

I know I didn't invent that message. I know it was from God. It has profoundly changed me and changed my life. After I heard those words, I looked out at the members of my community. I looked at the aged who are retired from teaching and are preparing for the great retirement of death. Being rather young and vibrant, I asked myself, "What is it like to be old? What does it feel like when the traffic of life goes whizzing by? When no one ever stops to ask about you? What does that feel like?" Then I looked at those who are physically and chronically sick. They wake up every morning with an agony in their guts called an ulcer, or an ache in their bones called arthritis. Having enjoyed a lifetime of almost uninterrupted good health, I asked myself, "What is it like to feel sick almost all of the time? What is it like to take pain to bed with you at night and wake up with it in the morning?"

Then I looked at the four or five members of my community who are members of Alcoholics Anonymous. "What is it like?" I asked myself. "What is it like to live with an addiction? What is it like to struggle to maintain sobriety one day at a time? What is it like to stand up at a meeting and say, 'My name is _____ , and I am an alcoholic'?" Then I looked at the men who are not very successful in their work. To be honest, God has blessed me with more success than I ever dreamed even in my most Technicolor dreams. "Do you feel like a failure?" I silently asked my less successful brothers. "Do you resent or envy the success of others? Do you ever wonder why everything seems to go wrong for you and right for others?"

Trying to walk for a mile in the shoes of another is not easy. It is the work of a virtue called empathy. Empathy is, I feel sure, the essential prelude to loving others. After my flood of empathic questions, I felt ashamed of my self-centered desire to impress these men. I had been praying for the grace to show them how good I was. I should have been praying for the grace to love them.

But God was not through with me that night. In another moment of grace, I remembered Mary Martin, the singer and entertainer. It was once said of her that "it would be difficult to sit in an audience of Mary Martin and to imagine that the audience loved her more than she loved the audience." Anyway, it was this Mary Martin who said that she never went out on any stage without first peeping through the stage curtains at her audience and whispering, "I love you! I love you! I love you!"

Love holds out to us the only substantial hope for lasting happiness.

Mary Martin maintains that you can't be nervous when you are truly loving. The only way to be nervous, she has said, is to be self-conscious. You can be nervous only if you are asking, "How am I doing?" But you can't be nervous when you are asking, "How are you doing?" This last question breaks the fixation that most of us have with ourselves.

So I looked out at my community on that memorable evening, and under my breath I promised, "I don't know if I have really loved you before, but I am going to love you, love you, love you." Almost as if a magic wand had been waved over my head, all the nervousness and tension vanished. Saliva came back into my mouth, and blood flowed again into my fingertips.

It was a lesson I had learned before, and would have to learn again and again. Someday, perhaps, I will be fully open to its meaning. Love is a liberation. Love is the lubricant that makes life a lot easier. Love breaks the tense and nervous preoccupation with ourselves. It frees us for a life of peace. Love holds out to us the only substantial hope for lasting happiness.

Remember! Love is a poor mathematician. It does not keep a careful count of what it has done. It just goes on doing . . . and smiling.

> *The path to full human living is impossible without choosing the life principle of unconditional love and service.*

Vocations of Love

According to what we have developed so far in this course, the path to personal fulfillment and happiness comes by (a) acquiring healthy Christian attitudes that enable us to more easily realize our potential to be fully human and fully alive, and (b) making our lives an act of love. The path to full human living is impossible without choosing the life principle of unconditional love and service. Full human living and the life principle of love go hand-in-hand; they are inseparable. Accordingly, instead of accepting and living one's life based on the life principles of power, pleasure, and avoidance of responsibility, the Christian sees happiness and fulfillment as by-products of a life of love and service.

As Christians, then, when we make decisions and choices, the essential question to ask is, What is the more loving thing to say, to do, to be? In short, the life principle of love and service is the *general vocation* that God gives each one of us. God wants us to be happy and fulfilled by loving God, other people (including our enemies), and ourselves. It is by loving and serving that we in turn actualize our potential to become fully human and fully alive. In addition to our general vocation to love, God also gives each of us a *specific vocation* to the single or the married life. Consequently, as we strive to make Jesus' vision of reality our own and accept his challenge to make our lives an act of love, it is important to consider the notion of "Christian Vocations" to the four states of life: the single life, religious life, orders, and married life.

Nonconsecrated Single Life

The nonconsecrated single life, whether chosen permanently or lived temporarily until marriage, is a valuable vocation in its own right. It is a vocation that reflects God's love in its own unique ways and is a positive means for a person to make his or her life an act of love. There are, of course, many different kinds of singleness. Some people are single because of circumstance—widowed or divorced—while others are single because of choice—have not yet married or are not called to marriage or the religious life. For many of you, however, the single life will more than likely be a temporary state until you decide to marry or enter the priesthood and/or religious life.

The life principle of love and service is the general vocation that God gives each one of us.

Yet, the Church recognizes that God may also call individuals to the permanent nonconsecrated single life.

The single nonconsecrated vocation is the most flexible of all vocations. Unlike the consecrated single vocation to the priesthood or religious life, the nonconsecrated single individual makes no lifelong commitment to a spouse and family or to a religious order. Therefore, the single person has the flexibility to decide whether he or she wants to be single permanently or temporarily. He or she may decide to marry later on, enter religious life, become a deacon or priest, or remain permanently in the single state. In turn, the flexibility of the single life offers the single person the freedom to relocate, change careers, enter different fields, and enter different ministries without having to consider how these decisions might affect a spouse, a diocese, or a religious community.

Moreover, the single individual has the freedom to choose to be involved in lay missionary work, in lay parish ministry as a Director of Religious Education, youth minister, eucharistic minister, or a catechist of religious instruction, and so on. A single person may also decide to be ordained to the deaconate and serve the Church in an official way. Even outside of the sphere of parish ministry, the single person may make his or her life an act of love by being dedicated to the sciences and medical fields or any other philanthropic endeavors. In any of these endeavors, parish or nonparish related, the single person is free to work and dedicate himself or herself to and for the common good and well-being of humanity. In these ways and many others the single person may specifically make his or her life an act of love.

Consecrated Single Life: Religious Life

Many individuals, called to the single life, may also discern a vocation to the religious life. The term *religious,* as it is used here, simply means "living by a rule." A religious person is a priest, brother, deacon, and/or sister who consecrates and commits himself or herself to a total, undivided commitment to the Church and the work of the kingdom of God. In the Church there are many different forms of consecrated, or vowed, religious life. Some religious communities are more devoted to prayer while others are devoted to action. What all religious communities have in common is a permanent or temporary commitment to follow a rule of life designed to help the individual and other community members to grow in the love of God, others, and oneself. The commitment of the consecrated single lifestyle includes three vows, or promises, that an individual professes. They are *celibacy,* a commitment chosen for the freedom it provides to love others nonexclusively and to give witness to the reality of God's love; *obedience,* a commitment to obey the Church and the individual's religious community; and *poverty,* a commitment to live a simple and uncluttered life free of material and nonmaterial possessions. These three vows, or promises, help the single person who is committed to living the consecrated single life live the values of the kingdom of God and make her or his life an act of love.

There are different consecrated lifestyles in religious life. Religious communities generally fall under two categories; they are either dedicated to the active life or the contemplative life. Augustians, Dominicans, Franciscans, Jesuits, Oblates, Salesians, Vincentians, and many other religious communities are dedicated to the active ministry. Their ministry includes, but is not limited to, teaching; missionary work; ministry to people who have disabilities, are abused, or disadvantaged; nursing and other medical fields; parish work; scientific research; social work; lobbying; communications media, the arts; and so on. On the other hand, other religious communities such as the Benedictines, Trappists, Carthusians, Poor Clares, and Carmelites, are committed to living the contemplative life. These religious communities live a cloistered lifestyle, which means they generally remain in the same residence (monastery or convent) and dedicate themselves to Jesus, the Church, and the work of the kingdom by disposing themselves to a deep prayer life.

Unlike active religious communities who go out in the marketplace, contemplatives generally remain at their residences and serve the people who visit them. For example, in Vallyermo, California, the Benedictines have an extensive retreat program for youth and adults at their monastery.

Consecrated Single Life: Holy Orders

The sacrament of Holy Orders consecrates and enables an individual to serve the Church community in an official role of leadership and service. Holy Orders includes the ministries of deacon, priest, and bishop.

The ministry of deacon is open both to religious and nonconsecrated single men as well as married men. All men who intend to be ordained to the priesthood are first ordained as deacons prior to being ordained priests. After six months to a year as deacons, they then are ordained to the priesthood. Besides being ordained to this *transitional deaconate,* a single or married man may be ordained to the *permanent diaconate.* The duties of transitional and permanent deacons are the same. As the term *deacon* implies, this vocation is a call to serve the Church as an official "helper." A deacon can baptize, teach, give homilies, witness marriages, assist at the Eucharist, offer pastoral counseling, visit the sick, and perform other ministerial duties. However, a deacon cannot preside at the eucharistic liturgy or be the presider at the sacraments of Confirmation, Reconciliation, and the Anointing of the Sick.

These three vows (celibacy, obedience, poverty), or promises, help the single person who is committed to living the consecrated single life live the values of the kingdom of God and make her or his life an act of love.

Priests, as helpers of bishops, are ordained to lead the Church community through a life of service. Diocesan (secular) priests work in a particular diocese under the authority of a bishop. *Religious* priests belong to a religious community and are under the authority of their religious superior. Whether an individual is a diocesan or religious priest, the priest's role is to rally the people to live as one body of believers, the Body of Christ, who mediate the presence of Christ to the world. A priest does this by (a) living after the example of Jesus, (b) dedicating himself to the work of the kingdom, and (c) leading people to true worship and true service of God.

A bishop is also ordained to lead the Church community through a life of service. He has the ministry to continue the work of the Apostles by serving the Church as the shepherd of a diocese. His role in the Church is to lead, teach, and shepherd the Church. By virtue of his ordination, a bishop belongs to the *magisterium,* the official teaching authority of the Church. Together with the pope and other bishops, the magisterium formulates and scrutinizes the orthodoxy of beliefs and practices of the Church community to lead the Church to live as authentic and faithful sign of Christ. Additionally, local bishops involve themselves in issues facing society in general and call the community of believers to respond to these issues in light of the Gospel.

Married Life

The vocation to the Christian married lifestyle is a sacrament of God's love for humanity and Jesus' union with the Church. When a man and woman commit themselves in marriage, they symbolize the covenanted and unconditional love of God for others. Together the married couple symbolize and mediate God's love of themselves and all others by their commitment to love and cherish each other, to remain together in good and bad times, in sickness and health until death do them apart.

Marriage in the Church is a special way of living one's life as an act of love. As a vocation of love, a married man and woman commit themselves to be open to family life, to service of others, and to worship of God. As God's love is *life-giving,* the natural outcome of married love is children. Similarly, as God's love is *life-nourishing,* married Christians are not to merely remain an isolated entity, but are to be of service to others in the world community. They do this first by raising a family founded on Christian values and attitudes. They nourish the family and help it grow and become the domestic church, or church of the home. It is in the family that parents are the first proclaimers and models of the faith to their children. Married Christians also minister to people outside their family. They dedicate themselves to the work of building the kingdom in the world. They strive to make the Christian family a clear sign of God's love for all people.

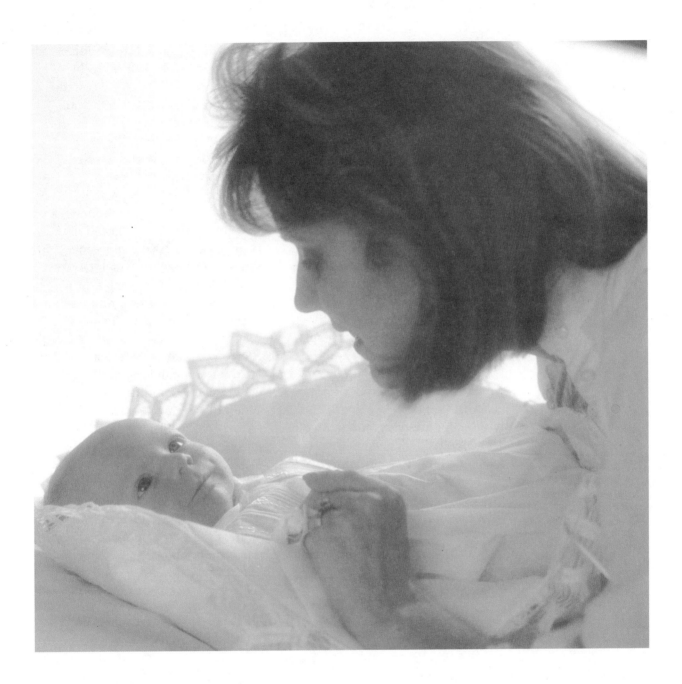

Discerning One's Vocation

Every vocation is a call from God to make our lives an act of love. The question before us then is: How do we know which vocation God is calling us to?

In your attempts to discern the vocation God is calling you to, there are certain concerns you might consider. First, it is highly important that you know yourself sufficiently well. This *self-knowledge* enables you to know how best you relate to others, in what ways you most easily serve others, what makes you happy, and what way of life (single or married) is the most meaningful for you.

The last chapter of this text, "The Christian Vision of the Will of God," will help you discern the specific vocation God calls you to. It will help you be more in tune with your deepest *inclinations* (attractions).

It is through the ordinary things of our life that God calls us to a specific vocation. Without being overly simplistic, we can place before our minds the different vocational lifestyles to which God might call us. After considering the alternatives, the one in which we find the greatest peace of heart most probably is the vocation God is calling us to choose. However, none of these decisions should be made in haste. It is important that you explore the different opportunities, that you converse with people of different lifestyles, and that you seek spiritual guidance before making a life-choice of marriage, single life, religious life, and/or orders.

In summary, God calls each one of us to live a life of love. In order to be fully human and fully alive, we are to love God, others, and ourselves. For it is through love that we enter the fullness of life and ultimately find happiness and fulfillment. But God also calls us to live this vocation of love in a specific way. God calls us either to the single consecrated life, nonconsecrated life, or married life.

Meanwhile, as you continue to learn more about yourself and begin to consider the different vocations of love to which God calls you, remember that your life right now is extremely important. In your present relationships with others, you now are called by God to live your life as an act of love. Learn to communicate kindness, encouragement, and challenge now. When making a specific decision of love, ask yourself: What is the more loving thing to say, to do, to be?

Begin now to live your life as an act of love. Then when you are ready to choose a permanent, lifelong lifestyle, you will know that much more about yourself and the vocation of love.

It is through love that we enter the fullness of life and ultimately find happiness and fulfillment.

FOR FURTHER REFLECTION

Chapter 17: We Must Make Our Lives An Act of Love

Review

1. Explain the following:
   a. Love is not a feeling.
   b. Love is a decision-commitment.
   c. Love should not be confused with the **need** to love.
   d. Love exists at different levels depending on the level of commitment.

2. How does Harvey Stack Sullivan's description of love connect love of others with love of self?

3. Distinguish "tough love" and "tender love." Give examples to illustrate the differences and their similar goals.

4. According to the chapter, what does it mean to love God with one's whole being?

5. Describe the **three parts of loving one another**. Given these three parts, how is love considered an art, rather than a natural phenomenon of humans?

6. We are called to love others unconditionally. Yet, what happens if a person repeatedly remains unfaithful to me? How do I reconcile my love of the person and love of myself in this kind of a situation?

7. How does a life of loving relationships lead to happiness and freedom?

8. What is the relationship between the **general vocation** and **specific vocations of love**?

9. Explain and comment on each vocation:
   (a) The non-consecrated single life, (b) religious life, (c) deaconate, priesthood, and episcopacy (bishop), (d) married life.

Discuss

1. Do you agree love is not a feeling? If it is not a feeling but rather a decision-commitment, what role do feelings have in the decision to love?

2. Have you ever had to offer "tough love"? Was it effective or not? Explain.

3. What are some concrete ways one may love, that is, make a decision-commitment to the happiness, security, and well-being of another person?

4. If we accept Harvey Stack Sullivan's understanding of **love**, what then does it mean to love even one's enemies? In other words, in what ways can "we make our lives an act of love" even to strangers or to those whom we might consider our enemies?

5. Powell claims that it's impossible to be nervous if you are genuinely loving others. Recall a situation in which your focus of attention was on another and not yourself, that is, a situation in which you were genuinely loving another or others. Describe how you felt. Were you nervous or comfortable? If you were nervous, was it because your attention was not totally on the other(s)? If you were comfortable, was it because you focused your attention on them?

6. In what ordinary ways might God reveal which specific vocation a person is called to?

7. If you felt called to the priesthood, how would you live that out: as a religious or a diocesan priest? Explain.

8. If you felt called to be a sister, would you be a contemplative or active? Why?

Scripture Activity

We love because God first loved us. If someone says he loves God, but hates his brother, he is a liar. For he cannot love God, whom he has not seen, if he does not love his brother, whom he has seen. The command that Christ has given us is this: whoever loves God must love his brother and sister also" (1 John 4 : 7–8, 12, 19–21, GNB).

Compose a prayer of your own about those people you tend to "write off" or hate. Ask God (in your prayer) (a) to help you see these people according to the Christian vision of others: "People are basically needy of love and understanding", and (b) to give you the courage and strength to love them.

Processing These Ideas about Love

1. **Write your own version of "What Love Does" and "What Love Doesn't."** Make a list of things that you think love would include and exclude. Based on this list, what do you think love is asking you to do or to avoid doing?

2. **Interview** a married couple, permanent deacon, a priest or bishop and specifically ask: (a) how the person discerned his or her particular vocation; (b) what are the advantages and disadvantages of their life; and (c) what advice they would give to someone else who felt called to their same vocational lifestyle? Record your findings.

Part Six

THE CHRISTIAN VISION

OF THE WORLD

18 *The Grandeur of God*

*God saw all,
and indeed
it was very good.*
From Genesis 1:31
(Jerusalem Bible)

Traditional World Rejection

After entering the seminary at the ripe old age of seventeen, my classmates and I were given most of our instructions by a Master of Novices. Father Master solemnly informed us that we had been called "out of the world." We were assured that this was a blessing because the three major sources of temptation were "the world" (usually listed in first place), "the flesh," and "the devil." Most of us novices were only teenagers, but we had ponderous discussions that sounded like those of aged veterans in an old people's home. We started many of our sentences with the sober, reflective introduction, "When I was in the world . . ."

One of our novices had to have his eyes checked, so he boarded the bus from our rurally situated novitiate for the big city of Cincinnati. He asked the bus driver, "What is the fare now?" The driver responded politely, "Thirty-five cents." The surprised novice countered, "Gee, when I was in the world it was only a quarter." The bus driver looked at him quizzically and asked, "Fella, I don't mean to get personal, but where do you think you are?"

Somehow, almost from the beginning of Christianity there were some who left the so-called world, escaping to the dusty deserts and hidden places to avoid temptation and contamination. Everything, but especially material things like the human body (often called "the evil and ugly prison of the delicately beautiful soul"), was to be despised. These escapees from the world believed that Christians were obliged to crawl through a long, dark tunnel of detachment until they came to the beatific light at the end, which was found only in death. There are probably very few Christians who think this way today, but we still have remnants of this thinking in prayers that portray us as "sending up our sighs," and crying because we are the "poor, banished children of Eve, mourning and weeping in this valley of tears, in this period of exile."

And God said it is very good.

Incarnational Spirituality: To Seek and Find God in All Things

The attitude of world rejection seems to ignore the words of Genesis that "God saw all he had made, and indeed it was very good." World rejection ignores the theologically sound, incarnational spirituality that "seeks and finds God in all things." Ignatius of Loyola could not look at the stars in the night sky without being moved to tears by God's beauty. Teresa of Avila found the sweetness of God in the taste of grapes. Philip Neri's two favorite books were the New Testament and his *Book of Jokes*. Gerard Manley Hopkins, a Jesuit priest and a poet, said that "the world is charged with the grandeur of God." Hopkins proclaimed that "Christ plays in ten thousand places" and that God should be glorified "for dappled things." "There lives the dearest freshness deep down things" because the Holy Spirit "over the bent world broods with warm breasts and with ah! bright wings."

So we must ask ourselves: How would a true Christian believer see this world? What is the liberating truth about this world with its many parts that I must know in order to be set free? If I truly "put on the mind of Christ," how would I perceive the world? If I could see through the eyes of Christ, what would the world look like? What attitude toward this world will free me to be a fully alive person for God's glory, to experience the peace and the joy that are the legacy of Jesus to his followers?

Definition of "The World"

Before attempting an answer to these questions, I would like to define what I mean by "the world." As I am using the term here, the world embraces all created reality, *except persons*. Consequently, the world in this usage would include all material things, but it would also include such immaterial things as personal talents and abilities, personal qualities and attainments. These are abstract terms, aren't they? Concretely, the list of created realities implied under "the world" would include such things as money, house, books, piano, type-writer, good looks, athletic ability, a charming smile, curly hair, straight white teeth, good health, academic degrees, artistic talent, a sense of humor, compassionate instincts, intellectual genius, love of nature, a reputation, power or influence, personal charm, and charisma. In our discussion, these are the types of things that I am including in the all-encompassing term "the world." All these things are part of my world. How am I, as a Christian believer, to regard them? If the gospel message were really in the marrow of my bones, if my mind and thoughts were drenched by the vision of Jesus, what would my attitude toward this world be?

If I could see through the eyes of Christ, what would the world look like?

The Spirits of Possession and Dispossession

As best I can understand Jesus and his good news, it seems that Christian spirituality involves both a spirit of possession and a spirit of dispossession. To be able to integrate and harmonize these two spirits is the genius of Christian spirituality. By possession I mean the ability to join God in his pronouncement over creation, " It is very good!" Possession would also include the ability to acquire knowledge of and to enjoy the good things of God's world, including one's own personal gifts and blessings. Possession reaches out to embrace life and all the parts of life. The glory of God is a person who is fully alive. The Christian spirit of possession sees a unique beauty in each of the seasons of the year, hears the music and poetry of the universe, smells the fragrance of a day in spring, and touches the soft petals of a flower. Possession tastes the deliciousness of every newborn day. Possession likewise includes experience of the whole galaxy of good feelings which are a part of our humanity: a sense of accomplishment when I have written a poem or have sung a song to the world, a feeling of appreciation when I am praised and thanked, a joy at being able to run fast or to tell a humorous story. In short, the spirit of possession tends to make me fully alive in my senses, emotions, mind, and will.

The spirit of dispossession implies that all these good and delightful things are never allowed to own and possess me.

The spirit of possession helps me become fully functioning in all the parts of my unique giftedness.

The genius of Christian spirituality is to integrate this spirit of possession with the spirit of dispossession. My possession of the world must be exercised in the spirit of readiness for dispossession. The spirit of dispossession implies that all these good and delightful things are never allowed to own, possess, or shackle me. Dispossession implies that I am always free, my own person, liberated from the tyranny that possessions can easily exercise over us. I always remain my own free person. The world may never dominate or manipulate me. The world may never be allowed to preempt my freedom to make my own decisions. All of us have some sense of what it is to be tyrannized, manipulated, or coerced by another human being. Things—even the good, delightful, God-made things of creation—can do the same to us. They can enslave us and deprive us of our freedom. What would it profit us if we should gain the whole world and suffer the loss of our own freedom, of our own persons? In a gospel parable, Jesus describes this tyranny of possessions.

> Jesus went on to say to them all: "Watch out and guard yourselves from every kind of greed; because a person's true life is not made up of the things he owns, no matter how rich he may be." Then Jesus told them this parable: "There was once a rich man who had land which bore good crops. He began to

> think to himself, 'I don't have a place to keep all my crops. What can I do? This is what I will do,' he told himself; 'I will tear down my barns and build bigger ones, where I will store the grain and all my other goods. Then I will say to myself, Lucky man! You have all the good things you need for many years. Take life easy, eat, drink, and enjoy yourself!' But God said to him, 'You fool! This very night you will have to give up your life; then who will get all these things you have kept for yourself?" And Jesus concluded, "This is how it is with those who pile up riches for themselves but are not rich in God's sight.

> *Luke 12:15–21 (GNB)*

Clenched Fists and Open Hands

There is an old adage, "We are all born with clenched fists, but we must all die with open hands." I personally like this symbolism of clenched fists and open hands. These two expressions aptly symbolize the spirits of possession and dispossession in incarnational Christian spirituality. I reach out to take into my hands the fullness of life and creation. But nothing is ever so fastened into my grasp that I cannot give it up. Nothing is really enjoyable unless we are free to release it, to give it up. Without this freedom we are possessed by our possessions. We become the slaves of our own addictions. We are not masters but mastered. Our spirits

"Watch out and guard yourselves from every kind of greed; because a person's true life is not made up of the things one owns, no matter how rich one may be."

are shackled and our souls are slowly shriveled. Recently I read a little story, a parable, that describes well what I am trying to say.

He asked me what I was looking for.

"Frankly," I said, "I'm looking for the Pearl of Great Price."

He slipped his hand into his pocket, drew it out, AND GAVE IT TO ME. It was just like that! I was dumbfounded. Then I began to protest: "You don't want to give it to *me*. Don't you want to keep it for yourself? But . . ." I said.

When I kept this up, he said finally, "Look, is it better to have the Pearl of Great Price, or to give it away?"

Well, now I have it. I don't tell anyone. From some there would just be disbelief and ridicule . . . Others would be jealous, or someone might steal it. Yes, I do have it, but there's that question—"Is it better to have it, or to give it away?" How long will that question rob me of my joy?[1]

The Biblical Imperative: Love Persons and Use Things

The biblical imperative is quite clear: We must *love* persons and *use* things. Jesus warns us that wherever our treasures are, there will also be our hearts. As I hear him, the Lord is saying, "Save your heart for love, and give your love only to persons: to the persons of

---

The biblical formula for a good life is this: "Love persons/Use things." When God made the world he say that is was very good. The world is charged, indeed, with the grandeur of God. And he calls upon us to join him in that pronouncement: "It is very good!" We are invited to use and to enjoy all God's good things. But we are warned: Don't ever let your heart be owned by things. If you love things, you will soon begin using persons to get, or get more of, the things you love. Save your heart for love, and save your love for persons.

The biblical imperative is illustrated by an example from the life of Martin Buber, the "I-Thou" philosopher. Buber directed his philosophical speculation toward "I-Thou" matters, toward the primacy of persons. after a very sad incident. A young man came to Buber's office one day, asking for some time. "I need to see you." Buber declined on the grounds that he was preparing a paper for delivery at a convention at a later date. That night the young man killed himself. His suicide touched Buber very deeply. In a renewed and painful way, he learned the importance of loving persons and using things.

This "Love persons/Use things" is a delicate equilibrium that is easily unbalanced. The moment that we start loving things we begin to use people to get the things we love. Consequently, the Bible does not say that "money is the root of all evil." it says that "love of money is the root of all evil." Where your treasure is there your heart will be. When we get hooked, for example, on praise and adulation, we allow entrance into our world only those who bring with them the necessary price of admission. When we get hooked on our own pleasures and satisfactions, we refuse to allow a place in our world for those who might be a burden or an inconvenience. We will not accept the challenge of love.

From *The Silent Holocaust*

---

yourself, your neighbor, and your God. Don't ever give your heart away to a thing. If you do, that thing, whatever it might be, will gradually become your master. It will own you and will lead you around on the leash of addiction.

[1] Theophane the Monk, *Tales of a Magic Monastery* (New York: Crossroad Publishing, 1981), p. 10.

Worry about it will keep you anxious and awake at night. But worst of all, if you give your heart away to a thing, you will soon begin the great inversion of priorities. When you begin to *love things*, you start to *use persons* to get those things, to get more and more of those things. And so, we notice that the Bible does not say that money is the root of all evil, but rather that love of money is the root of all evil. Having money isn't an evil, but giving your heart away to money is a tragedy. Wherever your treasure is, there your heart will be. If you give your heart away to the things of this world, you will soon begin competing with others to get all you can. You will begin to burn the candle at both ends in order to acquire more and more. It is the wide and well-traveled road to high blood pressure and ulcers, to anxiety and depression. If you choose to run down this road, you will eventually be tempted to cheat, to swindle, and to compromise your integrity for a "fast buck" or a "big deal."

The kingdom of God, which will be treated at length later on in this book, is an invitation on the part of God to belong to God in love. On our part, the kingdom of God is a response of love, a "yes" to this invitation. However, it is critically important to notice that the invitation of God is not extended to us individually as individuals. We are called into the People of God, into a faith community of love. We are invited to become a part of God's family. By the very nature of the invitation we can come to God only together; otherwise we cannot

come at all. This is the radical meaning of "Thy Kingdom come!" The bottom line is this: I cannot say my "yes" of responding love to God's invitation without saying a "yes" of love to you. It is impossible for me to love God and not to love you. Likewise it is impossible for you to love God without loving me. And so, as we have seen, Jesus tells us that if we come to place the gift of our love upon his altar, and we remember an unforgiving grudge, an estrangement from another, we should resolve that first. Only then are we invited to come and lay our gift of love upon God's altar. Jesus is very clear about this: We cannot love God without loving one another.

Sometimes, like a family squabbling over the material inheritance of a deceased relative, we are separated from this love of one another by the tyranny of things. You will remember the story of Jesus and the "rich young man." The poor fellow couldn't accept the invitation to follow Jesus in the kingdom because of his attachment to his possessions.

> Jesus said to him, "There is still one more thing you need to do. Sell all you have and give the money to the poor, and you will have riches in heaven; then come and follow me." But when the man heard this, he became very sad, because he was very rich. Jesus saw that he was sad and said, "How hard it is for rich people to enter the Kingdom of God! It is much harder for a rich person to enter the Kingdom of God than for a camel to go through the eye of a needle."
>
> *Luke 18:22–25 (GNB)*

We are called into the People of God, into a faith community of love.

The Tyranny of "Loved" Possessions

As I hear him, Jesus is saying that the tyranny of possessions is a very real danger: "Blessed are the poor in spirit . . ." means that only those will be truly happy who are ready to open their hands in dispossession. Happy are those who give their hearts only to love and who will give their love only to persons. Sometimes it is difficult for us to hear this message, just as it was for the rich young man. But if we fail to free ourselves from these attachments and addictions, it will mean the gradual death of love for one another; and this is what the kingdom of God is all about. When we begin to love things—whether they be material things such as money or immaterial things such as power, prestige, and status symbols—we will inevitably be trapped and enslaved. The people in our lives will soon begin to experience the sad truth: We do not really love them. Rather we love our "things." Our treasures and our hearts are elsewhere; they belong to our things.

I suspect that we have all experienced the difficulty of possessing without being possessed. When we got our first bicycle or car, the shiny new possession preoccupied our attention and concern. We were somehow diminished in our ability to think about the needs of others. Our availability to them and to their concerns was noticeably lessened. At the time, we could only think, "Heaven help anyone who puts a scratch on my bike or a dent in the fender of my car!"

I recall a story told to me by a young mother. It seems that she drove her children to the beach for a swim. When she finally got there in their ancient and balky family station wagon, the children eagerly flung open the doors, and one of the doors put a slight scratch on the BMW (Bavarian Motor Works = $40,000) in an adjoining parking space. The owner of the BMW, who was near his car, flew into an absolute rage, verbally scalding the children and abusing the young mother. "Do you know what this car costs?" he asked in a high-pitched scream. Finally, fearing for her own physical safety and the health of this poor outraged man, the young mother called a policeman, who had to look carefully before he finally found the almost undetectable scratch. The officer knitted his eyebrows and asked in puzzlement, "Is this what you are so excited about?" It is indeed difficult to be a rich man, to have many valuable possessions and still respond to the call and values of the kingdom. Where our treasures are, there our hearts will be, and the hands which are clutching many valued possessions do not open easily. And the simple fact is this: Open hands are needed to enter the kingdom of God.

I remember also an eighty-year-old millionaire telling me that he had slept only fitfully on the previous night. He explained that he himself wrote the radio commercials for his lucrative business, and it seems that he had tossed and turned his way through the dark hours of the previous night trying to think of a new commercial that would enrich him further.

> *Have I so invested my heart in any of these "untouchables" that I am diminished in my capacity to love myself, my neighbor, and my God!*

"The commercials," he observed, "bring in a lot of money, you know." I remember the heavy sadness I felt for this financially wealthy but personally impoverished old man. He had invested his heart in the currency of this world. He had deposited his soul in earthly banks. "Here you are," I thought, "worth many millions of dollars and you are near the end of your life. Still, you are losing sleep and turning your soul inside out in search of clever gimmicks that will make you even richer. You do not own your money, you poor old man; your money owns you."

The same kind of possessive addiction is possible, of course, with nonmaterial things: prestige, power, success, honor, reputation, public admiration, the pleasure of the senses, triumphs over and conquests of other people. I recall a televised interview with Jackie Cooper who had been a movie star as a child. Cooper reflected that most of the child stars of his day had become seriously embittered adults. When asked to explain this pervasive bitterness, he suggested that these people had once been the center of attention. They once stood in center stage, in front of the footlights, and had been given star billing and all that goes with it. Now, as the shadows of their lives began to lengthen, they were deprived of these things. The glitter of their early careers had disappeared. People ask about them only in the questions of "old movie trivia games." The loss of center stage and the bright lights is deeply painful and saddening for them, in the opinion of Cooper. Emotionally these child stars now feel cheated. Angry, they would like to demand a restoration of their lost star status.

A Personal Inventory

We could go on and on, of course. But the only really pertinent questions for me are these: Am I possessed and dominated by things? Where have I invested my heart? Have I so given my heart to a personal gift or to a piece of property that my capacity to love others, to be concerned for their needs and available to their requests, is proportionately diminished? These are questions, I think, that all of us who devoutly wish to be included in the kingdom of God must ask ourselves.

On the general principle that it is not wise to ask another to do what you yourself are unwilling to do, I would like to share with you my own list of "untouchables." As I was compiling this list I asked myself this question: Of all the things that are part of "the world" as I experience it, which would be the hardest for me to give up, to be without? Which of the gifts in my life do I regard as most important to my happiness? Here is my list:

1. Mental and emotional health
2. Physical health, especially eyesight
3. Faith and the meaning it gives to my life
4. My sharing in the priesthood of Jesus
5. Membership in the Society of Jesus
6. The nearness of several friends with whom I can be totally open and feel totally safe

7. Love of beauty and the gift of self-expression

8. The acknowledgment of others that I am a sincere and caring person

9. A sense of success: the knowledge that I am actually accomplishing at least in part what I would like to do with my life

10. A sense of humor and the spirit of enthusiasm.

The Bottom-Line Question

Now to the critical, subsequent questions: Have I so invested my heart in any of these "untouchables" that I am diminished in my capacity to love myself, my neighbor, and my God? Am I ready to open my hands to God, saying, "Thy will be done!" or am I rather insisting that God let me have my way and my will? Is there something on my list that I simply couldn't live without? This business of open hands is neither simple nor easy. For myself, I would expect that if God did in fact ask the surrender of one of my "untouchables," I would experience my own agony in the garden. However, I hope that with God's grace I could say, as Jesus did, "Nevertheless, not as I will but as you will. Thy will be done." I know that I can manage this only "with God's grace"; I know I could not do it on my own. Whenever I read the story of the rich young man in the gospels, I feel an easy and quick empathy for him. He was invited to go sell all that he had and to follow Jesus. It was no doubt the opportunity of a lifetime, but he was sad

because he had many possessions. I feel very sad for him because he missed the opportunity of his lifetime, but at the same time I think I understand something about his sadness. In my own way I think I have experienced it.

God's Tests in Our Lives

Once a brother priest told me that shortly before he was supposed to be ordained to the priesthood, he took a tranquilizer prescribed by a doctor to relieve the tension of "ordination jitters." By a strange biochemical irregularity, for him the tranquilizer proved to be a stimulant. He returned to the doctor and reported the deterioration of his condition. The well-intentioned doctor consequently doubled the dosage, and soon the young man's vision became clouded and his nervousness seriously worsened. Aware of these developments, the superior of the seminary called him into his office and sympathetically but firmly informed him that he could not be ordained.

My friend told me that he went to his room, knelt down at the side of his bed, and thrashed his arms down across the bed again and again, protesting, "Oh, God, you can't do this to me. You can't take thirteen of the best years of my life and then, within arm's reach of ordination, take it all away from me!" The agonized protest soon became a litany: "You can't . . . you can't . . . !" Finally, exhausted and emotionally spent, he fell across the bed and whispered, "But, of course, you can.

You can do anything you choose to do. You are my God. I am your creature. Thy will be done."

Then he added something that I did not anticipate: "It was the first time in my life that I had ever experienced complete peace. There were still many unanswered questions throbbing in my head, but my heart knew only the peace of surrender." Later, as the pages of the calendar were turned, the painful questions were answered in time and the young man was granted his desired goal of ordination. But the lesson of peace in the open hands of surrender will be with him all the days of his life.

Something similar once took place in my own life. In a sense it continues to happen in my life. In my early twenties, I visited an eye doctor, an ophthalmologist, for the first time. He seemed to be looking into each of my eyes, searching with his small beam of light, for a very long time. Finally, he stood back and, not looking at me, he asked if I knew about the condition of my eyes. When I responded that I did not, he said softly and somewhat sadly, "Someday very probably you will be blind."

The immediate result in me was an earthquake of shock. Like a sudden crack of lightning, I experienced a thousand painful emotions. No doubt the poor doctor sensed these reactions. Sympathetically, he told me that I was suffering from an inherited, congenital decomposition of the retina, called *retinitis pigmentosa*. He told me that there was no certain prognosis. "Many people with this disease," he explained, "are already blind at your age. Some have

partial vision all their lives." Then he added that I would probably receive some warning in the gradual loss of peripheral vision and the increase of night blindness. "If and when you have only tunnel vision, I would strongly advise that at that point you learn braille before you go blind."

I remember the heaviness and the fear, the grief of anticipation over the possible loss of vision. Leaving the doctor's office, I remember walking down the sunlit street trying to memorize all the visual beauty of that spring day. "Learn braille before you go blind . . ." played repeatedly on the tape recorder of my mind. I wondered how long it would be before I could no longer see the blue sky, the white clouds, the green leaves and grass, the faces of the people I love. I wondered what it would be like to make life's journey by night, stumbling around in a dark world. I recalled also a very emotionally stirring picture I had once cut out of a magazine and saved. It was the picture of a blind man, with white cane and tin cup, feeling along Park Avenue in New York City. The sign he wore read, "Please help me. My days are darker than your nights."

Of course, God has asked the surrender of vision from many other people. Some who are afflicted with my disease have been blind since childhood. For various reasons some people are born blind. They have never seen the sky, the clouds, the color green, the radiance of springtime, and the solemn, sad beauty of autumn. They have never seen the faces of those they love. But here was God

Jesus does remind us that we are pilgrims passing through this world.

warning me that he might ask me to return this precious gift of sight. Here was God asking me to hold out to him my own open hands.

I have often thought that the most common cause of our human inner turmoil is conflict of desires. Our highest expectations and our deepest desires are always struggling with reality. We conceive our own desires, make our own plans, and then hope that there will be a yellow brick road leading straight to fulfillment. Sadly, such success is often not in the script. We stumble and fail to achieve, we lose the contest we wanted so badly to win, and we have to give up the things we would so much like to keep. I have often wondered what it would be like if I wanted only the will of God, if I really took Jesus seriously, if I were really blessed by being poor in spirit, if my hands were open and held out in the readiness to surrender, if . . . "Is it really better to have the Pearl of Great Price or to give it away?"

Just as God did not ask the surrender of the priesthood from my friend, he may not ask my vision from me. It has been thirty years since the original diagnosis, and my vision is still adequate. However, the impairment of vision that I do experience, the loss of peripheral vision and the limitations of night blindness, is a daily reminder: The fullness of personal peace can be experienced only in the full surrender of my will and my desires to the will and desire of God. This is the theology of dispossession, the emptiness waiting to be filled by the presence of God. This is the price and the reward of open hands.

The Clenched Fists: Our Ability to Enjoy God's Gifts

But there is also a question at the other end of the spectrum. It is the question of clenched fists, the theology of possession. I am convinced that God wants us to use and to enjoy the beautiful world that God has made, to join in the pronouncement: "It is very good!" You and I have to reflect upon our vision of the world and ask about our capacity to enjoy, to find God's goodness in the good things of creation.

Jesus does remind us that we are pilgrims passing through this world, that this is not our lasting city. He assures us that in the end we shall be judged on how well we have loved. However, while warning us not to become attached to the good things we will experience along the pathways of our lives, Jesus does urge us to use and to enjoy these good things. We are to "find God" in all these things.

Virtue, the Romans used to say, stands in the middle. We must be able to use and to enjoy, to experience God's beautiful world of creation without ever being dominated by any of God's creatures. We must always remain free, never letting anything own us or make our decisions for us. Such cherished freedom is possessed only by the poor in spirit, the people of open hands.

The middle ground is this: to use and to enjoy, to experience and to admire God's world (the clenched fists) and at the same time to remain free from the domination of any creature, so that the love of our hearts may be given to God, our neighbor, and ourselves (the open hands).

The Biblical Imperative: Problems on Both Sides

Again, the biblical imperative: We are meant to use and enjoy the good things of God's creation, but to love only persons. Love persons, use things. For most of us, I would suspect, there are difficulties on both sides. Average people are said to use only about 10 percent of their potential to enjoy and to use fully the good things God has given

us. However, I would suspect that most of us also tend to clutch our possessions and gifts so tightly that when age or death demands surrender, our fingers have to be pried open. We are not ready to open our own hands.

Jesus compares death to two things: *a bridegroom* coming to claim his bride and *a thief in the night* coming to rob us of our possessions. I would think that whichever of these will be for each of us depends on our attitude toward this world. If we have used and enjoyed the good gifts of God along the journey of life but never held them tightly as our hearts' treasure, we have maintained the open hands of surrender. In this case death will be the *bridegroom* coming to bring his bride to the eternal banquet of celebration.

On the other hand, if we have given our hearts to earthly treasures and possessions, then death will come to us as the *thief* in the night, wrenching out of our tightly closed hands all that we have ever loved. This is the sadness about which Jesus warns us when he instructs us to love persons and to use things.

I have a deeply committed Christian friend who once wrote to me:

> I pray for you each day. And my prayer is that you will never be either rich or famous. Money and fame can so easily seduce us from our Christian calling. When we have a lot of money invested in the stocks and bonds of this world, it becomes so easy to pass over the human interest stories to get to the financial section of our newspapers. I thank God for your vow of poverty. And I do pray that you will be spared "celebrity status." Personal fame is really an inversion for a Christian. No one should ever be famous as a Christian. We should want our Jesus to be well known and famous, not ourselves.

Of course, my friend is right, even though something in me snickers: "With friends like this, who needs enemies?" All of us to some extent experience the seduction of various vanities, and we know that it must be a decision renewed every day, to love persons and to use things, to use and enjoy the good things of God's creation without being owned by any of them.

Security Operations: Playing It Safe and Having Enough

In the last years of my dear mother's life, she suffered from a seriously immobilizing arthritis. There were times when I would carry her up and down the stairs of our family home in Chicago. The routine was predictably regular. We would descend several steps, and then Mother would extend her hand and firmly grasp the banister. The dialogue that followed always went like this:

"Mama, you have to let go. We can't move unless you let go."

"I'm afraid you'll drop me."

"If you don't let go, I'm going to count to three and drop you. One . . . two . . ."

Mother always let go after the count of two, and then we could descend several more steps. However, after we had progressed several more steps, we rehearsed the same procedure and dialogue. Mama would grab the banister and I would warn her of her impending doom if she didn't let go.

On one such occasion, I reflected that the exchange between my mother and me must be something like the exchange between me and the Lord. Of course, he's got the whole world in his hands, including me, and he's moving me along to my desired destiny. However, I keep grabbing and holding on to the "security banisters" that help me feel safe.

We must be able to use and to enjoy, to experience God's beautiful world of creation without ever being dominated by any of God's creatures.

Jesus reminds me that we can't move as long as I hold on so tightly to the little gifts, possessions, and achievements that are part of my security operation. I hear him clearly asking me to "let go . . . ," but out of my ever-honest stomach comes the painful whimper: "I'm afraid you'll drop me." I am frightened by the prospect of open hands. What if I do say the "yes" of surrender? What will happen to me?

Security is such a deep need in us, isn't it? We have all those trembling and disquieting questions pulsing through our nerves and muscles: What will happen to me if I let go? Will I have enough—enough time, enough money, enough provisions for old age, enough people to care for me, enough intelligence, enough health . . . ? And so I hold on tightly to my security banisters. They make me feel safe. But they keep me stationary. They are an obstacle to grace.

The Lord must smile upon me as I once did upon my dear little mother, who was afraid I might drop her. He must want to meet my nervous, tremulous questions about "enough" with a comforting but challenging, "Trust me. I WILL BE YOUR ENOUGH!"

When we love another person, our love sometimes takes the form of comfort and sometimes the form of challenge. Jesus, who loves us, is both of these for us: a comfort and a challenge. There is an inestimable comfort in his presence and the reassurances of his unconditional love. There is also an endless challenge in his request for trust: "Let go. I will be your enough!" It is the challenge of love, asking for our open hands. There will be so many moments in your life and mine, like the stations along my mother's stairway, when we will let go and experience the freedom of being able to move. There will also be times of white knuckles, trembling fears about personal security, and not enough trust to "let go and let God."

"Love persons, use things!" This is the truth that will set us free if we only put it into practice. We must gamble on the gospel formula for happiness. Putting these insights into practice repeatedly will eventually make them habits, make them permanent attitudes. And then we will be truly Christian because our attitudes regulate our choices and our responses to life. Ultimately our attitudes will dictate the outcome of our lives.

An Irish Legend

Once there was a time, according to legend, when Ireland was ruled by kings and the reigning king had no sons. So he sent out his couriers to post signs on the trees in all the towns of his kingdom. The signs advised that every qualified young man should apply for an interview with the king as a possible successor to the throne. However, all such applicants must have these two qualifications: They must (1) love God and (2) love their fellow human beings.

The young man about whom this legend centers saw the signs and reflected that he indeed loved God and his fellow human beings. However, he was so poor that he had no clothes that would be presentable in the sight of the king. Nor did he have the means to buy

Love persons, use things! This is the truth that will set us free.

provisions for the journey to the castle. So he begged and borrowed until at last he had enough money for the appropriate clothes and the necessary provisions. Eventually he set out for the castle, and had almost completed his journey when he came upon a poor beggar by the side of the road. The beggar sat trembling, clad only in rags. His extended arms pleaded for help. His weak voice quietly asked, "I'm hungry and I'm cold. Would you please help me?"

The young man was so moved by the need of the poor beggar that he immediately stripped off his new clothes and put on the rags of the beggar. Without a second thought he gave the beggar all his provisions. Then, somewhat uncertainly, he proceeded to the castle in the rags of the beggar and without any provision for his journey home. Upon his arrival at the castle, an attendant to the king showed him in. After a long wait, he was finally admitted to the throne room of the king.

The young man bowed low before his king. When he raised his eyes, he was filled with astonishment.

"You . . . you were the beggar by the side of the road."

"Yes," replied the king, "I was that beggar."

"But you are not really a beggar. You are really the king."

"Yes, I am really the king."

"Why did you do this to me?" the young man asked.

"Because I had to find out if you really do love, if you really love God and your fellow human beings. I knew that if I came to you as king, you would have been very much impressed by my crown of gold and my regal robes. You would have done anything I asked because of my kingly appearance. But that way I would never have known what is really in your heart. So I came to you as a beggar, with no claims on you except for the love in your heart. And I have found out that you truly do love God and your fellow human beings. You will be my successor. You will have my kingdom!"

The Legend in Matthew's Gospel: The Last Judgment

This legend from Irish folklore reminds me of the twenty-fifth chapter in Saint Matthew's Gospel. There Jesus is describing the final judgment day of this world.

"Then the King will say to the people on his right, 'Come, you that are blessed by my Father! Come and possess the kingdom which has been prepared for you ever since the creation of the world. I was hungry and you fed me, thirsty and you gave me a drink; I was a stranger and you received me in your homes, naked and you clothed me; I was sick and you took care of me, in prison and you visited me.'"

At this the just are puzzled. They ask the Lord:

"'When, Lord, did we ever see you hungry and feed you, or thirsty and give you a drink? When did we ever see you a stranger and welcome you in our homes, or naked and clothe you? When did we ever see you sick or in prison, and visit you?'"

Matthew 25:34–39 (GNB)

> *"When, Lord, did we ever see you hungry and feed you, or thirsty and give you a drink?"*
>
> Matthew 25:34

The reply of Jesus, in effect, is this: "I was the stranger by the side of the road of your life. I came to you, not in the majesty and splendor of God, but as a poor and simple beggar. I had no claims on you except for the love in your heart. I had to find out if you could open your hands and heart to the needs of your neighbor. Where your treasure is, there your heart will be, and I had to find out where your heart was.

I have found great love in your heart. And so, you shall have a place in my kingdom forever. You will possess the joy that human eyes have never seen, that human ears have never heard, that the human imagination has never dared to dream. Come, my Beloved, into your Father's house, where I have prepared a special place just for you."

In the end, on the last day and in that final judgment, one thing alone will be important: On that day we shall all be judged on love. Our eternal destiny will depend on the love that Jesus the King finds in our hearts—the love that opened its hands to give away the things of time, the love that opened its hands to surrender human security and all of its banisters, to say yes to Jesus and to all the members of his kingdom.

The Vision of the World: A Summary

According to the vision proposed to us by Jesus, the committed Christian will not see this world as a source of temptation and be led to flee from it. The Christian believer knows that all those things which the Lord has made are good. However, while seeking and finding the goodness of God in all things, Christians will never become so wedded to this world through which they are passing that they cannot surrender it in open hands at the request of God or at the need of their neighbor. Christians will be fully alive in their senses, emotions, minds, and hearts. They will reach out to embrace life with all their powers. But always Christians will remain free, free from the domination and enslavement that results when we invert the biblical imperative, when we begin to love things and to use people to gain the further possession of those things. Where our treasures are, there our hearts will be. The Christian saves his or her heart for love, and that love is kept for God, one's neighbor, and oneself. In the spirit of possession and dispossession, the Christian will then enter into the kingdom of God.

So I ask myself: "If I were ever to be arrested for being a Christian, would there be enough evidence to convict me?"

In the next chapter, we will develop more fully the spirit of possession. Many of us find that we have a more difficult time "letting go" of the world, while others of us have a more difficult time "enjoying God's good world." As Christians who are called to be fully human and fully alive, we must live with "open hands" (dispossession) and "clenched fists" (possession). To be Christ-like, we are to love persons and enjoy things. In order to help us understand and practice the spirit of possession even more, we will look at (a) enjoyments as a mind-set, (b) some inhibitors that undermine enjoyment, and lastly (c) ways of learning to enjoy the good things of life.

FOR FURTHER REFLECTION
Chapter 18: The Grandeur of God

Review

1. Define (a) "the world," (b) "the spirit of possession," and (c) "the spirit of dispossession."
2. What is the "biblical imperative"? Comment on how this imperative summarizes the spirits of possession and dispossession.
3. According to Victor Frankl, life asks us questions. In other words, life exposes to us our attitudes. In what ways does life ask us questions about our attitudes toward the world?
4. What is the Christian vision of the world? In order to "put on the mind of Christ," how should a Christian see the world in the context of individuals who are fully alive in mind, emotions, senses, heart, and will, and who follow the biblical imperative?
5. How does Powell's Irish legend remind you of Jesus' description of the Last Judgment (found in Matthew 25)? How are the messages from these two stories saying the same thing?

Discuss

1. Why does Powell combine material things and immaterial things (personal qualities, abilities, and attainments) in his definition of "world"? In what ways can even immaterial things possess us and diminish our capacity to love?
2. Of all your immaterial possessions, which are you most grateful for?
3. Of all your material possessions, to which do you feel most strongly attached?
4. If you were to make a list of ten "untouchables" (material or immaterial possessions), which of these untouchables would you have the hardest time letting go of? How might this untouchable lessen your capacity to love yourself, others, and God?

5. When you meet people considerably wealthier than you, are your emotional reactions and resultant behavior different from when you are meeting people at your own economic level or less well off than you? What does your reaction indicate about your attitude?
6. If you were to lose a physical ability—for example, the use of a leg or arm, your eyesight, or your hearing—then what attitude might serve as a healthy way to deal with that loss? How might vision therapy help?

Scripture Activity

"God looked at everything he had made, and he was very pleased." (Genesis 1:31, GNB)

"[Jesus said:] "Love your neighbor as you love yourself." (Matthew 22:39, GNB)

Write a prayer of thanksgiving to the Lord. Recall all the material and immaterial possessions you have, and offer sincere thanks to God for them. Lastly, in order to show that you are more interested in the kingdom of God than in acquiring things for yourself, share with the Lord what you intend to do today for someone who is in need.

Processing These Ideas about the Christian Vision of the World

The spirits of possession and dispossession. Reflect upon your own vision (attitudes) about the world. Determine—according to how you respond emotionally, physically, or behaviorally—whether you have a harder time "enjoying God's good world and living a full life" (possession) or whether you have a more difficult time "letting go of your possessions" (dispossession). As a conclusion, attempt to get in touch with your underlying vision that makes the spirits of possession or dispossession harder for you.

19 We Must Learn to Enjoy the Good Things of Life

A glad heart is excellent medicine, but a spirit depressed wastes the bones away.

Proverbs 17:22
Jerusalem Bible

Enjoyment Is Also an Inside Job

Just as happiness comes from a source inside each of us, so does enjoyment. As the old Roman philosopher Epictetus tried to tell his contemporaries, "It's all in the way you look at it." Remember the two men who looked out of prison bars; one saw mud, the other stars. Enjoyment is more a mind-set than a set of circumstances. Enjoyment is actually more a choice than a chance. We all know that some people enjoy life much more than others do. And I think we all know that those who enjoy life are not necessarily more gifted or fortunate than the joyless. It's just that some have their interior dials set to enjoy life, while others seem to insist on struggling through life.

The intention to enjoy seems to be one of those attitudes or mind-sets that is with us from childhood. It almost seems that we came into this world asking, "What is life for?"

Somehow the answer got filled in, and we drew our own conclusions. Of course, it is impossible to say where or from whom we got the answer to our question. The important thing is that we did get an answer. What we heard may not have been what was said, but it did become our answer. It set our expectations, told us what to anticipate. The rest of our lives has been a self-fulfilling prophecy.

Eventually we learned to look at reality, at life itself, through the lenses of this developed mind-set. We came to expect life to be enjoyable or difficult. We woke up each day with this mind-set, and it colored all our days and all our experiences. Sometimes it is very hard for us to admit, but through this mind-set we ourselves have shaped and determined our own experiences. We have made our experiences, our days, and our lives happy or sad. Please understand that the basic attitude or mind-set was probably programmed into us very early in life. It was the result of suggestions from others and of our interpretation of these suggestions. In any case, this attitude or mind-set gradually became a part of us and has set the dials of our minds to struggle or to enjoy, or something in-between.

We are all pilgrims making a journey and we should try to enjoy the trip.

The Adult Children of Alcoholics and Early Programming

One of the more recent developments in the field of alcoholism recovery is a group called ACOA, the Adult Children of Alcoholics. Two college students whom I recognized as children of alcoholics helped me to understand what happens. In both cases the fathers had stopped drinking while the students were in early adolescence. However, the messages from an actively alcoholic parent were already recorded on the so-called parent tapes of both. The students described these messages as follows: "Don't touch . . . don't talk . . . don't get close to anyone . . . don't allow yourself to feel . . . don't touch or allow yourself to be touched . . . always stay on the alert and be ready to adjust to the unpredictable."

Of course, each adult child of an alcoholic looks and reacts differently, but in general, life is colorless through these lenses. There seems to be an emotional numbness, a fear of relating to others, a distrust of one's own reactions. Sometimes it looks as though the whole world is having a large and happy picnic. The adult child of an alcoholic doesn't feel invited. He or she stands alone, looking sadly through the fence.

The adult child of an alcoholic, like all of us, must readjust and revise. It can be done, but old habits will have to be unlearned and new habits will have to be practiced. Experiment with the next hour of your life. Decide that you are going to enjoy it. Determine that you will appreciate the good things of that hour, that you will take advantage of the opportunities offered in that next hour. Every time you do this, you will be cultivating the habit of enjoyment. Eventually this habit will become a permanent mind-set.

Once I taught a young woman who seemed to be very gifted. She was intellectually bright, physically beautiful, athletically talented. However, the expression on her face was always strained and pained. When she came in to talk to me, I mentioned that her face belied her goodness and giftedness. She explained to me that she knew all about it. "You see," she said, "I am adopted. My adoptive parents never told me this, but I always thought that if I ever displeased them, I would have to go back to the orphanage. I was always walking on eggshells. I felt sure of no one's love."

So she was spending her life continuing to walk on eggshells. She was trying not to displease people. She was afraid that they would send her back to the orphanage. It was again a case of an inherited vision in need of revision. But fortunately that revision is now in process, and the person in question is gradually being transformed into a happy person capable of enjoyment.

In ACOA meetings, letting someone else deprive you of happiness is called "stinkin' thinkin'." We worry about all the wrong things, we sweat the small stuff, and we become preoccupied with deadlines and worried about decisions. We allow other things and persons to deprive us of the enjoyment of life that is God's will.

A Woman Named Betty and a Man Named Frank

A former student of mine, a quiet and reserved young woman, came back to see me. We chatted for a few moments, and then I asked her if she was using her R.N. (nursing) degree. "No," she replied. "You see, I am dying. I have terminal leukemia." Of course, I gasped. When I recovered from the shock, I asked Betty what it was like. "What is it like to be twenty-four, when you think that your whole life lies ahead of you, and then suddenly you are counting the days left?" In her usual reserved and peaceful way, she replied, "I'm not sure that I can explain this, but these are the happiest days of my life. When you think that there are years ahead, it is so easy to put things off. You say

to yourself, 'I'll stop and smell the flowers next spring.' But when you know that the days of your life are limited, you stop to smell the flowers and to feel the warm sunlight *today*. Because of the disease I am suffering from, I have had several spinal taps. It is a painful procedure. However, my boyfriend held my hand during these spinal taps. I think I was more aware of the comfort of his hand in mine than of the needle being inserted into my spine."

We talked for a long time about dying and the perspectives it affords for full living. I had always heard that no one can live fully unless that person knows that life will someday come to an end. Betty helped me to understand why that is true. She is dead now. Leukemia eventually claimed her life.

Each of us has an inferiority complex. When we compare ourselves with others, failure can become the color of our days.

But she left me with a deeper understanding of the need to enjoy all the good things of this life. It was as if God was saying to me through her, "You are a pilgrim making a journey, but do try to enjoy the trip."

Another person who has helped me to understand the mind-set of enjoyment was a man named Frank. Everyone liked Frank. He was warm and kind. He was always smiling. Frank liked "little people" as much as he appreciated "little things." Then Frank suddenly died. Although he had at one time been rather wealthy, Frank did not leave much of an estate in property or investments. But much like Betty, Frank had left me a last legacy. It was two pages of "A List of My Special Pleasures." Good old Frank had actively cultivated his capacity to enjoy by listing his daily joys. He worked all his adult life at the "mind-set" of enjoyment. He had set the dials of his mind to enjoy all the humor, the rainbows and butterflies of life. According to his list, Frank enjoyed many things during his days on this earth, including scenic trails, sunrises, writing congratulatory notes, birds in flight, picture albums, the Boston Pops orchestra, playing Scrabble in front of a fireplace. The last four entries on his long list were all the same: "ice cream, ice cream, ice cream, ice cream." I'm sure that Frank had his private sufferings, but somehow he always managed to enjoy the good things of life. In this he will always be an important role model for me.

> *We allow other things and persons to deprive us of the enjoyment of life that is God's will.*

A Roll Call of Demons

I am sure that the mind-set of enjoyment cannot be an overlay type of mind-set. It cannot be used as a simple coverup for gloom and struggle. That would be putting one mask over another. We must first get in touch with the reasons we hold back from enjoyment. Psychologists have a picnic with this subject. There are so many possible reasons that can diminish our capacity for enjoyment. Each of us must explore our own inner spaces to exorcise our own personal demons. In *The Screwtape Letters,* C. S. Lewis describes the instructions of the chief devil to his henchmen. "Tempt this person in this way, but with this other person, don't use that technique. It would be wasted. Try this approach," and so forth. I'm sure that each of us is tempted by a unique and tailor-made obstacle to enjoyment.

With some of us, it may be a direct message from our childhood. It may be that no one ever told us, but we concluded from what we saw and experienced, that life is not to be enjoyed. Morbid messages heard and recorded by us during our early years tend to keep playing in us for life, unless we identify and disown them. We might have heard things like: "Life is a struggle. Don't expect a break from anyone. Wait till you get out in the cold, cruel world. You'll see."

Many of us are self-punishing. We remember chapter and verse of all our mistakes. We keep a librarian's record of our sins. One great psychiatrist says that there may be a God in heaven who forgives us our sins, but we are much more reluctant to forgive ourselves. It is as though we have judged ourselves and recorded our failures in every muscle, fiber, and brain cell of our being. A guilt complex is certainly one of the enjoyment inhibitors with which many of us human beings have to contend.

Elsewhere we have discussed the terrible toll of perfectionism. We called it "a suicide course" because it certainly deprives us of the fullness of life. Because we are not perfect, and because nothing we do is ever perfect, we leave ourselves only room for failure. And when failure becomes the color of our days and nights, discouragement and depression soon close in on us.

Every one of us has an inferiority complex. Those who do not seem to have one are only pretending. Their pretense may even become self-deceptive, but it is a deception. We all have areas of insecurity. Inferiority is a relative term. It is the opposite or counterpart of superiority. Inferiority always implies comparison. I compare myself with others. I find that others are smarter, better looking, more capable, or more virtuous than I am. Comparison is always the beginning of inferiority feelings. And it is almost impossible to enjoy anything else when we do not enjoy ourselves.

All-or-nothing thinking can also undermine enjoyment. For example, I could reason that because I am not all that I should be, I must be nothing. Or because I am not completely honest, I must be a total phony. It takes a little quiet time and some reflection to be comfortable as a fraction, but that is what we all are. Part of us is good and beautiful, but there is another part that remains unconverted. Part of us is light and part of us is dark. Part believes, another part doubts. Part is loving, part is selfish. Now, what we have called all-or-nothing thinking does not tolerate fractions very well. It does not like the gray area between black and white. And this all-or-nothing thinking doesn't even know the word *process,* let alone the reality. It obviously doesn't relish gradual growth and change because it wants to be all one cut of cloth, without shades and nuances of color. It has an enormous capacity to diminish and deny happiness. Everything has to go completely well, everyone has to be won over and convinced, and every grade has to be an *A* or it's the dark night of the soul.

Finally, we should check out our assumptions. Some of us have built our lives on irrational assumptions. For example, "I can't enjoy myself when I am alone." These irrational assumptions of ours have a way of turning into self-fulfilling prophecies. The person who assumes that there is no happiness in solitude will never be happy when alone. The person who assumes that other persons and things make us happy will always be disappointed in the end. Perhaps the most fatal assumption is to believe that "I am this way and that is that!" I remember having long discussions with a man who felt that since his early life was unhappy, he was doomed and destined to a life of unhappiness. Whenever I suggested that he could change, he protested that I was not listening. It was very difficult to shake his assumption.

> *Part of us is good and beautiful, but there is another part that remains unconverted.*

Driving Out the Demons

Behavior modification theorists assure us that we can change without understanding exactly how we got into our "denial-of-enjoyment" condition. The only important thing is to change, and this can be done by contriving a system of rewards and punishments. For example, let us suppose that your personal demon, whatever it is, rears its ugly head. If you win and enjoy something despite your demon, reward yourself.

Obviously (to me), it will help us to understand the nature of our problem. If I have an otherwise very pleasant evening, but allow one small incident to ruin everything, I should really try to get in touch with why I do this. Let us suppose that only one person in a large group doesn't seem to like me, although everyone else does. Let us further suppose that I get upset by this one person. This would seem to be a matter for personal investigation. Someone has said that if you name your demon, you tame it. It would be most helpful, I would think, to name and expose the little demon in charge of denying delight to me. As one psychiatrist put it: "We all know we could be happy, but there is always a big *if* or a big *but*. Well, I say it's time for us to get off our *buts*." What are the "ifs" and "buts" that limit my enjoyment of life? Sometimes, if the insight comes clearly and powerfully enough, it can bring with it a life-transforming effect.

Once I produced a long listing of the masks people wear. I gave the wearers nicknames, like Elmer Egghead, Peppermint Patty the People Pleaser, Dennis Doormat, Polly Porcupine. My hope was that each of us could find the mask we were wearing and proceed to take it off. Many friends of mine reported, "But I see a little of myself in all of your descriptions." When I thought about it, I had to agree. I also saw a little of myself in each of the proposed masks. I think I played each of the roles depending on the circumstances, and so forth.

When I go over the delight-denying demons, I see that all of them bother me at some time or another. But there is one, perfectionism, that seems to be my major problem. It then becomes a matter of divide and conquer. I have isolated my tendency to be a helper-rescuer-enabler and my penchant for perfectionism. Now I am working on them. I know that it is a question of gradual change, unlearning old and practiced habits and replacing them with new and life-giving habits. So, I am trying to be patient, but this is hard for us perfectionists. However, I have to be honest and say that every little victory seems to brighten the sky of my world and to widen my capacity for enjoyment and the fullness of life. And with the passage of time, I seem to enjoy the journey more and more.

Remember You will someday be called to account for all the legitimate pleasures you failed to enjoy. So, go ahead, Pilgrim, enjoy the journey!

> *The person who assumes that there is no happiness in solitude will never be happy when alone.*

FOR FURTHER REFLECTION

Chapter 19: We Must Learn to Enjoy the Good Things of Life

Review

1. Explain: "Enjoyment is more a mind-set than a set of circumstances."
2. From where and how does one acquire a mind-set or attitude of enjoyment or lack of enjoyment?
3. What mind-set or attitude is helpful for learning to enjoy the good things of life?
4. In what way is it "stinkin' thinkin'" to let other people deprive us of happiness?
5. How are "Betty" and "Frank" examples of people who learned to enjoy the good things of life? What do these two examples imply about the role of attitude in determining the quality of one's life?
6. Comment on how the following "inhibitors of enjoyment" affect one's capacity to enjoy the good things of life: (a) childhood messages, (b) self-punishing guilt, (c) perfectionism, (d) an inferiority complex, (e) all-or-nothing thinking, and (f) irrational assumptions.

Discuss

Enjoyment is certainly an essential part of the fullness of life. Each person draws enjoyment, however, from his or her own special sources: from wandering through a forest, reading a book, playing a sport or musical instrument, conversing with a friend, and so on. There is a special reward of peace at the end of a "perfect day," a day filled with these special sources of gratification.

1. The Talmud states that "everyone will be called to account for all the legitimate pleasures they have failed to enjoy." What is the difference between legitimate pleasures and selfish pleasures?
2. If you received news that you were to die within the next few months, how would you live your life differently in order to get the most enjoyment out of life?

Scripture Activity

"An argument broke out among the disciples as to which one of them was the greatest. Jesus knew what they were thinking, so he took a child, stood him by his side, and said to them, 'Whoever welcomes this child in my name, welcomes me; and whoever welcomes me, welcomes the one who sent me. For the one who is least among you all is the greatest.' " (Luke 9:46–48, GNB)

Read the passage and summarize its main point. Tell how it relates to the chapter, and share one or two ways that you will give yourself the gift of one hour this week to do something you particularly enjoy.

Processing These Ideas about Enjoying the Good Things of LIfe

Name your demon. Which of the devils discussed seems to haunt your personal premises most often and undermine your capacity for enjoyment?

1. *Parent tapes* (the messages that keep playing inside your head). Specifically, what are these messages?
2. *A guilt complex.* Do you think you are self-punishing? Do you hate yourself for your mistakes? Do you rehash your regrets?
3. *Perfectionism.* Do you attach your value to your productivity? Do you believe that you ought to be perfect? Is it important for you to impress and please others? Do you get discouraged by failure?
4. *Inferiority complex.* Do you feel inferior to many others to whom you compare yourself? How do you measure your worth? Do you believe that you are who you are supposed to be, and fully equipped to do what you are supposed to do?
5. *All-or-nothing thinking.* Do you really believe in slow growth and process? Are there gray areas for you, or just black and white? If you tell the truth a hundred times and lie once, what would you call yourself: a truth teller or a liar?
6. *Irrational assumptions.* Are there any enjoyment-denying assumptions from which you proceed? Do you really believe that you are supposed to be happy?

Part Seven

The Christian Vision

of God

20 *God Revealed in Jesus*

We ourselves know and believe the love which God has for us. God is love, and whoever lives in love lives in union with God and God lives in union with him. . . . There is no fear in love; perfect love drives out all fear.

1 John 4:16, 18 (GNB)

Two Exercises and Two Traditions

Back in Chapter 7, "The Christian Vision of Self," you were asked to see yourself sitting in a chair, face-to-face with yourself. It was an exercise of imagination, an attempt to evaluate your self-image. Before we get into this chapter on God, it might be good to repeat the exercise, but this time you are asked to see Jesus in that chair. So once more, warm up your imagination. Visualize the chair and then see a couple of people well known to yourself come successively and sit in that chair. Finally, let Jesus come and occupy the chair. Now you are face to face with Jesus. Be aware of how you feel in his presence. Notice the way he looks at you. What does his facial expression seem to be saying? What can you tell about his feelings for you from his manner and body language?

In a second exercise you might imagine yourself on your deathbed. You overhear the doctor saying to your family, "It won't be long now. It is just a matter of time. We've done all we can to make him (her) comfortable." What would your thoughts be? How would you feel about meeting God face-to-face? What kind of judgment of your life would you anticipate? The more vividly you can imagine this scene, the easier it will be to get at your root concept of God, the God in your muscles, fibers, and brain cells, the God of your guts. Each of us has a different concept of God. Based on these two suggested exercises, what would you say about your concept of God? Take some time now to try these exercises.

* * *

Christianity has preached, taught, and written about God for nearly two thousand years now. And certainly God has been given many different faces. It all depends on whom you are listening to and at what time in history that person is speaking. There has been a long and undeniably fearsome tradition that has given God an angry face. God is portrayed in this tradition as disgusted and short on patience. This is the so-called fire-and-brimstone tradition that gets a lot of mileage out of the so-called wrath of God. One approaches this God at his or her own great risk.

We cannot contain God in the measured dimensions of our thought or master God in the cages of our imaginations. God is love.

255

The demands of this God are so rigid and inflexible that they leave us room for little else besides failure, and our inevitable failures always stir the divine wrath.

A less strong and more recent tradition makes God a buddy-buddy type, a "Dutch uncle" God. This God is definitely pleasant, bland, and slightly wimpy. This God graciously asks nothing of us, but invites us only to be nice, to have a good time, and to hurt no one else in doing our thing. This God is called by familiar names like "The Man Upstairs" and "The Superstar."

The God I Don't Believe In

In the fine book of Juan Arias, *The God I Don't Believe In*. I found the summary at the end so moving that I would like to quote it more fully at this time.

No, I shall never believe in:
the God who catches man by surprise in a sin of weakness,
the God who condemns material things,
the God who loves pain,
the God who flashes a red light against human joys,
the God who makes himself feared,
the God who does not allow people to talk familiarly to him,
the grandfather-God whom one can twist around one's little finger,
the lottery-God whom one can find only by chance,
the judge-God who can give a verdict only with a rule book in his hands,

the God incapable of smiling at many of man's awkward mistakes,
the God who "plays at" condemning,
the God who "sends" people to hell,
the God who always demands 100 percent in examinations,
the God who can be fully explained by a philosophy,
the God incapable of understanding that children will always get themselves dirty and be forgetful,
the God who demands that if a man is to believe he must give up being a man,
the God who does not accept a seat at our human festivities,
the God whom only the mature, the wise, or the comfortably situated can understand,
the aseptic God thought up by so many theologians and canonists in their ivory towers,
the God who says, "You will pay for that!"
the God who says and feels nothing about the agonizing problems of suffering humanity,
the God whose disciples turned their backs on the world's work and are indifferent to their brother's story,
the God who does not go out to meet the person who has abandoned him,
the God incapable of making everything new,
the God who has never wept for men,
the God who is not light,

the God who prefers purity to love,

the God who is not present where [people] love each other,

the God in whom there are no mysteries, who is not greater than we are,

the God who, to make us happy, offers us a happiness divorced from our human nature,

the God who does not have the generosity of the sun, which warms everything it touches,

the God who is not love and who does not know how to transform into love everything he touches,

the God incapable of captivating man's heart,

the God who would not have become man, with all that implies,

the God in whom I cannot hope.

No, I shall never believe in such a God.[1]

I heartily agree with Juan Arias. All of my own instincts resonate profoundly with each of the statements quoted above. I don't believe in the God of fire and brimstone, nor do I believe in the "Sweet Old Man Upstairs" who never makes waves or dares to demand anything of us. Genesis tells us that God made us in God's image and likeness, and we seem to have a strong inclination to return the favor, to make God over in our human image and likeness. We make God an angry and mean God with a long white beard and a short temper. Or we paint a sweet pastel-colored patsy-God that can be manipulated to suit our moods and needs. Sometimes I think we don't want a God who would have the nerve to intrude into our lives and plans or suggest that God knows more than we do. "Don't you dare rain on my parade."

God Is Mystery

Something in me wants to insist, "None of the above!" First of all, God is infinite. If we ever think we've got God clearly focused in our mind's eye, the one thing of which we can be sure is this: we are wrong. No graven images or sharply focused photographs of God are possible. Because God is so utterly different from and so far beyond anything we can imagine, God is definitely a God of mystery. Sometimes we rankle at this. We want a God that we can fit snugly into our finite little minds, that we can carry around in our little prayer books. We do not want an ungraspable God. In these moments of struggle with mystery, we forget that if we could fit God into our minds, then we would have to pace back and forth in the prisons of those little minds for all eternity. We would certainly grow tired of such a small God.

We must remember that God made our awesomely complicated and vastly beautiful world by a simple act of the will. Just like that. God packed every atom of material with enormous power and potential. Our Creator strung beautiful stars across the sky of nighttime, and they still shine to us from millions of light-years away.

Genesis tells us that God made us in God's image and likeness, and we seem to have a strong inclination to return the favor, to make God over in our human image and likeness.

---

[1]Arias, *The God I Don't Believe In* (St. Meinrad, IN: Abbey Press, 1973), pp. 196–99.

God knows each grain of sand on the shores of our lakes and oceans. God knows the number of hairs on every human head. This is indeed a God of infinite majesty and power. The appropriate response would be, as Albert Einstein once suggested, an awesome reverence that bows its head and treads on silent feet.

God is to us like the sky to a small bird, which cannot see its outer limits and cannot reach its distant horizons, but can only lose itself in the greatness and immensity of the blueness. God is to us like the ocean to a small fish, which can never fathom the depths or dimensions of the vastness in which it swims. We should really be grateful and delighted that we cannot contain God in the measured dimensions of our thoughts or master him in the cages of our imaginations. We would be as bored with him as we are with a shallow and superficial person about whom there is nothing more to grasp or to understand.

God Is Love: God Only Loves

So the apostle John chooses dynamic rather than static words to describe and define God. God is like light, like a roaring wind. God is . . . *love!* We should be careful to notice that John does not say that God *has love*, but rather that God *is love*. This is the very nature of God. Just as we might say, "John is a man," to indicate John's nature, so Saint John writes, "God is love." God's very nature is to love. Just as every being acts always and only according to its nature, so God always and only *loves*. In a real sense this is all God can do because this is God's nature.

An analogy or comparison may help. It is the nature of the sun to give off warmth and light. The sun always shines, always radiates its warmth and light. Now you and I can stand under the sun and allow its warmth to make us warm. We can allow its light to fill our senses and surroundings with light. However, we can also separate ourselves from the sun, in partial ways or even completely. We can put a sun umbrella, a parasol, over our heads, or we can lock ourselves in a dark dungeon where the sun cannot possibly reach us. Whatever we do, whether we stand in the sun or separate ourselves from it, we know that the sun itself does not change. The sun does not "go out" if I lock myself in some barricaded dungeon.

Just so, God is love. Because we are free, we can separate ourselves from God's love. We can leave God just as we can leave the warmth and the light of the sun. But God, like the sun in our comparison, does not change because we go away. God is love and does not cease to love because we have left. Just as the sun always invites us to return to its warming and enlightening rays, so God is forever inviting us to return, even when we have distanced ourselves from the reaches of God's love. In a real sense, we can *refuse* the love of God but we can never *lose* the love of God. God does not stop sending out the warm and enlightening rays of love because I walk away. If this were so, God would be letting me decide how God is going to act.

It seems to me that it is something like this. Did you ever want to love someone, to share your life and your joy with another, but your offer was refused and your love was rejected? You always knew that the gift of love can never be forced, so you allowed the person whom you wanted to love to go out of your life, away from you. But, as that person was leaving, you called out, "If you ever want to come back, and I hope you will want to, my love will be here for you. I will be waiting for you with open arms and an open heart." This, I think, is something like God's own reaction when we choose to leave God. It is critically important to understand that God does not stop loving, does not become angry and vindictive, anxious to punish us in order to get even. That would be a God made to our human image and likeness when we are at our worst.

> Just as the sun always invites us to return to its warming and enlightening rays, so God is forever inviting us to return.

Covenanted love walks undemanded miles, goes far beyond the demands of justice and reciprocity. Covenanted love is never taken back or withdrawn. Covenanted love is forever.

I am sure that this understanding of God and God's love is borne out in the parable of the Prodigal Son. Jesus tells us that the father (God) allows his son to leave, but he waits patiently for the prodigal's return. In fact, he longs for the return of his son. In the parable, when the boy does come back, his own life and fortunes in shambles, the father runs down the road to embrace his son. The father quickly arranges a party to celebrate his return. "Get out the rings and the robes. Get some music makers in here. Kill the fatted calf. We're going to have a celebration. My son is home!" At the end of the parable Jesus adds that there is more joy in heaven over the one sinner who returns than over the ninety-nine who have never strayed.

God's Love: Covenanted and Unconditional

It is extremely important to realize that God's love is a *covenanted* and not a *contractual* love. In a business contract, if one party fails to meet its commitment, the second party of the contract is released from all the binding effects of that contract. For example, I promise to pay you twenty dollars to cut the grass in my yard. However, you do not cut the grass, and so I am not bound to pay you the promised twenty dollars. It is not this way in a covenant. A covenant implies a promise of unconditional love, a promise that is never canceled. A covenant promises a love that will go 100 percent of the way at

all times, no matter what is the response of the beloved. Covenanted love is not earned or won by the person to whom it is given. It is always a free gift. Covenanted love walks undemanded miles, goes far beyond the demands of justice and reciprocity. Covenanted love is never taken back or withdrawn. Covenanted love is forever.

In our human experience, there is usually very little to help us understand this kind of love. Sometimes we think that only a mother loves in this way. However, our great God assures us: "If a mother were to forget the child of her womb, I would never forget you. . . . I have carved your name on the palms of my hands so that I would never forget you." (Isaiah 49:15–16) "I will never ever leave you, nor will I ever forget you!" (Hebrews 13:5)

The "Wrath of God" and Other Anthropomorphisms

Sooner or later the question always arises: What about the so-called wrath of God mentioned in the Bible? Biblical scholars assure us that there is no wrath *in* God. God does not get angry, as we do. The scholars tell us that the "wrath of God" mentioned in the Scriptures is a figure of speech, an anthropomorphism. In such a figure of speech we ascribe human qualities or reactions to God. And while this particular anthropomorphism was probably intended to emphasize the incompatibility of God and sin, it has too often been used in a misleading way. It is true that we can't choose a sinful life, a life apart from God, and have a loving relationship with God at the same time. But it is likewise true that our sinning does not change God or arouse wrath in God.

It would be seriously misleading to imply that God gets angry because of something we have done. If that were true, we would be in control of God's reactions, which is unthinkable. It is likewise impossible to imagine that the Jesus who insists that we should love our enemies and forgive without limit would add, "But my Father will be very angry if you don't love him!" The only Father revealed by Jesus runs down the road, takes his son into his arms, and sighs with great relief, "You are home! It's all I have ever wanted. Wherever I am I want you with me, and wherever you are I want to be with you. If a mother would ever forget the child of her womb, I could never forget you!"

Once upon a time I used to think: "If I improve, become more charitable, eliminate my frequent faults of commission and omission, if I pray more and so forth, God will love me more." I am now convinced that this kind of thinking involves a serious misconception of our loving God. It is simply incompatible with a true vision of God. Again, it is making God to our human image and likeness. It ascribes to God that kind of "you have to earn it" type of conditional love with which we humans often pretend to love one another.

Each of us has his or her own unique and very limited concept of God, and it is very often marked and distorted by human experience. Negative emotions, like fear, tend to wear out. The distorted image of a vengeful God will eventually nauseate and be rejected. Fear is a fragile bond of union, a brittle basis of religion.

It may well be that this is why God's second commandment is that we love one another. Unselfish human love is the sacramental introduction to the God of love. We must go through the door of human giving to find the God who gives himself.

Those who do not reject a distorted image of God will limp along in the shadow of a frown, but they certainly will not love with their whole heart, soul, and mind. Such a God is not lovable. There will never be any trust and repose in the loving arms of a Father, there will never be any mystique of belonging to God. The person who serves out of fear, without the realization of love, will try to bargain with God, and will do little things for God, make little offerings, say little prayers, and so forth. Fear-riddled people try to embezzle a place in the heaven of their God. Life and religion are more like a chess-game, hardly an affair of love.

From *Why Am I Afraid To Love*

I now think that if we were to say to God, "I am going to improve; I am going to be better so you will love me more," God's response would be, "Oh, child of my heart, you've got it backward. You shouldn't think that if you become more virtuous I will love you more, because already you have all my love as a free gift. You don't have to change so I will love you more. I could not love you more. What you really need to know is how much I have always loved you. Oh, then . . . then you will really change."

> God's love for us is that of the love of an ever-faithful bridegroom for his bride.

Almost all of our human experience has been with conditional love: "If you change . . . if you do this or don't do that . . . I will love you." So we have to sit with this thought of God's unconditional, freely given love, and think about it for a long time. We have to soak in the realization of God's love in prayerful meditation. The truth of covenant, the truth that God could have made a world without you or me, but that such a world would have been incomplete for God— these are truths that are taken in slowly and realized only with the help of grace. God wanted you and me just the way we are, because . . . simply because this is the you and this is the me God has always loved. God *is* love. This is all God ever does.

The "Punishments" of God and the Fear of God

One more uncomfortable question: Does God punish? Again, I would like to step off from what has been a long and strong tradition in Christian rhetoric and preaching. I don't believe in a vindictive God who punishes to get even with us sinners. However, I do believe that we punish ourselves. When we leave the sunlight of God's love, we grow dark and cold, but this is self-inflicted punishment. I asked the classes I teach: "Suppose I were to teach this course, to offer you all the help and encouragement of which I am capable; but you chose not to do the required work, not to study for the examinations, and you flunked. In the end, did I punish you by flunking you, or did you punish yourself by flunking?" Most of my students, I think, immediately see the point. They also see the truth that God does not punish us, but that by our misuse of human freedom we can punish ourselves.

We are free. We are capable of sin. We can choose to reject God and the offer of God's love. And such choices have inevitable effects. Our sins always result in some suffering. When we leave the sun, we grow dark and cold. Still, we know that the sun is not punishing us for our absence. If we choose to be without God, because we want something more than we want God, we will begin hurting. However, it would be unfair to say that God is hurting us. We cannot truthfully accuse God of punishing us for our failures.

It is even possible that the final choice of our lives, what has been called the "fundamental and final option," is to be without God. If death comes to finalize this choice, we can even lose God forever. In the gospels Jesus warns us repeatedly about the possibility of this worst of all tragedies. But even in this case, the loss of our souls is the result of our own choices rather than God's punishment. God, who has carved us on the palms of God's hands and who will remember us even if our mothers should forget, wants to be with us forever. It is God's will that all of us be saved. (See 1 Timothy 2:4.) God is the father of the prodigal, always wanting hoping for our return.

If we choose otherwise, it will have to be our choice. It can never be God's. God can only accept our choice.

Finally, what is to be said about the "fear of God"? It is only a logical conclusion, I think, from what has already been said, that we might very well fear *ourselves*. We can fear the results of our human weakness, the misuse of our freedom in making deformed choices, but we need not fear our great and loving God, who wants only our happiness and salvation. One does not have to fear a mother or father whose love is unconditional and never withdrawn. One of the scriptural images employed to express

God's love for us is that of the love of an ever-faithful bridegroom for his bride. We, the bride, can and perhaps should fear the possibility of our own unfaithfulness. The fact is that we are all sinners. We have all been adulterous brides at times. We have been unfaithful to someone who has always been faithful to us. These times of unfaithfulness in my own life, I deeply regret. And I do very much fear the possibility of recurrence. Leaving love is the saddest and greatest of tragedies. But I could never believe in a God who demands that I fear God. I could never believe that God is inviting us into such a relationship.

Knowing God by Knowing Jesus

In fact, we have God's word for this. We have the Word that was with God from all eternity, the Word that is God: Jesus. Saint Paul calls Jesus "the visible image of our invisible God" (Colossians 1:15). Theologians have called Jesus our "window into God." And Jesus himself assures Philip, "Whoever has seen me has seen the Father." (John 14:9) Also, Saint John writes in his prologue:

> The Word became a human being and, full of grace and truth, lived among us. We saw his glory, the glory which he received as the Father's only Son. . . . No one has ever seen God. The only Son, who is the same as God and is at the Father's side, he has made him known.
>
> *John 1:14, 18 (GNB)*

God not only was in Jesus, reconciling the world to God (see 2 Corinthians 5:19), but was also revealed to us in Jesus. God was speaking our human language, as it were, in becoming a human being, like us in all things except sin. In uttering the Word into the world, God was revealing God's own self to us. The divine person of Jesus is the surest way to a more accurate attitude toward God, even though we can never hope to have a totally adequate view or concept of God. Again, it is obvious that God is simply too big, too magnificent for the finite lenses of our minds. However, we can get clearer and clearer insights into the mind and heart of

God by reflecting on the mind and heart of Jesus. The wisdom and power, the might and majesty of God reside in Jesus. Through Jesus they are revealed to us.

Jesus and the Law

Jesus began his rabbinical career at the appropriate age: thirty. He was by profession a rabbi. The word means "master," an honorific title that was accorded to the teachers of the Law. (See Matthew 23:7–8.) Consequently, Jesus was expected to give most of his time to the work of interpreting the Law. Rabbis were customarily consulted about questions of the Law. They would inform their questioners about the requirements of the Law in given cases that were presented to them.

A bit of historical background might help here. After the Babylonian Captivity (587–539 B.C.), the Jewish people were allowed by Cyrus the Persian, who had conquered the Babylonians, to regroup. At this time, in the five hundred years preceding the birth of Jesus, the regrouped Jewish people wrote down the Old Testament, including the Torah, or laws regulating the life of Israel. These laws were a part of the covenant between God and God's people. However, in this period the Law was given a new interpretation and a different emphasis. It became something of an ironclad and absolute norm, and for many of the people replaced a personal relationship with God. The Pharisaic tradition

Saint Paul calls Jesus "the visible image of our invisible God" (Colossians 1:15). Theologians have called Jesus our "window into God."

carried this absolutizing of the Law to exasperating extremes. The Pharisees actually started a new tradition. They added oral laws designed to interpret, apply, and preserve the Law by creating new, minute, and very exact precepts. In other words, they embroidered the Law with innumerable, straitjacketing regulations.

When Jesus came onto this scene to begin his rabbinical career, the fireworks of confrontation were almost immediate. Jesus kept saying that God is love, and that God is calling us into a relationship of love, not a legalistic relationship with God. Jesus insisted that the prescriptions of the Law can never replace a personal relationship of love. He further taught that the prescriptions of the Law are elevated, sublimated, and summarized in the law of the love of God and one's neighbor. (See Matthew 22:34–40.) Jesus made it clear that he had not come to do away with the Law, but to bring it to fulfillment and perfection in love. (See Matthew 5:17–20.) The first strategy employed by the Pharisees in dealing with this reluctant rabbi was an attempt to make him solve cases.

"Master (Rabbi), if a man's oxen have fallen into a ditch on the Sabbath, is he allowed to pull them out?"

"Master, are we supposed to pay taxes to Rome? How do you interpret the Law in this matter?"

"Master, how is it that your disciples pick the heads of wheat on the Sabbath when the Law prohibits this?"

"Master, we have caught this woman in the very act of adultery. In our Law Moses gave a command that such a woman must be stoned to death. Now, what do you say?" (The gospel goes on to say that they asked him this in order to trap him. See John 8:1–11.)

These were some of the "cases" which the Jews asked Jesus to arbitrate in an attempt to make him a legalistic rabbi. As the Scribes and Pharisees asked Jesus to judge the woman taken in adultery, he stooped over and started writing in the sand. An old Christian tradition suggests that he was writing in the sand the secret sins of the accusers. More recently it has been suggested that he was so bored with all this self-righteous haggling that he started doodling in the sand in an effort to find something more interesting to do.

What Jesus was saying to the Scribes and Pharisees was very important for them and for us: "You can keep the Law without loving, but you cannot really love without keeping the Law." The Pharisees, who were the most influential group among the Jewish people, could not handle this. They were quite complacent about themselves, and they rather openly despised fellow Jews who were not Pharisees. They called them the "people of the earth," the common people. Generally the Pharisees thought of them as ignorant of the Law and incapable of its observance. The Pharisees believed that these common people were therefore destined to perdition.

Jesus and Sinners

Jesus became even more objectionable to the Pharisees because by association he aligned himself with these common people—with the tax collectors, the prostitutes, the outcasts, and every kind of sinner. He seemed to prefer and to seek out their company. (See Matthew 9:9–13.) The Pharisees were outraged: "He even eats and drinks with sinners!" they gasped.

One day when many tax collectors and other outcasts came to listen to Jesus, the Pharisees and the teachers of the Law started grumbling, "This man welcomes outcasts and even eats with them!" So Jesus told them this parable:

"Suppose one of you has a hundred sheep and loses one of them—what does he do? He leaves the other ninety-nine sheep in the pasture and goes looking for the one that got lost until he finds it. When he finds it, he is so happy that he puts it on his shoulders and carries it back home. Then he calls his friends and neighbors together and says to them, 'I am so happy I found my lost sheep. Let us celebrate!' In the same way, I tell you, there will be more joy in heaven over one sinner who repents than over ninety-nine respectable people who do not need to repent."

Luke 15:1–7 (GNB)

Jesus was trying to tell them about the infinite love and mercy of God, which was being lived out in him and in his life. But he was also trying to tell them something else. He was saying that the observance of the letter of the Law can kill the spirit of the Law, which is the spirit of love. If one keeps the Law, keeps from all wrongdoing and legal infractions out of self-righteousness, because one is "above that sort of thing," such a person is like a "whitened sepulcher." One might be shiny-white on the outside, but inside, if there is no love, there can only be death and corruption. Somehow I am sure that the words "whitened sepulcher" were spoken with more disappointment and sadness than anger in the voice of Jesus. He was asking them, "Please don't be like that. Don't waste your life in that charade."

If you and I could locate ourselves in this Pharisee-dominated scene, if we could feel the shock waves of such reactions to the message of Jesus, if we could listen to the small-town gossip, I think we would hear something like this:

"Did you hear what he said when we asked him about his apparent weakness for the wicked, about his softness on sin? Did you hear? He actually said that he was 'the Divine Physician.' Honestly, that's what he said. He said he came 'to care for the sick, not the well.'"

"I once heard him say that he is the 'Good Shepherd.' Are you ready for that . . . the *Good Shepherd?* He claims that he is in search of his lost sheep! Just who does he think he is?"

"Well! I've never heard the likes of that!"

> *"You can keep the Law without loving, but you cannot really love without keeping the Law."*

Simon the Pharisee

One of them, a Pharisee named Simon, had a great story he liked to repeat. Simon had tried a patronizing gesture. He had invited Jesus and a few of his friends over for a dinner. Of course, he did not extend to Jesus the simple courtesies of an honored guest, like the washing of his feet. Why should he? Jesus should have been happy that he even received an invitation from a respected Pharisee. Well, things were going along pretty well until . . .

"You won't believe this. In comes a woman (they were never allowed at such banquets). And I don't mean *a* woman; I mean the town tramp, a common prostitute! I'm not fooling. This harlot staggers in and stages a big scene. She slobbers all over his feet, and then begins wiping away those phony tears with her bleached hair!

"Of course, I wondered why this good rabbi didn't kick the slut in the face and chase her away. No, he just reclines there and lets her carry on. It was really disgusting! You won't believe this next part, either. I cleared my throat as a little hint, and so the Good Master asks me a riddle. Honestly—a riddle! 'If two men owed a third man debts, one a large debt and the other a smaller one, and the good-hearted third man wipes both debts off his books, which would love him more?' Well, of course, I had to go with the one who owed the larger debt.

"Then he really outdid himself. Do you know what he asked me? He asked me, 'Do you see this woman?' I kid you not, he called her a 'woman.' She ought to be stoned to death because she is rotten and vile, and he asks me, 'Do you see this woman?' Then he proceeds to praise her for the love she has shown him. He says that her sins must be forgiven because no one can show such love unless God is in that person. All love, he says, is a gift from God.

"But here's the zinger: He concludes his little speech by saying that wherever the story of his life is to be told, down through the centuries and out to the ends of the earth, the story of 'this good woman and her kindness to me' will also be told. Did you ever hear anything like that? What a megalomaniac, eh? He obviously thinks his story is going to live after him, to be told for some years to come!"

See Luke 7:36–50

Simon's story was only one of many like it. There was a general consensus of opinion.

"He's making a mockery of the Law. He keeps insisting that the Law has been subsumed, elevated into the one great law of love! And you notice how he keeps talking about love, not sin. He is actually trying to imply that God loves sinners. And all of us know that God has only contempt for sinners. What a rabbi—soft on sin, and he even eats and drinks with sinners! He is corrupting everything we stand for."

The observance of the letter of the Law can kill the spirit of the Law, which is the spirit of love.

The Proposed Final Solution: The Death of Jesus

Then, for the first time, someone spoke of a final solution to end all this madness. Someone actually said, "Maybe we will have to kill him. It may be better that one man should die than that our nation should perish." The word was sweeping through the whispering galleries that he had raised a man named Lazarus from the dead. Everybody was talking about the power of miracles in his words and in his touch.

> So the Pharisees and the chief priests met with the Council and said, "What shall we do? Look at all the miracles this man is performing! If we let him go on in this way, everyone will believe in him, and the Roman authorities will take action and destroy our Temple and our nation!" One of them, named Caiaphas, who was high priest that year, said, "What fools you are! Don't you realize that it is better for you to have one man die for the people, instead of having the whole nation destroyed?" . . . From that day on the Jewish authorities made plans to kill Jesus.
>
> *John 11:47–53 (GNB)*

Jesus met their deepest suspicions head-on: "Do you think that I am preaching a watered-down, a superficial and diluted version of our responsibilities to God, that I am not demanding enough? When you see me seeking out those who have gone astray, do you really conclude that I am soft on sin? Don't you know that it is possible to love a sinner while regretting the sin? Really, what I am saying is that the observance of the Law without love is lifeless. Relating to God in a legalistic way is like playing a game with God. We make all the right moves and say all the right words, and in the end we proclaim to God with great self-satisfaction, 'See, I kept all your rules. I did everything I had to do. Now you can't damn me!' My Father is not inviting you into such a relationship. My Father loves you. My Father is love!"

Jesus was trying to explain to them that we deal in such a legalistic way only with someone we fear. We feel better when we are covered by the legalistic agreement with all of its clauses and provisions. We meet all that person's requirements, and then we can feel safe and satisfied. However, Jesus was insisting that God is rather calling us into a relationship of love. God is not like a demanding teacher who is intimidating his or her students with the fear of failure.

Love Is More Demanding Than the Law

The heart of the answer of Jesus is this: Love will ask much more of us than the Law could ever require. When a person enters into a legalistic relationship, there can come a time when that person can say, "I have now done enough. I have fulfilled all my obligations." The person can then prove it by citing chapter and verse in the provisions of the contract. However, true love can never say, "I have done enough. I have now fulfilled all my obligations." Love is restless, drives us on. Love asks us to walk many miles not demanded by justice or legalism. In effect, Jesus was saying, "When I confront your legalism with the law of love, I am not asking less. I am not diluting the demands of your relationship with God. Pan-scale justice can only regulate a human life; love will encompass and energize that life. And in the end, love is the only response that you can appropriately make to the loving invitations of my Father, who is love."

I think that Jesus was asking the people of his generation and is today inviting us to drench mind and spirit in the knowledge of God's love for us. We are the delight of God's smiling eyes, the children of God's warm heart. God cares for us more than any mother has ever loved her child. If we could only realize how much we are loved, we would of course want to respond, to make some return. "What can I ever do for the Lord in return for all the things he has done for me?" the psalmist asks in Psalm 116. When we have opened our minds and hearts to God's love, we will go far beyond the requirements of what we have to do. Justice and observance of the Law say that I must go just this far. Love will ask me to walk many undemanded miles beyond that point. If we love, we will want to do more than what we must. We will want to do all we can. Love is like this.

When we have opened our minds and hearts to God's love, we will go far beyond the requirements of what we have to do.

> *Love will ask much more of us than the Law could ever require.*

In the end, this effort to bring about a *metanoia*, the challenge to acquire a new outlook, proved futile with the people and the powers that prevailed in the generation of Jesus. So one day, near the end, they came to him. They did not try the usual questions of entrapment, but placed before him a direct accusation and a direct question. The accusation was that Jesus was too tolerant, too soft on sin, even going so far as to eat and drink with sinners. The direct questions: "Are you really suggesting that God would approve conduct like yours? How does God think of and treat a sinner?" Jesus looked long and sadly into their eyes, and then responded by telling them a parable: the parable of the Prodigal Son.

The Parable of the Prodigal

In a parable, two things are put side by side for the sake of comparison or contrast. A parable invites the listener to reflect on the comparison, so that the object or person in question can be illustrated and better understood by reason of the comparison. For example, Jesus says that the Kingdom of God, which he is trying to explain, is like "a man who goes out in his fields to sow seed." (See Mark 4:3–9.) Jesus invites the listener to see a scene from everyday life. By imagining the farmer at work, planting a harvest that will be some time in coming, the listeners could be helped to understand that the kingdom, the seed of God's invitation, will meet with a gradual, slow-in-coming response of humankind.

One other note to supply context for the parable of the Prodigal. The most shocking word that Jesus had ever used in all his dialogues with his contemporaries was the word *Abba*. Jesus insisted that God wants us to call God Abba, a tender name that implies belief in an unshakable and unconditional love, an understanding and enduring love. Abba is the name a small child calls his or her father, and the name itself summarizes their deep relationship of trust and intimacy.

At any rate, on the occasion of the confrontation of Jesus by the Pharisees, when Jesus was asked who God is and how God thinks of and reacts to sinners, Jesus told the story of the prodigal son. Perhaps we should really call this story the parable of the Prodigal Abba, because the central message concerns the father and his prodigal (extravagant), unconditional love.

In the story itself, it seems that a man and his two sons live and work together on a farm out in the country. The younger boy more and more comes to think of his father as outdated, and he gradually comes to be disenchanted with, even to resent, life with his father. He has had it with the chickens in the morning and the crickets in the evening. The boy dreams about the delights of the big city with its darkened lights and wicked pleasures. One day he comes to his father to demand his inheritance and to announce his impending departure. The father is sad, of course, but he finally gives his son the inheritance. The boy, without looking back over his shoulder, sets off to realize his high hopes and to actualize his daring dreams.

Jesus portrays the father as allowing his son to leave, but the father's heart is heavy with regret. During the long interval of the son's absence, the father sits nightly on the front porch of the farmhouse, watching with sad and longing eyes the road from the city. He cannot forget his son. He will always remember his little boy, the apple of his eye and the delight of his dreams. There will always be a special place in the heart of the father for his son. Only when the boy discovers the hollowness of his hopes and the delusion of his dreams, only when his inheritance has been spent and his friends desert him, does he come back down the long road homeward. He is hoping to be hired on as a farmhand, never daring to ask for reinstatement as a son.

Jesus pictures the father, looking as usual down the road that leads from the city, and suddenly recognizing the distant figure of his son. The father's heart pounds wildly, almost breaking with excitement. Overcome with joy, contrary to all the traditions of the time, the father runs down the road and gathers his lost boy back into his own finding arms. He doesn't even hear the boy's suggestion, "I can't hope that you will take me back as a son." After saying this, the boy feels the tight arms of his father encircling him,

and hears the relieved sobs in his father's chest. He feels his father's warm tears washing down the furrows of his own cheeks. The father moans softly, over and over again, "You're home . . . you're home!" Then the father gathers himself together, summons his loudest voice, and calls for rings and robes "for my boy." He gives an instruction to call in the music makers, to kill the prized fatted calf. There will be a party to end all parties. He repeats the joyful proclamation: "My son is home! My son is home!"

At the conclusion of this parable, Jesus looks squarely into the eyes of the Scribes, the Pharisees, and the high priests. "This," he says, "is who God is. This is how God feels about and reacts to a sinner." (See Luke 15:11–32.)

> *"Wherever I am, I want you to be with me. Wherever you are, I want to be with you. Wherever you go, I will go."*

Of course, his story sealed his fate. They would now set into motion the machinery of his death. It would come as no surprise. Jesus knew all the time what the result would be even before he started his parable. And he would gladly die for love. "I have a baptism wherewith I am to be baptized, and I am anxious to see it accomplished" (Luke 12:50). Under every crucifix commemorating his death, the followers of Jesus might well see an indelible caption: "This is what I mean when I say 'I love you!'" And down through the arch of the centuries, and out to the ends of the earth, the story would be told and the message would be repeated, and people would gradually come to understand: *God is love!*

Jesus Lives His Message

We have already suggested that when the apostles were first called by Jesus, they were very far from being finished products. If Jesus had eventually written them out of the script, history would probably have looked back with understanding. The apostles seemed so slow to grasp his message, to accept his vision, and to honor his values. We have already noted the frequency of the question of Jesus: "Are you yet without understanding?" On one occasion Jesus sighs with relief, "At last, you really understand, don't you?" (See John 16:31.)

The problem was neither lack of intelligence nor lack of good will. I suspect that the apostles ran an average race in these fields. As with most of us, the real problem was lack of metanoia—a change of

outlook, a new vision. The apostles had their own dreams, as we have said. They had made their own plans. They were sure about what would make them happy: personal importance, an earthly kingdom, a little security. They weren't asking all that much. But they weren't ready to open their hands to the Lord, to make their surrender, to say their yes. They weren't ready to invest their lives in a kingdom of faith and love. And the Lord was asking nothing less of them than this. Jesus was repeatedly telling them, by his words and his example, that those who want to be first shall be last. All authority in God's kingdom is a call to loving service. Don't worry about security, what you will eat and drink, what you will wear. Look at the lilies of the field, the birds of the air. Trust me. I will be with you. I will be your enough!

For the twelve apostles, as for most of us, it was a long road to metanoia. They did not easily give up their dreams, their plans, and their hopes. In much of their experience, Jesus had been the magnificent Lord who could give the blind sight and the deaf hearing, and who could cleanse lepers. He could even bring the dead back to life, and drive demons out of human hearts. During these bright and exciting days on the center stage of Palestine, the Twelve walked with Jesus, publicly identified themselves as his followers, and cashed in on the intimacy they enjoyed with him.

Then the lights went out and the tides of good fortune ran out on Jesus. The hosannas of Palm Sunday turned into jeers and demands for his death. The Lord of life, with miracles tingling in his fingertips, strangely became the Lamb of God, bruised and broken. The apostles quickly retreated to the upper room in search of the security that meant so much to them. They barricaded the doors, and talked only in frightened whispers. They anxiously calculated their chances of getting out of all this alive. What if the scourged Jesus should be crucified? What would happen then to them? Would the forces of darkness that killed him want to destroy them also? From Friday afternoon until Sunday morning, they paced back and forth, fretting and sweating in the hot confinement of the upper room.

Then Sunday morning broke, bright and clear and filled with a great surprise. A breathless Mary Magdalene comes pounding on the door of the upper room: "The tomb . . . the tomb is empty!" Peter and young John run to check out her report, and return to the others to confirm the fact: The tomb really is empty. It was the first small shaft of light in their darkened world. It was the first ray of hope to pierce their despair.

Then the majestic risen Jesus passes through the barricaded door. All the blood and bruises, the brokenness and ugliness of his dying are gone. He is again the most beautiful among the sons of men. The apostles had left Jesus alone to endure the terrible suffering of death by crucifixion. But Jesus comes back to them to share his victory over death. He says simply, "Shalom! Be at peace. I understand."

But they do not understand. As was suggested earlier, they conclude that they are suffering from mass hallucination, seeing a specter, a ghost. So Jesus gently invites them to touch him. As a further reassurance he eats their fish and honeycomb. "Shalom!" he reassures them. "Be at peace. I understand."

They must have remembered his story about the farmer and his two sons, the parable of the Prodigal Son. They must have remembered how the father ran down the road to embrace his wayward, disillusioned son, to welcome him home. The presence of Jesus in that upper room was so much like this story he had told. Jesus had come running down the road from the tomb where he had been laid in death, and he was embracing them with peace and understanding. "Shalom! Be at peace. I promised you that I would be with you. And I am here." It was just like the father in his story: "Wherever I am, I want you to be with me. Wherever you are, I want to be with you. Wherever you go, I will go."

All along, Jesus had been telling the apostles that God is love. But they had never experienced this kind of unconditional, covenanted love that never quits, that never ever gives up. When they first heard about this love, the apostles must have thought that it sounded like a myth, too good to be true. And then he came into that upper room and said to them, "Shalom! Be at peace." Perhaps it was at this moment that they really understood: So this is what love really means. So this is who God really is. There are so many things that we know only when we experience them. Apparently covenanted, unconditional love is one of these things.

The most shocking word that Jesus had ever used in all his dialogues with his contemporaries was the word Abba.

The Christian Vision of God, As Recorded by John

One of the men in that suddenly bright and hope-filled upper room was a young man, the youngest in fact, the apostle named John. John lived to a very ripe old age. By that time all the others in that upper room had long since died heroically for Jesus. Their witness had been martyrdom. John's witness was to be that of an old man telling the young people of his time and all the generations to come about Jesus. (This paraphrase of his meaning supplements his actual words.)

I want to tell you about the Word of life. I want to tell you what I have heard with my own ears and what I have seen with my own eyes. Yes, I have seen the Word and my hands have actually touched him. I want to tell you what I have seen and heard so that you can join with us in the covenant of love that we have with the Father and with his Son, Jesus Christ. I want to tell you this so that you may share our joy with us and that our joy may be complete. (1 John 1:1–4)

I have seen his always faithful goodness through the works of love which he performed. It was a slow process, but we came to believe in him. We came to believe in the comfort and in the challenge of Jesus. Jesus came to tell us all the things that he had heard from his Father. (John 5:19, 30) Jesus kept insisting with us that his kingdom was a matter of faith. (John 6:29) He invited us to see everything through the eyes of faith. And he asked us to gamble our lives on the only real force in this world, the force of love. (John 13:34–35)

He assured us that he is the way, the truth, and the life, and that if we followed him we would never walk in darkness. Jesus is the truth, the perfect revelation of the Father, and he shares with us the very life of God that is in him. (John 1:17, 14:6, 17:6) Slowly we came to know a God of love because Jesus introduced us to the meaning and the reality of love. He was so patient with us, as we gradually learned to accept a whole new way of looking at things, a whole new vision of reality. We Christians are those who know this truth because we see through the eyes of faith and we have put on the mind of Jesus. (1 John 2:3–6)

It is this truth, this vision that sets us free—free from all the crippling prejudices that wither the human spirit and cloud the skies of the world. The truth of Jesus sets us free from the tyranny of possession by the things of this world. His truth enables us to rise above the weakness of our human nature. (John 8:31–34; 1 John 2:4)

And this is the truth, the only really important truth, the truth about the Father who was in the Son, the Father who is known only through his Son. This is the truth that sets us free and gives our lives meaning, the truth that makes sense of this world and puts a song in our hearts:

> We ourselves know and believe the love which God has for us. God is love, and whoever lives in love lives in union with God and God lives in union with him. . . . There is no fear in love; perfect love drives out all fear.
>
> *1 John 4:16, 18 (GNB)*

FOR FURTHER REFLECTION
Chapter 20: God Revealed in Jesus

Review

1. Analyze the distortions of God as either the "fire-and-brimstone" fearful God or the "buddy-buddy" God. What is unhealthy and crippling about each of these visions of God?

2. What do we mean when we say "God is mystery"? In what sense must God always remain mystery, if God is infinite?

3. What is the difference between saying "God is love" and "God loves"? How is the sun an excellent analogy for illustrating God's covenanted and unconditional love for each one of us in spite of our sins and sinfulness?

4. In light of Powell's presentation on the many anthropomorphic descriptions of God, articulate healthy interpretations of the following: (a) the wrath and anger of God, (b) punishments of God, and (c) fear of the Lord.

5. Jesus is our "window" into God. In what ways does knowing Jesus help us to know God and to have a clearer vision of God?

6. In his teachings and miracles, in his life, death, and resurrection, Jesus reveals to us the kind of God we have—a God who loves us unconditionally. How is this revealed in the parable of the Prodigal Son? In Jesus' appearances to his followers after his resurrection? During these appearances, how does Jesus practice what he preached?

Discuss

1. How does your perception or vision of God relate to your vision of yourself, of other people, and of life itself?

2. In your relationship with God, do you generally believe that you must change (be nicer, more virtuous, pray more, and so forth) so that God will love you? Or do you believe that God already loves you, so therefore you can change?

Scripture Activity

"'Do not be worried and upset,' Jesus told them. 'Believe in God and believe also in me. There are many rooms in my Father's house, and I am going to prepare a place for you. I would not tell you this if it were not so. And after I go and prepare a place for you, I will come back and take you to myself, so that you will be where I am. You know the way that leads to the place where I am going.'

"Thomas said to him, 'Lord, we do not know where you are going; so how can we know the way to get there?'

"Jesus answered him, 'I am the way, the truth, and the life; no one goes to the Father except by me. . . . Now that you have known me, you will know my Father also, and from now on you do know him and you have seen him." (John 14:1–7, GNB)

Jesus reveals to us the kind of God we have. To know Jesus is to know God. Based on this passage, describe the kind of God Jesus reveals to us. How do Jesus' words about being "the way, the truth, and the life" not only reveal his divinity, but challenge us to follow his way, his truth, and his way of life in our own lives?

Processing These Ideas about God

1. **Identify and revise the common vision distortions of God.** Read through the list of "Some Common Vision Distortions about God" and offer a healthier and more Christian attitude toward God.

2. **Write a list of adjectives describing your God.** Make a list of adjectives that describe the God to whom you could *most easily relate* and with whom you would be *most comfortable.*

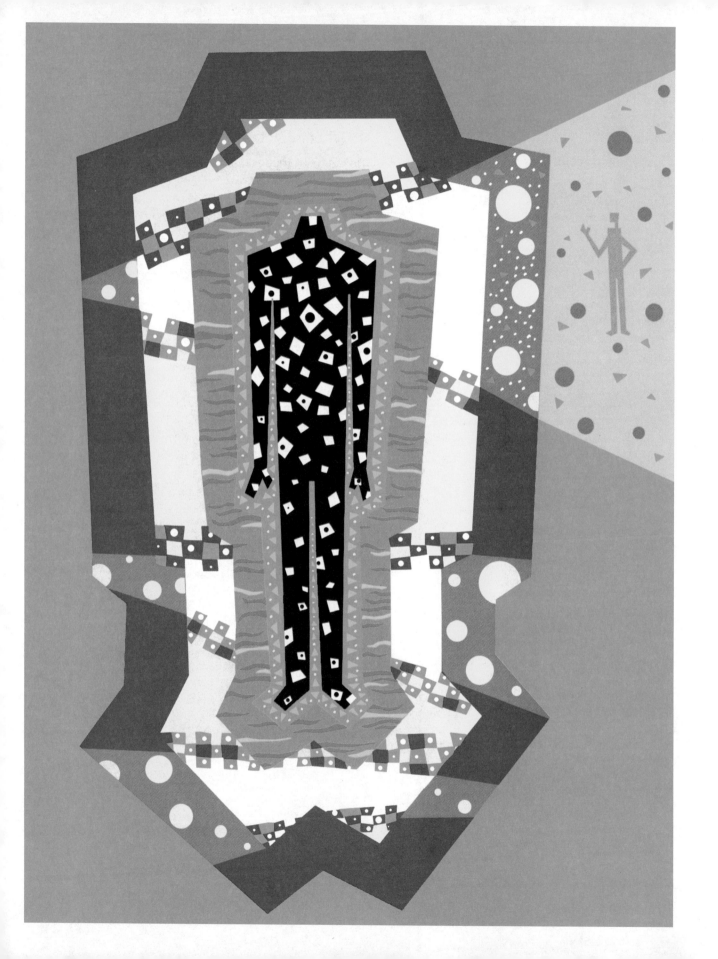

21 The Christian Vision of Suffering

For the message about Christ's death on the cross is nonsense to those who are being lost; but for us who are being saved it is God's power. The scripture says,

> *"I will destroy the wisdom of the wise*
>
> *and set aside the understanding of the scholars."*

So then, where does that leave the wise? or the scholars? or the skillful debaters of this world? God has shown that this world's wisdom is foolishness!

For God in his wisdom made it impossible for people to know him by means of their own wisdom. Instead, by means of the so-called "foolish" message we preach, God decided to save those who believe. Jews want miracles for proof, and Greeks look for wisdom. As for us, we proclaim the crucified Christ, a message that is offensive to the Jews and nonsense to the Gentiles; but for those whom God has called, both Jews and Gentiles, this message is Christ, who is the power of God and the wisdom of God. For what seems to be God's foolishness is wiser than human wisdom, and what seems to be God's weakness is stronger than human strength.

1 Corinthians 1:18–25 (GNB)

Believers and the Question of Suffering

It has been suggested that most people become preoccupied with their neuroses and personal problems. Paranoid people keep wondering why everyone is out to get them. Pessimists are constantly trying to convince the rest of the world that things really do look gloomy. In the same sense, I think that almost all of us keep probing the subject of suffering. It has certainly been an intriguing question in human history. Sometimes I think that we have faced the inevitability of suffering. What we are looking for is some meaningful explanation of the suffering and pain that touch our lives. The Book of Genesis struggles with the question of suffering in the persons of Adam and Eve and the sweat-and-toil suffering endured after their fall from grace. In the same book there is the record of Cain killing his brother Abel. Why? Also in the Old Testament, the Book of Job groans under the weight of this question: Why suffering? Jeremiah, who didn't want to be a prophet in the first place, couldn't understand why God called him to failure and rejection.

The suffering is saying to the person who will listen: When the pupil is ready the teacher will appear.

277

"You haven't made a prophet of me. You have made a fool of me!" (See Jeremiah 11:18–12:6, 15:10–21, 17:14–18.)

The question of suffering is constantly being explored and discussed by thinking people. In our own times there are many good books that take up this question, including the classic of C. S. Lewis, *The Problem of Pain*. Another of these books, the title of which seems significant, is Philip Yancey's *Where Is God When It Hurts?* Somehow I think that this title suggests the deepest source of our preoccupation with suffering. For believers, suffering is basically a faith question, I think, a question of God. Do you remember the old argument, the classic syllogism of atheism? It goes this way: God by definition is all-good and all-powerful. If God could prevent suffering but does not, then God is not all-good. On the other hand, if God would want to but cannot prevent suffering, then God is not all-powerful. In either case, the existence of suffering means that there cannot be a God who is all-good and all-powerful. Somehow I suspect that at least a deep part of our preoccupation with suffering is an effort to reconcile the existence of suffering with the existence of a loving Abba-God.

It would be only sanity, hardly modesty, for me to admit right from the beginning that I do not have all the answers. However, I do think that there are some helpful insights that assist us in formulating a Christian attitude, a healthy and profitable way of looking at suffering. In the end we will confront a wall of mystery. Whenever we use our finite intelligence in an effort to understand our infinite God, we are going to collide with the dead end of mystery. God's thoughts simply are not our thoughts. God's ways are just not our ways. In the end, at the wall of mystery, we will hear the small voice in the soft breeze: "Be still and know that I am God!" (Psalm 46:10)

Loving the Questions, Living the Answers

But God is not asking us to silence our curiosity or to cease our probing of this question of suffering. I think we should continue always to turn the question over in our minds in order to gain new insights and find new meaning. I often review the advice of the poet Rainer Maria Rilke:

> . . . be patient toward all that is unsolved in your heart and . . . try to love the *questions themselves*. . . . Do not now seek the answers, which cannot be given you because you would not be able to live them. And the point is, to live everything. *Live* the questions now. Perhaps you will then gradually, without noticing it, live along some distant day into the answer.[1]

[1] Rainer Maria Rilke, *Letters to a Young Poet*, trans. by M. D. Herter-Norton (New York: W. W. Norton, 1954), p. 35. Afterward, write what you have learned about the power of affirmation.

In the end, at the wall of mystery, we will hear the small voice in the soft breeze: "Be still and know that I am God!"

(Psalm 46:10)

I think that "loving the question until I am able to live the answer," in this matter of suffering, is a posture of faith. Suffering asks me to live with and to love the mystery of a God whom I cannot fully understand. Suffering asks me to make a submission of faith to this God who urges me at the edge of my pain: "Trust me!" Sometimes we can see by hindsight that our suffering in the past turned out to be for our own good. Sometimes we can see that if things had worked out as we wanted them to work out, the result would have been disaster. But this by no means suggests that we can ever accomplish total understanding. Even if God were to give us the answers right now, we would probably not be able to understand them.

God is working out a plan for our lives. However, we humans often foil his plans and God has to draw good out of our evil, write straight with our crooked lines. According to the blueprints of this divine plan we humans are free and can therefore fail. We can even hurt one another by misuse of our freedom. You and I cannot understand God's thoughts and ways. Why did he make us capable of sin? We can only love the questions and try to live in a trusting submission to mystery. Recently a fine Christian woman said to me, "Do you know what I want to ask God when I get to heaven?" "No," I responded, "what do you want to ask him?" Her answer was: "Everything!"

God's Response to Job's Questions

When Job asked God to tell him the reasons for his sufferings, God's reply was seemingly a strange one. It was not a doctrinal dissertation on the reasons for Job's difficulties nor an explanation of the motives of God for allowing Job to be so tested. This is what Job seemed to be asking for, and, I think, it is basically what you and I want: an explanation of suffering that we can understand. However, God's reply seems rather to take the form of a personal manifestation of God, a kind of vision of God and God's infiniteness that is overpowering. The magnificence and the majesty of God are spelled out in a long description of the wonders of God in the creation of this world. Having experienced God in this kind of overwhelming presence, Job says simply:

> I know that you are all-powerful:
>   what you conceive, you can
>   perform.
> I am the man who obscured
>   your designs
>   with my empty-headed
>   words.
> I have been holding forth on
>   matters I cannot understand,
>   on marvels beyond me and
>   my knowledge. . . .
> I knew you then only by
>   hearsay;
>   but now, having seen you
>   with my own eyes,
> I retract all I have said,
>   and in dust and ashes
>   I repent.
> *Job 42:2–6 (Jerusalem Bible)*

You and I cannot understand God's thoughts and ways.

There is a Zen proverb: "When the pupil is ready, the teacher will appear." God seems to be saying to Job and to all of us who demand complete and satisfactory answers: "This is not yet the time for answers. This is rather the time for trust. It may help you to trust in my goodness and power in these matters (your suffering) if you can experience me, my goodness and greatness, in the stunning world of creation. Of course, I have the answers you seek, but you are not ready yet. When you are ready, I will give you these answers. 'When the pupil is ready, the teacher will appear.' Meanwhile, be patient. Love the questions and live in trust. Someday I shall share all the answers and all my secrets with you."

Need for a Previous Mind-set

When we are asked by God to lie on the anvil of suffering, it is difficult to think clearly at that time. Suffering is like a loud and throbbing noise inside us. It is deafening and distracting. Suffering magnetizes all our attention, leaves us no peaceful and prayerful place. It is difficult, if not impossible, to reflect clearly in times of pain. And so I would like to suggest that what we need is a "previous mind-set," an attitude cultivated consciously in our pain-free moments of peace that will help us in our times of suffering.

Such a mind-set or attitude would seem to be built on and related to our concept of God. In answer to Job's questioning, God responds to Job's complaint by asking more questions.

> Where were you when I laid
> the earth's foundations? . . .
> Who decided the dimensions of
> it, do you know? . . .
> Who laid its cornerstone
> when all the stars of the
> morning were singing with
> joy? . . .
> Who pent up the sea behind
> closed doors
> when it leapt tumultuous
> out of the womb? . . .
> Have you ever in your life given
> orders to the morning or
> sent the dawn to its post? . . .
> Have you an inkling of the
> extent of the earth?
> *Job 38:4–18 (Jerusalem Bible)*

The power of God is awesome, and God is the master of this magnificent world. The mind of God can conceive the overwhelming solar system and produce the multicolored beauty of the seasons. The will of God can execute its own designs by a snap of the finger, as it were. In the presence of such awesome power and intelligence, we should reverently take off our shoes, bow our heads, and tread softly. It is this same God who assures us of the divine loving governance of the world and loving providence over our lives. It is this God of majesty and power who bends down to us, especially in our moments of suffering, and asks us for our act of trust in God. In our "previous mind-set," we must stand ready to trust God's infinite intelligence and God's awesome power, whatever is asked of us.

This God of majesty and power who bends down to us, especially in our moments of suffering, asks us for our act of trust.

Today much is being said about "positive imagining." This technique can be a helpful step toward positive thinking and attitude cultivation. It would definitely assist us in the preparation of the previous mind-set which we are discussing. Positive imagining involves a kind of dress rehearsal on the stage of one's imagination. For example, I want to think and react kindly to someone who is consistently obnoxious to me. So I imagine a situation in which I meet this person. I run through a dress rehearsal on the stage of my imagination. I see myself, in the imagined confrontation, being the kind and tolerant person I really want to be. I do not let the other person, who is offensive, decide my reactions. I am by choice an actor, not a reactor. Such an exercise in positive imagining will practice and reinforce the attitude that I want to make my own. And then, when the actual encounter takes place, it will most likely come off just as in the dress rehearsal. Such positive imagining can be as much a help toward positive and healthy attitudes as rehearsals are to the presentation of a stage play.

Our American astronauts were trained to function in the weightless atmosphere of space by practicing in a "simulator." The exact, gravity-free conditions of space were created inside a model space capsule. Here the astronauts went through their various routines. After the actual blastoff from earth and entrance into space, the astronauts were asked by ground control: "How well are you functioning?" The happy response of the astronauts was: "It is just like practice."

According to Ernest Becker in his book *The Denial of Death,* one part of the reality which we commonly refuse to confront is death. Most of us have no idea how we would react to impending death because we just don't want to think about it. And just as we fear the end of our finite existence, death, Becker maintains that we also fear the full experience of life. One integral part of a human life is the experience of pain—our own and that of others. However, when someone cries, the most common response is a plea: "Don't cry." It is probably good for people to cry, but most of us don't know how to handle tears.

When we cut off the experience of pain, we also separate ourselves from the full experience of the pleasures and the beauty of life. There is so much excitement and stimulation in the world of reality that surrounds us—the sights and the sounds, the light and the darkness, the agonies and the ecstasies of God's world. There is so much, in fact, that we are afraid of it. We are sure that we cannot handle it. We sense that we cannot cope with the charge of such high voltage; we are sure that we would suffer a short circuit. So we shut out much of reality and build a little house by the side of the road, laid back from the heavier traffic and surrounded by a hedge of small bushes. There we live a low-risk existence, with the sedations and distractions we need in order to cope with the limited part of the reality we are willing to confront.

It is obvious that you and I do have a limited capacity. We cannot take in all the suffering or all the beauty of our world. No one could rightly ask us to do this. It is rather a question here of using more of the capacity that we do have. It would be a waste of our human potential if we were to paint ourselves into a small corner of life and stay huddled there, frozen by the fear of a larger world and a fuller life.

In just this way, I would think, it is possible for us to practice the attitude of trust in God and submission to God's higher wisdom. We can cultivate a Christian attitude toward death, for example, by imagining ourselves on our deathbeds. Obviously such meditation on death and dying, recommended and practiced by so many saints, is not intended to be an exercise in morbidity. It is rather a dress rehearsal in which we practice the act of trust and surrender which we will all someday be called upon to make. Such practice will make our response in the actual moment of dying much easier. In a similar way, perhaps, we can prayerfully imagine ourselves in situations of suffering.

We can reflect that an encounter with suffering is truly an encounter with the God who is the Lord of our lives. We can recall in these moments of reflection that God is both tender and loving and at the same time awesome and omnipotent. We can realize and remember that God promises to sustain us in our suffering, to give us strength. Of us God asks only a trusting submission to divine wisdom and will.

A definite attitude toward suffering can be cultivated in such prayerful practices or rehearsals. Then in those moments when suffering, in one of its many forms, actually does touch our life and shake our world, we will be strengthened by these preparations and this prayerful anticipation. It will be "just like practice."

God is both tender and loving and at the same time awesome and omnipotent.

Suggestions for a Theology of Suffering

Some "theology of suffering" is also a necessary part in the preparation of this attitude. We have to come up with some answers to our questions seeking to reconcile a God who is love with the fact of suffering. First, I think, we have to face the fact that God had many options in the act of creation. God could have created other worlds, including a world without suffering. God could have created us already in heaven, confirmed in grace and filled with the utter happiness of the divine presence. Why God chose to create this world, the one we know, why God chose to create us free and capable of sin, capable of hurting one another—this, I presume, is a deep part of the mystery of God. The Russian novelist Dostoyevsky speculated that this was God's one mistake: to make us free. When I speculate about this choice of God, to create this and not another world, I think I have to admit with Job:

> I talked about things I did not understand, about marvels too great for me to know
>
> *Job 42:3, (GNB)*

However, I think that we can safely presume that God knew all the details of the world before creation took place. God did not create blindly and knew from all eternity that you would be born of your designated parents at a given day, hour, and minute. God knew the number of days you would live and the circumstances of your dying. From all eternity God knew the exact number of drops of water in the oceans. Of course, such intelligence and knowledge are inconceivable by our relatively tiny and finite minds. God is, as we believers have always said, infinite and beyond all measurement by human intelligence.

God knew you and me before forming us in the wombs of our mothers. (See Psalm 139:13–16; Jeremiah 1:4–5.) God knew of our days and of our nights. God knew there would be springtimes of delight and dark nights of lonely anguish, moments of human ecstasy, and other moments when we would feel very much alone and when we would wonder if there really is a God who cares. God knew that our gift of freedom would involve the possibility and fact of sin and that evil would touch your life and mine. God knew that we would at times refuse God's offer of grace to overcome temptation and that God would have to write straight with our twistedness and mend our brokenness. Yet, in full knowledge of all these things, God spoke the words of creation.

> "Let there be light. . . . Let there be a vault in the waters to divide the waters in two." . . . God called the vault "heaven." . . . "Let the waters under heaven come together into a single mass and let dry land appear." . . . God called the dry land "earth" and the mass of waters "seas," and God saw that it was good. God said, "Let the earth produce vegetation." . . . God said, "Let there be lights in the vaults of heaven to divide day from night." . . . God saw that it was good. . . . God said, "Let the waters teem with living creatures, and let birds fly above the earth within the vault of heaven." . . . God said, "Let the earth produce every kind of living creature." . . . God said, "Let us make man in our own image, in the likeness of ourselves." . . . God saw all that he had made, and indeed it was very good.

> *Genesis 1 (Jerusalem Bible)*

Someone has said that what we are is God's gift to us, and that what we become is our gift to God. It is true that God gives you and me the lumber of our lives, and offers to help us build from it a cathedral of love and praise. In this matter I have to face my own obvious responsibility. I will either use this lumber I have been given as a stepping-stone, or it will become for me a stumbling block. To use another analogy, day by day God gives me new pieces to fit into this gigantic jigsaw puzzle of my life. Some of these pieces are sharp and painful. Others are drab and colorless. Only God, who has planned and previewed the picture of my life, knows the beauty that is possible when all the pieces have been faithfully put into place. I will know that beauty only after I have put into place the very last piece, the piece of my dying.

Finally, no satisfying theological understanding of suffering can be achieved if one considers only this life which we know, in this world which we know. The context of an endless, eternal life must be in the

Someone has said that what we are is God's gift to us, and that what we become is our gift to God.

background of any Christian exploration of suffering. What happens in this life, in this world, can never make sense to the inquiring mind. There is no apparent fairness or equal distribution of blessings. But Christians have always believed that this life is a mere dot on the endless line of our human existence, which reaches from now into forever. Saint Paul consoles the church of Rome with this realization:

> I consider that what we suffer at this present time cannot be compared at all with the glory that is going to be revealed to us.
>
> *Romans 8:18 (GNB)*

Like Job, I do not have all the answers. After all, where was I when God made the world? But I do have some understanding of trust. And I do trust the God of love who is my Father. I'm sure you yourself must have been in such a situation, when you had to ask another to trust you. Do you remember that you couldn't really explain? You had to ask for an act of trust. Somehow, I think, in this matter of suffering God takes that very position with regard to us. The great and infinite God asks a very limited and finite you and me: "Can you—will you—trust me?"

An Analogy: The Man from Mars

Someone has suggested this analogy, which appeals to me. Imagine that someone from Mars or another distant planet were somehow and suddenly brought into the surgical operating room of one of our hospitals. The Martian might gasp at the inhumanity of what he would see there. He might describe what he saw in this way: "They put some poor person down on a white table. Then they forced a mask over the face of the poor victim. After rendering the person unconscious, masked men cut into her body and took out some of her organs. Their gloved hands were covered with the poor woman's blood. It was a cruel and revolting scene."

Somehow, I think this might be a good illustrative comparison. You and I know that the surgeon is trying to save the person's life. However, to someone who does not understand a surgical operation, it could look like the ultimate cruelty. Sometimes when you and I look at the suffering in the life of another, especially if it is someone we love and care about, we might be tempted to interpret as the Martian did. We might completely misconstrue what is going on, and demand to know why God allowed this to happen. A life-saving, a soul-saving operation of God might look to us like the ultimate in cruelty. In a sense, God deadens us, cuts into our lives, puts in and takes out parts of our selves and possessions of our lives. Just as we entrust ourselves to the surgeon's knowledge and skill, so we are called by faith to an act of trust in and submission to God's infinite knowledge, power, and love. Such an act of trust and submission is obviously a posture of deep faith. I remember reading about the reaction of a mother whose son

had been killed by an assassin's bullet. In the depths of her grief and anguish, she expressed a speculation that could have been made only by a woman of great faith. She said, "Maybe if Robert had lived, he might have disappointed the Lord." Such was the faith of Rose Kennedy.

Suffering As a Teacher

Carrying the cross with Jesus is both a posture and a practice of faith. But we can gain helpful insights into the reality and purpose of suffering. The philosopher Proust once suggested that nothing takes a person apart and puts that person back together again, with the result of greater self-understanding, more effectively than suffering. Without any doubt, suffering always teaches us something and often invites us to change and to grow. Again, the Zen proverb: "When the pupil is ready, the teacher will appear." In Chapter 4, "What's in Me?" we proposed the thesis that a distorted and crippling attitude always results in some form of discomfort. I am sure that if we are willing to trace our discomfort to its attitudinal roots, we will usually find the source of our problem and of our pain. Most of the time this discovery will be an invitation to change and to grow.

A physician who worked for many years in a leper colony once philosophized, "Thank God for pain!" The doctor explained that the reason lepers often lose fingers, limbs, and even features of the face is not the Hansen's disease (leprosy).

We are called by faith to an act of trust in and submission to God's infinite knowledge, power, and love.

It is rather the absence of sensation, the numbness, the inability to experience pain. A leper might well gouge the flesh of her fingers in twisting a stubborn key in a lock and not really know that she has cut herself. She might not realize that an infection is invading her torn flesh until a finger falls off. She has no sensation, no pain to warn her. Or a leper might hold the very hot handle of a pan over an open fire without realizing that his hand is being burned. He has no sensation, no pain to make him aware of this danger. So thank God for sensation and for pain! They often alert us to the presence of danger and harm. Likewise, the various discomforts we experience may well alert us to our distorted and crippling attitudes. But the lessons of pain can be learned only when the pupil is ready. And this means that we must be ready to enter into our pain, seeking to learn from it. It means that we must repress our instinct to run from pain; we must reject any inclination to drug ourselves into dullness so we won't feel anything.

For example, if people who repeatedly suffer from tension headaches enter into their pain to learn from it, they might well realize that they are unsuccessfully trying to please everyone. It may well be that they somehow attach their sense of self-worth to the approval of others. Consequently, everyone in such a person's life has the power to slash the jugular vein of this person's ego. Or perhaps the tension headaches indicate that the suffering person is a perfectionist, demanding perfection of self and of everyone else. The very possibility of imperfection and failure is a terrifying thought to such a person. Likewise it could be that these headaches result from taking oneself too seriously. Instead of seeing myself as a part of a greater human drama, I might be seeing myself as the only actor on the stage. The whole outcome of the human drama then seems to rest solely on my own performance. Finally, it could be that I am getting headaches from trying to entrust my happiness to others. As we have seen, it is futile for me to try to make others responsible for my happiness. Happiness is a matter of one's own attitudes. Happiness begins in the head.

All of the above attitudes are in some way distorted and neurotic. They imply a distorted and damaging way of looking at things. Anyone who consents to live with one of them is doomed to much misery and tension. But notice that the tension headaches are only the symptom, the signal. Pain is the teacher, constantly suggesting a lesson whenever the pupil is ready to listen. Such tension in another person might well take the form of depression or alienation from others. The point here is that the suffering, wherever and however it is felt, is a danger signal, a warning. The suffering is speaking, saying something to the person who will listen. "When the pupil is ready, the teacher will appear!"

Suffering: Its Lessons about Love and Life

Almost all the great figures in the history of psychology have believed that human unhappiness almost always results from a failure to love. When one considers that we must love ourselves, our neighbor, and our God, the truth of this psychological consensus becomes obvious. If we do not love ourselves, there is not much that can make us happy. There will always be the inner struggle, the inner loneliness, the unavoidable sadness. It is likewise true that if someone does not love others, that person will not be loved by others and will be condemned to live in a small and lonely world. Finally, if someone goes through life without a love relationship with God, much of the meaning of life and the motivation for a life of love will be lost. Such a life journey will be almost meaningless, and certainly old age will be deprived of all hope. The important thing is that suffering is a signal. Suffering, in any of its many forms, is very often underlining a failure to love: either ourselves, our neighbor, or our God. The pain is our teacher, if we pupils are ready to listen. We have to get in the habit of tracing our pain and human discomfort to their attitudinal sources.

A priest friend and confidant once asked me if I was enjoying my priesthood. Of course, I said some inspiring things about my deep sense of commitment and dedication. "Beautiful!" he replied.

"However, I did not ask you about that." So I told him about the meaning that I was finding in the exercises of my priesthood. "If I get one thing to do with my life, this is what I want to do!" said I. His reply was persistent: "I'm happy for you, but are you *enjoying* the priesthood?" Perhaps more to my own surprise than to his, I found myself stuttering, "Uh . . . um . . . no. I can't say that I am *enjoying* it." He sympathetically added, "You'd better find out why. God can demand heroism of us, but we shouldn't demand it of ourselves."

And so I did my own little investigation of the attitudinal roots of my dissatisfaction. I have already alluded to the discovery of my overresponsible "Messiah complex" and my attitude that tends to exaggerate my own importance. Seeing oneself as the Messiah and as being responsible for the whole world are certainly attitudes that exhaust, drain, and strain the resources of a person. By the way, when I traced the source of my pain to my exaggerated sense of responsibility, and when I had exposed my Messiah complex, I returned gratefully to my friend. I thanked him for prodding me to examine my lack of enjoyment. I admitted to him, "Do you know what? I was playing Atlas. I was holding the whole world up in my own hands." "Impossible!" he replied. "You couldn't have been supporting the whole world. Do you know why? I was!" Perhaps what we have here is an occupational hazard of those engaged in the priestly ministry.

> *If someone goes through life without a love relationship with God, much of the meaning of life and the motivation for a life of love will be lost.*

Suffering Motivates Us to Change

I have for some time been engaged in trying to learn more about alcoholism. The most constant advice I have heard given to the families and friends of alcoholics is absolutely and resolutely to avoid the role of "enabler." "Never cover up for the drinker or clean up their messes. Don't try to barter your affection for the other person's abstinence. Don't make it easier for the drinker to live with their addiction. Let them feel the pain of their addiction! People change only when the pain gets bad enough!" Of course, I have found this to be true not only with alcoholics but with all of us whose lives need revision. We all have a tendency to stay where we are, even if it is a place of stagnation. It is usually the discomfort or the pain in staying there that jolts us out of our rut toward revision and reform. As the doctor says, "Thank God for pain!" Certainly the most life-transforming insights of my own life have been connected with and have grown out of some experience of pain.

Like the birth of every baby, the bringing forth of human insights almost always involves the experience of pain. I have come to expect that when I enter into my pain rather than run from it, I will find at the center of my pain an amazing insight. Several years ago I remember feeling very angry and upset about a person with whom I had to relate. The very thought of this person seemed to turn my sweetest thoughts into rancid vinegar. I was surprised myself at the depth and dominance of my aversion. A psychologist friend of mine was chatting with me one afternoon in my office. I told him about my strong reactions, my antagonistic feelings with regard to this person. Within minutes he had me looking inside myself for the real source of pain. He reflected, "The world is filled with obnoxious people. When we let them get to us, it is because of something in ourselves." We began to explore my own inner space, and in a few moments he saw my shoulders sag with relief. He heard a soft sigh that said, "I've found it!" "What is it?" he asked. "Can you share it?" "Yes, of course," I said. "You see, the Lord has asked me to make my life an act of love. At the crossroads of every decision, if I am to be a Christian, I must ask only this: What is the loving thing to do, to be, to say? And I have committed myself with all my heart to being a Christian. This is my life-wager. However, I have *not* been loving this person at all. I have been wanting to wash this person out of my hair and out of my life. I have not been asking what I might do or be or say that could help this person find happiness and fulfillment. Very simply, I was not loving. The source of my pain is that I have compromised the fundamental commitment of my life."

Several years after that experience, I started to have similar feelings toward another person with whom I had to relate. However, the lesson of my previous pain came back as a forcible reminder. Right in the middle of a game of verbal one-upmanship with this second person, I realized what I was doing (trying to win an argument) and what I was not doing (loving). I put up my hands in a "T" gesture and said out loud, "Time!" Then I openly admitted, "Hey, I'm not loving you. I'm really sorry." So we laughed a little and hugged a little, and have lived happily ever after. Thank God for pain and its lessons. It motivates us to change. And, of course, Jesus was right: "If you make love the rule and constant motive of your life, you will be very happy!"

The psychologists are right, and of course Christian wisdom down through the centuries has always been right about this issue of human happiness. Our unhappiness somehow represents a failure to love. Our suffering and pain remind us, in ways that are difficult to ignore, that our metanoia is not complete. We try our own formulas for fulfillment, we put into practice our plans for personal happiness, and we dream our little daydreams of destiny. When these fail, the pain of frustration and the suffering of failure advise us to go back and look again at the gospel sources of beatitude. We have to refocus the lenses of our minds to restore a clear perception of what we are called to be. We must try to come to a clear knowledge that happiness can come to us only as a by-product of love and a life motivated by love.

Suffering and "Contact with Reality," the Reality of Me

It is unquestionable that suffering at times can put us into contact with reality as nothing else can. Sometimes we instinctively slap the face of a hysterical person. The surprise of pain can recall that person from the hysteria back into contact with reality. Physical suffering was once inflicted on mental patients in an effort to call them back to reality. Of course, this proved to be a useless and sometimes a dangerous application of the general principle. But it is a fact that very often our suffering strips us of our pretenses, removes our facades, and forces us out of the roles we are trying to play. Suffering demands that the "real me" stand up to be seen.

I am personally convinced that one of the most common reasons for failure in love relationships, including divorce, is this: We enter most of our relationships playing a role. We have a sign extended in front of us announcing our role. "I am a helper . . . I am an enabler . . . I am the friendly, smiling type who never gets angry . . . I am pure intellect . . . I am very religious . . . I am the perpetual nice guy . . ." The act, or role, announced by my sign is something like a bubble. It marks off "my space." I don't want anyone to pierce or puncture my bubble. In a sense I cordon off my space by the announcement and definition of my act.

We must try to come to a clear knowledge that happiness can come to us only as a by-product of love and a life motivated by love.

Obviously, in a truly intimate love relationship, another will come to know me very well. Such a person will inevitably puncture my bubble, will invade my space. Such a person will see that while I like to be a helper, I am also badly in need of help. Anyone who gets really close to me will know perhaps that I smile and don't get angry because I have a terrible fear of being rejected. Such a person will know that I continually smile because I am trying to please everyone. It is the price I am constantly paying for acceptance of others. And oh, I am religious, but I can think and say and even do some pretty irreligious things. Human intimacy exposes all these hidden things in you and in me. In the experience of human intimacy, we are left standing there naked, with all of our warts showing.

The pain will be like a two-edged sword. If I confront it, suffering will demand authenticity of me. It will force the "real me" to stand up and be seen. If I enter into the suffering rather than run from it, I can become a real person and have real relationships. Of course, I can run from my suffering, deny it. I can narcotize myself or distract myself so that I won't feel it. Or I can turn my suffering into projected blame, laying the responsibility on others. The sword of suffering, if I refuse to let it cut away my sham and pretense, can even slay me. Suffering can make us either better or bitter. It all depends, of course, on our attitude toward suffering.

> *Our very human temptation is to look for a place in the sun, and to pretend that we have here a lasting city.*

Our Pilgrim Status and Our Human Insufficiency

One fact of reality that suffering always drives home is that we are the *pilgrim* people of God. We are on our way home, but we are not there yet. We are only passing through this world. We are in fact moving toward a celebration and a fulfillment that eye has not seen, nor ear heard, nor the human mind ever imagined. It is the joy that the Lord has prepared for those who have loved him. But we haven't arrived yet. This is a fact. This is the reality with which we must live. Our very human temptation is to look for a place in the sun, and to pretend that we have here a lasting city. We want to make of our sunny little hillsides the "mountain of transfiguration." Like Peter we want to build permanent tents and stay in our cozy little place forever. We want to stop the insistent movement of the clocks and the perpetual counting of the calendars. We want to deny the reality of death. However, the suffering and the pain in our lives won't let us indulge in such daydreaming, in such unreality. Suffering is a constant reminder that we are still en route.

We also have daydreams of our self-sufficiency. We find a strange comfort in the delusions of our personal completeness. We can even hate the thought of dependency because it implies that our personal resources are not sufficient. So we cultivate these dreams of unreality until suffering awakens us. Poor Augustine, after thirty years of running from God, after thirty years

of brilliant self-deception, fell on his knees and confessed, "Our hearts were made for you, O God, and they will not rest until they rest in you. . . . Too late, too late, O Lord, have I loved you. . . . The ability to remember is indeed a sad privilege." In a sense, Augustine had to "hit bottom" to be grounded in reality. In his pain and restless emptiness he found his need for the God whom he tried to shut out of his life. Remembrance of the wasted years was very painful, a sad privilege. Almost always suffering has a unique way of unraveling the fabric of our delusions of self-sufficiency. Suffering can make us face and be our true selves as nothing else can. Of course, it is always possible to refuse these lessons, to run away from rather than enter into the meaning and lesson of our suffering. "When the pupil is ready, the teacher will appear."

The Secular Attitude toward Suffering

This Christian attitude toward suffering is obviously disowned and vigorously denied by the world we live in. The message of the media, which is constantly invading our senses and attempting to persuade our minds, is this: Go through life with the maximum amount of pleasure and the minimum amount of pain. All suffering must be shunned. Have a happy hour. Desensitize yourself with a few drinks. You only go around once. Grab all you can. Fly now, pay later. Let the good times roll. When in pain, pop a pill. Narcotize yourself. Promote pleasure. Eat, drink, and be merry; tomorrow we die. Remember: This is the "me generation." Be good to good old number one!

To some extent all of us have bought into this "good times" philosophy of life. One needs only to read the statistics to know how successful the world of advertisement and the media have been. In our own country there are enough aspirins and other analgesics sold each year to cure three billion headaches. In our country, the kind of drug most often prescribed is the tranquilizer. No other drugs even come close. Our little "valley of tears" is rapidly becoming the "valley of Valium." Another big business in the country is the illicit production and sale of marijuana. One former user and ardent promoter has said recently, "If you want to shut off your mind, to be really dumb and operate only at a sense level, smoke pot!" Snorting and free-basing cocaine have become the "indoor sports" of many of our idolized actors, actresses, and athletes. More than ten million Americans are addicted to the drug alcohol. One alcoholic told me that he drinks because when he doesn't, life hurts too much. Parents have been led to believe that they are not good parents unless they can keep their children perpetually happy. Throw gifts, food, money, anything at them, but keep them happy!

We are indeed a brainwashed people, ready to scratch before we even have an itch. The advertisers, many of the Hollywood heroes and heroines, and most of the scriptwriters who wash our brains see no value, no redemptive lessons, to be found in suffering. Let the good times roll.

Over and above the smoke of our dreams and delusions stands the loving but lonely figure of Jesus. In back of him, casting a long shadow, is a tall cross. To most of the people in our world, the cross is a stumbling block, a madness to be avoided. But to us who believe that there is in suffering the challenge of metanoia, the invitation to life transformation and personal growth, suffering is a valuable teacher. Thank God for pain. Jesus seems to be asking our generation, "Can you drink from the chalice of suffering with me? Can you trust me?" And then Jesus says softly, as he did two thousand years ago, "Whoever does not carry his own cross and come after me cannot be my disciple." (Luke 14:27, GNB)

For a Christian there is no other way to maturity, wisdom, and the fullness of life. We must all sit at the feet of this teacher. And we must stake our lives on the surrender of faith and trust that suffering always demands. "I consider that what we suffer at this present time cannot be compared at all with the glory that is going to be revealed to us." (Romans 8:18, GNB)

FOR FURTHER REFLECTION
Chapter 21: The Christian Vision of Suffering

Review

1. How does the story of Job in the Bible attempt to reconcile suffering with the existence of an all-loving God?

2. In order to deal with suffering in our lives, it helps to have already established a certain mind-set toward it. Describe what attitude(s) would help a person deal with an experience of suffering.

3. What suggestions or concepts are needed to help develop a healthy "theology of suffering"?

4. In order to further develop a healthy theology of suffering, the following concepts are important. Explain each one.
   (a) Suffering is a teacher.
   (b) Suffering teaches us lessons about life and love.
   (c) Suffering motivates us to change.
   (d) Suffering brings us into contact with reality and "the reality of me."
   (e) Suffering reminds us of our pilgrim status and our human insufficiency.

5. In what ways does the typical secular attitude toward suffering disown and deny the reality of suffering? What is the media's message regarding suffering? How does the media persuade people to deal with their suffering?

Discuss

1. Most people are better at enduring one form of suffering or pain than another. What forms of suffering or pain are most difficult for you? Why?

2. Is there any specific suffering or pain for which you have a particular fear or even dread?

3. From what do you most frequently suffer in your life?

4. Intellectually we know that suffering can be very profitable, and we may even realize that past sufferings have brought great blessings. Do you ever have grateful, welcoming feelings in the midst of suffering?

5. If someone could offer you a pill that would have no side effects but would eliminate suffering for the rest of your life, would you take it? Why or why not?

6. Do you feel an inner urgency to eliminate all suffering in your own life, and in the lives of those you love?

7. Do you often have feelings of satisfaction when another person is struggling and you have hopes that they will come out of it a better person?

8. What suffering or pain in the past year of your life has affected you most deeply?

Scripture Activity

"'Whoever does not carry his own cross and come after me cannot be my disciple." (Luke 14:27, *GNB*)

Reflect on what it means for you to "take up your cross and follow" Jesus. Compose a prayer of abandonment to, and trust in, God. Ask Jesus to enlighten and empower you so that through your suffering you might grow in maturity, wisdom, and the fullness of life. Ask him for the strength to carry your cross as you learn the important lessons about life and love.

Processing These Ideas about Suffering

1. *An interview with a person who has suffered.* Interview someone who has suffered a great loss or disappointment. Ask them to share how they coped with that suffering, and whether or not through hindsight they have discovered a great benefit from their experience of suffering. Record your findings.

2. *My own experience of suffering.* Recall an experience of suffering that you personally went through. Describe what happened and share what lessons you learned about life through it. Determine whether or not your experience of suffering helped you to grow in wisdom, maturity, and the fullness of life.

22 *The Christian Vision of the Church*

Another Exercise: The Church Is . . .

At various times I have asked people to do an association exercise about the Church. It's one of those really simple things. One just completes a sentence with the first thought that comes to mind. "The Church is . . ." In my experience, the most common response has been: ". . . a building." Frequent but less common: ". . . an organization run by priests and ministers" and ". . . where some people go on Sunday." The responses also get into the school systems, and occasionally a bit of sadness and bitterness finds its way into the exercises: ". . . a house for hypocrites." Obviously, there are various ways of seeing or perceiving the Church. And so we ask: How should a Christian see the Church? How does Jesus see the Church?

One of my former students, who is now a teacher himself, told me about a clever teaching devise he uses with his grade school students. It is meant to get across a simple, clear, and Christian way of looking at the Church. My friend goes to the chalkboard in his classroom and says, "I'm going to put the Church right up here, spell it out right here on the board." So he prints in large letters: CH CH.

Then he backs away, muttering to himself that "something is missing." Of course, his young and eager students tell him what is missing: UR . . . UR!" Then he looks enthusi-astically and points to his young students and exclaims, "Ah! *You are* at the center of the Church. And so there can be no Church unless *you are* there." I rather like that little teaching device. It presents a bedrock truth in a simple and memorable way.

The Need for the Church

The Church has many facets and can be perceived from many different vantage points. Just as I am a man, a teacher, a priest, a Jesuit and can be perceived as any one of these things, so the Church can be perceived as an organism, the Body of Christ, the prolongation of Jesus in time and the extension of Jesus in space, and so forth. It is undeniable that the Church is also an organization, an organization of the "Jesus People." Just as the organs of our bodies all have specific functions to perform, so every organization has a specific purpose. We don't start an organiza-tion and then look for something that it might do. Rather we first have a cause, something to be accomplished, a need to be met.

> *"God's plan is to make known his secret to his people, this rich and glorious secret which he has for all peoples. And the secret is that Christ is in you."*
>
> *Colossians 1:27 (GNB)*

295

Then we start an organization to work for that cause, to accomplish that goal, to meet that need. Like every other organization, the Church was formed to do something. God wanted something to be done, so God called together a Church, the Jesus People, to do it.

Likewise, all of us are aware that an individual cannot alone bring about widespread change in our world. An individual alone normally cannot accomplish a great cause. So we form political parties, racial equality committees, and organizations to preserve endangered species, to promote respect for life, to preserve the ecological balance, and to promote world peace. An individual who is not fed by the enthusiasm and support of others involved in the same cause usually gives up. Human dedication and enthusiasm for a cause, like everything human, are contagious. Dedication and enthusiasm are caught, not taught. Alone, apart from an organization, each of us would feel lost in the vast human wilderness. Alone we would feel drowned in a great sea of the unconcerned. Alone our voices would be like a soft whisper in the midst of a brass band concert. However, in chorus, the whole world can hear us. So God organized a chorus, the chorus of the Church, because God wanted the whole world to hear the good news.

Assuming these two truths about organizations, imagine now that you are God. (If it comes too easily, don't admit it. People will suspect you.) You are God and you have a cause. You want to gather all the individual human beings whom you have created into one family, your family. They are, as it were, the flesh of your flesh and the bones of your bones. They are made in your own image and likeness. But creatures are not the same as children, and you want to make them your adopted children so that you can share your life, your happiness, and even your home with them forever. You have already decided that these humans, made in your image and likeness, must always be free, and so you will offer your love and your life and your home, but you will not force these gifts upon the children whom you wish to adopt. Now, supposing you were God, what would you do?

What we know is that God became a man, called together a people, and formed an organization. This is the Church. What the members of this Church are supposed to do is to make the announcement, to spread the good news of God's loving intentions to make us God's family. This chosen people is meant to invite others into the experience of God's intimacy and into God's family. Sometimes we delude ourselves into thinking that the most important part of such an announcement and invitation is the words we use. Too often we get overinvolved with our words and even lost in them. In fact, the words we use are very often the least important part of the message-invitation entrusted to the Church. There is an old Chinese proverb: "What you are speaks so loudly that

God organized a chorus, the chorus of the Church, because God wanted the whole world to hear the good news.

I cannot hear what you are saying." All of us know that example is far more eloquent and persuasive than words. When others lecture and sermonize us, we often want to plead with them, "Show me. Don't tell me." People want only values that they have experienced, that they have seen "lived."

And so the most important and effective persons in this Church called together by God are not those who live by preaching, but rather those who preach by living. The most important persons are not the ones who tell us what love is, but rather those who actually love us. And those of us in the Church (like myself) who spend a large part of our lives mouthing the message must admit that words are, or can be, cheap. The true discipleship of a life of love is a far more costly and a far more eloquent testimony. The saints say more by their lives than all the books ever written, than all the sermons ever preached, than all the words ever spoken. However, whatever its diversity of people and roles, the task and function of the whole Church is to bring the human race together as God's family.

God's Cause, God's Plan: To Make Us God's Family

This you-and-I-Church, then, is God's effort and instrument to fashion a family. Saint Paul calls this cause or intention God's "plan." Paul says that this plan of God, to make us one family, was hidden in the heart of God from all eternity. Then, Paul says, it was revealed to us in the person and the preaching of Jesus. Finally, Paul insists that it must now be accomplished or achieved through us and among us. (See Ephesians, chapters 1–3.)

What does this plan involve? An adequate understanding would take us all the way back to the very act of creation. Before the world was made, there was only God: Father, Son, and Holy Spirit. In the boundless and infinite ecstasy of their mutual love, they wanted to share what was theirs. Love, of course, always does this. The deepest instinct of love is to share. Love is always self-diffusive. Love has an inner need to give away its possessions. And God is, by Saint John's definition, *Love*. In the act of creation, then, God wanted to share God's self— God's goodness and life, happiness and home. God did not create to get something but to give everything.

By a special choice God picked out each of us for God's own. The Creator could have made a world without a you or a me, but this Abba-God didn't want a world without you and me. That would have been an incomplete world. Likewise, God could have made us different, but it was this you and this me, just as we are, that God always loved. God wanted to share with this you and this me. However, God not only wanted to share *with* us, but also intended to share *through* us with others. God wanted us to share everything given to us individually with our human brothers and sisters.

> The deepest instinct of love is to share. Love has an inner need to give away its possessions.

> *The love of Abba-God which has been given to you and me is not intended to stop, to accumulate in you and me. Rather it is meant to be passed along through us to one another.*

Gathering a family means that the lines of loving must be horizontal as well as vertical. The reality of a human family clearly involves a vertical relationship between parents and each child. But the love which has its starting point and origin in the parents is also circulated horizontally among the children. The children become channels of love to one another rather than reservoirs which retain what they have in and for themselves alone. Love must flow through the whole network of the family relationship. Eventually such love unites everyone in a family.

Consequently, the love of Abba-God which has been given to you and me is not intended to stop, to accumulate in you and me. Rather it is meant to be passed along through us to one another. No grace of God is really accepted and fully used until it has been shared. There is a saying among the members of Alcoholics Anonymous: "The only way to keep your sobriety is to give it away, to pass it on to others." It is always this way with love. The only way we can keep the love that God has invested in each of us is to pass it on to one another. And it is this that will accomplish God's intention to have us bound together in love as God's family. So, of every other human being you and I can truly say, "He ain't heavy; he's my brother. She ain't heavy; she's my sister." And so, God who is Father and Mother to us has made us sisters and brothers in one family. This is God's cause and God's plan; this is to be the accomplishment of God's Church.

The Unity of God's Family

It has often been asked if it really does any good to pray for the dead, to pray to the saints, or to pray for one another. Good questions, aren't they? It seems obvious to me that God could have made this arrangement Since God can do anything God wants to. The point is that I feel sure that God does in fact make this arrangement because this kind of praying provides interaction and ultimately unity among us. It unites all of us in a network of human interdependency and mutual help. We are indeed God's family, brothers and sisters in the Lord. If one of us is hurting, we are all hurt. If one of us is successful, then we all rejoice. We are family, God's family.

So then, the eye cannot say to the hand, "I don't need you!" Nor can the head say to the feet, "Well, I don't need you!" On the contrary, we cannot do without the parts that seem to be weaker; and those parts that we think aren't worth very much are the ones which we treat with greater care; while the parts of the body which don't look very nice are treated with special modesty, which the more beautiful parts do not need. God himself has put the body together in such a way as to give greater honor to those parts that need it. And so there is no division in the body, but all its different parts have the same concern for one another. If one part of the body suffers, all the other parts suffer with it;

if one part is praised, all the other parts share its happiness. All of you are Christ's body, and each one is a part of it. In the church God has put all in place.

1 Corinthians 12:21–28 (GNB)

So God has called us together, united us into a people, the family of God, through and in Jesus. Jesus is the vine and we are the branches. Jesus is our God-connection. God's love flows through him and into us, and this life continues to circulate through us and among us. In the beginning, each of us is united to Jesus through the rite of baptism. Through this sacrament, we become parts of his body, live branches of his life-giving vine. We are nourished by all the sacraments, as also by the Scriptures, by personal prayer, and by living lives of love. In our Christian living, we begin our family life. We begin to receive our inheritance as the sons and daughters of our Abba-God. We become the heirs of God's promise.

In a very profound way we are in fact brothers and sisters to one another. Each of us has already received the first great gift of our spiritual inheritance: the gift of the Holy Spirit. The Spirit of God resides within each of us as the source of the divine life and the source of all the divine graces: peace, power, joy, health, and all the gifts of God. The life of God, which is not fully visible or experiential, is in each of us. From time to time we might experience the touch of God, tugs on our kite strings; but for the most part, we take this on faith. The life of God is in each of us, and this

---

All of us to some extent are enduring agonies of loneliness, frustration, emotional and spiritual starvation. Somehow these pains are radically due to failures in love. The essential sadness of such pain is that it magnetizes the focus of our attention; it preoccupies us with ourselves. And self-preoccupation is an absolute obstacle to a life of love.

I once asked a psychiatrist friend of mine, "How can you teach people to love?" His answer was mildly surprising, to say the least. He answered the question by asking one of his own: "Did you ever have a toothache? Of whom were you thinking during the distress of your toothache?" His point was clear. When we are in pain, even if it be only the passing discomforts of an aching tooth, we are thinking about ourselves.

The psychiatrist continued: "This is a pain-filled world in which we are living. And the pains that reside deep in the human hearts around us are not like toothaches. We go to bed with them at night and wake up with them in the morning. This is a pain-filled world, and so, a loveless world that we live in. Most human beings are so turned-in on themselves by their own pain that they cannot easily go out in love to others."

From *Why Am I Afraid to Love?*

---

means that we are all closely bonded to one another. We are more closely united by this living presence of the Spirit in us than we would be by family blood lines. The shared life of God, of which we are all temples, makes us family in a very profoundly personal way. This is the faith vision of the reality which we call the Church.

The plan of God then begins with God's generous gifts of life and love. And to those of us who have felt this life and love quicken in us, God directs a request that we share with our sisters and brothers what we have received.

The reality of the Church, in its most fundamental meaning, describes this network of channels through which the gifts of God run out to all creation. We are the means through which God chooses to bless the world, the means by which God gathers together our human race, to make us God's family, and to make us family to one another.

The Church and the Kingdom

Earlier we described the kingdom of God this way: On the part of God the kingdom is an invitation to us to come to God in love. On our part the kingdom is a "yes," a response of love: "Behold we come!" All the scholars of Sacred Scripture are agreed that "the kingdom of God" is the central message in the preaching of Jesus. The disputed question concerns the time of its coming. Jesus seems to be saying three different things about this. First he speaks of the kingdom as already present.

> After John had been put in prison, Jesus went to Galilee and preached the Good News from God. "The right time has come," he said, "and the Kingdom of God is near! Turn away from your sins and believe the Good News!"
> *Mark 1:14–15 (GNB)*

But Jesus also speaks about the coming of this kingdom as an event that would take place within his own generation. Some of the people to whom he was speaking would witness the coming of the kingdom.

> And Jesus went on to say, "I tell you, there are some here who will not die until they have seen the kingdom of God come with power." *Mark 9:1 (GNB)*

In a third set of gospel texts, Jesus speaks of the kingdom as coming at a day and hour that no one knows.

> "Then the Son of Man will appear, coming in the clouds with great power and glory. He will send the angels out to the four corners of the earth to gather God's chosen people from one end of the world to the other. . . . No one knows, however, when that day or hour will come—neither the angels in heaven, nor the Son; only the Father knows. Be on watch, be alert, for you do not know when the time will come.
> *Mark 13:26–27, 32–33 (GNB)*

The Timing of the Kingdom: An Explanation

Some scholars have felt obliged to choose one or the other set of texts, reasoning that they can't all be authentic. These scholars then declare the others incompatible and therefore not really the words of Jesus. Most, however, feel that the whole tradition of gospel interpretation moves away from this either-or position. They believe that one and the same kingdom can actually have three stages in its coming. The kingdom of God is like a planted seed, which will only gradually reach certain stages of growth. It will achieve these stages only in and with time.

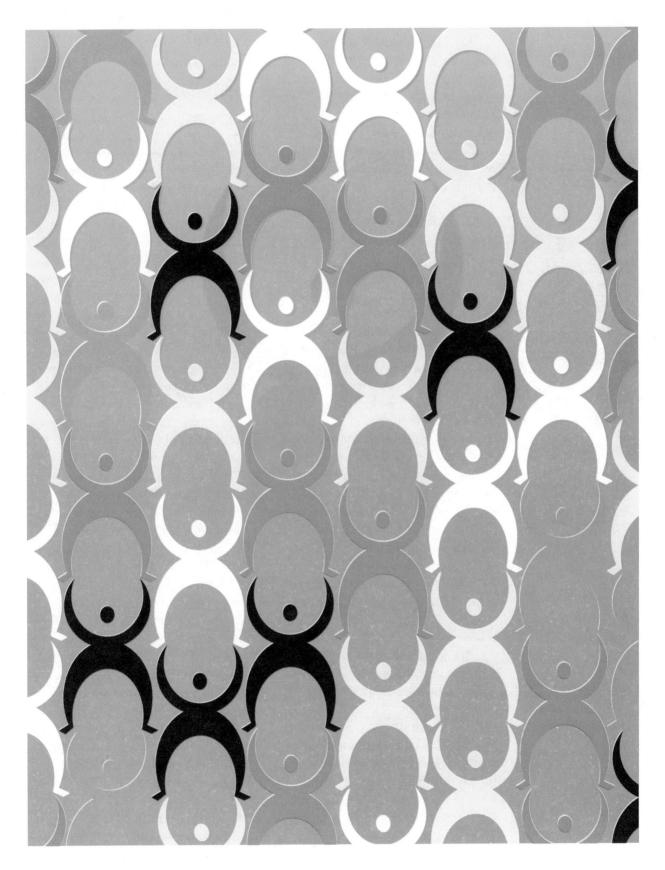

Literally, we know that the kingdom of God is an *invitation* on the part of God and an act of *acceptance* on the part of our human race. The invitation is extended in a series of requests and events, much as a young man in our culture invites a woman to share his life. There is the first date, the invitation into a special and exclusive relationship ("going steady"), the proposal of marriage, and the engagement period; finally there are the vows and consummation of marriage. In a similar way, God has extended to us through Jesus not one but rather a series of progressive invitations, calling us deeper and deeper into his intimacy.

In the New Testament, Jesus proclaims that the kingdom of God is here; it is at hand and among us. He is saying that his very presence, as well as his preaching and healing, is itself an invitation into the intimacy of God and into the sharing of God's life. Jesus' presence and his works are the first of the three invitations described in the New Testament. Of course, there were other invitations in the Old Testament, made through the patriarchs and prophets.

But Jesus speaks of a time, within a generation, when some of his hearers will see the kingdom coming in power. Here, I feel sure, he is referring to his death-resurrection-ascension and the outpouring of the Holy Spirit upon the faithful. This would be the second invitation described in the New Testament. Of this invitation, Jesus is in effect saying:

"Within a generation, you will see me hanging on a cross. My blood will run down onto the rocks of Calvary. Oh, but do not mistake this scene for tragedy. No one is taking my life from me. I am offering my life for those I love. My blood will be sealing a new and eternal covenant of love between God and God's family. Do not mistake my death for an end. It will really be only the beginning, because I shall rise and will go to my Father. who will then send the Holy Spirit into the hearts of men and women all over the world. And the Father, the Spirit, and I will take up our residence of love in human hearts."

The intervention-invitation will make possible a whole new dimension of intimacy: God will live and reign in the hearts of men and women as never before. And all this will come as the result of the death of Jesus, within a generation.

Finally, Jesus speaks of the coming of the kingdom on a day and at an hour that no one knows. He tells the people of his time that they will look up and see the Son of Man coming again on the clouds of the heavens. It will be the end of the world, as we know it. This is the third stage of God's invitation, described in the New Testament. Jesus will call all the just, God's family, into the eternal and definitive kingdom of God. Jesus will gather us all into his Father's house, which we call heaven. And then we will all enjoy forever the deepest intimacy: vision! We will see God face-to-face, which means that we will know God directly. There we will receive the full inheritance of

God's children: a profound and perpetual peace, the satisfaction of all our desires, and the answers to all our restless questions. We will experience forever the pure joy that God has wanted to share with us, God's beloved family, from all eternity. This is God's loving plan. These are the stages of God's kingdom as it is being carried out.

The kingdom of God, then, is an invitation of God, asking us to enter into, to say "yes" to, and to participate in God's plan of sharing. There are, as mentioned, three major stages of this invitation described in the New Testament: (1) the presence and power of Jesus in the world, (2) Jesus' death-resurrection-ascension and the sending of the Holy Spirit, (3) his second coming at the end of the world and the final judgment of the world.

Saying "Yes" to the Kingdom

When Jesus asks us to pray "Thy kingdom come," he is instructing us to ask for the grace to say "yes" to the loving invitation of God. Just as there are stages of intervention and invitation described in the New Testament, so there are various stages of intervention and invitation in your life and in mine. Your life and mine are like microcosms of the long, gradual coming of the kingdom in history. Each life, your life and my life, is a series of interventions inviting a response of love. We have to be ready, to watch, and to pray for one another that we will say "yes" to these invitations spaced throughout our lives. In his book *Prayers,* Michel Quoist writes:

> Help me to say "yes."
> I am afraid of saying "yes,"
>   Lord.
> Where will you take me?
> I am afraid of the "yes" that
>   entails other "yeses."
> I am afraid of putting my hand
>   in yours,
>   for you hold onto it. . . .
> Oh, Lord, I am afraid of your
>   demands,
> but who can resist you?
> That your Kingdom may come
>   and not mine,
> That your will be done and not
>   mine,
> Help me to say "yes."[1]

I think of this kingdom in my own life. Each day brings a new supply of "lumber" with which I must build a cathedral of love and praise. Each day brings new pieces of the jigsaw puzzle of my life, which I must fit into place. Each day challenges me to a new, to a deeper and more loving "yes." Some of these invitations are very pleasant, but others are sharp and painful. Sometimes God draws me into a night of suffering and shapes me over the painful fires of doubt. God challenges me forcibly to self-surrender. I feel the ringing blows of God's hammering grace on my soul. There are also many invitations that come as spring to melt my coldness. They bring back the grass, the leaves and flowers. The warm breezes of consolation invade my heart. The blood flows again through the veins of my soul.

Your life and mine are like microcosms of the long, gradual coming of the kingdom in history.

---

[1] Michael Quoist, *Prayers* (Fairway, Kans.: Andrews & McMeel, 1974), pp. 121, 123.)

Sometimes, of course, I am not watching and praying. I am not standing ready with my "yes." So the gracious and forgiving God who comes looking for me like the Good Shepherd looking for his stray sheep. God is always reinviting me, asking again for the "yes" of my love and surrender. With Michel Quoist I pray, "Lord, help me to say 'yes.' " And, in the Lord's own words, I pray, "Thy Kingdom come" in my life and in my world.

The "Horizontal" Kingdom

One implication of our call to the kingdom, which each of us must face, is this: I cannot say my "yes" of love to God without saying my "yes" of love to you. Neither can you say your "yes" to God without including me in your act of love. Jesus is very clear about this. If we come to place our gift of love upon his altar, and while there we remember that we are nursing a grudge of unforgiveness, we must turn back. We have to make peace with each other first. Only then can we come to him with a gift of self, the "yes" of love. He does not want my gift of love unless it is also offered to you. He does not want your gift of love unless you have shared that gift with me.

> "I have told you this so that my joy may be in you and that your joy may be complete. My commandment is this: love one another, just as I love you. . . . This, then, is what I command you: love one another."
>
> *John 15:11–12, 17 (GNB)*

In the kingdom of God I am never less than an individual, but I am never only an individual. I am always a member of a group, called by God to a response of love, which must include the whole group or it is literally unacceptable to God.

The Church is indeed God's family, and the Lord who calls us to a response of love takes as done to himself whatever we do to one another. "Whatever you do to the least of my children you do to me." There can be no relationship of love with God unless we relate to one another in love. Sometimes this seems to be the highest cost of being a Christian. It is so much easier to love the God I don't see than the neighbor I do see. But, as Saint John says:

> The message you heard from the very beginning is this: we must love one another. . . . We know that we have left death and come over into life; we know it because we love our brothers [and sisters]. Whoever does not love is still under the power of death. Whoever hates his brother [or sister] is a murderer, and you know that a murderer does not have eternal life in him. This is how we know what love is: Christ gave his life for us. We too, then, ought to give our lives for our brothers [and sisters]! If a rich person sees his brother [or sister] in need, yet closes his heart against his brother [or sister], how can he claim that he loves God? My children, our love should not be just words

In the kingdom of God I am never less than an individual, but I am never only an individual.

and talk; it must be true love, which shows itself in action.

1 John 3:11, 14–18 (GNB)
We love because God first loved us. If someone says he loves God but hates his brother [or sister], he is a liar. For he cannot love God, whom he has not seen, if he does not love his brother [and sister], whom he has seen. The command that Christ has given us is this: Whoever loves God must love his brother [and sister] also.

1 John 4 :19–21 (GNB)

A God with Skin

There is a well-circulated story about a child wanting to be held by his mother at bedtime. When the mother reminded her little boy that the arms of God would be around him all night, the child replied, "I know, but tonight I need a God with skin on." There is something profound, I think, in the child's reply. There are times when all of us need a God with skin on. Everything that we know in our minds must somehow come through the channels of our senses. Our senses are the organs of our contact with the external world. So, if God is going to come to us through the normal channels of our knowing, this must somehow occur through our senses. Somehow, God must allow us to see, hear, and touch God. In the Old Testament, God's voice is heard in the thunder and seen in the lightning over Sinai. God's voice booms out of the burning bush and out of the mouths of the prophets. God's is

the still voice that comes on the soft breeze, saying, "Be still, and know that I am God." Saint John, at the beginning of his first letter, says that he wants to tell us about Jesus.

We write to you about the Word of life, which has existed from the very beginning. We have heard it, and we have seen it with our eyes; yes, we have seen it, and our hands have touched it. When this life became visible, we saw it; so we speak of it and tell you about the eternal life which was with the Father and was made known to us. What we have seen and heard we announce to you also, so that you will join with us in the fellowship that we have with the Father and with his son Jesus Christ.

1 John 1: 1–3 (GNB)
The Christians of the early Church knew that all subsequent generations would need "a God with skin." Human beings can encounter Jesus, the source of all life and salvation, only if he is somehow available to their senses. The people of all generations, if they are to meet Jesus, must be able to see and hear and touch him, as Saint John did. It is a fundamental law of human psychology and of human experience.

And this is why God has willed to fashion a community of love which we call the Church. Saint Paul said that this plan of God, hidden in God from all eternity, has been revealed by Jesus and must be realized in and through us. Paul exclaims that this is God's plan: *Christ is in us!* (See Colossians 1:27.)

God's plan is that Jesus would live on in you and in me and in all the members of his Body, the Church. God would indeed be for all humans in all ages "a God with skin."

God put all thing under Christ's feet and gave him to the church as supreme Lord over all things. The church is Christ's body, the completion of him who himself completes all things everywhere.
Ephesians 1: 22–23 (GNB)

God's plan means this: Jesus will live in each of the members of his Church. This is the way that the people of this and of all generations to come can meet Jesus: in us, in you and in me! We are the flesh and blood, the bones and skin of Jesus, whose members we are. We are God's planned way of sharing God and God's love.

There is a familiar, post–World War II story about a statue of Jesus in the shell of a bombed-out German church. The figure of Jesus was portrayed in this statue as reaching out to the world. However, in the devastation of the bombing, the hands of the statue were broken off. For a long time afterward, the statue without hands stood as it was found. However, a sign was hung from the outstretched arms: "He has no hands but yours!" In a very real sense, this is true. We, the Church, the members of his Body, are his only hands, his only mouth, his only mind and heart. We are indeed the extension of Jesus in space and the prolongation of Jesus in time. We will continue his work of redemption, loving this world into life, or it will not be done at all.

The kingdom of God marches at the pace of our feet.

Of course, this could send shock waves through the nervous system. "I am Jesus to the world? Oh, no! I can't be that." After we get over the initial dread and the impulse to make a disclaimer, I think we all have to realize very calmly that this is not a call to walk on water. However, it is a call to stand up and be counted. Again, we recall the haunting question: If you were arrested for being a Christian, would there be enough evidence to convict you? The Jesus who asks to be recognizable in me isn't the perfect and all-good and all-powerful Jesus. I could never manage that. However, it is rather the Jesus who labors in me, who consoles me and supports me in my human weakness, that must shine out of me. It is the Jesus who said to Paul: "My strength will work through your weakness."

All of us carry the treasure of this loving Jesus, residing within us and working through us, in fragile vessels of clay. We cannot be expected to exhibit perfection, but we must be willing to stand up and to offer our personal testimonials to grace. You and I should want to say to the world, as best we can, by our words and our way of living, by our work and our worship: "Jesus has touched my life. By his kindness, by his encouragement, and by his challenge, Jesus has made all the difference in my life. I was blind and now I see. I was lost and now I'm found!" However, for myself I feel an inner urgency to add to this witness: "But please be patient. God is not finished with me yet."

> *God's plan means this: Jesus will live in each of the members of his Church.*

Stories of Faith: Testimonials to Grace

Today there has been a renewed interest in "stories of faith." More and more people are willing to come forth and tell the world about the touch of the Lord upon their lives. Having no delusions about their personal virtue and perfection, they can nevertheless say with certainty, "He has touched me, and after that nothing was ever the same!" For myself, I think I would be failing in gratitude if I did not say this to the world. No grace is ever fully used until it has been shared. I am certain that the Lord has touched my life, and I do recognize my obligation to share the graces which have been poured out upon me and my life. And so, I want to share God's goodness to me with others, with my sisters and brothers in God's family. Of course, the Lord is not finished with me yet. I am still very frail and flawed. I limp, and I know my own brokenness. I offer no other assurance except to say that I know he has touched and transformed my life.

So, when they ask, "Will the Jesus People please stand up?" I want to stand tall. I want to stand and be counted as one of the Jesus People. But I must share this with you: It would be very frightening to stand alone. I need you to stand with me in the ranks of the Church, the Jesus People. I need my weak voice to be joined by yours in the chorus that sings the Lord's praise and says the Lord's prayer. Yes, I have felt the touch of the Lord upon my life and I have felt the hand of the Lord in mine. But I would be very doubtful about my own experiences if you did not stand at my side and confirm me in my faith by your own testimonial to grace.

Confirming One Another in Faith

I once wrote a small book entitled *He Touched me: My Pilgrimage of Prayer,* at the request of an editor friend. For many years after the publication of that book, I received several letters each week from various parts of the world. Almost all these letters came from people who were grateful for the gift of being able to recognize their own experiences in mine. It was the joy of recognition, I suppose. "So much of your story parallels mine." It was very consoling and reassuring that the God who has touched me has also touched many others of my sisters and brothers. One of most moving of these letters was the sharing of a very beautiful and generous woman. She wrote:

> I decided to end my life, which had been utterly selfish and sinful. I was so miserable that I just wanted to end it all. I wanted to die by drowning. I imagined the ocean as a vast and watery mother who would rock me in the cradle of her waves and wash me clean in her waters.

> I got to the strand of beach along the ocean, where I was to die. I walked all alone along the deserted shoreline. However, that day the ocean was not a warm and watery mother.

No grace is ever fully used until it has been shared.

The weather was nasty, and the ocean was a snarling beast. Inside me I knew that I had to die, to end it all. If I had to give myself to a snarling beast rather than throw myself into the arms of a great mother, then so be it.

I had been walking along the sandy beach, and was about to turn into the water when I heard a very clear voice which seemed to be coming from within myself. It was very distinct and clear. The voice asked me to stop, to turn around and look down. There was something irresistible in the command, and so I did as I was asked. I could see only the waves of the ocean washing over, erasing my footprints in the sand. Then the voice returned: "Just as you see the waters of the ocean erasing your foot-prints, so has my love and mercy erased all record of your sins. I want you back in my love. I am calling you to live and to love, not to die."

It was like a shaft of blinding light in the darkness that was my life at that time. I turned away from the water and from all thoughts of dying. I have, with God's continued love and help, found a beautiful and satisfying life. I am now living and I am loving.

But I have never told anyone, not anyone, what happened to me that day on the beach. My whole life was changed forever by that experi-ence. Still I was afraid that, if I were to share it, someone might tell me that it was all a dream, a delusion. Someone might tell me that I didn't really want to die, and so I made up the voice which would tell me what I really wanted to hear.

Since so much of my life, the good and beautiful life I have found, is built on that moment, I could not risk its sacredness in hands that might be callous and insensitive. I could not bear to let someone take my most sacred secret and ridicule it.

After reading your book, I thought you would understand, and so I wanted to share this with you. You wrote at the end of your book that telling your story was your gift of love to us. Please accept this as my gift of love to you.

Of course, I will never forget that letter, even though I have never met its author. Something about the experience described in that letter sounds very authentic, and the author sounds truly balanced and blessed by God. When I occasion-ally reread this letter, the whole world seems a bit warmer, the sky always looks a bit brighter, and the loving presence of God in our world and among us seems much more real to me. The Jesus in that woman profoundly stirred in me a thousand remembrances of his goodness to me and through me. Her faith and her experience have really supported my own. The story of his goodness to her always starts in me a grateful count of my own blessings. For me she has been indeed, in her act of love, "a God with skin." She was, is, and will

> *God reaches out to me through you and out to you through me.*

always be for me an earthen vessel in whom I have experienced the presence of the Lord Jesus. It was indeed an experience of the reality and the meaning of the Church.

This is the deepest meaning and the fundamental function of the Church, as I see it. As mentioned, the question is not, *What* is the Church? The real question is, *Who* is the Church? "You are" (UR) is the heart and center of the very word *Church*. If we, if you and I, are to be the Church, then I know that I need you, and need you badly, to stand next to me, a God with skin. I need to hear your voice being raised with mine in prayer. I need to know by the experience of your nearness that God has made you my sister, my brother, and that we are together God's family. I need to pray with you for the coming of the kingdom. I need to hear you saying your "yes" which braces my own "yes" with a new strength. There is an inevitable contagion in everything human. And so I need the support of your presence, your love, and your person. God reaches out to me through you and out to you through me. And if, somehow and for your own reasons, you should choose to "leave the Church," please do not think that you have simply walked out of a building or an organization marked with weakness. The fact is that you have left us who need you and who will miss you and your love.

* * *

Sometimes some frightening questions surface in me: Is all this a dream, a lovely little fairy tale? Is this community of love which we call the Church a fact or a fiction?

Did God really make us in God's image and likeness, or have we made up a God of love? Oh, I do believe. I have believed with enough depth and enough strength to wager my life on the reality of the Church. In fact, I resonate very deeply to the words of Jean Anouilh's Becket when he says, "I have rolled up my sleeves and taken this whole Church upon my back. Nothing will ever persuade me to put it down."

Jesus is in us and works through us.

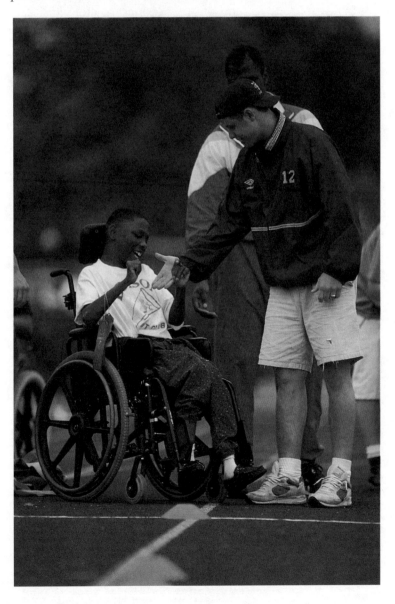

Still, there are parts of me that faith has not yet claimed. "Lord," I pray, "I do believe but please help me with my unbelief." I try to love my unbelieving questions until I can live the believing answers. One thing, however, seems certain: Every life must be based on some act of faith. Faith is basically a judgment, a judgment about whether the Word of God is true or not. If faith is a judgment about something for which there is no logical or scientific proof, then sooner or later all of us must make some decision, some act of faith in this matter. We must gamble our lives on something. Not to decide in this matter is really not a clever way to escape error. Not deciding is in itself a decision.

For myself I have made my judgment and my life commitment. I have also reflected that if the love of God, the call of the kingdom, and the reality of the Church are only a dream, then the opposite would be a nightmare. The opposite judgment or act of faith would see us as mere animals in search of prey. The strong would then devour the weak. The rich would buy and sell the poor. The handicapped would be destroyed as defective and unproductive. In the end, our only destiny would be to turn into dust and become food for worms.

I am reminded of what Dorothy Thompson, a journalist, once wrote. She was interviewing a survivor of a Nazi concentration camp. During the interview, she asked the survivor if any in those camps had remained human. His immediate reply was: "No, none remained human." Then he caught himself and remembered: "No, there was one group of people who did remain human. They were the religious people." The survivor said that all the others, even those who had great knowledge and skill, seemed to be using their abilities only selfishly for survival. The very architects of those camps had used their great knowledge and skill only to destroy. The knowledge and skills of a technological age without the compassion and wisdom of faith proved in Nazi Germany to be gruesomely dangerous and destructive. In her summary, Dorothy Thompson wrote: "I am beginning to think that when God goes, all goes." Her line was somewhat reminiscent of what George Washington said in his Farewell Address: "Morality cannot be maintained without faith and religion."

I am so grateful for the tugs on the string of my kite. I know that there is a God up there because I have experienced God's presence, power, and peace in my own life. I have also experienced God's presence and love in my sisters and brothers in the Christ, whose Church we are. In the end I must trust my own experience. I believe that Jesus is in us and works through us. I am satisfied with this truth on which I have wagered my life. Somehow I know that it has given me roots and wings: it has set me free.

FOR FURTHER REFLECTION

Chapter 22: The Christian Vision of the Church

Review

1. Why do we need the Church? What two images of the Church are helpful in acquiring a healthy Christian vision of the Church?
2. We are called to love ourselves, our neighbor, and our God. In light of this call to love, what does it mean to say that there are two lines of loving: the horizontal and the vertical?
3. Describe what God's plan or cause is. How does God utilize us as instruments to bring about God's cause and plan?
4. Explain: "The kingdom of God is here among us (present), but not yet totally realized (future) until the end of the world and the second coming."
5. How does the Church provide us today with "a God with a skin"? What about our human makeup causes us to need that kind of God?

Discuss

1. "The kingdom of God is an *invitation* on the part of God and an act of *acceptance* on the part of the human race." What does it mean for you to say yes to the invitation of the kingdom?
2. In what ways have you already accepted this invitation of the kingdom? In what ways do you still need to change, experience *metanoia,* in order to more fully accept the invitation?
3. We are the physical continuation of Jesus' presence in space and time. From your experience of the Church, the community of believers, does it seem that the community accepts and is aware of this concept that they are the Body of Christ on earth? Explain.
4. If you were on trial for being a Christian, would there be enough evidence to convict you?
5. What does the presence of hypocrites in the Church tell you about the stages of acceptance of the kingdom of God? In the last analysis, do you think all people who belong to the community of believers are or have ever been hypocrites?
6. Why can't you just go to a private place—such as the woods, your bedroom, your backyard—to worship God?

Scripture Activity

"Christ is like a single body, which has many parts; it is still one body, even though it is made up of different parts. In the same way, all of us, whether Jews or Gentiles, whether slaves or free, have been baptized into the one body by the same Spirit, and we have all been given the one Spirit to drink.

"For the body itself is not made up of only one part, but of many parts. If the foot were to say, 'Because I am not a hand, I don't belong to the body,' that would not keep it from being a part of the body. And if the ear were to say, 'Because I am not an eye, I don't belong to the body,' that would not keep it from being part of the body. . . . As it is, there are many parts but one body.

"All of you are Christ's body, and each one is part of it." (1 Corinthians 12:12–20, *GNB*)

What thoughts come to mind as you read this passage? Record in writing your answers to these reflection questions: (a) Does the passage offer you any new insights about the importance of each individual member of the church? (b) What does it say about the "weaker ones" of the community? (c) Does it shed any light on the importance of worshiping together as a community? (d) What does it say about causing or experiencing hurt and suffering or praise and happiness?

Processing These Ideas about the Church

The horizontal and vertical acceptance of love. Interview someone you believe has accepted the invitation of the horizontal kingdom—that is, a person who lives a life of loving service and contribution. How does that person's life seem different from the lives of other people you know? Ask that person about his or her attitude toward the Church. Ask the person to share his or her thoughts or feelings about worshiping together as a community, about personal prayer, and about loving service.

23 We Must Make Prayer a Part of Our Daily Lives

The Jesuit novitiate was spartan in those good old days. We talked in Latin, greeting each other with the Latin term Carissime, *which is translated, "Dearly Beloved."*

For me the most puzzling part of the novitiate experience was prayer. It was a wilderness. When the master of novices asked me if I had trouble with sleep during the morning meditation, I promptly assured him, "Oh, no, I go right off every morning." The most tantalizing part of it all was watching the "quakers and shakers" (as I secretly called them) in the chapel. I wanted to ask them, "Do you know something I don't? You're getting through, aren't you?" But this kind of questioning and sharing was not allowed, so I just kept wondering.

I identified with the poor moth who tried to get through the screen to the light on my desk. Poor guy kept hitting his head on the screen and trying again. He never made it.

Then came "Mayday." I was sure it was all a hoax. I was quite sure I didn't believe in any of it. But the master of novices told me to be patient, although I wasn't sure what it was that I was being patient for. I guess I forgot to ask what I could expect.

Then one night in the early spring, God touched me. I felt filled with God's undeniable presence. I remember thinking, "If this is what happiness is, I have never been happy before. A taste of new wine."

I remember standing there crying tears of relief. There really was a God. And this God had been inside me all the time.

The Critical Question

Perhaps the one question that most divides believers among themselves is this: Does God really interact with us? It is said that Thomas Jefferson, who considered himself a religious man, denied this willingness of God to interact with us. In fact, he is said to have razored out of his personal Bible all the passages that describe God entering human history and dialoguing with human beings. There are even some theologians who deny this willingness of God to become involved with us. And many of us who in theory may not want to accept a noninvolved God, in fact seem to think of God this way. There are many of us who really expect God to be silent and distant. Occasionally we throw our prayers and gifts over the high wall that separates us from God. We hope that God hears, but we do not expect an answer.

The question is critical because all relationships thrive on communication. Even on the purely human level, without an active communication there can be no relationship. I think that the same thing is true of our relationship with God. Only the communication in this relationship with God has a special name: prayer.

> Genesis tells us that we are made in God's image. But we also shape our concept of God in our human image.

313

The Barrier to Communication: The Masks We Wear

But communication is rarely easy. Unfortunately, most of us put on our masks, dress up in the costumes of our chosen roles, and begin reciting our well-rehearsed lines. The problem is that the masks, the costumes, and the lines are not really us. They are usually only our adaptations to reality. They are also barriers to real sharing and honest dialogue. You know this and I know this, in theory at least. If I put on an act, no matter what the act is, you cannot possibly interact with me. I have not given you a real person with whom to interact. So we try to meet somewhere on a stage, and we recite memorized lines to each other. I would like to submit as my opinion that God can truly interact with us only to the extent that we are real. And this, my sisters and brothers, is not easy. Being real, totally open and totally honest, usually takes a long time.

Of course, there are many types of prayers, just as there are many ways of communicating. But in essence, there is always in prayer some form of dialogue. It may not be a dialogue of words, though words usually find their way into the exchange. We humans often say more to each other by a smile or an embrace than we are able to say by words. But gestures and facial expressions can often be misinterpreted unless they are accompanied by words of explanation. Whatever the type of prayer one feels inclined to, the essence of communication is, as always, an honest sharing of self.

The Sincere Desire to Pray

Admittedly, there are times when we can engage in wordless prayer. But there is one thing without which we simply cannot pray. That is the *sincere desire to pray.* At first none of us wants to admit it, but we are all afraid of getting too close to God. A thousand questions and doubts flood into us at the very thought of being close to God. What will God say to me? What will God ask of me? Where will God lead me? The unknown is always a little frightening. And in this case, the stakes are high. My whole life is involved. God might shatter my whole construct, rearrange all my values.

Furthermore, I enter into every other dialogue as an equal. My thoughts are just as good as yours. My choices are mine, and you have no right to interfere. I did not come into this world to live up to your expectations, and you did not come into the world to live up to mine. It is quite different in the dialogue with God, who says, "Be still and know that I am God." As Albert Einstein once said, "When I approach this God, I must take off my shoes and tread lightly, for I am on sacred ground."

> *Whatever the type of prayer one feels inclined to, the essence of communication is, as always, an honest sharing of self.*

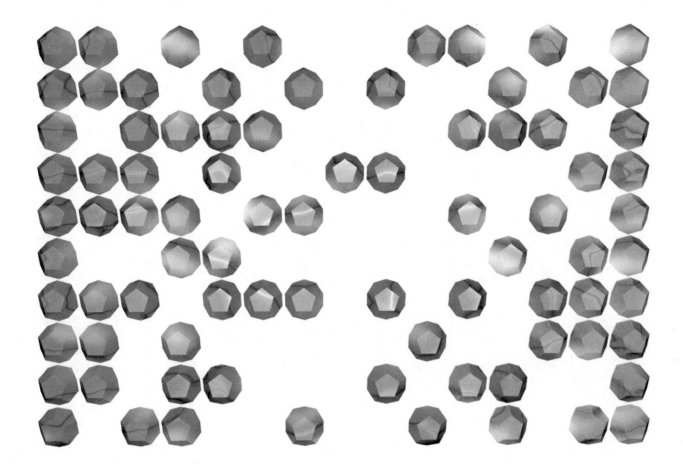

The High Price of Prayer: Surrender

Another essential condition for successful prayer is *surrender*. The very word usually terrifies us. But the fact of the matter is that the posture of surrender is a nonnegotiable condition for prayer. I remember reading a story written by a woman I have never met. In her article she described her humble origins—a cold-water flat, saving pennies for a "treat." Then she met her husband-to-be. He was the personification of her dreamed-about hero. She could not believe her ears when he asked her to marry him. Among other things, he had some wealth, so they moved to a suburb, where there was warm water, large windows, and green lawns. There were flowers in the summertime. And soon there was the marvel of children. It was all Jean had ever wanted.

Then she began feeling physically sick. Eventually she went to a doctor, and he put her in the hospital for tests. She was not at all prepared for it when her doctor looked at her sadly and said, "Your liver has stopped working." She almost screamed at him: "Are you telling me that I am dying?" With downcast eyes, he said solemnly, "We have done all we can." Then he turned and silently left her hospital room.

Relationships thrive on communication.

She felt a fire of anger ignite inside her. In her fury she wanted to tell God off. So, in her hospital gown and robe, she struggled through the corridors on her way to the chapel. It was to be a face-to-face confrontation. She felt so weak, she had to support herself by bracing against the wall as she moved along. When she entered the chapel, it was dark. No one else was there. So she proceeded up the center aisle on her way to the altar. Through what seemed like an endless journey from her room to the chapel, she had been preparing her speech: "Oh God, you are a fraud, a real phony. You have been passing yourself off as love for two thousand years. But every time anyone finds a little happiness, you pull out the rug from under her feet. Well, I just want you to know that I have had it. I see through you."

In the center aisle and near the front of the chapel, she fell. She was so weak, she could hardly see. Her eyes could barely read the words woven into the carpet at the step into the sanctuary. She read and then repeated the words: "LORD, BE MERCIFUL TO ME, A SINNER." Suddenly, all the angry words, all the desire to tell God off was gone. All that was left was: "Lord, be merciful to me, a sinner." Then she put her tired head down over her crossed arms, and listened. Deep within herself she heard: "All of this is a simple invitation to ask you to turn your life over to me. You have never done that, you know. The doctors here do their best to treat you, but I alone can cure you."

In the silence and darkness of that night, she turned her life over to God. She signed her blank check and turned it over to God to fill in all the amounts. It was the hour of God. It was the moment of her surrender.

Finding her way back to her room in the hospital, she slipped off into a deep sleep. The next day, after blood and urinalysis tests, the doctor gave her the hopeful news: "Your liver seems to be functioning again." Like Job in the Old Testament, God had led her to the brink, but only to invite her surrender. It is an important prerequisite for the communication of prayer. "Thy will be done!" is an enormous and frightening concession. It leaves us standing naked and defenseless. No more masks, no protective barriers. Just this: "Be still and know that I am God."

The Possibility of Prayer and Our Concept of God

We all have a different idea of God. Maybe intellectually some of us might define God using the same words. But we are more than just intellects. Of course, no one can say for sure where his or her idea of God has come from. But it is there, and it causes definite emotional reactions in us. Our concept of God propels us forward or it holds us back. Where did we get our idea of God? Our parent tapes and early religious instructions, our experiences, our imaginations, and even our programmed reactions to authority figures helped forge our concept of God. The Book of

> *Divine love is far greater than we could possibly imagine, but this we can know: whatever God does is done out of love.*

Genesis tells us that we are made in God's image and likeness, but it is inevitable that we also shape our concept of God in our own human image and likeness. We make God "one of us." We project impatience into God. We imagine God turning away from us. We think a thousand things that could never be. The fact is this: God is love, according to the Scriptures. God's nature is to love. Of course, divine love is far greater than we could possibly imagine, but this we can know: whatever God does is done out of love.

The Experience of God and Alcoholics Anonymous

One large group of believers in this God of love is the people in the Alcoholics Anonymous Fellowship. One of the founders of the movement and coauthor of the famous Twelve Steps program was a man named William G. "Bill" Wilson. Within the last several years, his correspondence with psychiatrist Carl Jung has been published. At the time the correspondence began, in January 1961, Bill Wilson wrote gratefully to Jung about Jung's role in the foundation of Alcoholics Anonymous. It seems that Jung had treated one Roland H. (The members of Alcoholics Anonymous protect anonymity by so designating themselves.)

After repeated treatments, Jung told Roland H. that he was hopelessly alcoholic. Wilson insists that Jung's acknowledgment of Roland's hopelessness became the first foundation

We do not need a theologically accurate portrait of God to begin the dialogue of prayer. If this were the case, none of us could ever begin to pray. Getting to know God is a dialogical process. We begin with mistaken impressions, distorted ideas, unfounded fears, and personal prejudices. But gradually, as we unfold ourselves to God and God is unfolded to us, we correct old erroneous impressions, gain new insights, experience new facets of the mysterious, tender God who cannot forget us even if a mother should forget the child of her womb. Having been wrong about God doesn't mean that we haven't been talking to God. It is only by perseverance in this type of prayer that we will come to be less and less wrong about God until that day when we shall know God even as we are known.

What I needed most, in arriving at this moment in my life, was the knowledge that God really wanted to be intimately close to me. I needed to be rid of the deistic concept of God as distant, uninterested, inoperative in me and in my human powers. But most of all, I needed some success in this method of prayer. I needed to feel the touch of God, to experience God's thoughts stretching my mind, to feel the firmness of God's strength and desires in my will, to hear God's voice and experience God's light in the darkness of my nights, to feel God's calm in the moments of my distress. Only then, in these meanderings into the mercy of this tender, present, and available Creator did I know that God really loved me and wanted to be the portion of my heart forever. Only then, with this success, did I know that God could never seem the same and I could never be the same again.

From *He Touched Me*

stone of Alcoholics Anonymous. The first of the famous Twelve Steps is to admit personal powerlessness, the unmanageability of one's life. After this, when Roland asked Jung if there was any other hope, Jung told him that there might be, provided Roland could become the subject of a spiritual or religious experience, in short, a genuine conversion.

> *It is extremely important to know the Jesus comes as the Divine Physician, making highly personalized house calls on those of us who are sick.*

Wilson thanks Jung effusively for pointing out how such an experience can provide the needed motivation when nothing else can. It was this suggestion that resulted in the second and third steps: belief in a loving and helpful God, and the turning over of one's life to this God.

It seems that Wilson himself was hopelessly addicted to alcohol at the same time that Roland H. was. Wilson's own doctor, a Dr. Silkworth, had also given him up for lost. Wilson admits, in his correspondence with Jung, that he cried out to God, begging for help. In the same letter he acknowledges that there immediately came to him an "illumination of enormous impact and dimension." Bill Wilson felt that he could never adequately describe this moment. He knew only that his release from the alcohol obsession was immediate. "At once, I knew that I was a free man."

Wilson acknowledged to Jung that he had also gained a great insight from William James's *Varieties of Religious Experience*. He wrote to the psychiatrist that this book had given him the realization that most conversion experiences, whatever their variety, do have a common denominator at their depth, namely, "ego collapse." This ego collapse is a giving up on oneself and one's own powers.

In the wake of his own spiritual experience there came to Bill Wilson a vision of a society of alcoholics. He reasoned that if each sufferer were to carry the news of the scientific hopelessness of alcoholism to each new prospect, such a sharing would lay every newcomer wide open to a transforming spiritual experience. It was this concept that proved to be the foundation of such success as Alcoholics Anonymous has achieved over the years.

It is not surprising, then, that Alcoholics Anonymous is very openly a spiritual program. Of the well-known Twelve Steps, only the first step mentions alcohol. All the others, directly or indirectly, mention God. But of special interest to us here and now are the first three steps. *The first step* is to face the unmanageability of my life. Even though I am not personally an alcoholic or a member of Alcoholics Anonymous, I have learned so much from the wisdom of this movement. I have come to recognize and acknowledge that there are so many areas of my own life that are riddled with irrationality. My perfectionism, my hypersensitivity, my immaturity when things don't go my way, my desire to pout and punish others—all confront me with the fact that these are unmanageable areas of my life. My life has indeed become unmanageable. I have tried to change, but know now that I cannot succeed without help. *The second step* is to come to believe in a God who loves me and wants to help me. I have to believe that this gentle and caring God will help me if I will only accept the help. (This step is really hard for us Harry Helpers.) Such openness to God's help involves *the third step,* which is to turn my life over to God. As many AAs put it: "Let go and let God."

No one has to convince the members of Alcoholics Anonymous that prayer is necessary. These are people who have had to take off all the masks of sham and pretense. These are people who have come to believe in a gentle and loving God, a "Higher Power" who mends what is broken, who straightens what has been twisted and distorted, who enlightens what is dark, and who revives what has died in us. These are the people who have turned their lives over to this God. Such a concept of and surrender to God is an important prelude to prayer.

Making Peace with My Weakness

Most of us have an instinctive fear of God that is based on our own weakness. We even fear other humans who we think can see right through us. We are indeed mistake makers, and sometimes our mistakes have been costly, to ourselves and to others. We either have to become comfortable with this human condition or go on pretending that it is not true. We have to go on hiding behind our pretending. Naturally, I am not suggesting that we simply cave in and give in to human weakness. I am suggesting that we must learn to be comfortable as fractions. We have all sinned and we will all sin again. For myself, it is extremely important to know the Jesus who comes as the Divine Physician, making highly personalized house calls on those of us who are sick. It is important for me to know the

Jesus who is the Good Shepherd. I have to keep remembering that he is looking for us lost sheep and rejoicing when he finds us.

Again and again I have gone over the parable of the Prodigal Son. I am the prodigal son who has squandered my gifts on so many vanities and immaturities. I feel a deep remorse. I have been so ungrateful. I prepare my words carefully and fearfully: "Oh, I can't ask to be taken back as a son. Take me back as a hired hand. Please, just take me back." Armed with my act of contrition born of loneliness and need, I start homeward. My steps are tentative and uncertain. But my Abba-Father sees me coming and rushes down the road. He takes me into his arms and sobs in relief, "You're home. You know, that's all I've ever wanted. You're home." In his parable Jesus assures me that I am welcomed in this way by my loving Abba-God. I have had to read that parable again and again. I have had to make the long journey home more than once. Gradually I am coming to know the gentle love and the gracious mercy of God.

The World of the Spirit

A friend of mine recently told me the story of two fish swimming in the ocean. The little fish swims up to the big one and asks, "Excuse me. Where is the ocean?" The big fish answers, "You are in it." The little fish does not understand and tries to ask his question again: "I mean, can you tell me how to get into the ocean?"

The surrender to God is an important prelude to prayer.

Again the big fish answers, "You are already in the ocean." The little fish swims away looking for someone else to answer his question.

My friend compares the question of the little fish to the question of those who ask, "What is spirituality? Where is the world of the spirit?" He pretends he is the bigger fish and says, "You're in it." Viktor Frankl, the Viennese psychiatrist, says that modern psychology has spent the last fifty years concentrating on the mind and the body. He complains that psychology has consistently neglected the human spirit and the world of the spiritual.

But we really have no choice. We are mind and body and spirit. We are "in it." We know when bodies are sick, and we bring them to our physicians. We know when minds are sick, and we entrust them to our psychiatrists. But spirits can get sick, too. Spirits can get starved, just as bodies can. They, too, need consistent nourishment and regular exercise. What are the symptoms when spirits get sick? We nourish grudges, we resent a lot of people, we find little meaning in life or human activity. We have a hard time enjoying. We are weak when strength is needed, and we become complainers and blamers. We are noticeably devoid of what the Scriptures call the "gifts of the Holy Spirit": love or charity, happiness, peace, patience, friendliness, kindness, loyalty, gentleness, and self-control.

When God made us, someone has suggested, we were made like Swiss cheese. We have a lot of holes in us that only God can fill.

> *I am told that whenever we think, we also verbalize our thoughts at least mentally. So verbalize to God who you are.*

If we do not ask God to fill our emptiness, we will foolishly try to fill it ourselves. We brag, we lie, we gossip, collect trophies, drop names, show off, compete for the limelight, try to gain power over others, gulp at the fountains of sensual pleasure, and look for kicks. But in the end, we are left with the painful emptiness that only God can fill.

The college years are usually years of risk and revision. So it did not surprise me when one of my former students returned to tell me of an experiment he had made. At the end of his college days, he was still not sure if he believed or was merely brainwashed. So on his own he decided to spend a week as though there were no God. He would refrain from prayer, from going to church, from doing everything that faith enjoins. Then in the following week, he would live a life of intense faith, including much prayer and everything that is part of the faith-filled life. When he finished telling me of his experiment, he smiled and added, "What a difference! If I were ever to deny the importance of faith and prayer, I would have to deny my own experience. I could never do that."

The Hour of God

Usually the term *hour* has a neutral significance. It is purely an indication of time. However, in the Scriptures, the "hour of God" has a special religious significance. The hour of God indicates a turning point in a life, or in human history, through God's special intervention.

The Lord asks us to be vigilant and ready because we cannot know in advance the "hour of God," the hour of God's coming to us with a special intervention. I am now old enough and wise enough to know that I cannot demand or produce this hour of God. God will come to me and to you in a way and at an hour of God's choosing. Sometimes we are tempted to stand like animal trainers, with our hoops. We urge God to come, to jump through our hoops, and now! But in the end we discover, sadly sometimes, that God is not a trained animal. God chooses the moments and the means. Ours is only to be ready for these special moments. Sometimes God's hour seems to come at the very limit of our endurance. However, part of our trust in God is that God will come to us, in the best possible time and in the best possible way. I have to let you be you, and you have to let me be me. And we have to let God be God.

A Suggested Form of Prayer

We have already said that there are many forms of prayer. I recently saw one I had never thought of. It starts out by looking at a "secular" picture and letting it stir prayerful thoughts and desires in the viewer. I like this approach because it seems to integrate faith into life. I look at the picture of a flower or a house, and I remember the special symbolism of love by flowers. Or, looking at the house, I recall that

we will all be gathered someday into God's house. My mind and heart move forward from there into further prayerful images and thoughts.

What I would like to suggest is something similar. Begin by trying to tell God who you are at this time. I am told that whenever we think, we also verbalize our thoughts at least mentally. So verbalize to God who you are. Force yourself to paint this verbal portrait.

At first it will be difficult. But going into deeper and deeper layers of self is a very helpful exercise in self-knowledge in addition to making for good prayer. And since everything is really God's gift, it helps to begin with a prayer for the gift of praying well. "Help me, loving God, to get to know myself and to know you. Help me to understand our relationship. Enlighten and empower me. Thank you." Then proceed with reflective questions like: Who am I? How do I feel today? What are the thoughts and feelings that have been rumbling around inside me during the last twenty-four hours? What has been most important to me? What person has meant most to me? What did I enjoy? What has caused me pain? Are there any special persons who played an important role in my recent life? What motives moved me into action? What did I really want to achieve, win, avoid? Overall, what am I doing with my life? Do I really want this?

I find that as I force myself to verbalize my answers to questions like these, I am actually getting to know myself better. Every day the answers are slightly different, as I peel off more layers and look into new corners of myself. Also, my moods change. Some days I feel tired of it all. Other days I am ready to move mountains. I also leave the "conversational door" open to God. We humans actually have many doors through which God can come into the dialogue. We have our *minds* into which God can put new ideas,

insights, perspectives. We have our *wills* or *hearts* in which God can implant desires and strength. We have *emotions* so God can comfort us in our affliction or afflict us in our comfort. God can come into our emotions with peace or with challenge. We also have *imaginations,* which means that in our dialoguing, God can say words or even suggest pictures to us. When Robert asks Joan of Arc in Shaw's *Saint Joan,* "Do you really hear God's voice or is it the voice of your imagination?" Joan replies, "Both. That is the way God speaks to us, through our imaginations." We also have *memories,* and God can stir our memories in the prayer of reminiscence. God can also heal our hurting memories or transform them into helpful memories. All in all, there are these five ports of entry for God to come into our reflective prayer. The important thing is to know that our limits are God's opportunities.

At the end of prayer, I ask God for my needs. "Enlighten me to see and empower me to do the loving thing with this day in my life. Fill my dry wells with your love so that I can pass it on." I then mention the names of people I have promised to pray for. I ask God to bless them. I pray for the people I have hurt—some knowingly, others unknowingly. But I was too distracted with myself even to notice. I thank God for loving me. I ask what God's got going today, because I would really like to be part of it.

FOR FURTHER REFLECTION

Chapter 23: We Must Make Prayer a Part of Our Daily Lives

Review

1. How is "wearing a mask" or "pretending to not be my real self" a barrier to communication with God? What is the advantage of being real in our prayer relationship with God?
2. Comment on how the following are prerequisites for prayer: (a) a sincere desire to pray, and (b) the willingness to surrender.
3. Identify the first three of the twelve steps Alcoholics Anonymous considers essential for dealing with the disease of alcoholism. How are these three steps also a prelude to, and foundational for, having a good prayer relationship with God?
4. What is the "hour of God" experience? What are the three criteria for determining whether or not an experience of God is valid? Why are these criteria important?
5. Paraphrase Powell's suggested form of prayer. Break down his form of prayer into steps.
6. We actually have many "doors" through which God can come into a dialogue of prayer with us. Identify these doors and explain how God dialogues with us through them.

Discuss

1. How and when do you pray?
2. When you pray, are you most often the "real you"? Or are you presenting yourself to God the way you feel God wants you to be?
3. Have you ever felt angry at God? (This is a perfectly legitimate emotion.) Do you feel comfortable expressing to God your anger? Why or why not?
4. What is, for you, the most frightening aspect about growing close to God through prayer? Are you afraid God might ask you to do something different, or to live in a different way? What are your fears?

Scripture Activity

Jesus also told this parable to people who were sure of their own goodness and despised everybody else. "Once there were two men who went up to the Temple to pray; one was a Pharisee, the other a tax collector. The Pharisee stood apart by himself and prayed, 'I thank you, God, that I am not greedy, dishonest, or an adulterer, like that tax collector over there. I fast two days a week, and I give you one tenth of all my income.' But the tax collector stood at a distance and would not even raise his eyes to heaven, but beat on his breast and said, 'God, have pity on me, a sinner!' "I tell you," said Jesus, "the tax collector was in the right with God when he went home. For everyone who makes himself great will be humbled, and everyone who humbles himself will be made great." (Luke 18:9–14, GNB)

Processing These Ideas about Prayer in Our Daily Lives

1. **Write a testimonial to grace.** Describe briefly an experience of yours when you felt God's presence (the "hour of God") in a strong way. What do you remember most clearly about this experience? How has it changed your attitude toward yourself, others, life, the world, or God?
2. **Write a fifth gospel.** The word *gospel* means "good news." In writing the gospels, the first Christians were trying to share their good news with all generations to come. Write a gospel about you and your life. Entitle it: "The Goodness of the Lord to Me." The writing of your faith story will help you to become more aware of God's gifts to you.
3. **Evaluate your relationship with God.** There are, for want of better words, "overdependent" and "underdependent" people. It is possible to be one or the other in our relationship with God. Some of us are overdependent. We constantly ask God to do things for us instead of asking God to enlighten us and to empower us to do those things. Others of us are underdependent. We proceed to make our plans and dream our dreams. We are sure that we know what is best for us. Then we ask God to support our plans. We are upset when God does not give us what we are asking for. The ideal, of course, is to ask God to enlighten and empower us to know and to do whatever God has sent us into this world to do. Write an answer to this question: Do I tend to be overdependent or underdependent, or am I on balance here?

THY
WILL
BE
DONE

24 *The Christian Vision of the Will of God*

For a Christian, in a very real sense, the bottom line of life is this: doing the will of God. This is the measure of what we call holiness. And for a Christian this is the only measure of success in life.

The late Padre Pio, the Capuchin stigmatic who bore the wounds of Christ on his body, was reputed to know everything. I once met this saintly man and was convinced by all that I saw and heard that indeed he did have a profound intuition of people; he had the gift of reading human hearts. Believing this, I wrote to him and asked him if he had any special message for me. In his response he said that he did indeed have something special to say to me. As I read this my heart started pounding and I could feel a sense of emotional anticipation rising in me. He wrote:

> *The strongest and most effective prayer, which you should make the center of your life, is this: "Thy will be done!"*

Somehow I felt disappointed. My heartbeats returned to a normal rhythm, and my emotions sagged back into place. My expectations shook their little heads sadly. I think I expected some clairvoyant statement, some startling revelation about my past or a dramatic prediction about my future.

"Thy will be done" just didn't do it. It seemed too basic, too fundamental, too taken-for-granted. It wasn't what I expected or wanted to hear.

I was relatively young at that time, anxious for excitement. As the years have moved on into middle age, I have more and more come to see that this desire to do the will of God is the heart of the matter. Seeking and embracing the will of God is the hallmark of Christian maturity.

Misunderstanding the Will of God

In the course of my own life experience, it seems that it has always been at the scene of some great or small tragedy that people have brought up the "will of God." I remember some years ago trying to console a woman who was sobbing almost hysterically just after the death of her husband. Unexpectedly someone in that room of grief remarked, "It is the will of God, you know." So abruptly did the woman stop crying that I stood there amazed, silently wishing that I had thought to say that. Now, of course, I realize that it would have been much better to let her release her grief and to express her sense of loss.

When Jesus had said this, a woman spoke up from the crowd and said to him, "How happy is the woman who bore you and nursed you!" But Jesus answered, "Rather, how happy are those who hear the word of God and obey it!"
Luke 11:27-28 (GNB)

But, the "will of God" is often used as a bromide to dull the sense of pain and to cover the pangs of grief. The "will of God" is often bottled with the label: "To be taken whenever things get rough."

I think that this crisis application is really a misunderstanding of the will of God. The will of God is, in fact, our happiness. That's why God created us: to share God's life and love, God's happiness, and even God's home with us. It would be a serious misunderstanding of God if we were to associate the will of God only with suffering, loneliness, and grief.

I think there is a usable analogy in the parent-child relationship. Almost all parents clearly want the happiness, the fulfillment of their children. They want exactly what the children themselves want: happiness and fulfillment. What parent and child may disagree about is the *means.* The child may not want to take vitamins or to stay in the safety of the backyard; the child may want to play with matches or sharp knives. At times like these the parents have to step in and assert their wisdom and their wills. The parents want the child to be happy and healthy; the child wants to be happy and healthy. It is only a question of who knows what *means* will best produce that desired state of happiness and health.

Most of the time, I would presume, the wills of parents and children are not in conflict. When Mom and Dad take the children to the beach or circus, when the whole family is eating dessert or playing some game, there is no conflict. Likewise, when God offers us all the good and beautiful things created for our enjoyment, there is no conflict. And we are certainly doing God's will when we are enjoying, appreciating, and being grateful for these many beautiful things: for good food, the moon and the stars, white sandy beaches, rippling streams and roaring oceans, the smiling faces of friends, the joy of a newborn baby, the encircling arms of love, the joys of success, the music and the poetry of the universe, rainbows, and Christmas trees. God has looked on all these things and pronounced them "very good!" And it is God's will that we join in that pronouncement, that we use and enjoy the marvelous and delightful works of God's hands. All this is definitely an important part of doing the will of God.

There are, of course, times when the will of a mother and father will not be the will of the young child. Most of the time, when we are very young, our parents do know what is best. Of course, it would really help if children could be convinced that their parents really do want only their happiness, even when their parents won't allow them to experiment with matches or play in the street or stay up all night. Likewise, it would really help us if we could really believe that what God wants is really our happiness, even when God challenges us with difficulties and asks us to endure failure or grief. The comparison between God

The general will of God asks us to do something loving with our lives, to glorify God by using all of God's gifts to the full.

and parents is valid, I think, except that parents can be wrong in some of their judgments. God, by definition, is infinitely intelligent and infinitely loving. God, cannot be wrong, knows much better than we what will make us happy. God clearly implied this in a question to Job: "Where were you when I made the world?"

A dear and good friend of mine, now deceased, had suffered more ill health than anyone I have personally known. A coronary heart attack at age thirty-five. Multiple surgeries for cancer, which left a gaping hole in the center of his face. This necessitated a prosthesis to replace his nose and cheekbones. Because of his consistent ill health, he was greatly limited and confined to sedentary occupations. He suffered prolonged bouts with pain and was often embarrassed by his affliction. Once I asked this man about his reaction. Did he ever get depressed? Was he ever bitter? I will never forget his reply: "These are the cards which God has *lovingly* dealt me, and these are the cards I will *lovingly* play." I will always remember and be grateful for that response of my friend.

God's Will: General and Specific

It is obvious that a necessary part of growing up is the chance to make our own decisions and choices. We will make some of these decisions and choices poorly, and in these cases we will have to learn from our mistakes. This is a part of the growing-up process. Consequently, parents must give their children an increasing liberty to make their own choices as the children grow older. If the mother and father were to dictate all the decisions of their children, the end result would be disastrous. The parents would wind up with indecisive, conformist, emotionally crippled children walking around in adult bodies. People who have been treated this way stumble and stutter through life, asking others, "What do you think I should do?" They hitchhike through life, carried along on the wisdom and maturity of others. All of us must have the liberty to make our own decisions and our own mistakes, to live with them and to learn from them. There is simply no other way to become mature.

So it seems to me that if God had a definite and detailed will for every one of our actions and in all our situations of choice, God would be aiding and abetting infantile delinquency. We would all end up indecisive, immature children, walking around in adult bodies. With our fingers laced nervously together, we would forever be praying to know the will of God. Should I go here or there? Should I paint my house this color or that? Should I locate my office on the second or third floor? The practice of faith, based on the supposition that God has a definite and detailed will for everything we do, would produce childish little robots instead of mature human Christians. God our Father would not do this.

The will of God is, in fact, our happiness.

> One of the most difficult parts of being a loving person is making all the decisions that love must make.

The only reason why a person might find comfort in believing that God does have a definite and detailed will in all things would be that it provides an escape from responsibility. The escapee from responsibility never has to make personal decisions, to take personal responsibility for his or her life, and never needs any inner reexamination of motive and attitudes. For such a person there is a hotline from heaven and all messages come directly from God, who bears all the responsibility. It is the formula for a stagnant life and perpetual immaturity.

My own belief is that God has, in our regard, a *general* and a *specific* will. I think that the general will of God asks us to do something loving with our lives, to glorify God by using all of God's gifts to the full. Indeed God has given each of us unique gifts and asks us to invest these gifts wisely and lovingly in the cause of God's Kingdom. Such a generalized life commandment to make our lives an act of love leaves many decisions up to you and me. In fact, one of the most difficult parts of being a loving person is making all the decisions that love must make: What is the loving thing to do, to say, to be? Love is not a simple matter. I must listen empathically to you and to your needs in order to learn where you are and what you need at this moment. At the same time, I must also love myself and my God. Consequently, I must weigh my own needs against yours. Which are the most urgent? I must also consider the needs of God's Kingdom in most of my

decisions. This general will of God that we make our lives an act of love allows us much room for the healthy exercises of maturity.

We obviously need God's *enlightenment* when we are trying to make these decisions of love. And I think that God is most happy to provide the graces of enlightenment. God will help us to see the issues involved in our decisions, issues that we might not have noticed. Divine grace will help us to gain a needed perspective, to take a longer and wider view, when we are making our choices. But as we go into that final room marked "decision," we must go in there alone. We must exercise and stretch our own muscles if we are to grow. Often we must learn from our mistakes and reverse our mistaken judgments wherever possible. This is necessary for all of us if we are to grow into mature and faithful Christians. When God gives me the lumber of my life and asks me to build a cathedral of love and praise, the request does not come with an architect's blueprint, complete in every detail. Rather, God's general will simply asks me to make love the rule and the motive of my life.

On the other hand, there may well be times in your life and mine when God will have a *specific* will, a call to something which is very definite. God has a providence over our world and over human history, which I think of as the "master plan." I believe that God has designed a whole network of crisscrossing causes designed to achieve the intentions of this master plan. While we probably live most of our days under the general directive of making our lives an act of love, there will be definite times when God will open a very specific door and ask us to go through it. There will be some deeds and accomplishments which are specifically entrusted to you and to me. No one else can do them.

I believe, for example, that I became a priest in response to a specific call of God. When people have occasionally asked me why I became a priest, I have replied, "If you want my reasons, I will be glad to try to impress you. But the real reasons are not mine. The real reasons are God's, and I do not know them." All I know is that once upon a time God opened a door and God's grace moved me through it. He allowed me at that time to think my own thoughts and to react to my own motives. But there was this greater plan, this providence of God over the history and over the world of humankind. In that plan of providence, there is indeed a set of specific things which God has called me to do. Why God chose these specific deeds of love for me or me for them I do not know. I am happy to love these questions until God graciously supplies the answers.

There have been quite a few times in my own life when I have felt the winds of God's grace in the sails of my small boat. Sometimes these graces have moved me in pleasant and sunlit directions.

I also believe that, in addition to God's general will, there is operative at definite times in our lives a specific will of God. I think it is certain that God has sent you or me into this world with a specific thing to do: a definite message to deliver, a song to sing, an act of love to bestow.

When we come to these times in our lives, God will nudge us with God's grace and will put into us a deep attraction, a sense of vocation. To us it may seem like a vague conviction, "I am supposed to do this." It may be that God will make us uncomfortable until we say "yes." God comes to comfort the afflicted but also to afflict the comfortable.

I think that I was called to be a priest by such a specific will of God. I think that God chose me to be a priest and so tailored the graces of my life that I would be attracted to the altar of my ordination. There have, of course, been other moments in my life when I somehow knew that God wanted something specific of me. God wanted me to help this person, to do that thing, to become involved in this cause, to be concerned about a given situation. In each of these times, I felt that God was asking me for a specific "Yes!"

From the audio program, *The Growing Edge of Life*

At other times the requested acts of love were born in the darkness of struggle and suffering. There have been springtimes and there have been long, cold winters of struggle for survival. God has come to me at times with the purest kindness, at times with the most affirming encouragement, and at other times with bold and frightening challenges. I think that all of us have to watch and pray, to be ready to say "yes" when God's language is concrete and God's request is specific— "yes" in the sunlit springtimes and "yes" in the darkness of winter nights.

Discernment: Through Attraction and Peace

The specific will of God is not always preceded by a great gong and an announcement in solemn tones. Most times we have to prayerfully "discern" or discover this specific will of God. How do we go about this? First, let me say that I think that the only person who can successfully and safely discern the will of God is one who really wants to know and to do the will of God.

There is a story, which I believe to be reliable, about one of our best-known Christian authors. It seems that this man had gone to spend a year in a monastery to deepen his own spiritual perceptions and to find his own spiritual directions. One day this subject of the will of God came up in conversation between the author and the Abbot of the monastery. The author asked the Abbot, "What is the most necessary step in finding the will of God?" The Abbot replied, "The most necessary step to find the will of God in a specific matter is to want the will of God with all your heart in all things and at all times."

The person who is seriously seeking and wanting God's will can trust that God's specific will can be found in his or her own deepest inclinations and attractions. Many of the saints have said that they knew a given action was the will of God for them because they experienced such a strong attraction within themselves for this course of action. Therese of Lisieux once said that she knew God wanted her to become a Carmelite sister because God had planted in her heart such a strong desire for this. Again, the main question which you and I must confront is this: Do I really want the will of God? Am I deluded first by wanting to make my own plans and then by insisting that God support and realize them? Or do I seek to find my place in God's plans, in God's "master plan" of providence? If the second, then I can safely and wisely consult my own deepest inclinations and attractions to find the movements and directions of grace.

The second method of discernment which I have found helpful is this. Again, the supposition is that I have made my act of faith and that I truly and above all want God's will. When we come to the frequent forks of decision in the roads of our lives, it is very profitable to imagine ourselves following each of the possible courses of action. Having placed before our minds all the alternatives, the one in which we find the greatest peace of heart most probably is the specific will of God for us.

Why? Imagine with me, if you will, that the grace of God is a physical force. This grace gently moves us in a definite direction. When we try to go in another, contrary direction, we have to exert force and we will feel the friction and the struggle of this opposition. However, if we move with, flow with the gentle but directive force of grace, we will feel rather the support and momentum of the gentle pressures of grace.

When we come the frequent forks of decision in the roads, we should always be guided by: What is the loving thing to do?

> *The most necessary step to find the will of God in a specific matter is to want the will of God with all your heart in all things and at all times.*

In a similar way, even though grace is not a physical but a spiritual reality, when we are moving in the direction of God's grace, there is an inner experience of harmony and peace. We are moving with the flow. There is a sense that "this is the right thing to do, to say, to be." On the other hand, when we are "kicking against the goad," as Saint Paul says, there is an experience of struggle. "There is another law warring in our members." The force of our wills is not flowing with the movement of grace, but pushing against it.

In the concrete, when I am trying to find out if there is a specific will or directive of God, more than anything else I have to try to become aware of my own basic and general intention: Do I really want the will of God? Am I willing to suspend or at least hold in check my own desires until I have found out God's desires? Am I ready to open my hands to God? Is my central and strongest prayer, "Thy will be done!" This desire always to do the will of God is the most important part of our discernment. This must always be the deepest desire of our hearts.

Discerning the Will of God: A Summary

You and I have to struggle through these profound and sometimes painful questions. I personally find it very costly to confront myself with the question, What do I really want? We can and should pray for the grace to want God's will, believing as we do that God's will is, in fact, the only way to our own true and deepest happiness. Only when we want God's will before all else can we safely consult our deepest desires and inclinations, trusting that these desires and inclinations have been born of grace.

At the crossroads of love's many decisions, we can place before our minds and hearts the alternatives, the possible courses of action. Wanting God's will, we will find in one of the alternatives greater peace of heart, an inner sense that "This is right!" On the other hand, we will experience some confusion, some inner struggle with the courses of action that are contrary to God's will. I have deliberately chosen the phrase "peace of *heart*" rather than "peace of *mind*" for a definite reason. Most theologians believe that the Holy Spirit works not only in our conscious thoughts but also in our subconscious. Many times the Holy Spirit does not share with our conscious minds all the reasons and motives for a given inclination, but moves us anyway, by forces we cannot recognize or name, to fulfill the Spirit's higher purposes and to attain our own ultimate destinies. We experience peace when we harmonize ourselves with this movement of the Spirit. The head may be left with a thousand questions, but the heart's intuition will sense that "This is right!" and will know a peace of its own.

Trusting the Lord

There is an ancient directive: "We pray as though everything depends on God but work as though everything depends on ourselves." Another version of the same goes this way: "When you are out at sea and a storm arises, pray with all your heart but row with all your might for the shore."

Recently I heard a story about a man whose house was located in a flooding area. When he looked out the window of the first floor of his house, he saw a man riding by in a boat. The man in the boat shouted, "Get into this boat and save your life!" "No," came the reply, "I am going to trust in the Lord." The floods kept rising and soon the poor fellow was looking out the window of the second floor of his house. Again a man in a boat rode by and implored him to get into the boat and save his life. "No," came the firm reply again, "I am trusting in the Lord." The floods continued to rise. Soon the man was forced to the highest peak of his rooftop. A helicopter flew by and hovered over his head. The pilot said over a loudspeaker, "We're going to drop a rope ladder. Climb into the helicopter and save your life!" Once more the stranded man, perched high on his rooftop, replied, "No, I am going to trust in the Lord!"

Well, it seems that the floods continued to rise and the poor man eventually drowned. At the "pearly gates" he encountered the stately figure of Saint Peter, snowy beard and all. "Say, I've got a complaint. I want to get it off my chest before I go into heaven. I understand that no one can complain in there. I want to tell you that I trusted in the powers of heaven and you let me down!"

Peter meditatively stroked his long white beard and replied, "I don't know what else we could have done for you. We sent two boats and a helicopter."

Sometimes trusting in the Lord can be used as an excuse for our own reluctance to work as though everything depends on us, to row with all our might for the shore. Wanting the will of God can never be a substitute for personal determination and hard work. We have to get into the boat, climb the rope ladder, use the means of achievement that God provides for us. God helps those who help themselves. If we really will the end, we must also will the means. We should ask God to help us with our work, but not expect God to do it for us. Trusting in the Lord should never be a cloak over our own cowardice or laziness.

Mary: Pieta

In the Gospels (Luke 1:26–38), we read of an angel coming to a young girl with a question she could not have anticipated: "Will you be the mother of the Messiah?" The overwhelmed girl had already promised her virginity to God. She did not understand how she could be a mother.

We should ask God to help us with our work, but not expect God to do it for us.

"The Pieta" by
Michelangelo
(1475–1564).

the Word was made flesh. The Son of God took his humanity from her body and from the power of God, took up his residence within her, under her immaculate heart.

When Mary said, "Let it be done!" she did not understand all the other "yeses" that would be inside her first "yes." Scripture scholars do not think she knew that the Messiah whom she had consented to mother would be in fact the Son of God. I am also sure that when she became visibly pregnant, she did not know how to explain her motherhood to Joseph, who was "making plans to divorce her." I think she wondered often about the future of the little baby she held in her arms that night in Bethlehem. Afterward, she did not understand that faraway look in the eyes of her little boy. It was a look that seemed to stare far into the future. It was almost as though he knew of his destiny to do something that would change the whole course of human history. Likewise, I think that Mary was puzzled by his response to her worried question, when he was lost in the Temple: "Son, why did you do this to us? Your father and I have been terribly worried trying to find you." He answered only, "Didn't you know that I had to be about my Father's business?" I am sure that Mary did not understand.

However, if heaven is where God is, that little cottage in Nazareth must have been for thirty years a heaven on earth for Mary. It must have been a heaven on earth that she had not dreamed about even in her most glorious dreams.

The angel proceeded to assure her that it would not be by the power of man but by the power of God that this would come about. "The Holy Spirit will come upon you."

Gathering her startled wits together, the young girl asks the only important question: "Is this really the will of God? Does God really want this of me?" This had always been her heart's desire: to do God's will in all things. The angel assures her that it is the will of God, and the young girl, Mary, bows her head with an immediate "yes!" "I am the Lord's servant. Let it happen to me as you have said!" (Luke 1:38) And so, in this moment

Then, after Joseph had died (as we presume), Jesus said that he had to leave her, to walk the long and lonely roads of Palestine announcing the Kingdom of God to the people of his time. After seeing him disappear down the road, Mary most probably walked back into that little house in Nazareth alone. There must have been a great emptiness in that house, the kind we experience when we return to our homes after the funeral of a family member. We know from the Gospels that sometime later Mary did celebrate a wedding of friends with him at Cana. She even alerted him to the embarrassment of the newly married couple: "They have no more wine!" Most probably she was puzzled by his reaction: "My hour is not yet come." Of course, she still trusted in the compassion and power she had always experienced in her son, and told the waiters, "Do whatever he tells you."

Apparently Mary was not with him on Palm Sunday. She did not hear the "Hosannas!" or experience the tingling excitement of his public acclamation and triumphant entry into Jerusalem. The final gospel portrait of Mary is the terrifying scene on Calvary. She stands there bravely at the foot of his cross, watching her son die slowly and painfully. And, as the sky darkens, she holds the dead body of her son in her trembling arms.

Michelangelo has carved out of marble a beautiful tribute to this young woman. It is likewise a tribute to her "yes" to God's will.

In the statue, Mary is holding Jesus in her arms, looking upon his torn body with a mother's tender and loving compassion. Michelangelo calls his statue the "Pieta." *Pieta* is an Italian word which means "faithfulness." Mary is the woman who with all her heart wanted only the will of God, who said her "yes" but did not understand all that it would involve. But she trusted God, trusted that God loved her, trusted God's wisdom and ways, even when she did not understand. Michelangelo's summary of her incredible achievement is the one word: PIETA.

Epilogue Prayer

God, my Father: Create in me a heart that hungers for your will alone—a heart to accept your will, to do your will, to be whatever you want me to be, to do whatever you want me to do.

When you chose to create this world, you knew the blueprint and the design of my life: the moment of my conception, the day and hour when I would be born. You saw from all eternity the color of my eyes and you heard the sound of my voice. You knew what gifts I would have and those that I would be without. You knew also the moment and the circumstance of my dying. These choices are all a part of your will for me. I will try lovingly to build an edifice of love and praise with these materials which you have given me. What I am is your gift to me. What I become will be my gift to you.

"I am the Lord's servant. Let it happen to me as you have said!" (Luke 1:38) And so, in this moment the Word was made flesh.

As to the future, I ask for the grace to sign a blank check and trustfully to put it into your hands, for you to fill in all the amounts: the length of my life, the amount of success and the amount of failure, the experiences of pleasure and of pain. I would tremble to do this except for one thing: I know you love me. And, of course, you know much better than I what will truly and lastingly make me happy.

In response to your will, I want my life to be an act of love. Whenever there is a choice, help me to ask only this: What is the loving thing to do, to say, to be? To make the decisions that love must, I seek and need your enlightenment. Touch my eyes with your gentle and healing hands that I might find my way along the winding course of love. Strengthen my will and direct my feet to follow that course always.

And whenever there is something special your love has designed for me to do in my life,

let me be found ready and waiting. Help me to become a sensitive instrument of your grace. I believe that you have a providential master plan for this world, and I want to be a part of it. I want to make my contribution to your Kingdom, the contribution you have entrusted only to me. I want you to use me to help love this world into the fullness of life.

Finally, my Lord and my God, let me be faithful in my commitment and dedication to your will, faithful until the end. Let "faithfulness" be the summary of my days and of my nights. Let the inscription on my tombstone read: PIETA.

I hope these thoughts on prayer, as well as all the other personal "beatitudes" presented in this book, will be helpful to you on your journey toward ever greater happiness. These pages have been my act of love for you. Thanks for your open mind and gentle hands. Remember me as loving you.

John Powell, S.J.

God, my father, create in me a heart that hungers for your will alone.

FOR FURTHER REFLECTION

Chapter 24: The Christian Vision of the Will of God

Review

1. What is the most common misunderstanding of God's will?
2. Distinguish the *general will* and the *specific will* of God. Explain how they are different and yet related.
3. Describe the steps for "discerning God's will" that are presented in this chapter. What specific questions might help you determine what God wants you to do?
4. Explain: "Although trust in God is important as we seek to do God's will, yet we cannot merely expect God to do everything for us."
5. How is Mary a model of a person who trusts, seeks to do God's will, and yet is personally involved in fulfilling God's will?

Discuss

1. How does your former understanding of the will of God differ from the description presented in this chapter? Why does Powell's description seem more healthy? How does it make a difference in one's day-to-day relationship with others and God?
2. When you have to make major personal decisions, do you ask God for inspiration to know God's will? Or do you go ahead and make your decision and hope God wants what you want?
3. If you were to actually accomplish God's will every time, do you think you would be a happy person?
4. What do you think God's specific will is for you today? How did you arrive at that conclusion?
5. What does it mean to say a person is "called" or has a "vocation" to a certain way of life? Do you think everyone has a unique vocation or calling? Or do you think we might have more than one calling in the course of a lifetime?

Scripture Activity

"When Jesus had said this, a woman spoke up from the crowd and said to him, 'How happy is the woman who bore you and nursed you!' But Jesus answered, 'Rather, how happy are those who hear the word of God and obey it!' " (Luke 11:27–28, GNB)

Reflect on this passage and share what you believe it means to "hear" and "obey" the word of God. Afterward, consider how you would answer the question, "Are you one of those happy people who hear the word of God and obey it?" Explain your reasons for saying yes or no.

Processing These Ideas about the Will of God

The general will of God. The general will of God is our happiness. God wants us to be happy by loving ourselves, our neighbor, and our God. Correspondingly, happiness is a by-product of a loving life. Look at your relationships, your goals in life, your ambitions, and your activities, and determine whether or not they promote the general will of God that you make your life an act of love.

Acknowledgments

Unless otherwise stated all Scripture quotations are taken from or adapted from the Good News Bible text, Today's English version. Copyright © American Bible Society 1966, 1971, 1976, 1993.

Robert Frost, "The Road Not Taken," from *The Poetry of Robert Frost*, edited by Edward Connery Latham. Copyright © 1916. Copyright © 1969 by Holt Reinhart and Winston, Copyright © 1944 by Robert Frost.

Poem by Archibald Macleish.

Frederick Perls. "Gestalt Prayer." Real People Press © 1969. All rights reserved.

Excerpts from John Powell, S.J.: *Abortion, The Silent Holocaust*, © 1981 by Tabor Publishing, Allen, Texas; *The Catholic Vision*, © 1984 by John Powell, S.J. Published by Tabor Publishing, Allen, Texas; *Fully Human Fully Alive*, © 1976 by Tabor Publishing, Allen, Texas; *Happiness Is an Inside Job*, © 1989 by John Powell, S.J. Published by Tabor Publishing, Allen, Texas; *He Touched Me*, © 1974 by John Powell, S.J. Published by Tabor Publishing, Allen, Texas; *Through Seasons of the Heart*, © 1987 by Tabor Publishing, Allen, Texas; *Unconditional Love*, © 1978 by Tabor Publishing, Allen, Texas; *Will the Real Me Please Stand Up?* © 1985 by John Powell, S.J. Published by Tabor Publishing, Allen, Texas; *Why Am I Afraid to Love?* © 1967, 1972, 1982 by Tabor Publishing, Allen, Texas; *Why Am I Afraid to Tell You Who I Am?* © 1969 by Tabor Publishing, Allen, Texas.

Excerpts from Juan Arias, *The God I Don't Believe In*, © 1973 by St. Meinrad Archabbey, Inc., St. Meinrad, Indiana.

Specified excerpt from *The Bell Jar* by Sylvia Path. Copyright © 1971 by Harper & Row, Inc. Publishers.

Walter Tubbs, "Beyond Perls," from *Journal of Humanistic Psychology*, 12 (Fall 1972), p.5.

Photo Credits

Martin Barraud/FPG International   178
Richard Berenholtz/The Stock Market   291
The Bettman Archive   23
Barry Blackman/FPG International   166
Philip Coblentz   5, 11, 238
Gerard Fritz/Superstock   Cover
Francekevick/The Stock Market   106
Full Photographics, Inc.   7, 26, 48, 74, 87, 103, 114, 125, 136, 163, 217, 221, 271, 309, 321
David Hundley/The Stock Market   118
Marburgy/Art Resource, New York   187
Scala/Art Resources, New York   334
R. Michael Stuckey/Comstock, Inc.   294, 394
Uli Weyland/Gamma Liaison   268

Illustrations

Matt Hall   226, 284
Ed Leach   254. 315
Pin Yi Wu   3, 10, 14, 21, 28, 30, 32, 38, 44, 53, 58, 63, 66, 73, 80, 91, 94, 100, 111, 116, 120, 129, 132, 139, 142, 148, 154, 161, 168, 171, 182, 188, 192, 195, 202, 211, 229, 244, 247, 258, 301, 312, 331